LECTURES ON JUDAISM
IN THE HISTORY OF RELIGIONS

SOUTH FLORIDA STUDIES IN THE HISTORY OF JUDAISM

Edited by
Jacob Neusner
Ernest S. Frerichs, William Scott Green, James Strange

Number 02
Lectures on Judaism
in the History of Religions

by
Jacob Neusner

LECTURES ON JUDAISM
IN THE HISTORY OF RELIGIONS

by

Jacob Neusner

Scholars Press
Atlanta, Georgia

LECTURES ON JUDAISM
IN THE HISTORY OF RELIGION

©1990
University of South Florida

Publication of this book was made possible by a grant from the Tisch Family Foundation, New York City. The University of South Florida acknowledges with thanks this important support for its scholarly projects.

Library of Congress Cataloging in Publication Data

Neusner, Jacob, 1932-
    Lectures on Judaism in the history of religions / by
  Jacob Neusner.
    p. cm. -- (South Florida studies in the history of Judaism : 02)
  Includes index.
  ISBN 1-55540-480-4 (alk. paper)
    1. Judaism--History--Talmudic period, 10-425--Historiography.
2. Judaism. I. Title. II. Series.
BM177.N476 1990
296--dc20   90-37025
                                                              CIP

Printed in the United States of America
on acid-free paper

FOR

CINDY LEIGH BENSON
DAUGHTER OF CECILE AND MAURICE BENSON

AND RAPHAEL JOSHUA KANTER
SON OF RABBI SHAMAI AND JEANNETTE F. KANTER

ON THE OCCASION OF THEIR WEDDING

JANUARY 14, 1990/13 TEVET 5750
IN LOS ANGELES, CALIFORNIA

A TOKEN OF CELEBRATION AND HOPE

BEARING THE PRAYER THAT CINDY & RAFI
WILL BE BLESSED
WITH JOY AND PEACE,
BUT ABOVE ALL,
WITH THE COURAGE THEY WILL NEED,
AS DO WE ALL,
TO LIVE OUT THEIR YEARS TOGETHER

Table of Contents

Preface ix

Prologue
JUDAISM WITHIN THE NEW HUMANITIES

1. FROM TEXT TO CONTEXT: THE POWER AND THE PATHOS OF THE HUMANITIES 3
   Keynote Address at Humanities Conference, Wayne State University, 1983

Part One
LECTURES ON JUDAISM AMONG RELIGIONS

2. THINKING ABOUT "THE OTHER" IN RELIGION: IT IS NECESSARY, BUT IS IT POSSIBLE?... 17
   Uomini e religione Conference, Warsaw, 1989, commemorating the fiftieth anniversary of the Start of World War II; The Beaven Lecture, University of Rochester, 1990

3. JUDAISM AND CHRISTIANITY IN THE FIRST CENTURY: HOW SHALL WE PERCEIVE THEIR RELATIONSHIP?...............33
   Pontifical Lateran University, 1989; National Council of Catholic Bishops, Brasília, 1989

4. RITUAL WITHOUT MYTH: THE USE OF LAW FOR THE STUDY OF JUDAISM..45
   Annual Religious Studies Lecture, University of Minnesota, 1975

5. THE TALMUD AS ANTHROPOLOGY..57
   The Friedland Lecture, The Jewish Theological Seminary of America, 1979

6. WHY NO SCIENCE IN JUDAISM?..81
   Tulane University, 1987

7. WHY DOES JUDAISM HAVE AN ECONOMICS? 119
   The Reinfeld Lecture, Connecticut College, 1988

8. HOW WE UNDERSTAND OUR TRADITIONS: IS JUDAISM A TRADITIONAL RELIGION? 147
   Seton Hall University, 1989

9. ARE JEWS "RELIGIOUS"?..165
   The Avram Endowment Lecture, Brooklyn, 1987

10. LITURGY IN CONTEMPORARY SOCIETY: WHY SOME RITES RETAIN POWER IN THE CASE OF JUDAISM 179
    Pontifical Anselm University, 1989

Part Two
LECTURES ON JUDAISM IN HISTORY

11. POLITICS AND THEOLOGY IN TALMUDIC BABYLONIA 193
    The Rudolph Lecture, Syracuse University, 1969
12. HISTORY AND PURITY IN FIRST-CENTURY JUDAISM 221
    On the Occasion of the Celebration of the Five-Hundredth Anniversary, University of Tübingen, 1977
13. THE TALMUD AS HISTORY 237
    The Allan Bronfman Lecture, Montreal, 1978
14. NEW PERSPECTIVES ON BABYLONIAN JEWRY IN THE TANNAITIC AGE 257
    Perspectives in Jewish Learning Series, The Spertus College of Judaica, 1964
15. FROM ENEMY TO SIBLING: ROME AND ISRAEL IN THE FIRST CENTURY OF WESTERN CIVILIZATION 287
    The Bokser Lecture, Queens College, 1986
16. WHAT, EXACTLY, DO WE MEAN BY "AN EVENT" IN JUDAISM? 319
    Collège de France, Paris, 1990

Epilogue
A LECTURE NOT GIVEN

17. METHODOLOGY IN TALMUDIC HISTORY 341
    Cancelled by the Israel Historical Society, Jerusalem, to have been given in 1984

Index 365

Preface

The University realizes itself in the formal academic lecture, often endowed and named, when it invites a scholar to speak to the academy as a whole, not to a small group of specialists or senior scholars alone, but to whom it may concern, student or senior professor, specialist, generalist, outsider to learning altogether. That is the moment at which, all together and all at once, the principal parts of the University come together to form a community of shared discourse. That explains why the named lecture presents a splendid opportunity, if also a major challenge, to scholars honored by the invitation to present such a public accounting of their work. It is the University's most distinctive way of expressing in concrete ways the rules of common discourse, the manners required by a decent respect for the opinions and intelligence of others.

A particularly demanding but attractive medium of scholarly expression, the academic lecture, imposes its own discipline. It requires an address to a broad and mixed audience of scholars about one's own specialization. That means the lecturer must speak to the academic world about quite particular results, therefore demanding the work of generalization: what do I have to say to people of intellect who want to know, for their studies, what I have learned in my scholarly undertakings? Not only so, but academic audiences include not only professors but sizable numbers of students, so that the mixture involves not only specialists in different disciplines and fields but also beginners and mature scholars alike. The upshot is that, at the academic lecture, the scholar speaks to the University in its richest sense: a group of engaged minds, working on different subjects, but eager to communicate what they have learned with one another – and with ages to follow.

In the past three decades, and particularly since I came to Brown University in 1968, I have delivered academic lectures on every continent, for every imaginable purpose and audience. I have given more than eighty such addresses, including conference papers and overseas lecture tours, in the average of one every three months for twenty years. Many of these lectures were published in one form or other, as books, as in the case of the Haskell Lecture at Oberlin College, which became *The Idea of Purity in Judaism* (Leiden, 1973: E. J. Brill), and the Richard Lectures at the University of Virginia, which produced *Ancient Israel after Catastrophe* (Charlottesville, 1985: The University Press of Virginia); many of them were issued as articles, or as pamphlets for the local audience. I have used these occasions to present to the University at large what seemed to me consequential and important in my own scholarship and thought. In these pages I have selected the few lectures, out of many dozens, that seem to me to warrant more permanent form than the original oral presentation and (commonly) *ad hoc* circulation in an offprint for the occasion.

My purpose in collecting and reprinting the lectures that seemed to me to sustain a second reading is twofold. First, I mean to set forth my conception of discourse appropriate for the academy. There are other conceptions that circulate; the concrete results of one choice in preference to some other seem to me worth placing on display. For even now debate on the character of the academy, on the nature of proper discourse within the academy, and on the calling of the scholar goes forward. That debate is framed both in general terms, in the public press, and also in special language, within the circles of professors of Jewish or Judaic studies and their counterparts in other fields of narrowly ethnic definition and interest. I maintain that every field of the humanities bears the common task of addressing the generality of the University and of doing so in intelligible language and in the framework of shared categories of thought. Since others in word and deed deny that position, I owe it to the academy to show what I mean, as others will show what they mean. Then people can examine the results and decide for themselves what they think is worthwhile.

I concentrate here on issues of history of religion (Part One) and of history (Part Two). In the former I deal with questions of general intelligibility and offer theses that are capable of generalization and application to a variety of religions, not Judaism alone. In the latter I deal with historical problems. I conclude with a lecture that I prepared upon invitation but never gave, the lecture on methodology in talmudic history invited by the Israel Historical Society, Jerusalem, for 1984 but cancelled by that Society when the hosts discovered that they did not wish to hear what I had to say. Specifically, I was asked to send the lecture in advance "for translation into Hebrew;" in fact the intent was to censor. So I sent the lecture in December, 1983, and was immediately disinvited. The disinvitation was because in my lecture I patiently explained to the Israeli talmudic historians why all of their work would now have to be redone and why nothing that their journal, *Zion*, had published in that field in its fifty years of existence could today stand the tests of critical learning. The action of the Israel Historical Society calls into question the academic character of historical learning in that setting, of course. That fact explains the importance of the papers in Part One, where I define my views of the academy as a setting for the study of religion in general, and of Judaism in particular. The anti-academic, sectarian, political, and, I think, simply unprincipled character of the Israel Historical Society and the community it represents contrasts with the humanistic and highly principled definition of the academy of the West.

I express my thanks to those whom I consulted in selecting these papers for publication: Professors Ernest S. Frerichs, Wendell S. Dietrich, and Calvin Goldscheider, Brown University, and William Scott Green, University of Rochester.

Jacob Neusner
The Institute for Advanced Study

Prologue
JUDAISM WITHIN THE NEW HUMANITIES

1

From Text to Context: The Power and the Pathos of the Humanities

*Keynote Address at Humanities Conference
Wayne State University, 1983*

Where we are powerful, there is our pathos. In the fields of humanistic learning we learn a great deal about something special, whether it is a particular history, philosophy, religion, literature, people or culture. But in our mastery of the particular, we lose sight of what we wish to know, what brought us to the work of learning a lot about a little. That motivation is always paradoxical, because it is to find out what we learn about ourselves in studying others. When we in humanistic fields of learning excel, we turn the particular into something exemplary, interesting beyond itself. When we fail, we turn ourselves into fact mongers, telling people things but teaching no suggestive lesson.

Our work at its best contains the power to show that what is most particular and special also speaks to the common human condition, but at its worst transforms us into eccentrics and mere erudites. What makes the difference? It is our use of our imagination to move from what we know to what someone else may also want to know. That is to say, by thinking through, but also beyond, the facts at hand, we may show how the facts speak to questions that transcend the merely private and parochial. So we may perform the miracle of making the whole add up to more than the sum of the parts. This we do by showing that the whole, seen all together, all at once, testifies beyond itself. What lies beyond, specifically, is the condition of humanity to which whatever we know points. The power of imagination transforms what we know into something exemplary of things we do not know.

Let me make this point more concrete. I cannot imagine why people who do not participate in a given particular history, literature, worldview or philosophy and way of life, would want to know a great deal about that system. The specificities at best produce curiosities to astonish us. But what happens when we take a way of life and worldview – a system – and ask ourselves what problems the group at hand has had to work out in framing its social world? "What would it be like if..." – if I were in their place? What would life demand of me, and how should I respond, for example, if I were ripped from my village and home and dragged in chains to a distant port, never again to hear the language that I understood? How would life appear to me if I were taken aboard a ship and sent off to a distant continent, there to work in wretched conditions until I died? And what sort of society would I be capable of reconstructing under such conditions of bondage and oppression as these? By asking me to use my imagination to contemplate the changes at hand, the range of possibilities for confronting and coping with those changes, I enter into the situation of the group under discussion. I then want to know the details of its history, philosophy, literature, way of life and worldview, because they exemplify something important and suggestive about how people respond to a world I can grasp, at least in mind. So the power of imagination – of asking myself, "What would it be like if...?" – that is what allows me to enter into a world that otherwise seems closed and private, particular to those who imagine their ancestors lived in that world, uninteresting to anyone else.

Our imagination throws a bridge from us to the other. To begin with, in our minds we translate the situation of the other into a framework we can grasp. That is what I meant to say by the question, "What if...?" Not many people likely care about what happened to a given individual, carried from village to plantation in a distant continent: He was taken there, he went there, he lost his family, he left behind anyone who could understand his language, he was sold for so many doubloons, he was taken on board a ship named such and such, the captain of the ship paid so and so many doubloons for the slop he fed the passengers, and so on and so forth. Yet when we translate the facts into the human experience at hand, we indeed want to know everything, every detail. And we accomplish the translation through our own imagination, our capacity to reach out in our minds to someone else's experience. What that requires is the power to imagine life other than as we know it, a human situation other than our own. The humanities conducted as human sciences endow us with the power to confront the other in all the difference and alien character of that other, yet both to see something of a common human experience in that other, and to see something alien and unknown even in ourselves. For we can reach out to the alien out of our own experience, shared with the other. Humanistic learning, conducted in all its concrete attention to detail, in the end speaks to that most general of considerations, the human condition, piece by piece, yet everywhere, if not the same, at least equally accessible to humanity.

The point is simple. The power of the humanities to spell out and unpack a specific literature, philosophy, religion, national history, derives from the patience and commitment of the scholar to mastering details. The pathos of the humanities flows from the scholar's incapacity, not to transcend, but to transform detail, to show the common in the uncommon, to turn the particular into something exemplary and suggestive beyond itself. I do not mean to say that the humanities matter only when they cease to be specific, so that our true function is to serve the curiosity of social scientists, looking for examples for their general rules or exceptions to them. Nothing could be further from the case. We serve the social scientists, particularly the anthropologists and sociologists, when we remind them that rule-seeking and generalization, the search for social laws and universally applicable truths – these great adventures in intellectual ambition always must fail. We play Cassandra to the social scientists. They founder on the rocks of the exceptional group, the unusual and the distinctive writing, the inconvenient fact of history. These always place obstacles against generalization. I am reminded of the impatience of my friend, Mary Douglas, who inveighs against what she calls "the argument from Bongo." That is to say, when confronted by a generalization, any group of anthropologists will turn up someone to proclaim, "But my tribe – the Bongo – do not do it that way." We in the humanities, collectively if not one by one, can be relied upon to produce the argument from Bongo. But that is not our interest. It is only our honesty to what we study, which is the infinite diversity of humanity: one by one, individually, in specific detail.

Now moving from these generalizations to specific problems, I turn to what I know best, which is my own work. I want to explain how I propose to transform what is technical and private into something any curious, questing mind would want to know. How do I find what is shared and human in what is distinctive to my particular Bongo? It is by translating the specific into the general, that is, by framing the issues of the texts on which I work in such a way that anyone can in the end make sense of them.

There are several stages of the work. First, I have to read the text in all its detail and accomplish a translation of the text into English. Why is that the necessary first step? The reason is that a text that has not been translated into a language other than its own also has not presented us in detail with the problem of what the other is saying to me. That is to say, if we do not ask the other, the alien – and the text in a language we do not speak always is alien – to speak to us in a language we understand, we have not made contact with the text at all. But as soon as we do make contact, we begin a process of subverting the text's splendid isolation from the rest of the humanity that speaks another language. To translate is to represent one thing in terms of some other. But then to translate is to seek analogies and metaphors for something that, in itself, ultimately remains beyond valid representation or replication in terms other than its own. We who work in foreign cultures and languages all know that. That is why, at the beginning of all humanistic learning about what is not our own, by which I mean, what is not private, utterly subjective and personal to us, we translate.

Now when I asked, then how do I find what is shared and human in what is distinctive and particular? I answered, I begin by translating. Yet what basis do I have for saying that what is distinctive can emerge in terms sufficiently neutral and accessible for outsiders to understand? You will notice I immediately conceded that the basis is shaky indeed. It ultimately rests on the power of analogy and metaphor. This word, in our language, works as does that word, in their language. This conception, in our cultural system, functions like, or corresponds to, that conception, in their cultural system. Translation constitutes a series of perceptive guesses, informed risks. But it is all we have. Recognizing that fact, we understand the parlous nature of our work, its inexact character, its reliance on feeling and experienced insight.

When we move to the step beyond translation, we confront a still less certain task. It is to build on the basis of the confrontation with the text a bridge to the context to which the text speaks. That is so much more a labor of risk-taking that many humanists prefer the more secure frame of philology, text criticism, and commentary, at the end, translation alone. Let me spell out what is to be done, how we move from text to context.

If in hand we have a text that purports to tell us about an event, or presents us with a law system, or takes up a sacred book and tells us what it means and how we are to use it, we commonly ask a set of questions dictated by the contents of the text itself. But we should ask a different set of questions entirely. How so? We often ask whether the event the text narrates happened as the text says it did, or in some other way, or not at all. So we are drawn into the arena of discourse dictated by the text itself. Or, in the case of a law system, we want to explain the laws at hand and relate them to the concerns of the people who believe them. Or, in the case of an account of how we are supposed to read a sacred literature, we allow ourselves to be captured by the details of the hermeneutical task at hand. We ask why they read the given text in one way rather than in some other. We want to know what generated the emphasis on one approach to the canonical document rather than another.

In all these ways we allow the text to divert our attention from the things we want to know and toward the things the framers of the text wanted to tell anyone who would read their text. That is the greatness, the art, of the great humanistic documents, their power to deceive us into thinking that we care about what the authors say in the language the authors chose and for the purposes the authors proposed to carry out. Being drawn into the text in its terms and values, we lose sight of all but what is particular and private – as the text at hand, by definition, tells what it wants to whom it wishes to speak.

If these are the wrong questions (although they are necessary in the address of right questions), then how shall we think through the right questions? Once we have completed the translation of our text, we have to stand back and discover those questions that meet two contradictory conditions.

First, they must be questions the text's authors clearly propose to answer or, at least, allow us to answer in their terms. The questions must be those that, read in one way rather than some other, the text permits us to raise.

Second, they also must be questions that we wish to have answered. We must be willing to stand still to hear the answers or, more concretely, we must find the quest for answers so urgent that we are willing to spend time and energy pursuing those particular questions in that particular text.

Questions inappropriate to the text prove brutal and destructive. An example, in the case of the biblical stories of Creation, would be questions of whether, in detail, the Creation myths of Genesis correspond to the results of contemporary geology and physics. Questions uninteresting to us transform our work into a narrow and technical fact mongering. Such questions turn the humanities into exercises in personal privilege, private whim, and self-indulgence. An example, in the Creation stories, would be questions about the number of letters in a given verse, or the word count in a given set of verses. Unless the information elicited by such questions contributes to literary critical study (and it often does), it is simply purposeless, producing a sense of knowledge when, in fact, all there is are inanity and gibberish.

Once we have translated our text, we have to take up a position on its margins, not too close, not too far. We cannot stand too close to the text, or we shall be drawn by its gravity into its heart and core. We shall then turn ourselves from interpreters on the margins, bilingual in two cultures, to participants and insiders, authorities not *about* the text but *of* the text. Standing too far, we see all things in so general a way that everything looks like everything else. Then the nuances of culture, the differences between societies, the diversity of stress and insistence that distinguish one text from another – all of these points of interest are lost. We end up producing banal generalizations. We reach the conclusion that, well, anyhow, after all, people are pretty much the same all over (or, it doesn't matter what you believe as long as you're a good person). That statement is untrue, except when it is true. I mean to say, if to begin with we know that any text, in any setting, is pretty much the same as any other anywhere, then we abandon our interest in specific worlds. We take up a position of Olympian universalism above them all. From such a height, with everything the same as everything else, we grasp nothing, understand nothing, learn nothing worth knowing. Why? Because no detail corresponds to our detailed context.

But if we seek to preserve our position on the margins, how are we to proceed? I see three steps. First, as I said, we translate the text. That is to move the text from one world to the other. We, on the fringes, attempt to understand both worlds and to speak of the alien world in terms accessible to the familiar one. For our part as marginal figures, we have to know with real feeling and accurate perception both of the worlds we claim to draw together: the one we study, the one we inhabit. Second, we turn to the matter of context; and third, we generalize. Let me now explain what I mean by context and generalization.

When I ask about the context of my text, I want to know (as well as I can) where and when it was written, in what circumstances people thought it important to deliver the message at hand, rather than some other message. I seek to explain why they chose to say what they wished in the kind of language and rhetoric they used, rather than in some other available ones. I ask how come they determined to employ the principles of logical discourse they do to make their ideal intelligible to others, rather than some other such modes of constructing intelligible statements. These questions then concern issues of history and society, on the one side, philosophy and aesthetics, on the other. The historical and social questions allow me to situate the text in a large world. I then may ask questions about the larger world and so establish the ways in which that setting proves congruous, or analogous to, a world I already know. What was the circumstance of the group that received the text? What was the social and political and economical character of the group (or the individual) that produced the text and won for it attention and authority? These two questions seem to me fundamental to all humanistic learning.

The philosophical question concerns logical discourse; the aesthetic one deals with rhetoric. The two cannot be separated from one another. What I ask is whether the text at hand constitutes a cogent statement or a collection of disconnected sentences or even meaningless sequences of sounds. How do the authors propose to make their ideas intelligible to me? What principles of logic join one fact to another, one sentence to the next, and turn the whole into a composition intent upon laying down a proposition? I cannot think of a more fundamental questions to bring to any text, than to ask how and why it is intelligible to me as it was to its writers. Like the historical, social, and economical inquiries, the philosophical and logical ones also aim at making the alien more familiar, overcoming the difference of the unlike and drawing the text at hand into the world of logic and intelligible discourse we all inhabit.

The rhetorical question proves no less critical. It leads to an inquiry into how the logical theorem is given specific wording, the ways in which authors make their ideas not only accessible but also persuasive. here too, we impose the criterion of our own comprehension. We ask the authors to speak, also, to us, we try to open to them our minds, our ears and eyes, and our hearts.

So the context we propose to describe, and interpret, encompasses matters of material culture – politics, society, economics, and class – and issues of the mind and intellect as well. In both dimensions of description, it is clear, we invoke, for the analysts of the other, the measure of ourselves and the dimensions of our world. That of course is pure anachronism. But it is all we have. We cannot go there, so they who wrote the text must somehow come, or be brought, here. But will they come when we call them? We must entice them. For we cannot claim that the text must stand as a monument, in all its purity and distinctiveness, untranslated, uninterpreted, repeated and worshipped but not read and appreciated. The beginning of humanistic learning comes when we insist that we want to grasp what other human beings have thought and felt and understood about themselves – that is, about themselves as human beings. Accordingly, we impose the criterion of meaning that emerges from our condition and ourselves, because we share with them a common humanity. That is a unity not to be disturbed or disordered by the diversities that make us what we are –

different from the other that we study – and define us apart from one another.

From description and analysis, the move to generalization demands no long steps. But it is the critical initiative. Once we have translated the text into our language, the context of the text into our setting, we have thrown across the abyss that bridge we seek to construct. For if we know what people have said and the social world to which they have said it, we may also generalize. We can compare that world to ours, that message to what is in our minds. We may propose a thesis that, in such-and-so circumstance, these are the messages wise women and men have laid forth. This is how people respond who face this set of circumstances rather than some other. Knowing ourselves and our world, we may then compare and contrast what they did to what we do, what they might have done to what we wish we could do.

The labor of generalization proves still more uncertain than the earliest stages I described. Few scholars undertake to speak out of what they know as learned people to the world in which they live. True enough, many address the world as citizens but cloak themselves in the mantel of scholars. But it is not common for the humanists to invoke what they know when addressing the world in which, no different from anyone else, they stumble and search for wisdom.

It may not sound like much. But it is no small thing in an age that perpetually totters on the brink, to be able to say what others did – people who were strangers in alien times, speaking incomprehensible languages, talking about topics we do not grasp to people we cannot imagine. In such an age, in such a circumstance as ours we can do worse than to invoke the metaphors and analogues contributed by the ages. How others kept their balance at the edge of the precipice after all may bring reassurance to us that we need not fall and should not despair. For an age such as ours, not to despair serves as an act of heroism.

I have come a long way in purporting to tell about my work and, in all this account, I have not once hinted at the world in which I spend my time. Let me say I speak of a defeated people, living out the centuries beyond their utter disaster. I study the writings of a small group of intellectuals within that people. I listen as they tell their own generation those lessons of social order and inner balance and cohesion that sustained the vanquished nation from their day onward. I deal with the losers, the wanderers, the loners in time, the ones whose triumph consists of mere survival and whose day never comes. From that description of my frame of reference, you could imagine that I deal with every continent and any age: with the Incas and the Mayas and the Aztecs after the Spanish came, or with the whole of Latin America in its self-understanding. You could suppose that I study the Zulus of the nineteenth century or the Finns of the twentieth, the Koreans from the end of the nineteenth century through World War II, or the islanders of the Pacific trust territories, the Inuit today or the peoples of the hills and the swamps, the lands no one covets and the languages no one speaks, the wanderers through the Sahel and through the outback in search of water and food. Any time, any place could define this scholar's study of the defeated who hung on and who hang on even today. You could guess that I work on the Germans after the Thirty Years War, the French after 1870, the English after 1066, the Scots after 1745, the Irish after Cromwell, or the Russian through nearly the whole of their sorry history as victims of foreign invasion. Or, given my stress on the issue of the mentality of survival and the social world constructed by the heirs of victims, you could even guess that I work on the future, thinking about public discourse of a rational character after the ultimate irrationality of humanity's self-destruction in the final war of history as we know it.

In fact, I work on the Jews from the first through the sixth centuries. They produced a literature with few rivals in the competition to write in an arcane and private way about subjects that to begin with interest no one. They created a society that went its way, separate from others, with few clear-cut points of contact with the larger world in which they lived. They developed a worldview that spoke essentially to their own group, with little interest in the outside world, which they viewed as undifferentiated and a realm of death. Why would anyone want to know about them and make the effort to translate not only their texts, but also their context, bringing both into a world so different from theirs as is our own? Even the generality of Jews today pay no attention to the documents at hand or, if they claim to honor these writings, treat them as a treasury of unconnected prooftexts and pretexts. And yet when I tell you that, among the group at hand – no more like us than the Asora mudmen of Kundiawa, in Chimbu Province in Papua New Guinea before the great Australian explorers came to the Eastern Highlands and to Kundiawa – when I tell you that these strange, incomprehensible, utterly alien minds said things about hope in an age of despair and order in a world of chaos, you will understand what is at issue. These Jews who wrote the Talmud sustained and nourished the Jewish people in its long journey through time. What they show the world at large is one route to survival, one resource for the power to endure. Since the issue confronting humanity in every age remains how to contend with disappointment without despair, how to deal with chaos with surrender, how to carry on and overcome and reaffirm ourselves against it all, despite it all – since the issue facing us all is always how to overcome, the message of the unimportant and utterly alien group at hand proves remarkably urgent.

So to conclude where I began, I spend my life studying something very specific. I want to learn more than anyone else about this diminishing circle of less and less. But I bring to the texts that occupy me a program of humanistic inquiry. Following the agenda of the humanities, I try to make what is particular into something exemplary, and what is private into something public and important. I seek to discern how large issues inhere in small actions. This I do not by ignoring the details that differentiate, but by trying to understand the system as a whole created and sustained only in detail.

To see the system as a whole, I have first to encounter the smallest glyphs of which it is made up, that is to say, the words that comprise its sentences, the sentences that add up to paragraphs, the paragraphs that express propositions and define the position of the system. Turning these glyphs and their tablets into a language other than the original – one we can grasp too – I draw the system as a whole into contact with a world beyond itself. In so doing, I seek points of contrast and comparison to determine what is like, and what is unlike, the known in the unknown, the unknown in the known. Once I accomplish that work of making the alien less strange and of isolating what must remain different (and even beyond comprehension), I proceed to the next stage. It is the definition in neutral and accessible categories and terms of what began as something highly special and wholly other. These categories and terms, drawn from our world but appropriate also to that other world, allow me to interpret the unknown in terms of the known, the world out there in the language of the world in here.

In the end, my judgment of what mattered then and in that faraway place depends upon the things I notice. I notice what strikes me as important. What seems important in the end emerges in our setting, not in theirs. Significance depends to begin with upon our entirely contemporary perspective on matters. So in the humanities we do not attain an objective stance, separate from our setting and also distinct from the setting of the world represented by the text at hand. Such a place on which to stand, above and beyond both them and us, would leave us too far away to see anything we can recognize. So we are left in our human circumstance to try to make sense, in terms always our own, of that other human circumstance. That other humanity, preserved in the history, the religion, the language, the literature, the social world that created and handed on the texts at hand, is not entirely like us. If it were, we humanists would live far easier lives, enjoy far more certainty than we do. But it also is not entirely unlike us. If it were, our work would prove impossible. So as we move from text to context, we build a bridge from ourselves to the other who, in the end, is also one of us.

For that reason our mode of learning cannot ever claim to attain that objective and universal standing alleged (mostly by nonscientists) to characterize scientific knowledge. Nor will the rules and theorems of the humanities (if there are any) ever compare to the certainties of mathematics and physics. The humanities work in such conditions that the results endure for only a moment, and then in small and limited circumstances. For the humanists as scholars never fully escape the uncertainty of the human condition, either of what they study or of the frail selves of those who do the work.

But we have gotten this far, and that is no mean accomplishment. We do know more, we do grasp and understand more, about ourselves as part of a common humanity, than we did before. For then all we were was believers, and all we did was repeat the words of the text in the language of the text to the people who revered the text. Today many of us propose to restore the text to the circumstance of shared discourse, to phrase the language of the text to speak to people who read the text for new reasons, with a new set of pressing issues. We are, and we speak to, people who need access as never before to all of those texts that, in our time and place, tell us what we as human beings have learned about life together on this planet.

Part One
LECTURES ON JUDAISM AMONG RELIGIONS

2

Thinking About "The Other" in Religion: It is Necessary, but Is It Possible?

Uomini e religione Conference, Warsaw, 1989, commemorating the fiftieth anniversary of the Start of World War II
The Beaven Lecture
University of Rochester, April 24, 1990

The single most important problem facing religion for the next hundred years, as for the last, is an intellectual one: how to think through difference, how to account, within one's own faith and framework, for the outsider, indeed, for many outsiders. True, people think that the most important problem confronting religion is secularity or falling away; but, it is clear from all studies, religious affiliation remains constant. Not only so, but when we look at the evidence of our own eyes, we find the vital signs of religion attested in the headlines everyday: Christian civil war in Ireland, monotheist civil war in the Middle East, the breakup of the Soviet Empire by reason of religious conflict – these attest to the power of religion. But they also remind us of its pathos, which is the incapacity of religions to form for themselves a useful theory of the other. That, not secularization, defines the critical task facing religions: their excess of success in persuading the believers, so that believers not only love one another, they hate everybody else.

The commonplace theory of religious systems concerning the other or the outsider, consigning to incomprehensibility the different and the other, finds ample illustration here. What do you do with the outsider? Find the other crazy (as we did Ayatollah Khomeini and Jim

Jones of Jonestown), or declare the other the work of the devil (as the Ayatollah did with us), or declare the other subject to such metaphors as unclean, impure, dangerous, to be exterminated, as the Germans – Christians, ex-Christians alike – did with the Jews. These will no longer serve, if they ever did. Religions will have to learn how to think about the other, not merely to tolerate the other as an unavoidable inconvenience or an evil that cannot be eliminated. For reasons I shall explain, they face the task of thinking, within their own theological framework and religious system, about the place, within the structure, of the other outside of it. And that is something no religion has ever accomplished up to this time.

Religions have spent their best intellectual energies in thinking about themselves, not about the outsider. Why should this be so? The reason is that religions form accounts of a social world, the one formed by the pious; they set forth a worldview, define a way of life that realizes that worldview, and identify the social entity that constitutes the world explained by the worldview and embodied in the way of life: world without end. The this-worldly power of religion derives from its capacity to hold people together and make them see themselves as not a given but a gift: special, distinctive, chosen, saved – whatever. But the very remarkable capacity of religions to define all that is important about a person, a family, a group also incapacitates religions in a world in which, it is clear, difference must be accommodated. For in explaining the social world within, religions also build walls against the social world without, and in consequence religions impose upon the other, the outsider, a definition and a standing that scarcely serve the social order and the public interest.

For theories of "the other" that afford at best toleration, at worst humiliation and subordination, may have served in an age of an ordered society, but they do not fit a time in which social change forms the sole constant. It is one thing to design a hierarchical society defined by religion when one religion is on top, all others subordinated, as was the case in the Islamic nation(s) from the seventh century, and as was the case in Christian Europe until the rise of the nation-state. A hierarchy based upon religion, with Islam at the apex, Christianity and Judaism tolerated but on the whole well-treated minorities, served so long as all parties accepted their place. So too, Christian European society before the Reformation had its dual theory of religious difference within the social order: the Christian state, headed by Pope, Christ's deputy, and monarch, the secular Christian counterpart. In such an order, Judaism found its place as testimony, Islam kept at bay across the Pyranees or Mediterranean and then was forced back in the Near East itself, and paganism would be eliminated. But with the shaking of the foundations, in the Reformation, for instance, the social order trembled, Christianity in the West became two, then many, and the hierarchical structure tottered. Then what of the other? Jews were driven to the east, the more tolerant, pioneering territories of Poland, Lithuania, White Russia, the Ukraine; Islam would then be ignored; and Christians would spend centuries killing other Christians – some theory of the other! some theory of the social order!

The solution of the seventeenth century was simple: the head of state defines the governing Church. That served where it served. The solution of the eighteenth century was still more simple: tolerate everything, because all religions are equally ridiculous. But no religion accepted either theory of religious difference, and it was with no theory of the other, of religious difference, formed within religious conviction and loyalty, that the West entered its great ages of consolidation and expansion and fruition, then dissolution and civil strife, in the nineteenth and twentieth centuries. The civil war of Western, then world, civilization proved no age for thinking about the social order, and the pressing problem of religious accommodation of religious difference hardly gained attention. The reason is that, from 1914 to nearly the present day, it was by no means clear that humanity would survive the civil war fought at such cost and for so long. With a million killed in one battle in 1915, with twenty million Soviet citizens killed in World War II after a prior ten million Soviet citizens were killed by their own government in the decade preceding the war, with six million Jews murdered in factories built to manufacture death – with humanity at war with itself, religions could hardly be expected to reconsider long-neglected and scarcely urgent questions.

Yet, it is obvious, religious theories of religious difference, that is, a theory formed within the framework of a religious worldview, way of life, and social entity, about those beyond that framework, do impose upon us an urgent task now. Part of the reason is the simple fact that we have survived the twentieth century. In 1945 no one knew we would, and many doubted it. But the atomic peace is holding, and while the competition between our own country and the Soviet Union will take other forms, the threat of armed conflict on a global scale diminishes, because the USSR at this time cannot mount such a war.

That adventitious fact by itself would hardly precipitate deep thought within religion on the requirements of the social order: how to get along with the outsider. But a more important fact does. It is that, as I said before, the two hundred year campaign against religion on the part of forces of secularization has simply failed. Faith in God, worship of God, life with God – these testimonies to the vitality of religions and therefore also of religion are measurable: people go to

Church or synagogue, they observe this rite and that requirement, they make their pilgrimages, and by these quite objective measures of the fact of human action, the vast majority of most of the nations of the world is made up of religious believers of one kind or another. All claims that secularization is the established and one-way process, and the demise of religion forms the wave of the future have defied the facts of religious power and (alas) worldly glory. Not only is religion strong in its own realm, religious affiliations and commitments define loyalties and concerns in the larger social world of politics and culture. Anyone who doubts it had better try to explain without religion the intense opposition to abortion manifested by from one third to nearly half (depending on the framing of the issue) of the voting population of this country – like it or not. In the formation of social groups, for instance, where we live, how we choose our friends, whom we marry, religion remains a critical indicator.

And that brings us back to the century rushing toward us, an age of parlous peace, a time in which, for the first time in human history, we have the opportunity of a period of sustained peace – but only if. We can have peace on earth only if we find sources of good will for one another, for, in the end, moved by hatred, we may well bring down upon ourselves the roof of the temple that is over us all. Hatred of the other, after all, forms a powerful motive to disregard love of self, and anyone who doubts that fact had better reconsider the history of Germany from July, 1944, through May, 1945. At that time, when everyone knew the German cause was finished, hatred of the other sufficed to sustain a suicidal war that ended with the absolute ruin of all Germany; more people died in the last nine months of World War II than in the first five years. And all that kept Germany going on the path to its own complete destruction was hatred: drag them all down with us. So much for the power of hatred. There is, then, no guarantee, despite the *pax atomica* that protects us now, of a long-term peace. There is good reason to tremble, when we consider how hatred, brewed within religious theories of the other as the devil for example, leads nations to act contrary to all rational interest; the war between Iraq and Iran suffices to prove that point.

So there really is a considerable and urgent task before religions today, the task of addressing a question long thought settled by the various religious systems that now flourish. It is the question of the other. And the question is to be framed in terms that only religions can confront, that is to say, the theological theory of the other. The theological question of the other has been framed in these terms: how, as a believing person, can I make sense of the outsider? And for a long time, that had to make do. But now we have to reframe the question:

how, as a believing person, can I make sense of the outsider with not mere tolerance of difference but esteem for a faith not my own?

To expand the question, how can I form a theory of the other in such a way that within my own belief I can respect the other and accord to the outsider legitimacy within the structure of my own faith?

I say very simply that no Western religious tradition has ever answered those questions. None has tried. The hierarchical theory of religions has served, by which, as I said, Islam at the apex made room for Christianity and Judaism and eliminated everything else; or Christianity at the apex (always in theory, sometimes in practice) found a cave, a cleft in the rock, for Judaism, kept Islam out of sight, and eliminated everything else. Judaism for its part expressed its hierarchical counterpart by assigning to undifferentiated humanity (Islam and Christianity never singled out for special handling) a set of requirements for a minimal definition of a humane and just social order, with holy Israel, God's first love, responsible for everything else. Of you God wants civility, of us, holiness: a hierarchy with one peak and a vast flat plain, no mountain of ascent in-between.

When we take note of how religions in the past and present have thought about the other, we may perceive the full weight of the task that is now incumbent upon us. For, looking backward, all our models tell us what not to do, but we have scarcely a single model to emulate. Let me give two examples of how religions have thought about the other, one out of times past, the other out of nearly our own age. The one concerns how Judaism thought about Christianity when, in the fourth century, it was forced to do so, the other, how British Christianity thought about Buddhism when, in the nineteenth century, it found it required a theory to make sense of chaotic facts. In both cases, we see religions thinking about the other solely in terms of themselves. We then discern the unprecedented character of the next phase in theological reflection: a Christian theology of the other in terms of the other – for faithful Christians; a Judaic theology of the other in terms of the other – for believing Jews. That effort at treating as legitimate and authentic a religion other than our own, and with it and on its account, treating as worthy of respect because of their religion religious people different from ourselves, we have never seen on this earth before, though in the past quarter century, the beginnings of the work have been attempted, so far as I know solely by Roman Catholic and mainstream Protestant theologians.

The case of Judaism tells us when and why a religion must frame a theory of the other. It is when political change of a fundamental character changes the social world that a religious system addresses, so imposing an urgent question that must be addressed. In the case of

Judaism, that change, at once political and religious, came about when in the fourth century Christianity became the religion of the Roman Empire. At that moment, the new faith, long ignored as a petty inconvenience at best, required attention, and, more to the point, the fundamental allegations of the new faith, all of them challenges to Judaism, demanded response. Christians had long told Israel that Jesus is Christ, so the Messiah has come, and there is no further salvation awaiting Israel; that they were now bearers of the promises of the Old Testament and in them the Israelite prophets' predictions were realized; that they were now Israel and Israel was now finished. The political change in government made it necessary for the people of Israel, particularly in the Land of Israel ("Palestine") to respond, as in the prior three centuries they had not had to respond, to Christianity.

What they did by way of response was not to form a theory of Christianity within the framework of Judaism, but to re-form their theory of Judaism, that is to say, of who is Israel and what is its relationship, through the Torah, with God. And to that theory, Christendom was simply beside the point. And within that theory – that religious system defining the holy way of life, worldview, and social entity that was Israel – Christianity did not find any explanation at all. Nor has it ever since. But at least, for a brief moment, Judaism thought about Christianity. Forced to do so by political change, that stunning shift in the political circumstance of a religion affected that religion's thought about, among other enduring questions, the outsider, the other, the brother and the enemy. And, as a matter of fact, in thinking about the other, that same religion reconsidered the enduring and long-settled issues concerning itself as well. The fact that thinking about the other means we have also to rethink the truth about ourselves explains, I think, why we are so reluctant to do so.

The particular case involves Judaism at the moment at which Christianity became first licit, then favored, then for a brief interval disgraced, and finally, at the end of the fourth century, the official religion of the Roman Empire.[1] The age of Constantine, the fourth century (dates for convenience: from 312, when Constantine extended toleration to Christianity, to 429, when the Jewish government of the Land of Israel ceased to enjoy the recognition of the state) marks the century in which Christianity joined the political world of the Roman Empire. In that century Christianity gained power, briefly lost it, and,

---

[1] I call upon the results of my *Judaism and Christianity in the Age of Constantine: Issues in the Initial Confrontation* (Chicago, 1987: The University of Chicago Press).

finally, regained the throne and assured its permanent domination of the state. Christians saw Israel as God's people, rejected by God for rejecting the Christ. Israel saw Christians, now embodied in Rome, as Ishmael, Esau, Edom: the brother and the enemy. The political revolution marked by Constantine's conversion forced the two parties to discuss a single agendum and defined the terms in which each would take up that agendum.

The politics of Rome in the fourth century therefore produced the first true confrontation between Judaic and Christian intellectuals. By confrontation I mean not actual, face-to-face discourse, but substantive debate, each party speaking to its own group in its own idiom, to be sure, on issues defined in the same terms, through the medium of the same modes of argument, with appeal to the same facts. This is the form in which thought about the other took place, and the only form: considering, at least, questions of interest to the outsider. That is something that did not happen before, and never happened again, until our own time. In the fourth century, the age of Constantine, Judaic sages and Christian theologians met in a head-on argument on a shared agendum and confronted the fundamental issues of the historical existence of politics and society in the West: doctrine, specifically, the meaning of history; teleology, specifically, the eschatological teleology formed by the messianic doctrine identifying Jesus as Christ; and the symbolism of the godly society, specifically, the identity of God's social medium – Israel – in the making of the world. Accordingly, for the first and probably the last time in the history of Judaism and Christianity in the West, differing people argued about the same things, sharing common premises and a single core of probative facts.

Political change shaped then theological discourse, and, I argue, political change now will reshape that same discourse Specifically, the reason that the two parties addressed issues defined in the same way – I maintain – derives from the political challenge facing them both. Each party, in its own setting, had to take up that challenge in terms essentially identical to those that confronted the other, in its context. When emperors convert and governments shift allegiance, the world shakes under everyone's feet. There was an argument on these issues, but no argument on any other issues for a simple reason. The issues under debate bore political consequences, and the others did not. True enough, both sides shared an interest in the issues of the scriptural canon and the exegesis of Scripture. But I cannot find points on which they argued on the same topic in the same terms invoking the same corpus of evidence. That is why I argue that the reason both parties could share a single program of debate is political.

Enormous shifts in the political facts of the world, represented by the growing control of Christianity over the institutions of state and government, raised for both Judaic sages and Christian theologians issues that, to begin with, the Scriptures of ancient Israel ("the Written Torah," "the Old Testament") had defined. These issues focused on the meaning of history, viewed by epochs, each with its message; the identity of the Messiah; and the definition of Israel, God's people, with special reference to the social metaphor and theological value imputed to that "Israel after the flesh" constituted by the Jews of the day. These three issues proved paramount specifically because the political revolution effected in the course of the fourth century by the Christianization of the Roman Empire made them urgent and transformed them into matters of public policy. Prior to that political change, Judaic and Christian thinkers had no common argument. Afterward, they wanted none.

No form of Christianity made an impact upon the systematic thought of any of the Judaic authorships known to us. That fact will become clear in the next section, in which we consider a Judaic system formed out of all relationship to interests of Christianity, for example, in the Messiah, the meaning of history, and similar eschatological questions. And the contrary also is the case. The formulation by Judaic thinkers of important theological categories, and the doctrines that imparted to those categories the meaning that they would have, never made an impact on the thought of the Church. What the Church knew was simply that the Jews did not believe in Jesus Christ. Before that time, the Christian theologians and Judaic sages had not accomplished that feat of framing a single program for debate. Judaic sages had earlier talked about their issues to their audience, Christian theologians had for three centuries pursued their arguments on their distinctive agenda. The former pretended the latter did not exist. The latter framed doctrines concerning the former solely within the logical requirements of the internal arguments of Christianity. There had been no confrontation of an intellectual character, since neither party had addressed the issues important to the other in such a way that the issues found a mutually agreeable definition, and that the premises of argument, the core of shared facts and shared reason, likewise formed a mutually acceptable protocol of discourse. Later on, as we shall see in the epilogue, the confrontation would shift, so that no real debate on a shared set of issues, defined in the same way by both parties, unfolded. The politics did not require it, and the circumstance prevented it.

In the fourth century by contrast issues urgent for Christian thinkers proved of acute, not merely chronic, concern for Judaic ones as well. In my view, this came about not because differences on Scripture and its meaning by themselves could produce debate. Those differences became urgent only when matters of public policy, specifically, the ideology of state (empire, for the Christians; supernatural nation or, as we shall see, family, for the Jews) demanded a clear statement on the questions at hand. When the Roman empire and Israelite nation had to assess the meaning of epochal change, when each had to reconsider the teleology of society and system as the identity of the Messiah defined that teleology, when each had to reconsider the appropriate metaphor for the political unit, namely, people, nation, extended family, only then did chronic disagreement become acute difference. It was the progressive but remarkable change in the character of the Roman government, at the beginning of the century pagan and hostile to Christianity, at the end of the century Christian and hostile to paganism, that was decisive. In the age of Constantine the terms of the fifteen-hundred-year confrontation between Judaism and Christianity reached conclusive formulation.

To state matters in a simple way, before the fourth century Judaism and Christianity (as defined by their intellectuals) comprised different people talking about different things to different people. In the fourth century the shape of discourse shifted. Because of a political event that Israel could not ignore and the Church deemed probative, discourse between Judaism and Christianity would find different people talking to different people about some of the same things. The reason for the shift and for the particular topics at hand is a common politics. There is a second factor, namely, common premises, deriving from common Scriptures, about the importance of politics, that is, history. Both parties to the common argument shared a single canon – the Hebrew Scriptures ("Old Testament," "Written Torah") and, more important, both parties confronted the same political facts and had to deal with them. The common argument proved possible, therefore, because the intellectuals of the two parties shared a single intellectual and social world. And that fact is critical today as well, for here again, living in our global village, we have no choice but to talk about the same things: what is theirs is ours, and what is ours is theirs.

So far I have argued that people talk about the same things when they have to, and that they talk about the same things, also, because they can. But, when they do so, what sort of discourse emerges? One answer to that question derives from Western theories of Buddhism. Indeed, because of recent research, we are able to compare how the West formed a theory of Buddhism at two different periods, the one medieval and Christian, the other modern and imperial. The medieval Christian response to Buddhism came about in a brief period when Mongol cavalry in 1211, like the United States Navy today, ranged from the western Pacific to the Black Sea. In the thirteenth century the Mongols became facts with which the Christian West had to deal. The possibilities for both Levantine and Latin Christianity, as D. A. Scott outlines them, were these: "They could cooperate with the Mongols against their common Islamic rivals and enemies....In religious terms the Mongols could be thought of as a prize to be won....As for the Mongols themselves, they fell more and more in the thirteenth century under the 'higher' universalistic religions of Christianity, Islam, and Buddhism."[2] Christianity through the Pope sent envoys to the Mongol Court; the Nestorians spread through Central Asia and China. For its part, Buddhism moved west through Transoxania, Persia, and Asia Minor.

How did Christianity respond to Islam between the earliest encounters, 1244, and the latest, 1349? The simple answer is this: they tried to make sense of Buddhism within the established categories of Christianity, explaining for themselves, and evaluating, Buddhist beliefs and practices by the analogy to Christian ones. Christian doctrinal priorities prevailed, as Christians entered into debate with Buddhism. It was argument by analogy, but only one party got to define the analogies. Buddhism of course would be considered a form of idolatry. But use of incense, chanting, imagery, scriptures, ornate robes – to all of these Christians could find analogies in their own experience. Scott concludes his account with these words: "None of the medieval writers...was systematically constructing a theology of religious encounter and dialogue; none of them was considering Buddhism in a deliberate phenomenological way."[3] But, then, the encounter was brief; the worlds were many; and when they collided, it was only for a moment.

The modern age is something else. Now, when Christianity once more meets Buddhism, it is in a permanent relationship in a world increasingly diminished as to distance and as to difference too. So while medieval Christians naturally looked for the familiar in the unfamiliar, therefore finding analogies within unfamiliar Buddhism to the known realities of Christianity, when the British reencountered Buddhism, now in the imperial age of the nineteenth century, they faced a more formidable task. It was both to make sense and also to justify: to make sense of a continuing presence, to justify their own presence within the Buddhist world. Philip C. Almond just now has demonstrated a fact that, so far as I know, none has appreciated before,

---

[2] D. A. Scott, "Medieval Christian Responses to Buddhism," *Journal of Religious History* 1988, 15:165-184. Quotation: p. 165.
[3] Ibid., p. 184.

which is that the very concept of "Buddhism" is an invention of the West. He says, "There was an imaginative creation of Buddhism in the first half of the nineteenth century, and...the Western creation of Buddhism progressively enabled certain aspects of Eastern cultures to be defined, delimited, and classified....The reification of the term 'Buddhism'...defined the nature and content of this entity."[4]

Almond's point is that, while thinking they were discovering Buddhism, in fact Western scholars were inventing it. For they formed a category of their own choosing so as to join and homogenize a vast variety of data that, in their own setting, were differentiated and not harmonized. Scholarship on Buddhism then forms a chapter in the Western response to the world made necessary by imperialism. As Western nations conquered foreign lands and took them over, they had to answer two questions: [1] what is this? and [2] why is it mine? The first question demanded making sense of nonsense, that is, the unfamiliar, and the second asked an equally nonsensical question: what am I doing here? The way in which the first question was answered differed from the medieval theory of the other. The medieval Christians looked for analogies to make the other familiar. The modern ones simply made the other familiar by remaking it into their own image, after their own likeness. Being scholars, they not only organized, they also selected the data with which they could conveniently cope, which is to say, books they could bring home, publish, and study in their libraries.

The work of definition — the British invention of Buddhism – came first. It involved seeing points in common, connections, between Ceylon and Thailand and China and Japan and Burma, the invention of a single classification, "Buddhism, the religion of Buddha" (by analogy to Christianity, the religion of Christ), to form of these vast territories a single entity, a single religion. Almond describes this phenomenon in these words:

> I have tried...to avoid giving the impression that Buddhism existed prior to the end of the eighteenth century: that it was waiting in the wings...to be discovered; that it was floating in some aethereal Oriental limbo, expecting its objective embodiment. On the contrary, what we are witnessing in the period from the later part of the eighteenth century to the beginning of the Victorian period in the latter half of the 1830s is the *creation* of Buddhism. It *becomes* an object, is constituted as such; it takes form as an entity that "exists" over against the various cultures which can now be perceived as instancing it, manifesting it, in an enormous variety of

---

[4]Philip C. Almond, *The British Discovery of Buddhism* (Cambridge, 1989: Cambridge University Press), p. 4.

ways....Buddhism, as constructed in the West, made manageable that which was encountered in the East by travellers, diplomats, missionaries, soldiers, traders, and so on. Buddhism as a taxonomic object organized that which the Westerner confronted in an alien space, and in so doing made it less alien, less other.[5]

Then where shall we find the sources for the characterization of this invention? The sources of Buddhism would be identified as the classical writings; these tell the authentic religion, and their picture defines the measure against which the contemporary, chaotic Buddhisms will be assessed (and found, as a matter of fact, decadent, degraded, inauthentic). Almond describes what I should call the "textualization" of Buddhism in these words:

> Buddhism had become by the middle of the nineteenth century a textual object based in Western institutions. Buddhism as it came to be ideally spoken of through the editing, translating, and studying of its ancient texts could then be compared with its contemporary appearance in the Orient. And Buddhism as it could be seen in the East compared unfavorably with its ideal textual exemplifications contained in the libraries, universities, colonial offices, and missionary societies of the West.[6]

So Almond proves, in his language,

> Buddhism was reified as a textual object. By the middle of the Victorian period, Buddhism was seen as essentially constituted by its textuality, and it was the Buddhism thus constructed and thus interpreted that was the criterion against which its manifestations in the "Orient" were measured, and generally...found wanting. A crucial product of this process of the textualization of Buddhism was the emergence of the historical Buddha. By the middle of the Victorian period the Buddha had emerged from the wings of myth and entered the historical stage. No longer identified with the ancient gods, distinct from the Hindu account of him and his mythical predecessors, the Buddha was a human figure – one to be compared not with the gods but with other historical personalities, and one to be interpreted in the light of the Victorian ideal of humanity."[7]

So, in a word, in developing a theory of the other, the British invented Buddhism, defined it as a textual object, published the texts, in all, "determined the framework in which Buddhism was imaginatively constructed, not only for themselves, but also in the final analysis for the East itself....This was an aspect of the Western creation of two qualitatively different modes of being human, the oriental and the occidental....This fundamental mode of organizing the East [provided

---

[5]Ibid., pp. 12-13.
[6]Ibid., p. 37.
[7]Ibid., pp. 139-140.

a] conceptual filter through which acceptable aspects of Buddhism could be endorsed, unacceptable ones rejected."[8]

The case of the British invention of Buddhism, of course, bring us close to our own day. For what we see is that the British intellectuals solved the problem of the other by making the other over into the self. These certainties, these self-evident truths and obviously valid judgments – all constituted a re-presentation of the other into the self. And that is at its foundations not vastly different from the fourth-century Judaic intellectuals' confrontation of the other wholly in terms of the self, and the thirteenth-century Christian intellectuals' reading of the other wholly in terms of the self. That is what people do, the difference between the religious fourth- and thirteenth-century versions and the secular nineteenth-century version being only the honesty and innocence of the former times, as against the ineffable snobbery of the moderns. Judaic theology did not like Christianity, but it did not hold it in contempt and it did not reinvent it; Christian theology did not like Buddhism, but, while misinterpreting through miscast analogies, it did not fabricate it; but the British intellectuals of the nineteenth century made up the other in their own image, after their own likeness – and in their own studies, turned into factories for the manufacture of mass-produced others, all of them in the model of the self.

And that brings us back to our own time, which is, after all, not the twentieth but the twenty-first century. Ours is an intellectual task, for if we cannot in a rational and rigorous way think religiously about the other, then the good works of politics and the ordering of society will not be done. And the dimensions of our task are formidable. For we have seen what does not serve. Tolerance works only in a climate of indifference; when you care, so it seems, you also hate. Toleration works where law prevails, but the limits of the law are set by sovereign power, and the range of difference on the other side of the border stretches to the last horizon. So are we able in wit and imagination, mind and intellect, to form a theory of the other coherent with the entire structure of the world that our religious worldview, way of life, account of the "us" that is the social entity, comprise? The issue of coherence is critical, and that matter of cogency with the whole religious system explains why at stake are theological propositions. Tolerance is a mere social necessity, but, we all recognize, simply not a theological virtue. Anyone who doubts should recall the ridicule that met the position, "It does not matter what you believe, as long as you're

---

[8]Ibid., p. 140.

a good person," not to mention, "it does not matter what you believe, as long as you believe something."

But beyond tolerance, and before theology – that is where we now stand. The history of religion is teaching us about the failures of the past, so closing off paths that lead nowhere. Can religious systems make sense of what lies beyond the system? In my judgment the answer must be affirmative, because the question comes with urgency.

Where to begin? I think it is with the recognition of the simple fact that the world really is different beyond its difference from us. By that I mean, religious systems differentiate within, but homogenize the world beyond. They find it possible to conduct a detailed exegesis of their own social order, forming their own hierarchy within; but when it comes to the world beyond the limits of the system, everything is represented as pretty much the same. And that is a component of the systemic coping with difference: we are differentiated because we matter, the outside is undifferentiated because there, difference is trivial. But Catholics hate Protestants, and the hatred has nothing to do with us Jews; and Protestants have contempt for Catholics, leaving us out as well. And we nurture our spite too. So difference is not only within the system, and that means, systems must think about more differences than until now they have tended to encompass.

When religious systems address the differences among outsiders, they will quite naturally reframe the question of difference in yet another way. They will not only understand that Christians are all Christians only to Jews or Muslims, but to Christians, Christians are profoundly divided. They will also understand that difference applies within: the participants of a system participate in many systems. Pluralism is existential, not only social; all of us live in many systems, working our way through many worlds, mostly serial worlds, but sometimes, synchronous ones. I am not quite sure how any of us holds together the worlds of work and home, vocation and avocation, or the considerable range of loyalties that divide our hearts. But most of us do. Then, in this context, we are not only systemically Judaic or Christian or Buddhist. We are systemically defined within other frameworks as well. Those of us who are intellectuals live within one framework, with its way of life and worldview and social entity; those of us who are politicians live within another, with its way of life, worldview, and political class; those of us who are athletes live by yet another schedule and do other things; and so it goes; and that is to speak only of the intersecting systems of the common life. What shall we then say of home and family and its confusion? In all, the happy chaos of our lives belies the neat and orderly hierarchy that religious systems impute to the social world. Whether in times past people lived so neatly ordered I cannot say; but today they do not. Religion matters not only because it integrates, it matters because it is one of the sole media of integration left to us. But for all of its power to define who we are and what we want to be and to what "us" we belong, religion too forms only one circle, concentric, perhaps, with more of the circles of our lives than others, but coexistent with the lives of only a few specialists. For the rest, religious difference is just another difference. Now that is something for theology to think about. And when theology addresses difference within, then quite naturally a theory of difference beyond will take shape. But it is, after all, asking much of a theology of Judaism to think about difference within the social world of Judaism. Recognizing that fact – and it is a fact – after all contradicts the integrating task that the religious system performs, and that theology is meant to explain. This is a time for intellectuals to do their work courageously.

3

Judaism and Christianity in the First Century: How Shall We Perceive Their Relationship?

Lecture, January 11, 1989,
Pontifical Lateran University
Lecture, August 23, 1989,
National Council of Catholic Bishops, Brasília

From the Nazi period onward, the Roman Catholic Church has formulated its relationship with Judaism in language and symbols meant to identify with the Jewish People, God's first love. To signal his opposition to anti-Semitism, Pope Pious said, "Spiritually, we are all Semites," and in the aftermath of "the Holocaust," successive Popes and princes of the Church have claimed for Roman Catholic Christianity a rightful share in the spiritual patrimony of Abraham. The epoch-making position of Vatican II marked only a stage forward in the process of conciliation and reconciliation that has marked the Roman Catholic framing of its relationship with both the Jewish People and with Judaism. As an American I have followed with enormous pride the particularly sustained and effective redefinition of that relationship, which has had its effect upon the civil order and public policy of my own country. The sages of Judaism define the hero as one who turns an enemy into a friend, and the present century's record of the Roman Catholic Church, seen whole and complete, must be called heroic.

And yet in consequence of that sustained and, I believe, holy work, a theory of the relationship between Judaism and Christianity in the first century has taken shape that I believe has exacted a price in both learning and also self-esteem. That theory stems from the correct claim of Christianity, in its embodiment here in Rome, to share in the heritage of Abraham, spiritually to be Semites. That claim in its initial formulation stands before us in the Bible, which is the systemic document of Christianity, and that Bible comprises the Old Testament and the New Testament. In this august body I need hardly rehearse the simple facts of the formation, by the Church of the second and third centuries, of the Bible, the Christian Bible, the Bible that made Christian the Hebrew Scriptures of ancient Israel. When the Church Fathers took their stand against Marcion and in favor of the Gospels' view of Christianity as the natural continuation of ancient Israel's faith, the fulfillment of ancient Israel's prophecy, they rejected the alternative position. It was that Christianity was something wholly new, plunged downward from Heaven without place, without origins, without roots. Quite to the contrary, they maintained (and so has Christianity ever since), in the line of the apostle, Paul, Christianity is the olive branch, grafted onto the tree; Christianity begins with the First Man; Christianity now fully and for the first time in history grasps the whole and complete meaning of the scriptures of ancient Israel. These and similar affirmations accounted for the rereading of those scriptures and enriched the faith of the Church with the heritage of the Torah, the prophets, and the writings, that, by that time, Judaism knew as "the Written Torah." That "Written Torah" for Christianity constituted "the Old Testament."

Now, along with Cardinal Ratzinger, I maintain that hermeneutics forms a chapter in the unfolding of theology, bearing no autonomous standing in the intellectual life of faith. And the hermeneutics that flowed from the formation of the Bible – New Testament and Old Testament – took the position that Christianity was "uniquely other," that is to say, a completely new intervention of God into the life of humanity – but. And the "but" stood for the appropriation of the life of humanity from the creation of the world onward, as the Evangelists and the author of the Letter to the Hebrews would maintain before Constantine, Eusebius afterward. Christianity did not begin with Jesus whom the Church called Christ, but with humanity, in the First Man, reaching its fulfillment in Jesus Christ, risen from the dead. That position left open the question of the place, in God's plan, for the Israel "after the flesh" that all of the Evangelists and Paul identified as the bearers of the grape cluster and the original children of Abraham, Isaac, and Jacob.

But that position left no doubt as to the autonomy of Christianity, its uniqueness, its absoluteness. Christianity did not suffice with the claim that it was part of ancient Israel, or that it had adopted the Torah of ancient Israel. The earliest Christians were not gentiles who

Judaism and Christianity in the First Century

became Jews; they were Jews who thought that their Christianity was (a) Judaism. More to the point, Christianity did not constitute a reform movement within Israel, that is to say, a religious sect that came along to right wrongs, correct errors, end old abuses, and otherwise improve upon the givens of the ancient faith. Whatever the standing of the old Israel, the new Israel was seen to be (if not the true, at least) truly Israel. And that meant it would not be represented as merely a reform movement, playing the role, in the drama of the history of Christianity, of the Protestant Reformation to Judaism's Roman Catholic Church. Christianity was born on the first Easter, with the resurrection of Jesus Christ, as the Church saw matters. And that event was unique, definitive, and universally significant for all of humanity. Christianity did not have to present itself as a reformation of Judaism, because it had nothing to do with any other formation within Israel, God's first love. Christianity was not a Judaism: it was Judaism, because it was Christianity, from Easter onward: so, I think, the Church understood. And, as part of that understanding, in later times, the Church gave birth, within its tradition, to the Bible.

But in representing Christianity as a reform movement within an antecedent and an ongoing Judaism, this received self-understanding of the Church was set aside. And, I am inclined to think, our century has witnessed a fundamental theological error, which has, as a matter of fact, also yielded an erroneous hermeneutics, in that order. It is, moreover, to speak plainly, a Protestant error. The theological error was to represent Christianity as a natural, this-worldly reform, a continuation of Judaism in the terms of Judaism. The New Testament would then be read in light of the Old, rather than the Old in light of the New. And that forms the hermeneutics that has predominated. We go to the Judaic writings of the age, or of the age thereafter, to discover the context in which Christianity was born; and Christianity then is understood to be represented by the Bible, or the New Testament in particular: a problem of reading writing, not of sifting through the heritage of tradition that the Church conveyed. The theological error of seeing Christianity as continuous and this-worldly, rather than as a divine intervention into history and as supernatural, affected not only the Christian understanding of Christianity. It also carried in its wake a theory of who is Israel, Israel after the flesh, that contradicted the position of the Church before our time.

The Church, in the tradition of the apostle Paul in Romans, affirmed the salvation of Israel through the heritage of Abraham and Sarah. But now, that "Judaism" that had become Christianity was given an autonomous standing, on the one side, and also assigned negative traits, on the other. Christianity became necessary in this-worldly terms to reform Judaism, and that reformed Judaism defined the theological verities for Christianity. It was a Christian theology of Judaism as an "if-only"-theology of Judaism: if only Judaism were done rightly, it would have been (and would be) all right with God. That theology yielded a hermeneutic in which the faults of "the Jews" or of "Judaism" were contrasted with the virtues of Jesus and of Christianity. Judaism then required reformation; Judaism now is a relic. Judaism then bore deep flaws, ethical flaws for example, so that the principal value of Jesus was not as Christ risen from the dead but as a teacher of ethics, as though the Sermon on the Mount contained much that would have surprised informed hearers on one's duty to the other or on the social responsibility of the society. And Christians, for their part, found themselves in a subordinate position in the salvific story of humanity, becoming not the true Israel by faith in Christ Jesus (as Paul would want us to maintain) but merely Israel by default, that is, by default of the old Israel.

The appeal of the Reformation Churches, their theology, and, consequently, their hermeneutics, to a theory of Christianity as a (mere) reform of Judaism, and of Judaism as hopelessly requiring a reformation, framed on the state of the first century the world-historical drama of the sixteenth century. In their picture of the founding of Christianity, the Reformation theologians imputed their own situation to that time of perfection that formed the authority and the model. Sola Scriptura carried with it not only an apologetic for the new, but also a reconstruction of the old; only by reference to Scripture shall we know what Christ really had in mind, and Scripture, read independent of the heritage of the tradition that the Church sustained, meant the New Testament in light of the Old. And that brings us back to our own century, its theology, and its hermeneutics.

The theology that saw Christianity as a reformation of Judaism, so identifying the Reformation as the new, and sole, Christianity, yielded a hermeneutic that would read the life of Jesus as continuous with the Judaism of his day, and the salvation of Christ as an event within the Judaism of the first century. What that meant is that scholars would turn to the Judaic writings of the time not merely for information about how things were, and were done, at that time, but for insight into the meaning and message – the religious message, the theological truth – of the New Testament. It was kind of a reverse-Marcionism. Instead of rejecting the Old Testament in favor of the New, the hermeneutics that has guided thought on the relationship of Judaism and Christianity in the first century has appealed to "the Talmud," that is to say, to the literature of the ancient rabbis broadly construed, as the keystone and guide in the reading of the New. The

Old Testament then would be set aside as merely interesting; salvation would come of, not the Jews, but of the rabbis.

And that observation about the current state of New Testament hermeneutics draws us back to the point at which I began, namely, the affirmation of the Church as "Semitic," the declaration, in the very teeth of Nazism, that "spiritually, we are all Semites," the insistence upon the Judaic heritage of the Church and of Christianity. Given the tragedy of Christianity in the civilization of Christian Europe, perverted by Nazism and corrupted by Communism, given the natural humanity that accorded to suffering Israel, Israel after the flesh, for the first time an honorable place within the faith, we must admire the intent. Everyone meant well, and today means well. But the result is an unChristian reading of the New Testament, and, as a matter of fact, a misunderstanding, from the viewpoint of the history of religion, of the New Testament and the whole of the Bible as well.

I have already made clear what I mean by an unChristian reading of the New Testament. It is the hermeneutic that appeals for the solution of exegetical problems to Judaic sources, in the manner of Strack-Billerbeck, for instance. And that manner, E. O. Sanders has shown, was anti-Semitic to the core. But of interest here is a different matter, namely, the hermeneutic, and the hermeneutic of Billerbeck scholarship about Jewish parallels or the Jewish *Umwelt* flows from the theology of Christianity as a continuation of, and mere improvement upon, Judaism. But if, as I have pointed out, Christianity understands itself as autonomous, unique, then Christianity cannot be a mere reformation. And not only so, but if, as we Jews maintain, the Torah of our Rabbi Moses, encompassing both the Written Torah and the Oral Torah, bears no relationship whatsoever to any other revelation that God may have had in mind, if, as we hold, what God wants of all humanity rests in the commandments to the children of Noah, then we cannot find a compliment in this same notion. We are no relic; ours is not the unreformed sediment, nor are we the stubborn and incorrigible heirs of a mere denial. We bear the living faith, the Torah, of the one true God, creator of Heaven and earth, who gave us the Torah and who implanted within us eternal life: so is the faith of Israel, God's first love. But in the context of this tragic century, we too have found reasons to affirm the picture of the first century as an age of reform, of Christianity as profoundly interrelated with Judaism in the way in which Protestant theology maintained.

The theological error does not dwarf the one that has characterized the historical account of the religions, Judaism and Christianity. The error as to history of religion is distinct. It is in two parts, one theological, the other religious. The theological error concerns history, not belief but (mere) description. As Cardinal Ratzinger warned as to theology and hermeneutics, it too represents a hermeneutical error, concerning the reading now of history, flowing from a theological position. The theological error, in this case, comes not from Christianity but from Judaism. It is the position that there was, is, and can forever be, only one Judaism, the Orthodox one. Speaking from the perspective of Sinai, one surely affirms that view. But translating theological truth into historical fact reduces theology to a matter of description, and that is an error. And it consequently imposes upon history the burden of faith. And that is as grave an offense against religion as asking science to conform in its results to Scripture in its crudest interpretation. In the case of the first century, we have been asked to see one Judaism, the Orthodox one, and to see that Judaism in the first century as an exact representation of what would emerge, in the Talmud of Babylonia seven hundred years later. It would follow that if we want to know what Judaism, the one, Orthodox, Judaism was in the first century, we have simply to consult the later writings in which that Judaism came to full and complete expression. That Orthodox theology of Judaism stands behind the possibility, represented by Strack-Billerbeck, of interpreting the New Testament as an essentially Judaic book, the life of Jesus as the story of a great rabbi, the formation of the Church as an aberration, and the work of the apostle Paul as a betrayal, an invention of a Christianity Rabbi Jesus never contemplated – and on and on.

The theological error on the Christian side is to read Christianity as a continuation and reform of Judaism. That makes possible the hermeneutic, supplied by Orthodox Judaism, by Jewish apologists, by Christian friends of the Jewish People, by pretty much everybody of good will in our own awful century, that reads Christianity as contingent upon Judaism, secondary to Judaism, not absolute, not unique, not autonomous. The theological error on the Judaic side is to seek in the social facts of the history of the here and now the replication of God's Torah's picture of holy Israel. It was (and is) a positivist conception that the facts of history settle the affirmations of faith, that the sanctity of holy Israel living by the Torah is to be affirmed because in the first century (first only for the Christians, after all), there was that one true, orthodox, Orthodox Judaism that pretty much everybody affirmed (even Jesus), and that, as a matter of mere fact, Christianity distorted – so runs the apologetic.

I spoke of an error as to history of religion, and, in correcting that error, I propose to set forth a constructive program, one that accords with the theological self-understandings of unique Christianity and absolute Judaism alike. Out of the history of religion I want to form the possibility of a new classicism in theology of Judaism and theology of Christianity – no mean ambition. This program aims at allowing Christianity to be absolute, Judaism to be unique, and the two to define, for the twenty-first century, a shared range of genuinely religious discourse, one to which the facts of history are not critical, but the confrontation with God, central. I wish, in a word, for Judaism to be Torah, the one whole Torah God revealed to Moses at Sinai, not subject to the uncertainties of time or the varieties of circumstance; and I want, for Christianity, that autonomous standing, that confidence, that permits the end to the question, addressed here, there, and everywhere: why not? (that is, why not become like us), and permits the asking of the question: how? (that is, how shall we all find, in Christian language, each his or her cross, in Judaic language, each in the face of the other the image and likeness of God).

No small task, no mean ambition. Where to begin? Just as faith comes prior to hermeneutics, so religion comes prior to hermeneutics. We have therefore, in the realm of history of religion, to undertake first to define what we mean by religion, then to carry that definition onward to the reading of the holy books that concern us. A shift in language is required, however, from "religion" to "religious system." When I speak of "religious system," I refer to the cogent statement, framed in supernatural terms, of a social entity concerning its way of life, its worldview, and its definition of itself. When a group of people, whether numerous, whether few, share a conception of themselves as a social entity, when they explain by appeal to transcendent considerations the very everyday pattern that defines what they do together, then the conception they set forth to account for themselves comprises their religious system. In simple terms, a religious system is made up of a cogent theory of ethics, that is, way of life, ethos, that is, worldview, and ethnos, that is, social entity.

Religions seen in this way form social worlds and do so through the power of their rational and symbolic thought, that is, their capacity to explain data in a (to an authorship) self-evidently valid way. As to hermeneutics flowing from this theory of religion, the framers of religious documents answer urgent questions, framed in society and politics to be sure, in a manner deemed self-evidently valid by those addressed by the authorships at hand. Religious writings present striking examples of how people in writing explain to themselves who they are as a social entity. Religion as a powerful force in human society and culture is realized in society, not only or mainly theology; religion works through the social entity that embodies that religion. Religions form social entities – "churches" or "peoples" or "holy nations" or monasteries or communities – that, in the concrete, constitute the "us," as against "the nations" or merely "them." And religions carefully explain, in deeds and in words, who that "us" is – and they do it every day. To see religion in this way is to take religion seriously as a way of realizing, in classic documents, a large conception of the world.

That brings us to the systemic hermeneutics in the reading of the formative documents of Judaism or of Christianity. Writings such as those we read have been selected by the framers of a religious system, and, read all together, those writings are deemed to make a cogent and important statement of that system, hence the category, "canonical writings." I call that encompassing, canonical picture a "system," when it is composed of three necessary components: an account of a worldview, a prescription of a corresponding way of life, and a definition of the social entity that finds definition in the one and description in the other. When those three fundamental components fit together, they sustain one another in explaining the whole of a social order, hence constituting the theoretical account of a system. Systems defined in this way work out a cogent picture, for those who make them up, of how things are correctly to be sorted out and fitted together, of why things are done in one way, rather than in some other, and of who they are that do and understand matters in this particular way. When, as is commonly the case, people invoke God as the foundation for their worldview, maintaining that their way of life corresponds to what God wants of them, projecting their social entity in a particular relationship to God, then we have a religious system. When, finally, a religious system appeals as an important part of its authoritative literature or canon to the Hebrew Scriptures of ancient Israel or "Old Testament, we have a Judaism.

We describe systems from their end products, the writings (and the rituals that the writings portray). But we have then to work our way back from canon to system, not to imagine either that the canon is the system, or that the canon creates the system. The canonical writings speak, in particular, to those who can hear, that is, to the members of the community, who, on account of that perspicacity of hearing, constitute the social entity or systemic community. The community then comprises that social group the system of which is recapitulated by the selected canon. The group's exegesis of the canon in terms of the everyday imparts to the system the power to sustain the community in a reciprocal and self-nourishing process. The community through its exegesis then imposes continuity and unity on whatever is in its canon. The power of a system to persist expresses or attests to a symbolic transaction. That symbolic transaction, specifically, takes place in its exegesis of the systemic canon, which, in literary terms, constitutes the social entity's statement of itself. So the texts recapitulate the system.

(In the language of Roman Catholic Christianity, the Bible is the Bible of the Church, which is to say, Scripture and tradition form the authority and criterion of Christian truth, not Scripture alone.) The system does not recapitulate the texts. The system comes before the texts and defines the canon. The exegesis of the canon then forms that ongoing social action that sustains the whole. A system does not recapitulate its texts, it selects and orders them. A religious system imputes to them as a whole cogency, one to the next, that their original authorships have not expressed in and through the parts, and through them a religious system expresses its deepest logic, and it also frames that just fit that joins system to circumstance.

The whole works its way out through exegesis, and the history of any religious system – that is to say, the history of religion writ small – is the exegesis of its exegesis. And the first rule of the exegesis of systems is the simplest, and the one with which I conclude: the system does not recapitulate the canon. The canon recapitulates the system. The system forms a statement of a social entity, specifying its worldview and way of life in such a way that, to the participants in the system, the whole makes sound sense, beyond argument. So in the beginning are not words of inner and intrinsic affinity, but (as Philo would want us to say) the Word: the transitive logic, the system, all together, all at once, complete, whole, finished – the word awaiting only that labor of exposition and articulation that the faithful, for centuries to come, will lavish at the altar of the faith. A religious system therefore presents a fact not of history but of immediacy, of the social present.

By the definitions just now given, can we identify one Judaism in the first centuries B.C. and A.D.? Only if we can treat as a single cogent statement everything all Jews wrote. That requires us to harmonize the Essene writings of the Dead Sea, Philo, the Mishnah, the variety of scriptures collected in our century as the Apocrypha and Pseudepigrapha of the Old Testament, not to mention the Gospels! That is to say, viewed as statements of systems, the writings attest to diverse religious systems, and, in the setting of which we speak, to diverse Judaisms. There was no one orthodoxy, no Orthodox Judaism. There were various Judaisms. In that context, the formative writings of what we call Christianity form statements of systems, and whether we call the Judaisms or Christianities really does not affect how we shall read them – in that context. For reading a text in its (systemic) context and as a statement of a larger matrix of meaning, requires us to accord to each system, to each Judaism, that autonomy, that uniqueness, that absoluteness, that every Judaism has claimed for itself, and, it goes without saying, that all Christianities likewise have insisted upon.

How does the approach to the study of religion define an answer to the question with which we began, the relationship of Judaism to Christianity in the first century? And what hermeneutic flows from the theory of religion I have outlined? Each document is to be read in its own terms, as a statement – if it constituted such a statement – of a Judaism, or, at least, to and so in behalf of, a Judaism. Each theological and legal fact is to be interpreted, to begin with, in relationship to the other theological and legal facts among which it found its original location. A specific hermeneutics emerges.

Let me speak of both Judaism and Christianity. The inherited descriptions of the Judaism of the Dual Torah (or merely "Judaism") have treated as uniform the whole corpus of writing called "the Oral Torah." They have further treated Christianity as unitary and harmonious; so it may have become, but, in the first century, I think both the founder of this place and his protagonist, Peter and Paul, will have found that description surprising. When we define religion in the way that I have, we have a different task from the one of harmonization. It is the task of describing the Judaisms and the Christianities of the age, allowing each its proper context and according to each its correct autonomy. What of the relationship between (a) Judaism and (a) Christianity? There we have to appeal to Judaic writings where they bear facts that illuminate Christian ones, but we must not then reduce Christian writings to the status of dependence and accord to them a merely recapitulative intent: reform, for instance.

Some facts are systemically active: Jesus Christ rose from the dead. Some are systemically inert: they wrote writs of divorce in the first century; some people observed cultic purity even at home; they kept the Sabbath. We cannot assign to systemically inert facts an active position that they did not, and as a matter of fact, could not, have had, and we cannot therefore frame our hermeneutics around the intersections of facts deriving from one piece of writing and occurring in another, later piece of writing. In New Testament hermeneutics, salvation is not of the Jews, because the New Testament is a component of the Bible, and the scriptures of ancient Israel form the other component of that same Bible: all read as the Church has been taught to read them, whole and complete, the story of salvation.

Among the religious systems of the people, Israel, in the Land of Israel, one of which we call "Christianity," another of which we call "Judaism" – and both names are utterly post facto – we find distinct social groups, each with its ethos and its ethics, each forming its distinctive ethnos, all of them constituting different people talking about different things to different people. As bearers, all of us, of the heritage of Israel and the fundament of truth of Sinai, we have therefore to affirm that God works in mysterious ways. We Jews can live with that mystery. That is why the seven commandments to which all humanity everywhere is subject make so much difference to Judaism: it is the theory of the other. God asks that much, and, if you do it, you are what God wants you to be, no less, but also no more. Why so much is asked of us and so much less of others? That is the mystery of eternal Israel. We not only live with that mystery. We are that mystery. Can Christianity live with that mystery? I think that, with the Christian theology of Judaism that has taken shape in Vatican II and since that time, in the American bishops' framing of matters in particular, Christianity too says its amen to God's work.

In that context, we now look back at the first century from a new perspective. We understand that Christianity is Christianity not because it improved upon Judaism, or because it was a Judaism, or because Christians are "spiritual Semites," or (to complete the catalogue) because Christianity drew upon Judaism or concurred in things that Judaism taught. Christianity is Christianity because it forms an autonomous, absolute, unique, and free-standing religious system within the framework of the scriptures and religious world of Israel. It suffices therefore to say that the earliest Christians were Jews and saw their religion as normative and authoritative: Judaism. That affirmation of self then solves the problem that troubles Christians, when they (wrongly) see themselves as newcomers to the world of religion: why Judaism as a whole remains a religion that believes other things, or, as Christians commonly ask, "Why did (and do) the Jews not 'accept Christ'?" or "Why, after the resurrection of Jesus Christ, is there Judaism at all?" Often asked negatively, the question turns on why the Jews do not believe, rather than on what they do believe.

Christians want to know why not. To me as a rabbi, the answer to that question is simple: Judaism and Christianity are completely different religions, not different versions of one religion (that of the "Old Testament," or, "the Written Torah," as Jews call it). The two faiths stand for different people talking about different things to different people. And that explains why not: Judaism answers its questions in its way, and it does not find itself required to answer Christianity's (or Islam's, or Buddhism's) questions in the way that these are phrased. Judaism sees Christianity as aggressive in its perpetual nagging of others to accept salvation through Jesus Christ. The asking of the question – why not? rather than why so? – reflects the long-term difficulty that the one group has had in making sense of the other. And my explanation of the difference between Christianity and Judaism rests on that simple fact. Each religious tradition talks to its adherents about its points of urgent concern, that is, Judaism and Christianity, respectively, stand for different people talking about different things to different people.

If we go back to the beginnings of Christianity in the early centuries of the Christian Era, we see this picture very clearly. Each addressed its own agenda, spoke to its own issues, and employed language distinctive to its adherents. Neither exhibited understanding of what was important to the other. Recognizing that fundamental inner-directedness may enable us to interpret the issues and the language used in framing them. For if each party perceived the other through a thick veil of incomprehension, the heat and abuse that characterized much of their writing about one another testifies to a truth different from that which conventional interpretations have yielded. If the enemy is within, if I see only the mote in the other's eye, it matters little whether there is a beam in my own. But if we see the first century from the perspective of the twenty-first, that is not how matters are at all. Now we can affirm what has taken twenty centuries for us to understand, which is that we all believe in one God, who is the same God, and whom alone we serve in reverence. And that shared life in God and for God defines the relationship of Judaisms and Christianities, then as it does now. But now, through the suffering of us Jews, eternal Israel, and through the response to our suffering of you Christians, Israel with us, we can see that truth, as before we did not and could not. So our awful century has left some good for the age that is coming.

4

Ritual without Myth: The Use of Law for the Study of Judaism

*Annual Religious Studies Lecture
University of Minnesota, 1975*

While some religions, Christianity and Islam for example, are rich in theological writings, and others in myth, still others make their statements about the nature of being and of the realm of the sacred primarily through law. In the case of early rabbinic Judaism, upon which we shall concentrate, we have a considerable corpus of laws which prescribe the way things are done but make no effort to interpret what is done. These constitute ritual entirely lacking in mythic, let along theological, explanation. Accordingly, the processes and modes of thought of earlier rabbinic Judaism, the Mishnah, in fact was not practiced; indeed, the earlier rabbis scarcely claim that it was. For example, we have two immense sections of Mishnah, one third of the whole, devoted to the conduct of the cult of the Temple on the one side, and rules of purity, on the other, and the rabbis of whom we speak, who lived from A.D. 70 to A.D. 200, flourished after the destruction of the Temple and in no way could have legislated for the conduct of the actual cult. Further, the laws about ritual cleanness or purity, so far as they had to be kept so that a person could enter the Temple, bore no more concrete relevance to everyday life than did the cultic laws, and only a small part of the Jewish population of Palestine was expected to keep those laws outside of the cult. Accordingly, we have before us the paradox presented by most serious effort to create a corpus of laws to describe a ritual life which did not exist. I shall try to show that the processes of making those laws themselves constituted the rabbis' mode of thinking about the same issues investigated, in other circumstances, through rigorous theological thought, on the one side, or profound mythic speculation, on the other.

My primary point is that *so far as the laws describe a ritual, the ritual itself is myth,* in two senses. First, the ritual is myth in the sense that it was not real, was not carried out. Second, while lacking in mythic articulation, the ritual expresses important ideas and points of view on the structure of reality. What people are supposed to do, without a stage of articulation of the meaning of what they do, itself expresses what they think. The explanation of the ritual, the drawing out of that explanation of some sort of major cognitive statement, is skipped. The world is mapped out through gesture, the boundaries of reality are laid forth through norms on how the boundaries of reality are laid forth.

Accordingly, we deal with laws made by people who never saw or performed the ritual described by those laws. It is through thinking about the laws that they shape and express their ideas, their judgments upon transcendent issues of sacred and profane, clean and unclean, It follows that thinking about the details of the law turns out to constitute reflection on the nature of being and the meaning of the sacred. The form, the ritual lacking in myth, is wholly integrated to the content, the mythic substructure. The structure of the ritual is its meaning.

We turn now to a particular ritual, the burning of the red cow for the preparation of ashes, to be mixed with water, and sprinkled upon a person who has became unclean through contact with a corpse. The ritual is described in two sources, Numbers 19:1-10, and the tractate of Mishnah called Parah, the cow.

Let us first consider the way the priestly author of Numbers 19:1-10 described the rite, the things he considers important to say about it:

> Tell the people of Israel to bring you a red cow without defect, in which there is no blemish, and upon which a yoke has never come. And you shall give her to Eleazar the priest, and she shall be taken outside the camp and slaughtered before him. And Eleazar the priest shall take some of her blood with his finger and sprinkle some of her blood toward the front of the tent of meeting seven times. And the heifer shall be burned in his sight; her skin, her flesh, and her blood, with her dung, shall be burned; and the priest shall take cedarwood and hyssop and scarlet stuff and cast them into the midst of the burning of the heifer. Then the priest shall wash his clothes and bathe his body in water, and afterwards he shall come into the camp and the priest shall be unclean until evening. He who burns the heifer shall wash his clothes in water and bathe his body in water and shall be unclean until evening. And a man who is clean shall gather up the ashes of the heifer and deposit them outside the camp in a clean place; and they

Ritual Without Myth

shall be kept for the congregation of the people of Israel for the water for impurity, and the removal of sin. And he who gathers the ashes of the heifer shall wash his clothes and be unclean until evening (Num. 19:1-10a).

How is the ash used? Num. 19:17 states:

For the unclean they shall take some ashes of the burnt sin-offering and running water shall be added in a vessel; then a clean person shall take hyssop and dip it in the water and sprinkle it upon the tent...(in which someone has died, etc.).

Let us now ask, what to the biblical writer are the important traits of the burning of the cow and the mixing of its ashes into water?

The priestly author stresses, first of all, that the rite takes place outside of the camp, which is to say, in an unclean place. He repeatedly tells us that anyone involved in the rite is made unclean by his participation in the rite, thus, 19:7, the priest shall wash his clothes; Num. 19:8, "the one who burns the heifer shall wash his clothes"; Num. 19:10, "and he who gathers the ashes of the heifer shall wash his clothes and be unclean until evening." The priestly legislator therefore takes for granted that the rules of purity which govern rites in the Temple simply do not apply to the rite of burning the cow. Not only are the participants not in a state of cleanness, but they are in a state of uncleanness, being required to wash their clothes, remaining unclean until the evening, only then allowed back into the camp which is the Temple. Accordingly, the world outside the Temple cannot be clean; only to the Temple do the cleanness taboos pertain; and it follows that a rite performed outside of the Temple is by definition not subject to the Temple's rules and is not going to be clean.

What is interesting, when we turn to the Mishnah tractate on the burning of the red cow, Parah, is its distinctive agendum of issues and themes. If I may now summarize rapidly the predominant concerns of Mishnah-Tosefta Parah, they are two: first, the degree of cleanness required of those who participate in the rite and how these people become unclean; second, how the water used for the rite is to be drawn and protected, with special attention directed to not working between the drawing the water and the mixing of the ashes referred to in Num. 19:17. The theoretical concerns of Mishnah-Tosefta Parah thus focus upon two important matters of no interest whatever to the priestly author of Numbers 19:1-10, because the priestly author assumes the rite produced uncleanness, is conducted outside of the realm of cleanness, and therefore does not involve the keeping of the levitical rules of cleanness required for participation in the Temple cult. By contrast, Mishnah-Tosefta Parah is chiefly interested in that very matter. An important body of opinion in our tractate demands a degree of cleanness higher than that required for the Temple cult itself. Further, the matter of drawing water, protecting it, and mixing it with the ash, is virtually ignored by the priestly author, while it occupies much of our tractate and, even more than in quantity, the quality and theoretical sophistication of the laws on that topic form the apex of our tractate. Accordingly, the biblical writer on the rite of burning the red cow wishes to tell us that the rite takes place outside the camp, understood in Temple times as outside the Temple. The rite is conducted in an unclean place. And it follows that people who are going to participate in the rite, slaughtering the cow, collecting its ashes, and the like, are not clean. The mishnaic authorities stress exactly the opposite conception, that people who will participate in the rite must be clean, not unclean, as if they were in the Temple. And they add a further important point, that the water which is to be used for mixing with the ashes of the cow must be mixed with the ashes without an intervening act of labor, not connected with the rite.

At the outset I pointed to two facts. First, the authorities of the Mishnah describe a ritual which, in fact, they have never seen, and about which they claim to have few historical traditions. The ritual under description is, as I said, a myth in two senses. The first has just now been stated: it is something which is not part of observed reality. But the second remains to be spelled out. The laws of the ritual themselves contain important expressions about the nature of the sacred and the clean, I shall now attempt to illustrate how the articulation of the laws, through the standard legal disputes of the late first- and second-century authorities, contains within itself statements about the most fundamental issues of reality, statements which, in describing the form of the ritual, also express the content of the ritual, its myth.

The first dispute concerns which hand one uses for sprinkling the blood toward the door of the Holy of Holies; the second asks about how we raise the cow up to the top of the pyre of wood on which it is going to be burned; and the third deals with whether intending to do the wrong thing spoils what one actually does. The texts are simple and pose no problems of interpretation. The first is at Mishnah Parah 3:9:

> They bound it with a rope of bast and place it on the pile of wood, with its head southward and its face westward.
>
> The priest, standing at the east side, with his face turned toward the west slaughtered it with his right (northern) hand and received the blood with his left (southern) hand.
>
> R. Judah says, 'With his right hand did he receive the blood and he put it into his left hand, and he sprinkled with (the index finger of) his right hand.'

Ritual Without Myth

Before analyzing the pericope, I should add the corresponding Tosefta supplement (Tosefta Parah 3:9):

> They bound it with a rope of bast and put it onto the wood pile.
>
> And some say, "It went up with a mechanical contraption."
>
> R. Eliezer b. Jacob says, "They made a causeway on which it ascended. Its head was to the south and its face to the west."

In the present set, therefore, are the first two of the issues mentioned earlier: which hand we use for sprinkling the blood, and how we raise the cow to the top of the pyre of wood.

Let us notice, first of all, the placing of the cow and the priest. The rite takes place on the Mount of Olives, that is, to the east and north of the Temple Mount in Jerusalem. Accordingly, we set up a north-south-east-west grid. The cow is placed with its head to the south, pointing in the direction of the Temple Mount, slightly to the south of the Mount of Olives, and its face is west – that is, toward the Temple. The priest then is set east of the cow, so that he too will face the Temple. He faces west – toward the Temple. When he raises his hand to slaughter the cow, he reaches over from north and east to south and west, again, toward the Temple. We have, therefore, a clear effort to relate the location and slaughter of the red cow, which takes place outside the Temple, toward the Temple itself. In fact each gesture is meant to be movement toward the Temple. Just as Scripture links the cow, outside the camp, to the camp, by having the blood sprinkled in the direction of the camp (a detail which Mishnah takes for granted), so that the sprinkling of the blood, which is the crucial and decisive action which effects the purpose of the rite – accomplishes atonement, or *kapparah*, in mishnaic language – so all other details of the rite here are focused upon the Temple.

This brings us to Judah's opinion, which disagrees about slaughter with the left hand. As observed, we have to set up a kind of mirror to the Temple, with the whole setting organized to face and correspond to the Holy Place. The priest in the Temple slaughtered with his right hand, and received the blood in his left. Likewise, the anonymous rule holds, the priest now does the same. In other words, our rite in all respects replicates what is done in the Temple setting: What is done there is done here. Judah, by contrast, wants the blood received with the right hand and slaughtered with the left. Why? Because we are not in the Temple itself. We are facing it. Thus if we want to replicate the cultic gestures, we have to do each thing in exactly the opposite direction. Just as, in a mirror, one's left is at the right, and the right is at the left, so here, we set up a mirror. Accordingly, he says, if in the

Temple the priest receives the blood in his left hand, on the Mount of Olives and facing the Temple, he receives the blood in his right hand. All parties to the dispute, therefore, agree on this fundamental proposition, that the effort is to replicate the Temple's cult in every possible regard.

This brings us to the dispute about how we get the beast up to the top of the wood pile. The anonymous rule, shared by Mishnah and Tosefta, is that we bind the sacrificial cow and somehow drag it up to the top. But in the Temple the sacrifices were not bound; they would be spoiled if they were bound. Accordingly, Eliezer b. Jacob, a contemporary of Judah, imposes the same rule. He says that there was a causeway constructed from the ground to the top of the woodpile on which the cow will be slaughtered and burned, and the cow walks up on its own. Self-evidently, both parties cannot be right, and the issue is not what really was done in "historical" times – let us say, seventy-five years earlier. As in the dispute between Judah and the anonymous narrator, the issue is precisely how we shall do the rite, on the Mount of Olives, so as to conform to the requirements of the rite on the Temple Mount itself. To state matters in general terms, it is taken for granted by all parties to the present pericope that the rite of the cow is done in the profane world, outside the cult, *as if* it were done in the sacred world constituted by the Temple itself.

How is the contrary viewpoint expressed? The simplest statement is in Mishnah Parah 2:3B-D:

B. The harlot's hire and the price of a dog – it is unfit.

That is to say, if the red cow is purchased with funds deriving from money spent to purchase the services of a prostitute or to buy a dog, the cow is unfit for the rite. The pericope continues:

C. R. Eliezer declares fit,
D. since it is said, 'You will not bring the harlot's hire and the price of a dog to the house of the Lord your God (Deut. 23:18). But this (cow) does not come to the house (of the Lord, namely, the Temple).

The issue could not be drawn more clearly than does the glossator (D). Eliezer holds that since the burning of the cow takes place outside of the Temple, the Temple's rules as to the acquisition of the cow simply do not apply.

A more subtle question appears at Mishnah Parah 4:1 and 4:3. The manuscript evidence here is in conflict. Some manuscripts give us the operative ruling in the name of Eliezer, others read Eleazar, a different authority; and in point of fact, there are several Eliezers and Eleazars. Tosefta supplies a parallel which gives us Eleazar b. R. Simeon, and I

Ritual Without Myth

am inclined to think that the Mishnah's Eliezers and Eleazars are Eleazar b. R. Simeon. But it hardly matters, since the viewpoint is identical to that assigned to Eliezer (certainly b. Hyrcanus, ca. 70-90) in the foregoing passage. The first item, Mishnah Parah 4:1, is as follows:

> The cow of purification which one slaughtered not for its own name (meaning, not as a cow of purification, but for some other offering), or the blood of which one received and sprinkled not for its own name, etc., is unfit.
>
> R. Eliezer (Eleazar) declares fit.

What is at issue? In the sanctuary, we have correctly to designate the *purpose* of a sacrifice. Eleazar holds that this is not a rite subject to the rule of the Temple cult. The rule continues,

> And if this was done by a priest whose hands and feet were not washed, it is unfit.
>
> R. Eliezer declared fit.

Priests of the Temple of course had to be properly washed. Since the rite is not in the Temple, Eliezer says that the priest need not even be washed. In this connection, Tosefta supplies:

> If one whose hands and feet were not washed burned it, it is unsuitable.
>
> And R. Eleazar b. R. Simeon declares fit, as it is said 'When they come to the Tent of Meeting, they will wash in water and not die' (Ex. 30:20) – So the washing of the hands applies only inside (the Temple, and not on the Mount of Olives).

The issue seems to me fully articulated, and the glosses in both the matter of the harlot's hire and the matter of washing spell out the implications. The law which describes the ritual – the *structure* of the ritual itself – also expresses the meaning of the ritual. The form imposed upon the ritual fully and completely states the content of the ritual. If now we ask, What is this content? we may readily answer. The ritual outside of the cult is done in a state of cleanness, as is the ritual done inside the cult. The laws of the cult, furthermore, apply not only to the conduct of the slaughtering of the cow (the cases I have given here), but also to the preservation of purity by those who will participate in the slaughtering (cases not reviewed here).

Mishnah presupposes what Scripture takes for granted is not possible, namely, that the rules of purity apply outside of the Temple, just as the rules of Temple slaughter apply outside of the Temple. And the reason is, of course, that the Mishnah derives, in part from the Pharisees, whose fundamental conviction is that the cleanness taboos of the Temple and its priesthood apply to the life of all Israel, outside of the Temple and not of priestly caste. When Israelites eat their meals in their homes, they must obey the cleanness taboos as if they were priests at the table of God in the Temple. This larger conception is expressed in the acute laws before us.

Let us now proceed to a matter which is by no means self-evident, and which was not understood in the way in which I shall explain it even by the second-century authorities. It concerns the issue of drawing the water. The rule is that if I draw water for mixing with the ashes of the red cow, and, before actually accomplishing the mixture, I do an act of labor not related to the rite of the mixing of the ashes, I spoil the water. This is stated very succinctly, "An act of extraneous labor spoils the water." This conception is likely to have originated before the destruction of the Second Temple in 70, because a very minor gloss on the basic rule is attributed to the authorities of the period immediately after 70, of Yavneh:

> He who brings the borrowed rope in his hand (after drawing the water with bucket suspended on a rope, the man plans to return the rope to the owner) – if (he returns it to the owner) on his way (to the rite of adding ashes to the water), it is suitable (that is, the bucket of water has not been spoiled by the act of extraneous labor), and if it is not on his way, it is unfit.

Appended is the following observation:

> (On this matter) someone went to Yavneh three festival seasons (to ask the law), and at the third festival season, they declared it fit for him, as a special dispensation.

Taken for granted, therefore, is the principle, evidently deriving from Pharisaism before 70, that an act of extraneous labor done between the drawing of the water and the mixing of ashes and water spoils the drawn water.

The rule lies far beyond the imagination of the priestly writer of Numbers, because he tells us virtually nothing about the water into which the ashes are to be mixed. But that is of no consequence. What is interesting, second, is the language which is used, *unfit,* not *unclean.* So the matter of the cleanness of the water – its protection against sources of contamination – is not at issue. Some other consideration has to be involved. Third, the drawing of the water is treated as intrinsic to the rite. That is: I burn the cow. I go after water for mixing with the ashes of the cow. That journey – outside of the place in which the cow is burned – is assumed to be part of the larger rite.

Now this matter of extraneous labor is exceedingly puzzling. We have to ask, to begin with, for some sort of relevant analogy. Do we know about other rites in which we distinguish between acts of labor which are intrinsic and those which are not? And on what occasion is such a distinction made? The answer to these questions is obvious. We do distinguish between acts of labor required for the conduct of the sacrificial cult, and those which are not required for the conduct of the sacrificial cult, in particular we make that distinction *on the Sabbath.* On the Sabbath day labor is prohibited. But the cult is continued. How? Labor intrinsic to the sacrifices required on the Sabbath is to be done, and that which is not connected with the sacrifice is not to be done.

When we introduce the issue of extraneous labor (and the issue extends to the burning of the cow itself, but I think this is secondary), what do we say about the character of the sanctity of the rite? Clearly, we take this position: The rite is conducted by analogy to the sacrifices which take place in the Temple, so that the place of the rite and all its participants must be clean, exactly as the place of the Temple and all the participants in the Temple sacrifices must be clean. So too with the matter of labor. When we impose the Temple's taboos, we state that the rite is to be conducted in clean space. When we introduce the issue of labor, we forthwith raise the question of holy time, the Sabbath. For it is solely to the Sabbath that the matter of labor or no labor, labor which is intrinsic or labor which is extrinsic, applies. When we impose the taboos applicable to the Temple on the Sabbath, we state that the rite is to be conducted in holy *time.*

The cleanness laws in the present instance create in the world outside of the cult a *place of cleanness* analogous to the cult. The Sabbath laws in the present instance create in the world outside of the cult a *time of holiness* analogous to the locus of the cult. The ritual constructs a structure of clean cultic space and holy Sabbath time in the world to which, by the priestly definition, neither cleanness nor holiness (in the limited sense of the present discussion) applies.

The laws, it is clear, do not contain explanations. The issues themselves are trivial, ritualistic, yet even the glossators at the outset introduced into the consideration of legal descriptions of ritual extra-legal conceptions of fundamental importance. Accordingly, the processes of thought which produce the rabbis' legal dicta about ritual matters also embody the rabbis' judgments about profound issues. The final stage in my argument is to consider other sorts of sayings, in which the rabbis speak more openly and directly about matters we should regard as theological, not ritual, in character. These sayings are general, not specific, treat questions of salvation, not of the conduct of a ritual, and constitute a quite distinct mode of expression about these same questions, These theological sayings contrast, therefore, to the ones about ritual law, showing a separate way in which the authorities of the same period form and express their ideas. The issue at hand, in particular, is the relationship between cleanness and holiness. We have already considered the matter in our interpretation of the ritual laws, showing that cleanness is distinct from holiness, and the two are related to and expressed by the laws about burning the red cow. Pinhas b. Yair gives us a statement (translated following ms. Kaufman) which links the issue of cleanness and holiness to salvation:

> R. Pinhas b. Yair says, "Attentiveness leads to (hygienic) cleanliness, cleanliness to (ritual) cleanness, cleanness to holiness, holiness to humility, humility to fear of sin, fear of sin to piety, and piety to the holy spirit, the holy spirit to the resurrection of the dead, and the resurrection of the dead to Elijah of blessed memory."

Pinhas therefore sees cleanness as a step in the ladder leading to holiness, thence to salvation: the resurrection of the dead and the coming of the Messiah. Maimonides, much later, introduces into the messianic history the burning of the cow of purification. Referring to the saying that nine cows in all were burned from the time of Moses to the destruction of the Second Temple, he states (*Red Heifer* 3:4):

> Now nine red heifers were prepared from the time this commandment was received until the Temple was destroyed the second time...and a tenth will King Messiah prepare – may he soon be revealed.

Maimonides thus wishes to link the matter of the burning the red cow which produces water for ritual purification to the issue of the coming of the Messiah. Both sayings, those of Pinhas b. Yair and Maimonides, show that is is entirely possible to speak directly and immediately, not through the language of ritual law, about fundamental questions. And when we do find such statements, we no longer are faced with ritual laws at all. Yet it seems to be clear that Pinhas b. Yair and Maimonides saw in the issues of purity, even in the very specific questions addressed by the rabbinic lawyers who provide the ritual law, matters of transcendent, even salvific, weight and meaning.

Let us now return to the issues raised at the outset and summarize the entire argument. It is now clear that the mishnaic rabbis express their primary cognitive statements, their judgments upon large matters, through ritual law, not through myth or theology. Indeed, we observe a curious disjuncture between ritual laws and theological sayings concerned with the *heilsgeschichtliche* meanings of the laws. The ritual laws themselves describe a ritual.

Since the ritual was not carried out by the authorities of the law, the purpose and meaning of legislation in respect to the ritual of burning the cow are self-evidently not to describe something which has been done, but to create – if only in theory – something which, if done, will establish limits and boundaries to sacred reality. The issue of the ritual is *cleanness* outside of the Temple, and, if I am right about the taboo connected with drawing the water, *holiness* outside of the Temple as well. The lines of structure, converging upon, and emanating from, the Temple, have now to be discerned in the world of the secular, the unclean, and the profane. Where better to discern, to lay out these lines of structure, than in connection with the ritual of sacrifice not done in the Temple but outside of it, in that very world of the secular, unclean, and profane. As I have stressed, the priestly author of Numbers cannot imagine that cleanness is a prerequisite of the ritual. He says the exact opposite. The ritual produces contamination for those who participate. The second-century rabbis who debated the details of the rite held that the rite is performed just as it would have been done in the Temple. Or, in the mind of Eliezer and Eleazar b. R. Simeon, the rite is performed in a way different from the way it would have been done in the Temple. The laws which describe the ritual therefore contain important judgments upon its meaning. With remarkably little exegesis of those laws – virtually none not coming to us from the glossators themselves – we are able to see that their statements about law deal with metaphysical reality, revealing their effort to discern and to define the limits of both space and time.

The structure of the ritual contains its meaning. Form and content are wholly integrated. Indeed, we are unable to dissociate form from content. It follows that what is done in the ritual, the sprinkling with one hand or other other, the binding of the cow or the use of a causeway to bring it to the pyre, the purchase of cows with the wrong sort of money, the employment of unwashed priests, the exclusion of the issue of the wrong intention – all of these matters of rite and form *alone* contain whatever the rabbis will tell us about the meaning of the rite and its forms. The reason, as I have stressed, is that the rabbis think about transcendent issues primarily through rite and form. When, as I showed at the end, they choose another means of discourse and a different mode of thought entirely, matters of rite and form fall away. Theological and mythic considerations to which ritual is irrelevant take their place. Judah, Eliezer, Eleazar b. R. Simeon, Eliezer b. Jacob, and the others cited, however, refer to no myth, make use of neither mythic nor theological language, because they think about reality and speak about it through the norms of the law. Since, as I have stressed, the law concerns a ritual which these authorities have never seen and certainly would never perform, *the law itself constitutes its own myth,* the fabulous myth of a ritual no one has ever done, and the transcendent myth of the realm of the clean and the sacred constructed through ritual and taboo in the world of the unclean and the secular. That is why I claim that the ritual *is* the myth. What people are told to do is what they are supposed to think, the gestures and taboos of the rite themselves express the meaning of the rite, without the mediation of myth.

5

The Talmud as Anthropology

The Friedland Lecture
The Jewish Theological Seminary of America, 1979

At the outset I thank Chancellor Gerson D. Cohen for the honor of his invitation to give this lecture. The Friedland Lectures enjoy enviable distinction, and that is not solely because the first of them, Mr. Cohen's on the Song of Songs, still is read as a model of scholarly argumentation and insight. For me, therefore, participating in this series is a gesture of weight and meaning. I express my delight at the invitation. By way of response, I take as the purpose of my lecture the illustration of an important proposition first laid out by Mr. Cohen: assimilation is a blessing when it means creative competition. Chief among the proofs for that proposition, he holds, is the fructification of Jewish learning through the methods and insights of world scholarship.

Chancellor Gerson D. Cohen speaks of "the blessing of assimilation in Jewish history," by which he means "the healthy appropriation of new forms and ideas for the sake of our own growth and enrichment." He says, "Assimilation properly channeled and exploited can...become a kind of blessing, for assimilation bears within it a certain seminal power which serves as a challenge and a goal to renewed creativity."[1] There is no area of Jewish expression more distinctive and intimate to the Jewish people, more idiomatic and particular to its inner life, than the study of the Talmud. In the present age, in my view, it is the study

---

[1] Gerson D. Cohen, "The Blessings of Assimilation in Jewish History," in J. Neusner, ed., *Understanding Jewish Theology. Classical Issues and Modern Perspectives* (New York, 1973: KTAV Publishing House), pp. 251-258. Quotations: pp. 257f.

of the Talmud which has experienced[2] and must continue to undergo the fructifying and vivifying experience of assimilation. The reason is that it is precisely there that the Jewish intellect expresses itself.[3]

Now there have been two approaches to learning which already have stimulated students of the talmudic and cognate literature to ask new questions and therefore to understand and perceive new dimensions in that literature. The first is the study of the language of the Talmud in the light of other Semitic languages, on the one side, and of Indo-European ones, Greek, Latin, and Iranian, on the other. Comparative philology in fact is very old, since its first great monument appears in the eleventh century, after the Islamic conquest of the Mediterranean world.[4] The result of the modern phase of that project, which has been continuous since the nineteenth century, has been a clarification of the meanings of specific sentences, the specification of the origins and sense of words used in one place or in another, in all, a great improvement upon our understanding of the concrete and specific meanings of the

---

[2] The ways in which Talmud scholarship has confronted, if not wholly assimilated, some of the approaches and methods of the nineteenth- and twentieth-century humanities (and even social sciences) are sketched in J. Neusner, ed., *Formation of the Babylonian Talmud: Studies on the Achievements of Late Nineteenth and Twentieth Century Historical and Literary-Critical Research* (Leiden, 1979: E.J. Brill), and in J. Neusner, ed., *The Modern Study of the Mishnah* (Leiden, 1973: E.J. Brill). A broader analysis of the relationship between Jewish learning and the secular university, to which Jewish learning comes only in the twentieth century (and, for the most part, in the third quarter of that century) is in my *The Academic Study of Judaism. Essays and Reflections* (New York, 1975: KTAV Publishing House) and *The Academic Study of Judaism. Essays and Reflections. Second Series* (New York, 1977: KTAV Publishing House). Later in this essay I point to two points in which assimilation has been completed, philology and Semitics. The third point at which, I think, assimilation to a fresh mode of thought will be fructifying is in the area of social and cultural anthropology, as I shall make clear.

[3] I hasten to add that that is not the only classic and distinctively Jewish document. The Hebrew Scriptures are still more important and, read as Judaism has read them, equally distinctive. This point should not be given more weight than is intended here.

[4] I refer to *Arukh Hashshalem* by Nathan b. Yehiel of Rome, 1035-c. 1110, who gives the meaning and etymology of the talmudic lexicography in Latin, Greek, Arabic, and Persian. This is not to suggest he is the only important "comparativist" in post-talmudic times. For their part, talmudic rabbis themselves are acutely aware of linguistic origins, differences in word choice, and other aspects of what we should now call comparative philology and lexicography. There are, moreover, pericopae in the Babylonian Talmud which can have been composed specifically with the interest of sociolinguistics in mind. But it was in the time of the beginnings of modern Semitics that the true weight and meaning of these facts were grasped and taken seriously.

Talmud's various discrete words and phrases. This step forward in exegesis, however, has not vastly improved our understanding of the method and meaning of the Talmud. But it has given greater clarity and accuracy to our search for its method and meaning.[5]

The second approach is the study of the Talmud for historical purposes. It has been in three parts, first, use of talmudic evidence for the study of the general history of the Near and Middle East of its own times;[6] second, use of historical methods for the study of what was happening among the Jews and especially the people who created the Talmud itself;[7] third, use of historical perspectives in the analysis and

---

[5]I do not make reference to important modern and contemporary advances in the exegetical methods brought to bear upon the interpretation of the talmudic literature, because these appear to me to emerge essentially within the limits of classical talmudic exegesis. They exhibit only casual, and, in any event, unsystematic interest in exegetical and hermeneutical experiments outside of talmudic studies or on its fringes. The reason is that the exegesis of the text is, alas, of interest principally to people who teach in *yeshivot* and Jewish seminaries or in Israeli university Talmud departments. These scholars have no access to, or interest in, the work of exegetes in the larger fields of hermeneutics in secular universities. Still, the noteworthy achievements of David Weiss Halivni in *Meqorot ummesorot* (Tel Aviv, 1968, 1975) [English titles: I. *Sources and Traditions. A Source Critical Commentary of Seder Nashim*, and II. *A Source Critical Commentary on the Talmud. Seder Moed. From Yoma to Hagiga*] should be ample evidence of what can be achieved even within an essentially traditional ("*aharonic*") frame of reference.

[6]Historians of the Near and Middle East who have turned to talmudic materials as a routine part of their examination of the sources are not numerous. In general well-trained Semitists will be apt to turn to the talmudic corpus more readily than Classicists and Byzantinists, for obvious reasons. Still, I cannot point to a single major work on the history of the region from Alexander to Muhammed which intelligently and sustainedly draws upon talmudic evidence. As a general overview, though, I recommend F.E. Peters, *The Harvest of Hellenism. A History of the Near East from Alexander the Great to the Triumph of Christianity* (New York, 1979: Simon and Schuster).

[7]All the historians of the Jews of this period, by contrast, draw extensively upon the Talmud's evidence. But most of them draw solely upon that evidence. The best examples of well-crafted historical accounts of the period, making ample and, *for their day* (which has passed), reasonably critical use of the talmudic evidence are Salo W. Baron, *Social and Religious History of the Jews*, Vol. II (New York, 1952: Columbia University Press), Michael Avi-Yonah, *The Jews of Palestine. A Political History from the Bar Kokhba War to the Arab Conquest* (Oxford, 1976: Basil Blackwell), and Mary Smallwood, *The Jews Under Roman Rule* (Leiden, 1976: E.J. Brill). Each volume in my *History of the Jews in Babylonia* (Leiden, 1965-1970) I-V, opens with a chapter on the political history of the Jews at a given period in the history of the Parthian and Sasanian dynasties; in these chapters the evidences of the talmudic stories are brought together with those deriving from other sources entirely, Christian, Iranian, Greco-Roman, and the like. The second chapter of each of those books then

elucidation of the Talmud's own materials.[8] None of these three methods has attracted a great number of practitioners. In a moment I shall explain why use of historical methods for the study of the world of the Talmud has, on the whole, produced results of modest interest for people whose principal question has to do with the discovery of what the Talmud is and means. At this point it suffices to say that the assimilatory process has worked well. The Talmud is no stranger to historical discourse, just as it is a familiar and routine source for the pertinent philological studies.

In my view there is yet a third approach to the description and interpretation of texts and to the reconstruction of the world represented in them. It is the approach of anthropology, the science of the description and interpretation of human culture.[9] Anthropology

---

deals with the inner political history of the Jewish community, and for this purpose Iranian and talmudic evidences are utilized as well.

[8]I am inclined to think that historical perspectives have clouded the vision of those who attempt them for exegesis of talmudic literature. The most ambitious, and, consequently, the most unsuccessful such effort at a kind of historical exegesis of the Talmud and its law is in Louis Finkelstein, *The Pharisees* (Philadelphia, 1936: The Jewish Publication Society). But in this regard he merely carried forward the perfectly dreadful approach of Louis Ginzberg, for example, in "The Significance of the Halachah for Jewish History," 1929, reprinted in his *On Jewish Law and Lore* (Philadelphia, 1955: The Jewish Publication Society of America), pp. 77-126. My reasons for regarding this approach to the exegesis of the law of the Talmud as untenable and the results as capricious and unsystematic are amply spelled out in my *The Rabbinic Traditions about the Pharisees before 70* (Leiden, 1971: E.J. Brill), Vol. III, pp. 320-368. There I review a very wide range of historical writings about the Pharisees and place into context the work of Finkelstein and Ginzberg (among many others). I am able to point to the underlying and generative errors in their approach to the interpretation of the legal materials for historical purposes and in their claim to interpret the legal materials from a historical perspective as well (a totally confused work).

[9]In what follows, I point to the work of a few specific anthropologists. In doing so, I do not pretend to have mastered the corpus of contemporary anthropological theory or to know more than the works I cite. Nor do I even claim fully to grasp all of the writings of the scholars whom I find, at some specific points in their corpus, to be strikingly illuminating for the work of understanding the talmudic literature. In pointing toward social and cultural anthropology as a source of helpful questions and methods, moreover, I do not mean to take a stand on any of the mooted issues of that field. Nor do those whose names I omit make no or little impact upon me. Indeed, the scholar whose works I should most want to emulate is not cited here at all, namely, Melford Spiro. If I could write for Judaism an equivalent to his *Buddhism and Society*, I believe I could make a contribution of lasting and fundamental importance to the study of Judaism within the study of religions. So, in all, what follows should be understood as a preliminary and tentative account of some of

began its work, as Marvin Harris points out, "as the science of history." It was meant to discover the lawful principles of social and cultural phenomena. In the past half century "anthropologists sought out divergent and incomparable events. They stressed the inner, subjective meaning of experience to the exclusion of objective effects and relations...with the study of the unique and non-repetitive aspects of history."[10] In our own day there is a renewed interest in generalization and in regularities, for instance, in underlying structures of culture. Now what makes anthropology fructifying for the study of the Talmud is a range of capacities I discern in no other field of humanistic and social scientific learning. To me, anthropologists are helpful because they ask questions pertinent to the data I try to interpret.[11] We who spend our lives investigating and trying to master the talmudic and cognate literature and to gain valid conceptions of the world created by that literature are overstuffed, indeed, engorged, with answers. Our need is for questions. Our task is through the exercise of taste and judgment to discern the right ones.

Information by itself nourishes not at all. Facts do not validate their own importance. Unless they prove relevant to important questions, they are not important. As I shall explain, among anthropologists of various kinds, who would not even agree with one another in many things, I find a common core of perspectives and issues which make their work stimulating for talmudic learning of a particular sort. It is, specifically, because they show me the meaning of the data I confront that their modes of thought and investigation demand attention and appreciation.

II

Before specifying those things to be learned from anthropology, let me spell out what I find wrong with the approaches of that field which, to date, has predominated in the academic study of the talmudic literature, I mean, historical study. There are two kinds of problems which in my view call into question the fruitfulness of historical study of the Talmud. It is because of these two problems that

---

what I have learned from a few interesting people in a field presently altogether too remote from mine.

[10]Marvin Harris, *The Rise of Anthropological Theory. A History of Theories of Culture* (London, 1968, Routledge & Kegan Paul), pp. 1-7. It goes without saying that I do not wish to take a position on the controversy generated by this stimulating book. I learned much from Harris's history and critique.

[11]I cannot overemphasize the priority: anthropology here is important *because* it serves the exegetical project of the Talmud. Whether the Talmud is important for anthropological work I do not know.

I turn to a field other than history to find some useful questions for those many answers which we have at hand.

The first problem is very obvious. The Talmud simply is not a history book. To treat it as if it were is to miss its point. That is to say, the Talmud and related literature were not created to record things that happened. They are legal texts, saying how people should do things (and, sometimes, do do things); or they are exegetical texts, explaining the true meaning of the revelation at Sinai, the Torah; or occasionally, they are biographical texts, telling stories about how holy men did things. They are put together with an amazing sense of form and logic, so that bits and pieces of information are brought into relationship with one another, formed into a remarkably cogent statement, and made to add up to more than the sum of the parts. talmudic essays in applied logic rarely are intended to tell us things which happened at some one point. They still more rarely claim to inform us about things that really happened.

For in the end the purpose of the talmudic literature, as talmudists have always known, is to lay out paradigms of holiness. The purpose is to explore the meaning of being human in the image of God and of building a kingdom of priests and a holy people. For that purpose, the critical questions concern order and meaning. The central tension in the inner argument lies in the uncovering of sacred disciplines. The Talmud describes that order, that meaning, which, in society and in the conduct of everyday life, as well as in reflection and the understanding of the meaning of Israel and the world, add up to what God wants. The Talmud is about what is holy.

Now in the quest for the holy order, things of interest to historians, that is, the concrete, one-time, discrete and distinctive events of history, are obstacles. For order lies in regularity. But history is the opposite. It is what is interesting, which is what is unusual. That is what is worth reporting and reflection. So it will follow that the last thing of interest to people of the sort of mind who made the Talmud is whether things really happened at some one point.[12] What they want to know is how things always happen and should happen. If I may

---

[12] I stress that this issue is simply beside the point. It is not relevant to talmudic discourse. Therefore to accuse the rabbis of lying because they tell didactic tales and moral or theological fables, rather than writing history like Tacitus or Josephus, is to miss the point of what the rabbis of the Talmud mean. By their long arguments of analysis and applied and practical reason they propose to bring to the surface underlying unities of being. It is the most naive sort of anachronism to accuse them of being uninterested in truth because they do not record events, or record them in fanciful ways, since it denies the logicians their task but expects them to work like historians instead.

project upon the creators of the talmudic literature what I think their judgment would be, they would regard history as banal. My basis for thinking so is not solely that they wrote so little of it. It is principally that they wrote something else. So history misses the point they wish to make.

Besides the triviality of history there is a second problem, of a quite different order. It concerns how history is done today. For a long time in Western culture we have understood that merely because an ancient source says something happened, that does not mean it really happened that way, or even happened at all. An attitude of skepticism toward the claims of ancient documents was reborn in the Renaissance and came to fruition, in the religious sciences, in the eighteenth and nineteenth centuries. From that time onward, it was clearly understood that, in trying to figure out who did what and why, we are going to stand back from our sources and ask a range of questions not contained in them. When we come to the talmudic sources out of which some sort of history (biography, politics, or a history of ideas) may be constructed, so that we have a sense of what came first and what happened then, we have therefore to reckon with the problem of the accuracy and reliability of our sources. That problem would confront us in the examination of any other source of the period of which the Talmud is a part. It is not an insurmountable problem, but it must be met.

Now when we combine these two problems, the first, the problem of the intent of our sources and the meaning they wish to convey, and the second, the problem of the accuracy of our sources for the doing of that sort of work which people generally call historical, we realize that the historical approach to the Talmud requires a considerable measure of thoughtfulness. Studying the Talmud as history demands the exercise of restraint, probity, and critical acumen. Unfortunately, these traits, when Heaven divided them up, were not lavished upon the sorts of folks who think that the important thing to ask the Talmud is what really happened on the particular day on which Eleazar ben Azariah's hair turned white, or – for that matter – on which Jonah was swallowed by the whale. Let me give just one instance of this fact – the obtuseness of those who ask the Talmud to tell us about people who really said and did the things reported about them – so that I not be thought to exaggerate.

For this purpose I choose the most current book available to me, which is Samuel Sandmel's *Judaism and Christian Beginnings*.[13] Sandmel provides an account of what he at the outset admits are "legends" about some of the holy men of the talmudic literature. These

---

[13]New York, 1978: Oxford University Press. Under discussion: pp. 236-251.

stories he tells specifically in the context of his description of the state of Judaism in the formative century of Christianity. It is self-evident that he would not write about these particular men if he were discussing the Judaism of the third or fourth centuries. But these are the centuries in which the stories he cited first are attested. When Sandmel chooses Hillel and Shammai, he clearly wishes the reader to believe that he is telling about people who are contemporaries of Jesus. When we listen to the fables Sandmel brings in evidence of these contemporaries, what do we hear? This is characteristic of Sandmel's wide-eyed and credulous narrative as a whole:

> Hillel loves his fellow man as deeply as he loved the Torah, and he loved all literature of wisdom as much as he loved the Torah, neglecting no field of study. He used many foreign tongues and all areas of learning in order to magnify the Torah and exalt it..., and so inducted his students.[14]

The voice of this paragraph is the historian, that is, Sandmel, claiming to tell us about dear old Hillel (and mean old Shammai). He puts nothing in quotation marks, and his footnotes lead the reader to unanalyzed, unquoted sources, as though he had any basis whatsoever, other than third and fourth century fables, for every single sentence in this paragraph. But that paragraph in fact is nothing but a paraphrase of materials found in rabbinic sources of a far later age than Hillel. None of the sources emerging from the late second century (a mere two hundred years after Hillel is supposed to have lived) knows about Hillel's vast knowledge. Indeed, in an age in which the sources report conflict on whether Jews should study Greek, and in which only a few highly placed individuals are allowed (in the mishnaic corpus) to do so, no one thought to refer to the "fact" of Hillel's having known many languages. The reason, I think, is that no one knew it, until it was invented for purposes of storytellers in an age in which the story was told, whatever these purposes may have been. It follows that, to represent Hillel in this way (and Sandmel runs on for fifteen pages with equivalent fairytales) is simply meretricious. If it is the Hillel legend, then it is a legend which testifies to the state of mind of the storytellers hundreds of years after the time of Hillel (and Jesus). The stories Sandmel tells us on the face of it record absolutely nothing about the age, let alone the person, of Hillel himself. If they do, Sandmel does not show it. In my judgment, this kind of historiography is deceiving and childish. If Hillel were not interesting to Christians, Sandmel would not tell about him.

---

[14]*Ibid.*, p. 237.

But even if this were true, *historical* Hillel, what difference would it make? By that I mean, what important information, relevant to profound and interesting questions confronting ancient or contemporary culture, should we have, for instance, in the knowledge that "Hillel loved his fellow man," and in similar, didactic statements? The study of stories about saints is interesting, from the perspective of the analysis of culture and society, because it opens the way to insight into the fantasy and imagination of that culture and society. We learn from the hopes which people project upon a few holy men something about the highest values of the sector of society which entertained those hopes and which assigned them to those men. Or we may learn something about the fears of that group. But the one thing which I think is dull and unilluminating is a mere repetition of stories people told, because they told them. In other words, when Sandmel claims to tell us about the time of Jesus and then arrays before us perfectly routine, third-, fourth-, or fifth-century rabbinical hagiography, he is engaged in a restatement, *as history*, of what in fact are statements of the cultural aspirations and values of another age. It was one in which – in the present instance – some storytellers appear to have wanted people to appreciate Torah-learning in a broad and humanizing context (if we may take a guess as to what is at hand in these particular allegations about Hillel). But if, for the turn of the first century, we have evidence that the ideal of Torah-study was not associated with the very movement of which Hillel is supposed to have been a part, but of a quite different set of people entirely, then I am inclined to think Sandmel engages in deception.[15] If Hillel had not lived in the time of Jesus, Sandmel would not be interested in him for a book on Judaism and Christian beginnings, and he would not be asking us to believe these fairy-tales as history of a particular man, who lived at a particular time, *and who therefore tells us about the age in which he lived*. This is nothing short of an intellectually despicable deceit. But it is how things are among the historians, though, I admit, Sandmel's case is somewhat extreme.

---

[15]See my "Oral Tradition and Oral Torah: Defining the Problematic," in *Method and Meaning in Ancient Judaism* (Missoula, 1979: Scholars Press for Brown Judaic Studies). This same argument is made in my *Rabbinic Traditions about the Pharisees before 70*, which, naturally, Sandmel fails to cite. I hasten to add that Sandmel is taken solely to show something acutely contemporary. I could adduce in evidence a great many others over the past two hundred years, as I indicated in *Rabbinic Traditions*, III, pp. 320ff., cited above. That discussion, too, thus far has elicited not a single contrary opinion. I think the reason is that the other side has not got much to say in its own behalf.

III

Of the two problems just now outlined, it is the first which I think more consequential. Merely because historians work unintelligently or without candor is no reason to wonder whether we have to turn elsewhere than to history to find useful questions – appropriate routes toward the center and heart of our sources. But if, as I suspect, historians do not ask the critical and generative questions, then we have to look for help to those who do. Perhaps the most difficult problem is to overcome our own circumstance, our own intellectual framework. For in thinking the Talmud important, we tend to claim it is important for our reasons.[16] We ask it to address questions interesting to us, without finding out whether these are the right questions for the Talmud too. Let me now spell this problem out.

The distance between this century and the centuries in which the Talmud was brought into being is not simple to measure. For it is not merely that the rabbis and most others of their day thought the world was flat, and we know it is not. It is that the way in which they formulated the world, received and organized information about life, profoundly differs from that of our own day. We are not equipped to interpret the Talmud's worldview if we bring it to our own. We drastically misinterpret earlier rabbinic documents when we simply seek places on the established structure of issues and concerns on which to hang whatever seems relevant in the talmudic literature.[17] Let me illustrate the matter very simply.

---

[16]Since in my years in rabbinical school and graduate school, the two paramount humanistic disciplines were history and philosophy (philology was a poor third), and since my undergraduate concentration had been in history, it was perfectly natural to me to ask historical questions of the talmudic sources. I still think these are important questions. In the end, my hope is to contribute to the intellectual and cultural history of the period in which the Talmud came into being. But, as I stress, there are more important questions than the ones with which I (and so many others) began to work.

[17]This is the sort of thing characteristic of theologians of talmudic Judaism, whose theological categories are imposed upon, and do not flow from, those of the talmudic literature. I have spelled this problem out, in one concrete instance, in "Comparing Judaism," *History of Religions* 18, 2, 1978, pp. 177-191, and, in another, in my essay-review of Urbach's *The Sages, Journal of Jewish Studies* 27, 1, 1976, pp. 23-35. I think the only modern student of talmudic Judaism to confront this problem and to try to overcome it is Max Kadushin. See for example his *Worship and Ethics. A Study in Rabbinic Judaism* (Evanston, 1964: Northwestern University Press). My impression is that his failure lies in his trying to do too much, on too broad a canvas; for his results are

When the rabbis of the late first and second centuries produced a document to contain the most important things they could specify, they chose as their subjects six matters, of which, I am inclined to think, for the same purpose[18] we should have rejected at least four, and probably all six. That is, the six divisions of Mishnah are devoted to purity law, tithing, laws for the conduct of sacrifice in the Temple cult, and the way in which the sacrifices are carried on at festivals, four areas of reality which, I suspect, would not have found a high place on a list of our own most fundamental concerns. The other two divisions, which deal with the transfer of women from one man to another, and with matters of civil law, including the organization of the government, civil claims, torts, and damages, real estate and the like, complete the list. When we attempt to interpret the sort of world the rabbis of the Mishnah propose to create, therefore, at the very outset we realize that that world in no way conforms, in its most profound and definitive categories of organization, to our own. That is why we need help in interpreting what it is that they propose to do, and why they choose to do it that way and not in some other.

It follows that the critical work of making sense and use of the talmudic literature is to learn how to hear what the Talmud wishes to say in its own setting and to the people addressed by those who made it up. For that purpose it is altogether too easy to bring our questions and take for granted that, when the rabbis of the Talmud seem to say something relevant to our questions, they therefore propose to speak to us. Anachronism takes many forms. The most dangerous comes when an ancient text seems accessible and clear.[19] For the Talmud is separated from us by the whole of Western history, philosophy, and science. Its wise sayings, its laws, and its theology may lie in the background of the law and lore of contemporary Judaism. But they have been mediated to us by many centuries of exegesis, not to mention experience. They come to us now in the form which theologians and scholars have imposed upon them. It follows that the critical problem is to recognize the distance between us and the Talmud.

---

entirely unhistorical and undifferentiated. But the effort is impressive and not to be forgotten.

[18] As if we knew their purpose!

[19] I think theologians and historians of talmudic theology most consistently commit the sin of anachronism. In this regard the list of examples covers the bibliography of available monographs and books. I cannot think of a single theologian who begins with consideration of the character of the sources and what he proposes to say about them. Everyone works as if "we all know" what we are doing.

The second problem, closely related to the first, is the work of allowing strange people to speak in a strange language about things quite alien to us, and yet of learning how to hear what they are saying. That is, we have to learn how to understand them in their language and in their terms. Once we recognize that they are fundamentally different from us, we have also to lay claim to them, or, rather, acknowledge their claim upon us. The document is there. It is interesting. It is important and fundamental to the definition of Judaism. When we turn to the humanities and social sciences of our own day with the question, who can teach us how to listen to strange people, speaking in a foreign language, about alien things, I am inclined to look for scholars who do just that all the time. I mean those who travel to far-off places and live with alien tribes, who learn the difficult languages of preliterate peoples, and who figure out how to interpret the facts of their everyday life so as to gain a picture of that alien world and a statement of its reality worth bringing back to us. Anthropologists study the character of humanity in all its richness and diversity. What impresses me in their work is their ability to undertake the work of interpretation of what is thrice-alien – strange people, speaking a strange language, about things we-know-not-what – and to translate into knowledge accessible to us the character and the conscience of an alien worldview.

When I turn to anthropology for assistance in formulating questions and in gaining perspectives on the talmudic corpus, what I am seeking is very simple: fresh perspectives, fructifying questions.[20] To illustrate what I have found, let me now take up three specific problems solved for me by anthropologists, all three problems directly related to the study of early rabbinic Judaism and its classic texts.[21]

IV

First, the most difficult task we have is to learn how to decipher the glyphs of an alien culture. For example, in the case of the Talmud,

---

[20] It is far from the truth that historians do not bring fresh perspectives on ancient or medieval sources. I point for contrary evidence to the splendid work of Peter Brown, for instance, in readily accessible form, his *The World of Late Antiquity. From Marcus to Aurelius to Muhammed* (London, 1971: Thames & Hudson). There is a certain insightfulness in Brown's work which some may call ad hoc and not unimpressionistic, but I think it is genius.

[21] Once more I emphasize that I do not pretend to be a master of contemporary anthropological thought or research. I point only to a few of the writings of a handful of people who have given much to me and made me see things in a fresh way. I have no news to bring to anthropologists, and little enough to talmudists.

if we have a story about how a holy rabbi studied many languages and mastered all knowledge in his pursuit of Torah – as we do about Hillel – what is it that the storyteller is trying to express? And what communion of language and forms, perceptions and values makes it possible for him to speak to his listener in just this way about just this subject? In other words, once we concur that we want to create more than a paraphrase of the sources, together (in the case of the historians of conscience) with a critical perspective upon them, what is it that we wish to discover? We need to learn how to read these stories and so how to become sensitive to their important traits and turnings, both those of language and those of substance. Literary critics make their living on their sharpened mind and eye. For the purposes of ancient Jewish and Israelite sources, so too do people who learn to think like anthropologists.

Let me cite, as a stunning example, the perspective of the great structuralist-anthropologist, Edmund Leach, upon the story of the succession of Solomon to the throne of Israel. This is how he introduces his work:

> My purpose is to demonstrate that the Biblical story of the succession of Solomon to the throne of Israel is a myth which "mediates" a major contradiction. The Old Testament as a whole asserts that the Jewish political title to the land of Palestine is a direct gift from God to the descendants of Israel (Jacob). This provides the fundamental basis for Jewish endogamy – the Jews should be a people of pure blood and pure religion, living in isolation in their Promised Land. But interwoven with this theological dogma there is a less idealized form of tradition which represents the population of ancient Palestine as a mixture of many peoples over whom the Jews have asserted political dominance by right of conquest. The Jews and their "foreign" neighbors intermarry freely. The synthesis achieved by the story of Solomon is such that by a kind of dramatic trick the reader is persuaded that the second of these descriptions, which is morally bad, exemplifies the first description, which is morally good.[22]

This brief statement of purpose tells us that Leach will show us, in stories we have read many times, meanings and dimensions we did not know were there. When we follow his analysis, we realize that we have been blind. For he shows us what it means to see.

V

Second, the most difficult question is to find out what are the right questions. Precisely what we want to know when we open the pages of

---

[22] Edmund Leach, "The Legitimacy of Solomon," in Michael Lane, ed., *Introduction to Structuralism* (New York, 1970: Basic Books), pp. 248-292.

the Talmud is not simple to define. To be sure, these documents have been studies for centuries by people who knew just what they wanted to find out. The questions shaped and brought to the Talmud by the rabbinical scholars of earlier ages made sense both for the Talmud and for the social and intellectual circumstances of the scholars of the Talmud.[23] But, as I have made clear, the information and insight we seek, the problems we wish to solve, and the questions we find urgent are not those which flow, directly and without mediation, from the pages of the Talmud itself. It is one thing to point out that history provides us with the wrong questions. It is quite another to lay forth right ones.

For this purpose, I am much in debt to theorists of social anthropology for showing, in the study of other artifacts and documents of culture, the sort of thing one might do, too, with this one. I refer, for one important example, to the conception of religion as a cultural system. This conception proposes that we view a document of a culture as an expression of that culture's worldview and way of life.

In this context, for example, there is much to be learned from the statement of Clifford Geertz:

> Sacred symbols function to synthesize a people's ethics – the tone, character, and quality of their life, its moral and aesthetic style and mood – and their worldview – the picture they have of the way things in sheer actuality are, their most comprehensive ideas of order. In religious belief and practice a group's ethos is rendered intellectually

---

[23] The *yeshivot* in Europe trained masters of the Talmud able to exemplify and apply its teachings (in that order of importance) and who could serve as judges and clerks for the Jewish community. That is why the Talmud was studied by them as it was; for instance it explains the tractates they chose. Their larger cultural tasks – to perpetuate the relevance of the text through continuing and extraordinarily brilliant work of exegesis, and application – were wholly successful. So what they did was congruent to their social and cultural context. Indeed, in large measure, because of their success, they imparted to that context its distinctive social and cultural traits. (If universities in the Western countries would enjoy an equivalent success, then the populations of those countries would enjoy the power to think clearly and analyze an issue critically.) Precisely why *yeshivot* and Jewish seminaries in the USA and Canada study the texts which they do, and ignore the texts they ignore (out of the same corpus of Torah-writings) is not so clear. My impression is that the curriculum, once crucial to the formation of Jewish culture, has not changed, so that the things the students might know in order to have something worth sharing with their own age are not given to them. The results among *yeshiva*-alumni I have known are rather sad, people who cannot, for example, operate in a world in which statements are verified by reference to empirical testing, not by what sounds right or seems reasonable (let alone what some holy rabbi tells them). In the end they tend to make things up as they go along and call it Torah-true.

reasonable by being shown to represent a way of life ideally adapted to the actual state of affairs the worldview describes, while the worldview is rendered emotionally convincing by being presented as an image of an actual state of affairs peculiarly well-arranged to accommodate such a way of life.[24]

What Geertz's perspective contributes is the notion that the worldview and way of life laid forth by a religion together constitute a system, in which the character of the way of life and the conceptions of the world mutually illuminate and explain one another. The system as a whole serves to organize and make sense of all experience of being. So far as life is to be orderly and trustworthy, it is a system which makes it so.

Now it would be difficult to formulate a more suitable question to so vast and encompassing, relentlessly cogent a document as the talmudic literature than this simple one: How does this document inform us about the ethos of the community it proposes to govern? For this document does present a picture of the proper conduct of life, expressive of a cogent ethos. In this immense mass of ideas, stories, laws, criticism, logic, and critical thought, we are taught by Geertz to look for the center of it all and to uncover the principal conceptions which unite the mass of detail. Geertz for his part emphasizes that there is nothing new in his perspective: "The notion that religion tunes human actions to an envisaged cosmic order and projects images of cosmic order onto the place of human experience is hardly novel." But, he notes, it is hardly investigated either.[25] And, it goes without saying, all those who have spoken of the Talmud as an ocean share a single failing: none has offered us much by way of a chart.[26]

---

[24]Clifford Geertz, "Religion as a Cultural System," in his *The Interpretation of Cultures* (New York, 1973: Basic Books, Inc.), pp. 87-88. I may point out that this is not the first point in my work at which I have drawn upon Geertz's thoughtful proposals. His "Religion as a Cultural System" originally appeared in Michael Banton, ed., *Anthropological Approaches to the Study of Religion* (London, 1966). It made an immediate impact upon my approach to the history of the Jews in Babylonia, which I made explicit in the preface to the concluding volume, *A History of the Jews in Babylonia* (Leiden, 1970) V. *Later Sasanian Times*, p. xvii. In fact, it was from Vol. III onward that the shape of the work changed in some part in response to what I was able to learn from Geertz.

[25]I think the most difficult thing to investigate in the talmudic ethos is also the most obvious: the character of the literature, its logic and the sorts of arguments and analyses it presents. I have tried to present such an analysis in my *Invitation to the Talmud. A Teaching Book* (New York, 1973: Harper & Row), particularly on pp. 223-246, and in "Form and Meaning in Mishnah," *Journal of the American Academy of Religion* 45, 1, 1977, pp. 27-54. But these papers, I should claim, only scratch the surface.

[26]Though, as I said, some have tried, Kadushin being the one worth noting. Among *yeshiva*-trained talmudists none has even tried.

VI

While the contributions of Leach and Geertz serve to make us aware of the potentialities of our sources, we may, third, point to yet another anthropologist, who has realized a measure of these potentialities. Some of the work of Mary Douglas already has made a considerable impact upon the analysis of students of the Hebrew Scriptures and earlier strata of the rabbinical literature. *Purity and Danger*,[27] for example, opened new perspectives on the issues and meaning of the laws of Leviticus. Her contribution is both to the theory and the substantive analysis of a society's culture. her stress is upon the conception that, "each tribe actively construes its particular universe in the course of an internal dialogue about law and order." So, she says,

> Particular meanings are parts of larger ones, and these refer ultimately to a whole, in which all the available knowledge is related. But the largest whole into which all minor meanings fit can only be a metaphysical scheme. This itself has to be traced to the particular way of life which is realized within it and which generates the meanings. In the end, all meanings are social meanings.[28]

These judgments, which I think form a common heritage of social analysis for the work before us, present a challenge. It is how not only to decipher the facts of a given culture, but also to state the large issues of that culture precisely as they are expressed through minute details of the way of life of those who stand within its frame. Mrs. Douglas has done a fair part of the work. So she has given an example of how the work must be done. This is in her work on the Jewish dietary code, especially as laid out in the book of Leviticus. She introduces one of the most suggestive examples of her work in the following way:

> If language is a code, where is the precoded message? The question is phrased to expect the answer: nowhere....But try it this way: if food is a code, where is the precoded message? Here, on the anthropologists' home ground, we are able to improve the posing of the question. A code affords a general set of possibilities for sending particular messages. If food is treated as a code, the messages it encodes will be found in the pattern of social relations being expressed. The message

---

[27](London, 1966). I point out, also, that Mrs. Douglas was kind enough to read in manuscript and to write an important critique of my *Idea of Purity in Ancient Judaism* (Leiden, 1973), pp. 137-142. This critique was my first exposure to the interesting perspective of anthropologists. Further discussions with her and (of a quite different order) with Melford Spiro have proved stimulating.

[28]Cf. *Implicit Meanings. Essays in Anthropology* (London, 1975: Routledge, Kegan & Paul).

is about different degrees of hierarchy, inclusion and exclusion, boundaries and transactions across the boundaries.[29]

What should be striking is that she treats as suggestive and important those very rituals in which the Talmud and the form of Judaism created and expressed in it abound.

VII

While I have pointed to three specific contributions of anthropologists, I do not ignore a more general contribution of anthropology as a mode of thought. When we speak to anthropologists about the details of the Talmud's laws, not merely about its intellectual results, we do not have to feel embarrassed or apologetic, as we do when we talk to historians and theologians. Let me spell this out.

A critical problem facing us when we come to the Talmud is that it simply does not talk about things about which people generally want to know these days. The reason that historians have asked their range of questions is in part a counsel of desperation: Let us at least learn in the Talmud about things we might want to know – wars, emperors, or institutions of politic. The theologians and historians of theology similarly bring a set of contemporary questions, for instance, about the Talmud's beliefs about sin and atonement, suffering and penitence, divine power and divine grace, life after death and the world to come, because people in general want to know about these things. Both kinds of scholars do not misrepresent the results when they claim that the Talmud contains information relevant to their questions.

But neither the historian nor the theologian and historian of theology would ask us to believe that the Talmud principally is about the questions they bring to its pages. As I said, it is not divided into tractates about kings and emperors, or about rabbis and patriarchs, for that matter. It also is not organized around the great issues of theology. There is no tractate on the unity of God or on prayer, on life after death or on sin and atonement. Nor does the Talmud speak openly and unambiguously on a single religious and theological question as it is paraphrased in contemporary discourse. So the two kinds of work done in the past, theology, including history of theology, and history, have asked the Talmud to speak in a language essentially alien to its organizing and generative categories of thought.

What does the Talmud tell us? To take three of its largest tractates: it speaks about who may and may not marry whom, in

---

[29]*Ibid.*, p. 249.

Yebamot; about what may and may not be eaten, in Hullin; and about the resolution of civil conflict, courts of law, property claims, and similar practical matters, in Baba Qamma, Baba Mesia, and Baba Batra. If, to go on, we speak about yet another vast tractate of Mishnah, we address the issues of Kelim, thirty chapters, longest of them all, which analyze the questions of what sorts of objects are subject to cultic uncleanness, and what sorts of objects are not subject to cultic uncleanness. What follows is an amazing agendum of information, answers to questions no one would appear in our day to wish to ask: marriage, food, property relations, cultic cleanness.

Yet it is not entirely true that no one wants to know about these things. When an anthropologist goes out to study a social group, these are the very questions to be asked. As Mary Douglas says, "If food is a code, where is the precoded message? Here, *on the anthropologist's home ground*, we are able to improve the posing of the question."[30] The stress is in her words, *on the anthropologist's home ground*, because when we want to tell scholars of religious studies and theology about the things important to the Talmud, their interest perishes at the frontiers (however wide) of their courtesy. How I slaughter an animal is not deemed a question relevant to religion among philosophers of religion and theologians. But it is a critical questions to an anthropologist of religion. The difference lies in the understanding of the task. The anthropologist wants to understand the whole of a social and cultural system, the group's way of living and its worldview. As Geertz points out, the anthropologist seeks to tell us important things about how these interrelate and define a coherent system. Douglas holds that we uncover a cogent set of conceptions and social events, which, when uncoded, tells us something important about the human imagination. Viewed in this way, things which seem trivial are transformed into the very key to the structure of a culture and the order of a society.

Matters are not to be left in such general terms. When we speak about the human imagination, we are addressing a particular issue. It is how people cope with the dissonances and the recurrent and critical tensions of their collective existence. What lies at the heart of a group's life, and what defines both its problem and its power? In the case of ancient Israel, it is the simple fact that a small people lives upon a land which it took from others, and which others wish to take from it. So what is critical is the drawing and maintaining of high walls, boundaries to protect the territory – both land and people – from encroachment. As Douglas phrases matters:

---

[30]*Loc. cit.*

Israel is the boundary that all the other boundaries celebrate and that gives them their historic load of meaning.

In the very next sentence, she says:

Remembering this, the orthodox meal is not difficult to interpret as a poem.[31]

It is this mode of thought which I think makes us see the pages of the Talmud in a way in which we have never seen them before. It makes us realize we have never seen what has been there all the time. And it gives us confidence that others too should see what we do. Douglas concludes:

It would seem that whenever a people are aware of encroachment and danger, dietary rules controlling what goes into the body would serve as a vivid analogy of the corpus of their cultural categories at risk....the ordered system which is a meal represents all the ordered systems associated with it.[32]

This is the sort of thesis which, I think, we are able to explore and analyze by reference to the documents of early rabbinic Judaism. For this purpose they are perhaps more compelling than some more theological ones.

VIII

Yet a second more general contribution accruing from the anthropological mode of thought is to be specified. We have to learn not only how to describe and make sense of our data. Once we have discerned the system which they evidently mean to create, we have the additional task before us of comparing that system to other systems, yielded both by Judaism in its various stages, and by other religious and cultural contexts entirely. For a system described but not juxtaposed to, and compared with, other systems has not yet been interpreted. Until we realize what people might have done, we are not going to grasp the things they did do. We shall be unable to interpret the choices people have made until we contemplate the choices they rejected. And, as is clear, it is the work of comparison which makes that perspective possible. But how do we compare systems?[33]

---

[31]*Cf. ibid.*, pp. 272-273.
[32]*Loc. cit.*
[33]Much that is called "comparative religions" compares nothing and is an exercise in the juxtaposition of incomparables. But it does not have to be that way.

In fact, whenever we try to make sense for ourselves of what alien people do, we are engaged in a work of comparison, that is, an experiment of analogies. For we are trying to make sense specifically by comparing what we know and do to what the other, the alien culture before us seems to have known and to have done. For this purpose we seek analogies from the known to the unfamiliar. But the work of comparison is exceedingly delicate. For, by using ourselves as one half of the equation for a comparative exercise, we may turn out to impose ourselves as the measure of all things.[34] That of course is something anthropology has taught us not to do, which is another reason for its critical importance in today's labor. In fact, matters prove more insightful when we reverse the equation and regard the other as the measure, and ourselves as the problem. That is, we have to recognize these are the choices those people made, which help us to understand that we too make choices. These are the potentialities discerned and explored by those folk who have made this document and this system. Now we may measure ourselves by whether, for our part, we too recognize potentialities beyond our actuality, whether we see that we too have the capacity to be other than what we are. These are critical questions of culture and sensibility.[35]

That is the point at which the talmudic literature proves especially interesting to students of culture, on the broad stage of humanities, and to scholars of contemporary Judaism, on the narrow one of theology of Judaism. It provides us with the richest documentation of a system of Judaism among all the Judaic systems of antiquity, from the formation of the biblical literature to the Islamic conquest. When we consider that the Talmud also is formative for the systems of Judaism of later times, we realize how promising it is as a fulcrum for the lifting of that unformed mass of the ages: the making sense of the Judaic tradition in all its diversity, complexity, and subtlety. Clearly, I deem anthropology to be a useful instrument. Let me conclude the argument by

---

[34] It seems to me any pretense that we stand outside of the equation of comparison is misleading. When we teach a foreign language to our students, it is, in significant measure, by trying to locate analogies to facilitate memorization, and, at the outset, to relate the unknown to the known. That is so in any sort of interpretive enterprise, I think, and it is best to admit it at the outset. But it is specified not as what must be, only as what is anachronistic and must be avoided.

[35] This point is especially important in the academic study of religions. I have spelled it out at some length in my lecture, "Stranger at Home," the inaugural lecture for the Department of Religious Studies at Arizona State University, Tempe, published by Arizona State University in October, 1979. The role of the academic study of religions in the maturing of students' educational and cultural perceptions and perspectives is what is analyzed in that paper.

specifying that thing I wish to make with diverse tools, one, but only one, of which is the anthropological instrument.

IX

What I seek is the insight into the world of ancient Judaism.[36] This is in part so that contemporary Jews may have a clearer picture of themselves, but in still larger measure so that contemporary humanists may gain a more ample account of a tiny part of the potentialities of humanity, that is, that part expressed within the Judaic tradition in its rabbinical formulation. We have to find out what others have made of that system, what it is that the talmudic system contains within itself, so as to find yet another mode for the measure of humankind. The human potentialities and available choices within one ecological frame of humanity, the ancient Jewish one, are defined and explored by the talmudic rabbis. (As it happens, we know a great deal about the results.) This same question – the possibilities contained within the culture of ancient Judaism – is to be addressed to the diverse formations and structures of Judaism, at other times in its history besides that of late antiquity. But we have to learn how to do the work in some one place, and only then shall we have a call to attempt it elsewhere. What we must do is first describe, then interpret. But what do we wish to describe?

I am inclined to think the task is to encompass everything deemed important by some one group, to include within, and to exclude from, its holy book, its definitive text: a system and its exclusions, its stance in a taxonomy of systems. For, on the surface, what they put in they think essential, and what they omit they do not think important. If that is self-evident, then the affirmative choices – which are not the only ones about which we know – are the ones requiring description and then interpretation. But what standpoint will permit us to fasten onto the whole and where is the fulcrum on which to place our lever? For given the size of the evidence, the work of description may leave us with an immense, and essentially pointless, task or repetition: saying in our own words what the sources say, perfectly clearly, in theirs. That is not an interesting task, even though, in some measure, it must be done.

So when I say that a large part of the work is to describe the worldview of the rabbis of the Mishnah and the Talmud, at best I acquire a license to hunt for insight. But I have not come closer to the definition of the task. What brings us closer, indeed, what defines the work as well as I am able, is the conception to which I have already

---

[36]In a moment I make this banal statement much more specific.

alluded, the idea of a system, that is, a whole set of interrelated concerns and conceptions which, all together, both express a worldview and define a way of living for a particular group of people. (That word, system, yields a useful adjective, systemic: the traits pertinent to a system.) The work I do is to describe the system of the rabbis of the Mishnah and the Talmud. That is, I propose to bring to the surface the integrated conception of the world and of the way in which the people should live in that world. All in all, that system both defines and forms reality for Jews responsive to the rabbis.

Now all worth knowing about the rabbis and the Jews around them is not contained within their system, as they lay it out. There is, after all, the hard fact that the Jews did not have power fully to shape the world within which they lived out their lives and formed their social group. No one else did either. There were, indeed, certain persistent and immutable facts, which form the natural environment for their system. These facts do not change, but do have to be confronted. There are, for instance, the twin facts of Jewish powerlessness and minority status. Any system produced by Judaism for nearly the whole of its history will have to take account of the fact that the group is of no account in the world. Another definitive fact is the antecedent heritage of Scripture and associated tradition, which define for the Jews a considerably more important role in the supernatural world than the natural world obviously affords them. These two facts, the Jews' numerical insignificance and political unimportance, and the Jews' inherited pretensions and fantasies about their own centrality in the history and destiny of the human race, created (and still create) a certain dissonance between a given Jewish worldview, on the one side, and the world to be viewed by the Jews, on the other. And so is the case for the rabbis of the Mishnah and the Talmud, and that seems to me a critical problem to be confronted in the talmudic system.[37]

But, as I have stressed, we cannot take for granted that what we think should define the central tension of a given system in fact is what concerns the people who did create and express that system. If we have no way of showing when our surmise may be wrong, then we also have no basis on which to verify our thesis as to the core and meaning of our system.[38] The result can be at best good guesses.[39] A mode for interpreting the issues of a system has therefore to be proposed.

---

[37]The conception of an "ecology of religion" is spelled out as best I can in the third edition of my *Way of Torah: An Introduction to Judaism* (Duxbury Press, 1979).

[38]Furthermore, *if we cannot show it, we do not know it.* I am tired of the appeal to "it seems reasonable to suppose," and "this has the ring of truth," which fills

The Talmud as Anthropology

One route to the interpretation of a system is to specify the sorts of issues it chooses to regard as problems, the matters it chooses for its close and continuing exegesis. When we know the things about which people worry, we have some insight into the way in which they see the world. So we ask, when we approach the Talmud, about its critical tensions, the recurring issues which occupy its great minds. It is out of concern with this range of issues, and not some other, that the Talmud defines its principal areas for discussion. Here is the point at which the great exercises of law and theology will be generated – here and not somewhere else. This is a way in which we specify the choices people have made, the selections a system has effected. When we know what people have chosen, we also may speculate about the things they have rejected, the issues they regard as uninteresting or as closed. We then may describe the realm of thought and everyday life they do not deem subject to tension and speculation. It is on these two sides – the things people conceive to be dangerous and important, the things they set into the background as unimportant and uninteresting – which provide us with a key to the culture of a community, or, as I prefer to put it, to the system constructed and expressed by a given group of people.

I have outlined what must appear to be a formidable and serious agendum for scholarly work. Yet the truth is otherwise.

The work of learning is not solemn but is like the play of children. It is an exercise in taking things apart and putting them back together again. It is a game of seeing how things work. If it is not this, then it is a mere description of how things are, and that is not engaging to active minds. If I do not have important questions to address to the facts in my hands – the documents which I study – then I am not apt to discover anything interesting. I am unlikely to make of the documents more than a statement of what already is in them. But the Talmud and its cognate literature have exercised a formidable and continuing power over the minds of the Jewish people for nearly twenty centuries. They contain the artifacts of a foreign culture, exhibiting distinctive traits, and capable of sustaining quiet searching scrutiny by scholars of culture. Therefore, merely saying what is in the Talmud and its cognate literature is not sufficient.

The central issues, those questions which generate insight worth sharing and understanding worth having, therefore are to be defined in these terms: What does the Talmud define as its central problems? How does the Talmud perceive the critical tensions of its world? We

---

the pages of talmudic history. It is just as weighty an argument as is the common criticism, "not persuasive."

[39]That is, pure subjectivity and impressionism. These can be avoided.

want to describe the solutions, resolutions, and remissions it poses for these tensions. We propose to unpack and then to put back together again the worldview of the document. When we can explain how this system fits together and works, then we shall know something worth knowing.[40]

---

[40]I do not mean to suggest there are no problems in anthropological approaches and methods. For one thing, we address ourselves to historical data and seek to accomplish the interpretation of a world known through its literary remnants. But anthropologists tend to do a better job on living societies than on books. Leach and Douglas are exceptional, I think. Further, there is a range of questions I have not confronted here, specifically, about whether, when we speak of systems, we mean merely philosophico-religious ones – that is, intellectual constructs, or we refer also to social-cultural groups – "real people." The talmudic literature begins in Mishnah, which is an essentially theoretical account of a nonexisting world (see "Map Without Territory" and "History and Structure" in my *Method and Meaning in Ancient Judaism. Essays on System and Order* (Missoula, 1979: Scholars Press for Brown Judaic Studies), but ends in the Jewish community formed under rabbinical authority and governed by the Talmud. So there are more ambiguities than I have suggested – many more.

6

Why No Science in Judaism?

Tulane University, 1987

The Judaism of the Dual Torah has coped only with considerable difficulty with the three definitive components of modern life, specifically, fundamental changes of behavior and belief in politics, economics, and intellect. Democracy, capitalism, and science including technology emerged elsewhere than from within the mind and imagination of thinkers nurtured by the canonical writings of that Judaism. While Jews sustained by intellectual resources in addition to the Judaism of the Dual Torah, for example, in medieval times by the Western philosophical tradition of Greece mediated by Islam, or in modern times by a different Judaism, or by no Judaism at all, found in democracy, or capitalism, or, for medieval times, science, medicine, and technology, valued sources for tight thinking and worthwhile living, the institutions and intellect of the Judaism of the Dual Torah did not.[1]

---

[1] And it is the fact that they do not today, as the so-called *haredim* in the State of Israel, absolutely authentic in their grasp of the disciplines of the Judaism of the Dual Torah, demonstrate day by day. In the State of Israel today, the dominant sector of the Judaism of the Dual Torah, in its institutions and attitudes, carries forward the quite different ideals in politics, economic action, and intellectual life received from Sinai (as the system would say). The simple fact is that the expression of the Judaism of the Dual Torah effected by the *Haredim* can be correlated, point by point, with the received canonical Torah, and the claim to authenticity seems to me subject to ample demonstration. But in my view, it is also the fact that the Judaism of the Dual Torah in this, its clearly classical statement for the contemporary world, also has no way of dealing with science and technology, democracy, and capitalism (or, for that matter, socialism). Whether or not the reversion to the authentic tradition (as defined in this context) therefore constitutes a valid choice for contemporary women and men seems to me a question worth considerable theological inquiry, since this particular version of romantic religion, while bearing its

Decision-making, individual and institutional, referred to the authority of sages. Sustained, systematic, rational economic activity took a subordinate place, well behind study of the Torah, as the paramount activity of men's (but not women's) lives. Scientific learning, empirical testing and sustained experiment in the sorting out of hypotheses and evaluating of propositions, systematic skepticism concerning received truths – all of these routine contemporary modes of thought were held to be matters of triviality, wasting time best spent only in Torah study. When we consider the Protestant Christian sources of democracy and (it is commonly maintained) also of capitalism, and the Christian Orthodox, Protestant, and Roman Catholic origins of science among the faithful of the Church for long centuries prior to the outbreak of the war between religion and science, we recognize through the comparison and contrast that a question of considerable interest awaits attention: Why there, not here?

I propose to explain why the normative modes of thought and intellect which I call "the mind" of the Judaism of the Dual Torah did not generate the kind of thinking that produced science, the division of philosophy known until nearly our own day as natural philosophy. By thought I mean, specifically, two things, first, how people connect one thing to something else, one fact to another, in literary terms, one sentence to another; and, second, how they draw conclusions from the particular connections that they make in their minds. These two stages – the perception of connection, the discernment of (self-evidently valid) conclusions based on the connection – characterize mind. They further allow us to explore the potentialities and also the limitations of intellect, what people are likely to see or to miss. In particular I show

---

ineluctable attraction, also demands denial of the presence of the world alongside ample exploitation of the goods of the world, deriving as they do from democracy, allowing free choice; capitalism, providing the surplus of wealth necessary to support full-time Torah study for vast numbers of males; and science and technology, defining the material conditions of everyday life fully enjoyed, also, by the *Haredim*. The formulation of a consistent position by the *Haredim*, affirming the received Judaism but also rejecting the goods and services of science and technology, capitalism, and democracy, will surely afford to the *Haredim* a moral authority, not to mention an inner cogency and consistency to their position, that presently appear wanting. A consistent position on the part of Jews who do not share the position of the *Haredim*, e.g., who sustain other Judaisms or no Judaism at all, is equally demanded. Conceding the claims to authenticity and providing ample financial support for the *Haredim* on the part of American Reform or Conservative or secular Jews as well as on the part of Zionist Israeli Jews (inclusive of both the Zionist-secular and the Zionist Religious parties) and their government seem not entirely honest and attest to a different kind of participation in the same romantic religion as the *Haredim* have worked out for themselves.

the range of choices available in the making of connections and the drawing of conclusions. I call them "logics," meaning, specifically, the modes of intelligible discourse. Specifically, how do I join one thought to another, therefore also one sentence to another, in such a way as to make a point that you can grasp. Let me give a simple example.

It rained heavily today./A ship came up the Mississippi River.

In our world of cogent thought, sentence one standing by itself bears no relationship to sentence two.

It rained heavily today./No ship came up the Mississippi River.

In our world of cogent thought, sentence one explains sentence two; because of the rain, joined with heavy winds, shipping in the Mississippi River ceased. We could make sense out of the first of the two instances also, for example, by adding "despite the fact that...," and the like. But the point is clear. We have rules in our minds that permit us to link one fact to another and that prevent us from doing so as well. When we know those rules, that is, the logics of cogent discourse and therefore also of intelligible thought, we know how our minds work. And the same is so in the case of the Judaism attested by the canonical writings from the Mishnah through the Bavli. Specifically, the way in which a given authorship composes cogent thought will be limited to a repertoire of four logics – modes of joining one sentence to another to make an intelligible statement – which allow that authorship to say things in one way and not in some other, and to say some things and not others. Linking in a cogent way one sentence to another, one thought to another, these logics exhibited by the canonical writings of the Judaism of the Dual Torah are four, propositional, teleological, metapropositional, and fixed associative, as I shall explain. Two of the four came to predominate, serving exceedingly well the tasks of thought of Judaism. But the fact that the two of the four predominated in the way in which they did accounts for the failure of Judaism in terms of its own indigenous logic to generate philosophy, including science.

The specific question I answer, therefore, is a very simple one of how the mind of Judaism sees the connections between one thing and something else and draws conclusions from the connections that are discerned. Stated in more general terms, my proposition is that an explanation of mind matters because it tells us how an intellect common to a number of authoritative writings – hence, to a textual community – altogether makes sense of things. Modes of thought transform information into knowledge, identify questions and answer them. Intellect endures in language, modes of thought in syntax and sentence structure, which realize in concrete ways abstract processes of reasoning. The mind of Judaism reaches us only in its results, the sentences formed into paragraphs, the paragraphs into chapters, the chapters into books: the truths deemed self-evidently valid, the propositions held beyond all debate, yielding the intense disagreement on this and that that serves as the wherewithal of everyday thought. The stakes are higher still. For the books of a long-dead past live on and shape the everyday reality of Judaism today. The mind of Judaism exists in the here and now of decisions on what I should do and why I should do it, the meaning of things, the past and future, the hope and destination, the sense of the whole and the fittingness of each part. The stakes are very high. If therefore we wish to understand what people think, we had best first ask how they think. That means explaining the ways in which they choose the problems they find urgent, know that one set of data pertains and another does not. So we have to account for how the writers of authoritative documents make connections between this and that. All of these abstractions come to immediate and concrete expression not in sentences but in paragraphs, that is to say, in the composition of two or more sentences. These points of union, the joining of two facts into a proposition that transcends them both, the making of a whole that exceeds the sum of the parts – these acts of intellectual enchantment wonderfully form the smallest whole units of propositional thought. When, therefore, we know why this, not that, why a paragraph looks one way, rather than some other, we find ourselves at the very center of the working of a mind: its making of sense out of the nonsense presented by the detritus of mere information.

I

Let me begin from the beginning. An ongoing social entity inculcates in age succeeding age modes of thought that, shared by all, impart self-evidence and enduring sense to transient propositions. Minds may change on this and that. But mind does not, mind meaning modes of patterned thought on ephemera. Accordingly, while the social entity undergoes change, rules of deliberation dictate the range of permissible deed, and the realm of choice knows limits set by sense deemed common. How people think dictates the frontiers of possibility. What they think – the exegesis, in accord with a fixed hermeneutic of the intellect – knows no limit. When we can describe the mind of a social entity through sorting out the rules governing the reaching of discrete and disparate conclusions, then we can claim to understand how the mind of a society of like-minded people is formed, those generative rules of culture and regulations of intellect that succeeding generations receive from infancy and transmit to an unknowable future. Attitudes shift. Values and beliefs change. One generation's immutable truths come to the coming age as banalities or nonsense. But processes of reflection about the sense of things, modes of thought concerning how we identify and solve problems, above all, the making of connections between this and that – these endure like oceans and mountains. Shifting only in tides and currents so vast as to defy the grasp of time, so that, when they do quake, the whole earth moves, these processes and modes of mind in the end dictate structure and establish order, the foundations of all social life, the framework of all culture. A well-composed and powerfully framed mode of deliberation, a manner of seeing things one way rather than some other, took shape in the formative age of the Judaism of the Dual Torah that has constituted the Judaism that was normative from the seventh century to nearly our own time. That manner of seeing things, in particular told people how to make connections between one thing and another, which is to say, how to make sense of detail and hold the whole together. My claim to describe, analyze, and interpret the mind of Judaism appeals to the paramount status of a single, normative and norm-defining document, to which people turned for the details of how to conduct themselves, and which, in consequence, imparted not only information, but, through recurrent acts of consultation, a mode of thought as well. That single document, the Talmud of Babylonia or Bavli, so dominated the life of Jews in both Christian and Muslim civilizations that that writing formed the academy of the mind of Judaism. Therefore when we can characterize the mind conveyed within the pages of that writing, we may accurately assess the intellect of those whose lives found structure and sense there and nowhere else.

II

The way in which people add up two and two to make four always requires the appeal to the *and,* and that is what endures, that *and* of the two and two equal four, and, too, the *equal,* which is to say, the conclusion yielded by the *and*. The logic lasts: the *and* of making connections, the *equal* of reaching conclusions. This endures: the certainty that X + Y are connected and generate conclusion Z, but (to make up an example) that the symbol # and the number 4 are not connected and therefore, set side by side, produce a mere nonsense statement. The mind of Judaism flourishes in processes of thought and comes to expression in the premises of self-evidence, more lastingly and more certainly than in the propositions of conviction and confession. That is why I choose to focus upon the simple matter of making connections and reaching conclusions: how people know that one connection between two matters is obvious, another pure nonsense. If I am correct in insisting that the logical repertoire of the canonical writings of the Judaism of the Dual Torah is limited, then any component of the canon serves as well as any other for an inquiry into the matter.[2] We turn directly to a single text and survey the several answers its authorship gives to a simple question: how do one *and* one *equal* two? We want only to define the *and* and the *equal,* simply parts of speech, so to speak. For a sample document, I have chosen Sifré to Deuteronomy. It is of indeterminate origin in time, but certainly coming after the formation of the Mishnah, in ca. A.D. 200, and before the closure of the Talmud of Babylonia or Bavli, in ca. A.D. 600. The authorship cites the Mishnah verbatim and the document is cited in the Bavli. An educated guess would place this compilation in the same general time as that of Sifra and Sifré to Numbers, and a convenience date of 300-400 is not wholly without justification. But the point, within the unfolding of the canonical writings of the Judaism of the Dual Torah, at which this one reached closure has no bearing upon our problem; our concern is with the fixed structures of rhetoric and logic characteristic of its authorship, not with the larger social and political world in which the authorship did its work.

III

In the document at hand I see four different logics by which two sentences are deemed to cohere and to constitute a statement of consequence and intelligibility. One is familiar to us as philosophical logic, the second is equally familiar as the logic of cogent discourse attained through narrative. These two, self-evidently, are logics of a propositional order. The third logic yielded by the sample document

---

[2]In my *Making of the Mind of Judaism. The Formative Age,* I survey the more important documents' logical repertoires. What I found is that all documents but two appeal to a uniform logic for both the composition of individual propositions of thought, fully exposed, which we should call "paragraphs," and also the joining of many such compositions into a cogent and sizable statement, which we should call a chapter or a document. If propositional logic governs the making of cogent statements out of two or more sentences, then propositional logic will also govern the joining of such statements into a large and encompassing composition. That is also the case for teleological logic, and, in the main, for metapropositional logic as well as fixed-associative logic (all of which I shall define presently). The two exceptional documents are the two Talmuds, which ordinarily form cogent statements of two or more sentences through propositional logic but then join these cogent statements together into sustained discourse through fixed associative logic. That will form the centerpiece of my concluding analysis, below.

Why No Science in Judaism?

before us is not propositional, and, as a matter of fact, it also is not ordinarily familiar to us at all. It is a mode of joining two or more statements – sentences – not on the foundation of meaning or sense or proposition but on foundations of a different order altogether. Presenting and explaining this unfamiliar logic of making connections (commonly without drawing conclusions that transcend the things connected) will present the greatest difficulty in exposition, though numerous examples will show beyond doubt that our authorship took for granted the mode of connection I shall define and describe. The fourth logic, distinct from the prior three, is a mode of establishing connections at the most abstract and profound level of discourse, the level of methodical analysis of many things in a single way, and that forms the single most commonplace building block of thought in our document. It is, as a matter of fact, stunning in its logical power. But, in a limited sense, it also is not propositional, though it yields its encompassing truths of order, proportion, structure, and self-evidence.

Let us first consider the two familiar modes of turning two sentences into a coherent statement with weight and meaning, the propositional logic. It is the one that connects two or more sentences, forming them into a whole that in meaning and intelligible proposition transcends the sum of the parts. Philosophical discourse is built out of propositions and arguments from facts and reason. I first give one example of the philosophical mode of stating and proving propositions, that is, repeatedly deriving one thing from many things. I give only part of a passage that shows how philosophical logic is realized.

Sifré to Deuteronomy

CCCXXVI:I

1. A. "For the Lord will vindicate his people and repents himself for his servants, when he sees that their might is gone, and neither bond nor free is left" (Dt. 32:36-43).
   B. "For the Lord will vindicate his people:"
   C. When the Holy One, Blessed be He, judges the nations, it is a joy to him, as it is said, "For the Lord will vindicate his people."
   D. But when the Holy One, Blessed be He, judges Israel, it is – as it were – a source of grace to him.
   E. For it is said, "...and repents himself [JPS: take revenge] for his servants."
   F. Now "repents" can only mean "regret," for it is said, "For I regret that I made them" (Gen. 6:7),
   G. and further, "I regret that I made Saul king" (1 Sam. 15:11).

We shall now see a systematic demonstration of the proposition that, when things are at their worst and the full punishment impends, God relents and saves Israel. The facts, or, in the rhetorical terms, sentences, are joined together into a cogent statement because all of them point toward a single proposition.

CCCXXVI:II
1. A. "...when he sees that their might is gone, and neither bond nor free is left:"
   B. When he sees their destruction, on account of the captivity.
   C. For all of them went off.
2. A. Another teaching concerning the phrase, "...when he sees:"
   B. When they despaired of redemption.
3. A. Another teaching concerning the phrase, "...when he sees [that their might is gone, and neither bond nor free is left]:"
   B. When he sees that the last penny is gone from the purse,
   C. in line with this verse: "And when they have made an end of breaking in pieces the power of the holy people, all these things shall be finished" (Dan. 12:7) [Hammer's translation].
4. A. Another teaching concerning the phrase, "...when he sees that their might is gone, and neither bond nor free is left:"
   B. When he sees that among there are no men who seek mercy for them as Moses had,
   C. in line with this verse: "Therefore he said that he would destroy them, had not Moses his chosen one stood before him in the breach" (Ps. 106:23)....

The completion of what God sees is diverse but on the whole coherent. No. 1 introduces the basic theme invited by the base verse, namely, Israel's disheartening condition. Then the rest of the items point to the unfortunate circumstance of Israel and the absence of effective leadership to change matters. To state the logic in more general terms, the sentences, 1, 2, and 3, standing entirely by themselves convey not a proposition but merely statements of a fact, which may or may not be true, and which may or may not bear sense and meaning beyond itself. Sentence 1 and sentence 2 by themselves state facts but announce no proposition. But the logic of syllogistic discourse joins the two into No. 3, which indeed does constitute a proposition and also (by the way) shows the linkage between sentence 1 and sentence 2. But there are more ways for setting forth propositions, making points, and thus for undertaking intelligible discourse, besides the philosophical, and syllogistic one with which we are familiar in the West. We know a variety of other modes of philosophical-propositional discourse, that is to say, presenting, testing, and demonstrating a proposition through appeal to fact and argument.

While philosophers in the Greco-Roman tradition will have made their points concerning other topics entirely, modes of proof will surely have proved congruent to the systematic massing of probative facts, all of them pertinent, all of them appropriate, to the argument and the issue. Collecting data and classifying them by their indicative traits, permitting identification of unities and diversities – the genus and the species – form the definition of one kind of scientific thinking. Here we see that kind of thinking. In propositional logic, which is the one we know best, connection is shown in a conclusion, different from the established facts of two or more sentences, that we propose to draw when we set up as a sequence two or more facts we claim to be connected and further claim out of that sequence to propose a proposition different from, transcending, the facts at hand.

We come next to a different form of linking sentence to sentence, which is narrative. Narrative connects facts into propositions in ways that for us are equally familiar to the philosophical mode, because narrative connections are, in their way, as propositional as the connections of philosophical logic. In this mode of thought, we prove propositions by appeal to teleology – the direction or purpose of facts, for example, events. A proposition (whether or not it is stated explicitly) may be set forth and demonstrated by showing through the telling of a tale that a sequence of events, real or imagined, shows the ineluctable truth of a given proposition. The logic of connection demonstrated through narrative, rather than philosophy, is simply stated. It is connection attained and explained by invoking some mode of narrative in which a sequence of events, first this, then that, is understood to yield a proposition, first this, then that – because of this. That manufactured sequence both states and also establishes a proposition in a way different from the philosophical and argumentative mode of propositional discourse. Whether or not the generalization is stated in so many words rarely matters, because the power of well-crafted narrative is to make unnecessary explicitly drawing of the moral.

The third logic is a sustained and highly cogent propositional discourse carried on at two levels, the immediate and the generalizing, in which one analytical method applies to many sentences, with the result that many discrete and diverse sentences are shown to constitute a single intellectual structure. This too is a highly scientific way of thinking, since it asks for unities in diversity, the rule that underlies diverse data, the regularity and order that explain the surface of things. A variety of explanations and amplifications, topically and propositionally unrelated, will be joined in such a way as to make a point beyond themselves and applicable to them all. Here we have a fixed way of connecting diverse things, so showing that many things really conform to a single pattern or structure. It is the promiscuous application to a range of discrete facts of a single mode of thought, that is, a cogent analytical method. Methodologically coherent analysis then imposes upon a variety of data a structure that is external to all of the data, yet that imposes connection between and among facts or sentences, a connection consisting in the order and balance and meaning of them all, seen in the aggregate. One of the most common modes of intelligible discourse is to ask the same question to many things and to produce a single result, wherever that question is asked: methodical analysis of many things showing pattern and therefore order where, on the surface, none exists.

Methodical analysis in fact imposes stunning cogency on otherwise unrelated facts or sentences, showing one thing out of many things. For unity of thought and discourse derives not only from what is said, or even from a set of fixed associations. It may be imposed by addressing a set of fixed questions, imposing a sequence of stable procedures, to a vast variety of data. That will yield not a proposition, but what I call a metaproposition – a rule that covers a variety of cases. This then is a different mode of cogency, one that derives from showing that many things follow a single rule or may be interpreted in a single way. It is the intelligible proposition that is general and not particular, that imposes upon the whole a sense of understanding and comprehension, even though the parts of the whole do not join together. What happens, in this mode of discourse, is that we turn the particular into the general, the case into a rule, and if we had to point to one purpose of our authorship overall, it is to turn the cases of the book of Deuteronomy into rules that conform, overall, to the way in which the Mishnah presents its rules: logically, topically, a set of philosophically defensible generalizations.

This brings us to the fourth logic of cogent discourse, which is one with which we are not ordinarily familiar. But in Judaism it is paramount in making up large and cogent structures of thought. I call it "the logic of fixed association," and when I set forth how it works, it will emerge as not at all alien in theory, even though it is uncommon in the discourse of the West. I begin with a negative definition. Fixed associative logic does not yield a proposition. But, on the positive side, that logic tightly links one fact to another. It does so not by joining the two through a proposition shared among them both, that is, through an intrinsic intersection, but through a property shared by them both and extrinsic to them both, namely, intersection with a common point of connection formed by an available set of associations, hence, fixed (or available) associations (or extrinsic connections). I underline the fact that the sense of the logical connection and sequence of things that links in one composition sentence 1, then sentence 2, then sentence 3, *though there is no propositional connection between* 1 and 2 or 2 and 3, rests upon principles of intelligibility hardly commonplace in our minds. Nothing links one sentence (completed thought or fact) to the ones fore or aft. Yet

Why No Science in Judaism?

the compositors present us with sequences of episodic sentences that they represent side by side with sentences that do form large propositional compositions, that is, that are linked one to the next by connections that we can readily discern. In the following simple example, the source of the fixed associations is Scripture, specifically, a verse of Scripture, the clauses of which are spelled out systematically, fact by fact. Between and among the facts ("sentences," "comments") are no intrinsic connections or even ample points of intersection. But the facts join together in a – to the authorship of our document, self-evident – connection. The source of the connection between and among facts then is the fixed association of clauses of the verses of Scripture that stand at the head of each discrete individual fact or thought or comment or sentence. I give part of a sustained passage held together through the logic of fixed association, in this case, to a cited verse of Scripture.

Sifré to Deuteronomy

XXV:I
1. A. "What kind of place are we going to? Our kinsmen have taken the heart out of us, saying, ['We saw there a people stronger and taller than we, large cities with walls sky-high, and even Anakites']" (Dt. 1:25-28):
   B. They said to him, "Moses, our lord, had we heard these things from ordinary people, we should have never believed it.
   C. "But we have heard it from people whose sons are ours and whose daughters are ours."

XXV:II
1. A. "We saw there a people...taller than we:"
   B. This teaches that they were tall.
2. A. "...and greater...:"
   B. This teaches that they were numerous.

XXV:III
1. A. "...large cities with walls sky-high, and even Anakites:"
   B. Rabban Simeon b. Gamaliel says, "In the present passage, Scriptures speak in exaggerated language: 'Hear O Israel, you are going to pass over the Jordan this day to go in to dispossess nations greater and mightier than yourself, cities great and fortified up to heaven' (Dt. 9:1).
   C. But when God spoke to Abraham, Scripture did not use exaggerated language: 'And we will multiply your seed as the stars of the heaven' (Gen. 26:4), 'And we will make your seed as the dust of the earth' (Gen. 13:16)."

XXV:IV
1. A. "...and even Anakites did we see there:"

B. This teaches that they saw giants on top of giants, in line with this verse: "Therefore pride is as a chain about their neck" (Ps. 73:6).

That each unit of thought, signified by a Roman numeral, stands by itself hardly needs proof, since it is a self-evident fact of discourse here. I cannot imagine how, apart from the mere statement of the facts, I can show more vividly that a sequence of utterly unrelated sentences has been laid forth before us. They occur in context of sequences of highly propositional units of thought. In terms of our language, we have a sequence of sentences that constitute discrete paragraphs, in the midst of sets of sentences that, themselves, compose quite cogent paragraphs of size and substance. These episodic sentences/facts then present no proposition and are not meant to, yet they clearly are deemed by the compositor of the document to cohere. This they do in a way different from the manner in which the sentences that make paragraphs (that is to say, facts that form propositions) cohere. The logic of connection of the one is different from the logic of connection of the other.

The logic of fixed associations rests upon the premise that *an established sequence of words joins whatever is attached to those words into a set of cogent statements, even though it does not form of those statements propositions of any kind, implicit or explicit.* The established sequence of words may be made up of names always associated with one another. It may be made up of a received text, with deep meanings of its own, for example, a verse or a clause of Scripture. It may be made up of the sequence of holy days or synagogue lections, which are assumed to be known by everyone and so to connect on their own. The fixed association of these words, whether names, whether formulas such as verses of Scripture, whether lists of facts, serves to link otherwise unrelated statements to one another and to form of them all not a proposition but *an entirely intelligible sequence of connected or related sentences.* The *and* therefore derives from a fixed association among traits or formulas common to sequential sentences but external to them all. Some may suppose that we have nothing more than a fancy statement of the plain old (il)logic of free association. But that is far from the case. Free association means, "There is this, and, by the way, this reminds us of that." But the logic of fixed association invariably appeals to an available structure to form connections between otherwise unconnected sentences or facts. And we can always identify the source of the fixedness of association, for example, in a sequence of verses of Scripture, or in an established order of sages' names, or in a known set of historical events, deemed always to fall in a given order, or in the synagogue lections, and the like.

IV

Among the four logics I have outlined, all documents of the Judaism of the Dual Torah find ample guidance for making cogent statements. But one of those documents, the Talmud of Babylonia or the Bavli, took paramount place and served, from the seventh century to the present, to define Judaism. Accordingly, if we want to know how the mind of Judaism works, we turn in particular to the Bavli. What we find there is that two of the logics predominate, each for its own purpose. One, the logic of propositional discourse, defines how completed units of thought, which we should call "paragraphs," are composed. That is, two or more facts join together to make a point, prove a proposition, comprise an argument. The other, the logic of fixed association, is paramount when it comes to joining completed units of thought to one another. The upshot is that the Bavli's authorships' completed compositions of thought – the propositions, whether philosophical, or teleological, or metapropositional, in logical cogency – are laid out like a commentary to the Mishnah. Each of its discussions, cogent in itself because of the inner relationships of sentences in making points or establishing propositions – is placed where it is located specifically to amplify in some way or another a statement of the Mishnah (or of Scripture). So the discussions one by one turn out, in the aggregate, to be highly propositional, to intend to say some one thing and to prove it. But the discussions are joined to one another not through proposition and argument, but rather, through a position assigned to them, without regard to continuous argument and sustained meaning, because of their pertinence to the sequence of sentences or paragraphs of the Mishnah or of Scripture.

Let me give a single example of a passage of the Bavli, which shows us how the intermediate units of discussion form propositions and demonstrate them, and then are strung together not as a sequential discussion, with beginning, middle, and end, but rather in accord with the principle of fixed association, which I defined earlier.

Bavli-tractate Sanhedrin to Mishnah-tractate Sanhedrin 2:3

A. [If] [the king] suffers a death in his family, he does not leave the gate of his palace.
B. R. Judah says, "If he wants to go out after the bier, he goes out,
C. "for thus we find in the case of David, that he went out after the bier of Abner,
D. "since it is said, *'And King David followed the bier'* (2 Sam. 3:31)."
E. They said to him, "This action was only to appease the people."
F. And when they provide him with the funeral meal, all the people sit on the ground, while he sits on a couch.

The exposition of the cited passage of the Mishnah begins with a propositional composition. The proposition is presented at B, C, and then Judah, C, is given an argument, with a counter argument at F.

I
- A. Our rabbis have taught on Tannaite authority:
- B. In a place in which women are accustomed to go forth after the bier, they go forth in that way. If they are accustomed to go forth before the bier, they go forth in that manner.
- C. R. Judah says, "Women always go forth in front of the bier.
- D. "For so we find in the case of David that he went forth after the bier of Abner.
- E. "For it is said, 'And King David followed the bier' (2 Sam. 3:31)."
- F. **They said to him, "That was only to appease the people [M. 2:3D-E].**
- G. "They were appeased, for David would go forth among the men and come in among the women, go forth among the women and come in among the men,
- H. "as it is said, *'So all the people and all Israel understood that it was not of the king to slay Abner'* (2 Sam. 3:37)."

The Bavli's authorship now inserts a sizable exposition on David's relationship with Abner, and this goes its own way, without regard to the amplification of M. Sanhedrin 2:3D-E, cited just now. The following not-very-cogent unit of discourse makes no single point but holds together because of the systematic amplification of the cited verses, and the amplifications yield clear-cut propositions. II stands by itself and sets the stage for III, so I skip directly to the following item, III.

III
- A. Said R. Judah said Rab, "On what account was Abner punished? Because he could have prevented Saul but did not prevent him [from killing the priest of Nob, 1 Sam. 22:18]."
- B. R. Isaac said, "He did try to prevent him, but he got no response."

What we have is once more a set of propositions, and what follows holds together in a logic of syllogistic argument.

- C. And both of them interpret the same verse of Scripture: "And the king lamented for Abner and said, Should Abner dies as a churl dies, your hands were not bound or your feet put into fetters" (2 Sam. 2:33).
- D. He who maintains that he did not try to stop Saul interprets the verse in this way: "Your hands were not bound nor were your feet put into fetters" – so why did you not try to stop him? *"As a man falls before the children of iniquity so did you fall"* (2 Sam. 3:33).
- E. He who maintains that he did try to stop Saul but got no response interprets the verse as an expression of amazement: "Should he have died as a churl dies? Your hands were not bound and your feet were not put into fetters."

F. Since he did protest, why "As a man falls before the children of iniquity, so did you fall"?
G. In the view of him who has said that he did protest, why was he punished?
H. Said R. Nahman bar Isaac, "Because he held up the coming of the house of David by two and a half years."

The framer refers to the Mishnah passage and proceeds. What we have now is the familiar program of Mishnah exegesis: amplification of words and phrases in the instance of No. IV of which I present only a few stichs, for these will suffice to make my point quite amply, which is that the Mishnah's order dictates the joining, in logical order and sequence, of one completed, propositionally cogent unit of thought to the next. The logic of the sequence is therefore that of fixed association.

IV
A. And when they provide him with the funeral meal, [all the people sit on the ground, while he sits on a couch] [M. 2:3F]:
B. What is the couch?
C. Said Ulla, "It is a small couch [Shachter, p. 106, n. 3: not used for rest but placed in the home merely as an omen of good fortune]."

The ongoing discussion of the matter provides a secondary development of the rules pertaining to the couch under discussion and need not detain us. What is important is simple. Each of the units signified by a Roman numeral finds cogency in propositional logic. Sentence A joins sentence B because both address a common point and intend to deal with that point. So the principle of cogency of the facts, or sentences, signified by letter is that familiar logic of propositional discourse that we use every day. But what joins the large-scale compositions which, in our own terms, we should call paragraphs? If we ask what has made the compositors or authorship of the whole link everything signified by Roman number I with everything signified by Roman numerals II, III, and so forth, it is not a sequential argument to which each "paragraph" contributes at all. It is, in fact, something else: the requirement of Mishnah exegesis or of Scripture exegesis.

What defines the *and*, and what defines the *equal*, of the sentence, *two and two equal four*? What I see here is a mixed mode of putting two and two together, one propositional, for the paragraphs or the whole units of completed thought, the other not, for the linkage of the paragraphs into a sustained composition or discourse. The one makes points through juxtaposing facts, that is to say, sentences, which are meant to bear an intrinsic relationship to one another because they point toward a common conclusion. The other puts two units of discussion side by side not because of an intrinsic relationship, established by a shared proposition, but because of an extrinsic relationship, imposed and imputed from the outside by the simple fact that the sentences of the Mishnah or of Scripture demand this relationship and order and not some other or no relationship and order at all. So much for the way in which the four available logics of discourse work within the Bavli. And that brings us to the question with which I commenced: why no science in Judaism?

V

Science as a mode of though bears two distinct, though related meanings; it is not a subject matter alone; it is preeminently a mode of thought. As subject matter, science concerns natural phenomena. As a mode of thought, science involves orderly and systematic comprehension, description, and explanation of natural phenomena,[3] which, in my terms, I should call the making of connections between one thing and another and the drawing of conclusions based on the making of connections.[4] And the critical component of science is the making of connections in one way rather than in some other: this relates to that, but it does not relate to the other thing. These connections – and also rejection of connections – are discovered or intuited, then tested empirically, not supplied, not received, and not dictated by convention. It is science in the latter sense, as a mode of thought, but encompassing the former, an interest in natural phenomena, that I claim not to find in mind exhibited by the formative states of the canon of the Judaism of the Dual Torah. It is for the same reason, that is, the indicative traits of mind defined by the canonical writings of that same Judaism, that that mode of thought – I also allege – did not flourish within Jewry so long as that Judaism predominated in the past, and that does not flourish today where that Judaism remains normative. The premise of my argument therefore is that thinking in one way, and not in another,

---

[3] I paraphrase Marshall Clagett, *Greek Science in Antiquity* (New York, 1955: Aberlard Schuman), p. 4.

[4] The matter of experimental science is not at issue here. I focus only on modes of thought, with particular reference to the making of connections. Stories on conducting experiments to test hypotheses are found, as a matter of fact, in talmudic literature and indicate that the critical mode of thought was entirely characteristic of its authorships. I laid heavy emphasis upon the critical and skeptical attitude of mind characteristic of the Bavli's authorships in my *Invitation to the Talmud* (San Francisco, 1985: Harper & Row), second edition, and nothing in the thesis and argument of that book contradicts the discussion that follows. Indeed, since the centerpiece of my thesis in this chapter – the correspondence of dialectical argument to the logic of fixed association – forms a counterpart to the focus of my argument in that book, which concerns the extraordinarily pure spirit of criticism and skepticism manifest in dialectical argument in the Bavli, the two books form a complement to one another.

involves the making of connections and the drawing of conclusions in this way, not that, with the consequence that philosophy, encompassing natural philosophy or science, as we now call it, will or will not emerge. If I make connections in one way, I shall also, by the way, think philosophically and produce science, in both mode of thought and (given the world in which we live, inevitably also) subject matter encompassing natural science, and if I make connections in another way, I shall produce other kinds of thought and – in the nature of things – also deal with other subjects entirely. The way in which connections are made between one thing and something else will also affect the things I choose to connect – and then explain.

The Judaism of the Dual Torah on its own produced little philosophy, both in general and also in the particular natural and social forms that flourished in Christianity and Islam in the same time and circumstance. That claim of mine is captured by the simple fact that Copernicus was a monk in Poland in the sixteenth century and that the Church for purposes of accurately calculating the calendar assigned him the task that he performed, with unanticipated results to be sure. In Poland in that same century flourished countless towering intellectual figures within the Judaism of the Dual Torah; none of them known to us pursued questions of a scientific character in a philosophical manner, in the way in which their countryman and contemporary, Copernicus, did. And, of course, Copernicus stood in a long line of tradition, extending backward to the origins of Christian philosophy in Greece and forward into the seventeenth century. Nor did the Christian impetus for science end there; Mendel, founder of genetics, we recall, was an Austrian Roman Catholic Christian monk. And the role of Protestant Christian philosophers, including scientists, in both the Reformation Churches and the free churches, hardly requires a sizable repertoire of instances. I may therefore stipulate as fact that until the seventeenth century science, as a division of philosophy, formed an important component of the intellectual life of the principal systems of Christianity, east and west, Greek and Latin. I maintain that the Judaism of the Dual Torah did not yield science, while, in the same times and circumstances, diverse Christian systems did. And I want to know what characterized the mind of Judaism that made philosophy, including natural philosophy, an uncommon outcome of intellectual inquiry: why this, not that?[5]

---

[5]A systematic characterization of the philosophy and history of ancient and medieval science is not required for the argument at hand. I consulted these books: Marshall Clagett, *Greek Science in Antiquity* (New York, 1955: Abelard-Schuman); S. Sambursky, *The Physical World of Late Antiquity* (London, 1962:

Any claim that the mind made by the Bavli could not do science because speculative thinking of a philosophical order was prevented by traditional thinking of an unsystematic character, incapable of either pursuing curiosity or generalizing, contradicts the character of the Bavli itself. That negative explanation demands sustained attention, since the proposed reason for the essentially unphilosophical, therefore also unscientific, mind of Judaism will not be grasped so long as people dismiss as merely traditional and subservient the intellect that Judaism did create. In fact, the mind of Judaism as the Bavli defined it was not traditional at all. "Tradition" may refer to "truth [thought] received," hence to the way in which revealed truth is transmitted. The word also may speak of "thought in process of formation," truth that results from a spell of agglutination and long-term sedimentary formation. What I have said to this point has prepared the way for my final proposition, which is that a system cannot be traditional in the sense of coming into being through a sedimentary process. A system can, and, in the case of Judaism, always is, traditional in that other sense: truth revealed and faithfully nurtured and handed on. That is to say, a system may lay claim to the status of traditionality when its framers say that what they teach derives from a remote past, revelation at Sinai for example, transmitted faithfully from that point onward. The Bavli, viewed whole and at the end, is not a traditional document. It is one that at each point presents its ideas as a system, whole, complete, ordered and properly balanced. So far as a document is traditional in that in origin and in composition, it is agglutinative, the Bavli is not a traditional document but one deriving from that sort of systematic and orderly thinking that we associate with the philosophical mind. In the sense that "traditional" teachings derive from a long process of a sedimentary order, accumulation and conglomeration, tradition is incompatible with the notion of system, and the Bavli states its ideas,

---

Routledge & Kegan Paul). See also his *Physics of the Stoics;* Lynn Thorndike, *History of Magic and Experimental Science During the First Thirteen Centuries of Our Era* (New York, 1923: MacMillan): A. C. Crombie, *Augustine to Galileo. The History of Science A.D. 400-1650* (Cambridge, 1953: Harvard University Press); A. C. Crombie, *Medieval and Early Modern Science* (Cambridge, 1963: Harvard University Press). I. *Science in the Middle Ages. V-XIII Centuries.* II. *Science in the Later Middle Ages and Early Modern Times: XIII-XVII Centuries;* Herbert Butterfield, *The Origins of Modern Science 1300-1800* (New York, 1957: The Free Press); Marie Boas, *The Scientific Renaissance. 1450-1630* (London, 1962: Collins); Richard S. Westfall, *The Construction of Modern Science. Mechanisms and Mechanics* (Cambridge, 1977: Cambridge University Press); and Edwin Arthur Burtt, *The Metaphysical Foundations of Modern Physical Science* (London, 1932: Routledge & Kegan Paul).

whole, complete, and systemically. That statement that the Bavli as a whole makes, specifically, bears many traits that point to cogent and systematic thought – system-building – but few literary or historical traits of that long-term agglutination and conglomeration, such as a sedimentary process yields. In so framing matters, I contrast thought derived from active rationality. And so far as the Bavli exhibits traits of intellect, these are of the same order of rationality and critical acumen as those of any other product of philosophical thinking. Nothing out of the past can be shown to have dictated the Bavli's program, which is essentially the work of its authorship. That authorship took command of the whole of the received Torah, both oral, the Mishnah, and written, Scripture. Their remarkable contribution was to turn both documents into sources for the connection of fixed association that defined the Bavli's principle logic of composition, namely, cogency among and between intermediate and the largest units of thought.

The authorship of the Bavli constructed the document that formed the centerpiece of the Judaism of the Dual Torah from the seventh century onward.[6] Access to the Torah, written and oral, both Scripture and the Mishnah for the Judaism of the Dual Torah that predominated, commenced in the pages of the Bavli. The Bavli defined the curriculum of Judaism in its schooling of all males from birth to death. Study of the Torah formed the principal religious activity, and when people studied the Torah, what they learned, in particular, is what they found when they opened the pages of the Bavli. True, other writing went forward; the Bavli hardly marked the end of the intellectual activity of the Judaism of the Dual Torah. That representation of the Bavli as the culturally definitive statement of the Judaism of the Dual Torah still understates the impact of the Bavli upon the intellect of Judaism because it sets forth the fact but does not explain it. Why the Bavli imposed upon the mind of Judaism its

---

[6]Various explanations for the paramount status of the Bavli in the history of Judaism circulate. To evaluate them and to offer a judgment upon the question would require knowledge of the post-talmudic sources and scholarly traditions, which I do not have; it would lead us far afield, since political and economic explanations have been offered. From the viewpoint of the argument of this paper, these explanations are beside the point. I simply take as fact the preeminent standing of the Bavli in the life of Judaism from the seventh century onward, and I know no work of scholarship that has called that fact into questions. My interest is in the intellectual consequences of the dominance of that document, rather than some other, or no particular writing at all, in the educational and cultural affairs of the community of Judaism, at that time coextensive with Jewry throughout most of the world.

particular configuration is not explained by the enduring and definitive influence of the Bavli. Why people turned to the Bavli is beside the point; what happened to their intellectual lives because they did forms the center of interest. What I propose to explain is why the Bavli, because of its particular character as a piece of writing, exercised remarkable formative power upon the mind of Judaism. And that explanation is central to my answer to the question, Why no science in Judaism?

The reason for the Bavli's power in defining for the community of Judaism the shape and structure of intellectual life – the process, not only, or even not mainly, the propositions thereof – is hidden in the character of the Bavli as a piece of writing. The authorship of the Bavli taught not only *what* to think, but *how* to think. The authorship of the Bavli exhibited in public the reasoning behind its results. It would follow that generations nurtured on the study of the Bavli would be educated to find self-evident not only the propositions of the Bavli but also its processes of thought, specifically, of analysis, the making of connections, and of synthesis, the drawing of conclusions. Because the Bavli records an ongoing conversation, a dialectic without a final stopping point, the conversation never ended, and later generations could locate for themselves a place within it. And making intelligible statements within the intellectual syntax and structure of the Bavli, age succeeding age carried forward those principles of cogency and argument that found initial definition in the pages of the Bavli itself. That is why process, not only proposition, imposed upon the intellect of succeeding generations that character that the shared mind of Judaism exhibited. And from our perspective, a particular aspect of that dialectic, which the Bavli's ebb and flow of argument conveys, takes on special importance.

The reason – the source of the Bavli's power to shape intellectual life – is that the sustained discourse of the Bavli exposed the processes of reasoning, the making of distinctions, the discerning of connections, the drawing of conclusions, that lay behind decisions of law and theology. Indeed, the bulk of the writing is devoted not to the presentation of facts but to the exposition of the connections between them. What makes possible the very distinctive character of the Bavli's discourse, its moving, or dialectical, argument, which flows from point to point in an unbroken stream of conversation, is the sense of the connectedness of thought that animates the whole. Even the brief snippets we examined show how the authorships have put together discrete sentences in such a way that the connections between one and the next, or between one set and the next, derive not from proposition – "let us prove this, by appealing to the following facts" – but from a shared, prior, and *a priori* program. The fundamental logic of the dialectical argument, the principle by which cogency is imputed to two or more sentences in succession, is that same logic of fixed association that joins the very largest units of thought into a single sustained document, a treatment of a Mishnah paragraph, a treatise on a Mishnah-tractate, upward to the Bavli as a whole. True, earlier we noticed how smaller units of discourse, paragraphs in common parlance, hung together because of a shared proposition. Yet a second glance shows us that even here, a sizable component of discrete and individual sentences finds its place as well. And well it should, when what links three independent facts or sentences, not of the same classification at all, for instance – in my earlier representation, episodic statements of the classification A to 3 to # – is simply the movement itself, this, then that, then the other thing, connected every which way, and, more than a few times, adventitiously at best. Let me state the link I perceive between dialectic and the logic of fixed association emphatically:

Given the clear sense of the compositors that they have, in fact, composed a cogent document made up of cogent compositions themselves comprising connected sentences, we have to conclude that dialectical argument appeals in the end to that logic of fixed association. That is what makes it necessary to maintain and sustain the movement that defines dialectical argument. Moving from one thing to the next, and by the way, there is this also to consider, but then this leads to that – that characterization of the dialectical argument tells us what holds the whole together. And it is that sense of the givenness of connection that makes unnecessary the disciplined composition of a sustained and well-constructed argument, proposition, proof, argument, and the like.

The fixed association of one thing to the next bears two traits. First, it is fixed, excluding free association. Second, it is imputed or supplied, not discovered or achieved by the engaged participants to discourse. The former trait insures rational discourse. The latter precludes inquiry into matters beyond the framework of the convention of fixed association (whatever it is), except within the limits of reason defined by that convention. So while scientific argument may move in a dialectical manner, talmudic argument would not yield science. That is why it is the very power of the Bavli, namely, its exposition of its modes of thought and the steps of argument, that also constitutes its pathos, its strength, its weakness.

For the two absolutely necessary traits of mind of philosophy, including natural philosophy, require, first, systematically thinking about propositions in a philosophical manner, and, second, highly speculative pursuit of wherever curiosity leads. Connection therefore cannot be imputed and must be discovered. Dialectical argument, which appeals for connection to extrinsic points of intersection, for example, with a common third element, may or may not yield philosophical argument about propositions. But a logic of fixed association, which, I argue, to begin with makes possible the dialectical argument that distinguishes the Bavli, assuredly imposes limits upon the free run of curiosity hither and yon. For fixed association is just that: fixed, defined from without. The fixedness of association is what makes possible dialectical argument, without the danger of chaos and descent into caprice and irrationality. But it also is what makes unlikely the free pursuit of curiosity wherever it leads: why this, not that? Once more, power and pathos meet: the strength of dialectic rests upon fixed association, which protects the integrity of discourse; the weakness of dialectic is this same fixed association, limiting, as it does, the potentialities of inquiry to a preassigned program and predetermined limits.

True, when we ask whether the Bavli's authorship has defined a mode of thought that would facilitate, or discourage, propositional discourse, we answer in the affirmative. The interior obstacle to philosophical inquiry is not set by the Bavli's basic mode of thought, which is indeed propositional. Intermediate units of discourse and thought (paragraphs, in common language) such as we reviewed demonstrate a strong interest in sustained and cogent, philosophical discourse, the mounting of arguments, the drawing of conclusions. The Bavli's was, moreover a mode of thought fully able not merely to stimulate the rehearsal and classification of received information, the sifting and refining of tradition, but also, and especially, to provoke free and wide-ranging speculation on hitherto-unimagined possibilities. The Bavli's authorship inaugurated an ongoing tradition of thought, in which later generations found for themselves a distinctive position. Commentaries pursuing issues not suggested within the Bavli itself, codes of law organizing the result of thought in entirely fresh ways, decisions on questions wholly outside of the program of the original document – all three modes of fresh speculation testify to the potentialities of the Bavli to precipitate and generate speculation of a systematic and also a propositional order. So at the center of matters is not the issue of propositional thought, of which the Bavli presents an ample and sophisticated example. It is the manner of making connections and – consequently, inexorably and unavoidably – also the drawing of conclusions, that is, that very centerpiece of mind that I identified at the outset as characteristic of the writings of the Judaism of the Dual Torah. The mode of argument, and not the character of the propositions, is what made unlikely the development of science as part of the philosophical tradition.

Why No Science in Judaism?

Since the authorship of the Bavli set the example of writing in a highly speculative manner and scarcely engaged in the mere rehashing of tradition, it follows that heirs to their mode of thought, properly trained, also would think in ways that were highly speculative, not simply rehashing "tradition." But the authorship of the Bavli, while exhibiting attitudes of speculative and propositional character entirely congruent with those of philosophy, were not philosophers in large scale processes of overall procedure. They joined facts in a way different from the philosophical, and they drew conclusions from facts in a way different from that of philosophy. Once connections came from without, the making of connections and drawing of conclusions would derive from that same received program of inquiry. The received program of fixed associations hardly stimulated looking to the world beyond the Torah, whether the world of nature or the world of social history. It is not because people within the Bavli's intellectual framework avoided making generalizations or presenting conclusions in an orderly and systematic way. That is beside the point, and it also is not true. It is because people used to receiving associations within a fixed and available program found slight stimulus to observe associations on their own, to ask why this, not that in circumstances in which this and that join together not in fixed and available intersection but solely in the mind of an observer. Nature and social history did not form realms in which people would anticipate associating facts and explaining the association by drawing conclusions. The received program of the Torah, written and oral, set forth those realms in which people would expect to associate two unrelated facts and explain their intersection, unity, difference or harmony. I underline that nothing in the topicality of nature or the history of nations set those subjects beyond the pale; the reason that the heirs of the Bavli did not pursue natural philosophy or social philosophy – we should today call the one natural science, the other social science or (more narrowly) history – is not that the Bavli ruled out as inconsequential those vast areas of knowledge. It is – to repeat – because those areas of learning contained within themselves no program of fixed association, except as they found their way into the pages of the Torah, written and oral, set forth in the Bavli. Creation, the history of humanity – natural and social science – found ample consideration in those pages, but solely within connections dictated not by the intrinsic traits of natural and social science but through points of intersection and association imputed, wholly extrinsically and from without, by the adventitious character of the Torah, oral and written, set forth by the Bavli. and, in the nature of things, on that basis there could be no science, whether natural or social. To state matters very simply, the Mishnah, with its propositional and syllogistic argument concerning the nature of things, can have generated natural and social science; the Bavli could not and did not.

And that is why they produced philosophy only by abandoning the Bavli, and also why those who did not abandon the Bavli produced no philosophy, nor, therefore, science. The Bavli's *and*, and not the *equal*, formed the insuperable obstacle to science. Let me state matters simply: why in the mind of the Judaism of the Dual Torah was there no science in particular, even when there could be philosophy?

Because in a system of fixed texts, you need a fixed text to make connection, and nature provides no fixed texts.

Let me state the next step in my proposition with heavy emphasis:

In forming the large world in which everything would be contained in some one thing, the Bavli's authorship relied for connection upon the received text and necessarily drew conclusions resting upon connection solely within the dictates of an a priori and imputed system of making connections. These constitute connections supplied and not discovered, structures ultimately imputed through extrinsic process of thought, and not nurtured through the proposal and testing of propositions intrinsic to the matter at hand.

In the rather odd language I introduced earlier, in the mind of Judaism you have an *and* and you have an *equal* or a *therefore*, but you do not have both an *and* and an *equal* or a *therefore*. The *and* comes from an extrinsic source, a source not deriving from connections we see among facts we think congruent or even interesting, and any *equal* or *therefore* that we then propose will not attend to the propositions implicit in the facts (whether those of nature, leading to natural philosophy or natural science, or those of history, leading to social philosophy or social science). At issue then is not the topics defined as important by the received writing, either Scripture or the Mishnah. Science found no interest not because it dealt with subject matter found trivial, since, after all, Scripture begins with the creation of the world, and in the Mishnah, issues of natural science, physics as then practiced, as well as psychology, for example, do occupy a place of importance. Philosophy, including natural philosophy, began in the making of connections, in asking, why this *and* also that? The answers, the conclusions drawn, proved adventitious and merely interesting; the making of connections between and among facts is what precipitated the processes of intellect that, by the way, yielded answers. But for the authorship of the Bavli, large structures, encompassing connections among many things – these to begin with derived from without, from the received documents, which joined this to that and so precipitated inquiry into connections

Why No Science in Judaism?

between this and that supplied, ultimately and exhaustively, for thought at the largest scale of intellect, by the Torah.

The mode of thought that yielded connections of this kind – connections I have characterized as those imposed through fixed association – thus made no room for a mode of thought that required the mind itself to discover its own points of intersection or confluence and then – but only then – to ask why. Connection supplied left no space, so it appears, for connection discovered. True, in the Bavli we find both the making of connections and the drawing of conclusions. But in the logic of fixed association that holds the whole together, the connections are provided by fixed associations, and – so it follows – the *equal* or the *therefore* does not emerge from the same sort of logical thinking that formed the foundation of the fixed association. The *equal* or the *therefore* derives from rigorous thinking, the making of distinctions, the search for regularity and order and rule. But to fixed association, proposition, regularity order and rule – these are simply not pertinent. Fixed association puts things together in one way, propositional connection in a different way, and the Bavli's authorship mixed two essentially distinct logics, the one at the intermediate, the other at the fundamental, level of the construction of thought. Thinking philosophically about connections formed nonpropositionally, therefore framed in an other-than-philosophical way, in the end produced thought that took for granted the very thing that philosophy, and especially natural philosophy, found at the center of interest, the subject of the most intense curiosity: the connection, why this *and* that?

Now this characterization of the paramount mode of effecting connection and explaining it contradicts a simple fact. The Judaism of the Dual Torah from the advent of Islam did encompass an ongoing and vital philosophical movement.[7] But the Judaism of the Dual Torah did not produce philosophy, since its philosophers invariable mastered another mode of thought and argument, in addition to the Judaic one and produced their philosophy of Judaism out of that other tradition altogether. Only where intellectuals mastered a second, and separate intellectual tradition did the modes of thought of philosophy, including science, make an important impact. That fact once again

---

[7] A comprehensive and accessible account is provided by Salo Wittmayer Baron, *A Social and Religious History of the Jews* (Philadelphia, 1958: The Jewish Publication Society of America). Second edition, revised and enlarged. *High Middle Ages. 500-1200: Volumes III-VIII.* VIII. Philosophy and Science, pp. 55-138. For science, including medicine, pp. 138-268. All allegations as to fact in what follows derive from Baron.

underlines my simple assertion that distinctive modes of thought derived from distinct sources of learning, and that the mind of the Judaism of the Dual Torah as defined by the Bavli proved ultimately not propositional and assuredly not philosophical. Institutions devoted to the study of the Bavli and related writings proliferated; the community of Judaism turned to the Bavli for guidance in the conduct of public business and private life. The schools and public bodies devoted to the Bavli vastly outweighed in influence the philosophical movement. That movement was made up of individuals, who read one another's books and wrote for one another; few philosophers defined public discourse or greatly shaped the shared intellectual life of the community of Israel. Among the philosophers within Judaism issues of philosophy and science did enjoy ample attention; but the Judaism of the Dual Torah even in their time went its own way, essentially unchanged by the philosophical movement and its propositional logic of discourse. So the exception proves the rule: the Judaism of the Dual Torah defined discourse as the Bavli taught it to, and that discourse in the aggregate of the world of Judaism made slight provision for philosophy, including natural philosophy.[8] The correlation between the presence of the philosophical mode of thought and exposure to philosophy, in addition to talmudic study, strongly sustains the proposition at hand.]

A second important objection to my account of why the mind of Judaism did not encompass science in particular is that, of course, it did. That is to say, within the rich philosophical tradition of Judaism in medieval times flourished a scientific and medical one, so Baron:

---

[8]That is not to underestimate the role of rationalism in the period, e.g., in the twelfth century, as is stressed by Isadore Twersky, *Introduction to the Code of Maimonides (Mishneh Torah)* (New Haven and London, 1980: Yale University Press), p. 86. But as Twersky concedes, the role of rational thought gauged just by its "formal literary history from the works of R. Saadiah Gaon and R. Solomon ibn Gabirol through those of R. Abraham bar Hiyya and R. Joseph ibn Saddik to R. Judah hal-Levi and R. Abraham ibn Ezra" is not considerable. Twersky takes the view that the impact and influence of rationalism "transcended these classics and must be sought in other literary genres as well as in oral discussion and oral commitment. Rationalism was a modalist of thought, with its own deep structures and models of perception." All this is entirely beyond doubt. But the main point is simply that modes of thought paramount in the Bavli did not produce a predominant and broadly influential philosophical movement at all, and the rather slight dimensions of the philosophical movement, which can be written up, beginning, middle, and end, in a few pages in an encyclopaedia article, underlines the simple fact that it was other than philosophical and propositional thought that, in the aggregate, derived from the Bavli.

> With the same passionate faith in the power of reason that characterized their quest for metaphysical and theological certainty, the Jewish thinkers under Islam began coping with the expanding horizons of scientific knowledge.[9]

Baron points to the impetus for scientific thinking and even research. It did not derive from the Bavli or any other document of the inherited Torah. It derived from knowledge of Greek science and Roman science: Euclid, Ptolemy, Galen, for example. Not only so, but conflict between doctrines as to facts of the natural world deriving from science and observation and those implicit in the Torah, encompassing the Oral Torah, testifies to the simple claim I have made. The impetus for scientific work, the modes of pursuing it both in intellect and in observation and even experiment – these came from sources of thought other than the talmudic, and they also appealed for self-evidence in observation and explanation – making connections, drawing conclusions – to a mind other than the Bavli's. It is one thing to allege that medieval scientists who were Jews characteristically cited biblical or rabbinic prooftexts for scientific propositions or proposed to harmonize their results with the Torah, oral or written. It is another to maintain that the modes of thought guiding scientific work accord with the modes of thought imbued by talmudic learning. Here too, the impetus and the method came from elsewhere. That mathematics was held to waste time better spent in Torah study is only one obvious piece of evidence pointing toward the simple conclusion I have drawn.[10] The simple fact is that the Bavli and associated writings defined both what was worth knowing and what knowing required; the claim was exclusive and those who thought otherwise, in both philosophy in general and natural philosophy in particular, found need to justify and validate doing the work they did, not to mention holding the conclusions that they reached.

Given the extraordinary power of the Bavli, exercised from its closure to our own day, to shape the mind of Judaism, we must find entirely natural the continuing formative power of that document's principal modes of thought even today. Those educated only in the Bavli and related sacred sciences take for granted that that writing is the only thing worth knowing, and that knowing meant knowing the Bavli and its exegetical literature in one way and not in some other. Historical study is no more welcome than scientific inquiry, and for the same good reason. The reason is not that people will reach wrong

---

[9]Baron, op. cit., p. 138.
[10]Baron, op. cit., p. 149.

results, but that people will both study the wrong things and also carry out study in the wrong way. I find it difficult to point to a more cogent, more self-confident, or more successful intellectual tradition in the world history of mind than the talmudic one. And yet, even with its tough and enduring experience, the mind of Judaism, as formed in ancient times, finds a challenge. Where that mind flourishes, the challenge derives not from different minds, that is, competing opinions or modes of thinking, but from the loss of access to, and accurate understanding of, Judaism's own mind as the Bavli has defined it. People deemed to embody, in our own century, the brightest and most intelligent, as well as the best and most learned, exhibit traits of mind that in form run true to the Judaic, but in fact do not replicate its discipline at all.

Two traits of the mind of Judaism proved definitive, we recall, first, rigorous propositional argument at the middle range, second, appeal to an *a priori* principle of connection, via fixed associations defined in a manner extrinsic to the proposition, at the broad horizon. The understanding of the logic of fixed association proves the key, since, when misunderstood, fixed yields free association. If propositions do not dictate connection between two facts or among three or more facts, so that the presentation of a statement encompasses facts, argument, and conclusion, then what does? In the received mind, it is the text that joins facts together within its own structure. For those who do not grasp the logic of the mind of Judaism, there is no fixed association that dictates what belongs and what does not, and that yields only association without proposition and also without a principle of inclusion and exclusion. That association beyond all rationality that tells two or more minds equally what belongs and can be exchanged is what we call free association: there was this, and then, by the way, I just thought of that – but the other thing too comes to mind, and so forever and ever.

Let me then show in a concrete way what has happened as the logic of fixed association has yielded for latter-day modes of thought characteristic of the world formed by the Bavli and its secondary literature a logic not to be anticipated. It was one that misunderstood the remarkably *disciplined* character of the paramount logic of fixed association. If we review the literary form indigenous to the logic of fixed association, we note that the commentary or exegesis serves better than any other literary medium for expressing the discourse generated by that logic. The reason, self-evidently, is that once we have a fixed association defined by a text, then we do well to exploit what we have in hand, joining sentences one after the other not through shared propositions, nor even through a common teleological enterprise, but

Why No Science in Judaism? 109

merely through appeal in common to an imputed cogency. What would happen, however, when the entire conception of argument and proposition fell away, and when even the notion was lost that discourse of fixed association would register points, concerning the base text, that were susceptible to generalization and systematic propositional statement? What would be left, then, would be simply the collecting and arranging of information pertinent to a given sequence of statements, for example, a list of words or clauses or even whole sentences.

What would happen, concretely, was that fixed association, with its remarkably subtle mode of effecting connection, was misunderstood as a license for *free* association, in which nothing joined anything to anything else. Merely collecting and arranging vast quantities of information, without a semblance of a point or a proposition, is not the same thing as collecting what pertains immediately and directly to a sequence of words, or phrases or topics that stand in a fixed and precise relationship with one another. The logic of fixed association dictated not only what fit, but also what did not. Reduced to a scheme of collecting and arranging masses of information composing a whole of a merely thematic order, the logic of free association ended up no logic at all, because no one could say what did not belong to discourse. Everything fit as well as everything else, because, in a logic of free association, nothing was to be excluded on principle, on logic.

The long-term result was to yield public discourse, in the Judaic sciences, lacking all cogency, a mode of setting forth sentences in which beginnings and endings of paragraphs, that is to say, of whole discourses or expositions of ideas, played no role and served no purpose. For in free association, not only does any thing enter or leave merely as a matter of whim, but the very notion of connection is lost. And that forms the end of logic, of cogent discourse of a public character that, in one way or another, produces if not propositions then a kind of discourse deemed cogent and sensible, with rules of intelligible exchange of thought, public laws governing what one may say and what is forbidden, in all, a syntax and structure of mind. In our own day the world made by the Bavli tended to lose sight of the discipline and order implicit in the logic of fixed association and to understand as the principle of intelligible discourse generated by the Bavli the legitimacy of utter free association.

To provide an example of the movement from refined and subtle practice of fixed association in the classical writings of ancient and medieval times to the rather crude imitation by modern and contemporary writers we need not go far afield, or even attempt to translate the gibberish that passes for thought in Hebrew into a corresponding gibberish in English. We have ample evidence in writings of distinguished and well-regarded writers deemed within the circles of the faithful brilliantly to represent the best and the bright in the mind of Judaism. Let me give a single example of the result of the misapprehension of what is at stake in the logic of fixed association by (self-styled) heirs of the Bavli's intellectual heritage. A single sequence of paragraphs suffices to show us how the mind of a kind of Judaism does its work. For that purpose I turn to Saul Lieberman,[11] because, in centers of Judaic intellectual life in the classical sciences, he is deemed a paragon of learning. He may therefore serve as an authentic avatar of the contemporary state of mind of the Judaism of the Dual Torah. What we find in Lieberman is simply the incapacity either to generalize or to compose a competent paragraph, that is to say, present a propositional statement of a cogent character in which connections between two facts are made to yield a conclusion. Fixed association has in Lieberman's mind, as shown in his writing, given way to free association. He presents us with an exemplary figure excelling in the hunting and gathering, the collecting and arranging of information, which is always best presented – predictably – in the form of a commentary. But even within the units of thought of the commentary, for example, on the Tosefta, Lieberman found it exceedingly difficult to state two or more cogent thoughts in not only succession but also cogent relation. But Lieberman in English presents us with an accurate portrait of the workings of the mind, and to that we turn.

In mid-career attempting to write a historical article,[12] Lieberman found himself unable to conduct historical study and never again attempted to write a book or even an article on a historical problem. Nor, indeed do we find in Lieberman's corpus of writing much further effort to compose propositional discourses of a sustained character; his other work in English is essentially lexicographical and by nature episodic; the vast assembly of information in his Tosefta commentary is conceptually utterly chaotic and bears no propositional character extending beyond two or three successive sentences. Over vast stretches of dreary fact mongering, it is mere erudition, collecting and arranging lacking all logic. When we examine the sequence of topic sentences of

---

[11]Rabbi Joseph B. Soloveitchik's writings in English would have served just as well, but they do not enjoy the scholarly position of preeminence that is commonly accorded to those of Saul Lieberman, and it would not be fair to subject to a close reading writings that, in any event, the author himself characterizes as unsystematic.

[12]Saul Lieberman, "Palestine in the Third and Fourth Centuries," *Jewish Quarterly Review* 1946, 36:329-370, 37:31-54.

the sample at hand and secondary developments of paragraphs on an announced subject, we see how limited was the intellectual equipment provided to an exemplary figure of learning by training principally in the received canonical writings, secondarily in philology pertinent to them. Lieberman wishes to present an argument on "taxation and imaginary religious persecutions."[13] A survey of his topic sentences of sequential paragraphs yields the following:

> We read in Aboth de R. Nathan, "Therefore shalt you serve..."
>
> Similarly, we read in the Palestinian Talmud...
>
> Here again the precariousness of riches at the beginning of the third century is well demonstrated.

We have already lost the topic "taxation," and persecution is not at stake. The point of joining of the three topic sentences of course is an implicit text, or sequence of texts deemed to relate to one another, thus a fixed association, if one lacking an explicit text. So the procedure is not topical, even though the form is. But we proceed to recover the announced topic. Lieberman says, "The burden of *leitourgiai* of the third century is also well mirrored in rabbinic literature." Here the matter of taxation does emerge. We proceed to Lieberman's next topic sentence:

> R. Johanan himself summarized the situation....
>
> Besides the liturgies, rabbinic literature of the time mentions a great number of taxes...
>
> Similarly, Graetz gives a Midrash which demonstrates the crooked ways of the Roman legal procedure in trying the Jews.
>
> Again, we read in the Palestinian Talmud: "Diocletian oppressed the inhabitants of Paneas."
>
> The petition of the people of Paneas was probably worded according to the usual formula.
>
> Similarly, we read in the Midrash:
>
> Again, we read in the Palestinian Talmud:
>
> I think it very probable that the purpose of Proclus' entering Sepphoris is revealed in another passage of TP [The Yerushalmi].
>
> Moreover, the rabbis were not unaware of the fact that the Romans tried to put a face of legality on their robberies.
>
> An interesting discrimination between the arbitrary and the 'legal' actions of the officials is noted in the following passage:
>
> It is obvious from the names of the rabbis who visited the Hot Springs of Gadara that the question was raised in the first half of the third century.

---

[13]Ibid., pp. 344-370.

> Herein lies the main point of the discussion of the rabbis in the above passage of the Palestinian Talmud.
>
> The Jews were in exactly the same situation as the other provincials.

The topic headings of Lieberman's paragraphs leave the strong impression that we deal with a kind of stream of consciousness, not with a program and a well-crafted argument. The topic sentences do not produce the outline of a program, for example, a propositional argument, a systematic inquiry – even a discussion of a sustained and orderly character. The topic sentences attest to a stream of consciousness that in other circumstances we call free association. It is just this, that, and the other thing, starting somewhere, ending somewhere else. What has happened is that the dialectical argument as a mode of sustained discourse yields only the dialectic – the movement. The argument is lost, or left behind, or simply forgotten in the onrush of information and episodic, ad hoc observation concerning this and that.

That is not to suggest that Lieberman invariably proved incapable of composing a sustained argument, setting forth a well-composed statement with a beginning, middle, and end. Nor is it to claim that all he had to offer was an enormous mass of disorganized information, given some semblance of order by essentially meretricious appeal to a topic ("persecution," "taxation") or a text (the Tosefta). It is only to show that Lieberman, this century's single most distinguished product of the intellectual tradition of the Dual Torah in its centers of acknowledged greatness, exhibited an infirm grasp on the requirements of propositional discourse and relied rather heavily upon imputed connections which, a glance at his rather odd sequence of topic sentences suggests, look suspiciously like the outcome of little more than, "first there was this, and then, by the way, I just thought of it, also there was that." So much for the composition of a large-scale discussion, the counterpart to the resort to fixed association by the mind of Judaism. Let us then turn to the other principal mode of thought, the propositional, within the limits of a completed unit of thought, a paragraph. Here too we see the same evidence of a limited grasp, on Lieberman's part, of the mixed modes of thought of the received intellectual discipline in which Lieberman was educated and which he was widely held to embody better than anyone else in his time.

The reader may find patience to work through a sequence of two complete paragraphs, in which the full flavor of Lieberman's writing shows us how free association leads hither and yon but never to a cogently stated proposition, at best only to an implicit and somewhat confused one:[14]

> [1] We conclude our short survey with the position of the Patriarch and the Jewish scholars in the Roman system of taxation. [2] The role of the former in the distribution of the tax-burden and his responsibility towards the government are not clear. [3] However, it is certain that the Patriarch had to pay vast sums to the government and offer gifts to the officials. [4] The Midrash relates that the Patriarch asked R. Simeon b. Laqish to pray for him, because "the government is very wicked," and this is demonstrated by the following episode: "A woman brought the Patriarch a small salver (*diskarion*) with a knife on it. He took the knife and returned the salver to her. Then a courier (*beredarios, veredarius*) of the government came and he saw it, coveted it, and took it."

I have numbered the sentences so that the simple point may be visibly clear. Nos. 1-3 form a cogent statement. The break at No. 4 is stunning. In fact we have no paragraph at all, only a set of generalizations followed by a case which in no way proves commensurate with, or even congruent to, the generalizations, and, in my judgment, has not been demonstrated to be even relevant to the issue. Let us conduct the same analysis of the following paragraph in context, for we shall see precisely the same problem exhibited by Lieberman's writing in sustaining a thought and mounting an argument at the intermediate level of discourse, that of a propositional character, that we noted in mounting a cogent statement at the large level of discourse, that in accord with the logic of fixed association:

> [1] As for the scholars, there is enough evidence to show that they were at certain periods...exempt from some taxes and especially from *leitourgias*. [2] But it is unlikely that all scholars enjoyed the tax immunities. [3] It is much more probable that only the ordained scholars benefited from this privilege, scholars who could be placed in the category of priests, *sacerdotes*. [4] From the Palestinian Talmud we learn that Simeon b. Abba was not ordained because he happened to be in Damascus when an opportunity to ordain him presented itself. [5] We also find that R. Jonah refused to be ordained prior to his teacher, R. Zeminah.

I have simply to point out that between sentence [3] and sentence [4] is an abyss, another between [4] and [5]. So the paragraph consists of three absolutely unrelated thoughts – and no proposition joins the thoughts. The pattern in both paragraphs is manifestly the same. Lieberman starts with something very like a generalization, then resorts immediately to a "case." But the case stands on its own. There is no

---

[14]Ibid., pp. 359-362, passim.

clear connection between the case and the generalization. In the first paragraph, the "wickedness of the government" is not very clearly linked to the generalization, and Lieberman's reason for introducing the case is scarcely made explicit, nor are the conclusions we are to draw. But his persistent introduction of the Greek and Latin for the Hebrew counterparts suggests that a secondary motive was simply to show off knowledge of the Greek and Latin counterparts for the Hebrew, since that information plays no role whatsoever in making the point, if any, that he wished to make. In Lieberman's defense, I have to point out that the next paragraph refers back to "these incidents" and alludes to this and that, so that, if we stay the course, we can get some sense out of the whole.

But it seems to me amply demonstrated that Lieberman found exceedingly difficult the composition of a cogent paragraph, with a beginning, middle, and end, and that he was remarkably adept at collecting and posting interesting pieces of information. These pieces of information manifestly lacked all cogency between and among themselves, but were joined to some larger whole only by reason of an assumed composition, an implicit set of unstated associations of another-than propositional character. With no evidence of an available program of fixed associations (except as Lieberman's own mind defined for him the points of contact or intersection between one thing and the next), we have to conclude that the Judaic mind of the Bavli in our own day is imitated but not understood. For Saul Lieberman, exemplary of the world which received this kind of writing (whether in English or in Hebrew) and valued it, and Lieberman's audience too, obviously took for granted that free association, when executed by a scholar of sufficient public notoriety or political influence in the limited world at hand, constituted logical discourse. And that is not at all how the mind of Judaism was meant to think.

For the mind of Judaism appealed to four logics in its quest for what linked one thing to another. Three of these logics – the propositional, the metapropositional, and the teleological – are entirely commonplace for the West, and the fourth – the fixed associative – can be understood as well. All four carried forward that same program of thinking that we in the West have always understood to be the address and task of philosophy and today quite reasonably identify with science. It is the effort to put two and two together and therefore to explain four, or, stated more abstractly, to find, in the language of Robin Horton, "unity underlying apparent diversity...simplicity underlying apparent complexity,...order underlying apparent disorder...regularity underlying apparent anomaly."[15] I identity two discrete facts with diversity, complexity, disorder, anomaly, and the making of connection between them as the quest for unity, simplicity, order, and regularity. The proposition yielded by the making of connection, the drawing of conclusions or the offering of hypotheses – tradition or of science, that contemporary classifications of thought identify. We recognize that the distinctive union of two modes of thought, the propositional and the fixed associative, trained the mind of Judaism to find unity, simplicity, order, regularity – in all, self-evident explanation – in a distinctive way. That way served to draw together tradition and system, to allow systematic thought to generate propositions, and also to present those propositions in such a way as to affirm and validate the received Torah of Sinai, written and oral. Systematic thought arranged as if it came from revelation constituted the mode of discourse that Judaism defined, and that served exceedingly well for a very long time.

If I had to offer a single reason for the subordination of philosophy and proposition at the dimension of intermediate discourse to the principle of large-scale organization defined by received associations at the far horizons of orderly thought, I should point to the outcome. It is a sense for the received, revealed character of truth that is in fact discovered and validated in a this-worldly framework of argument. The effect of organizing large-scale discourse in one way, intermediate in the other, is to present the result of thought in such a way as to underline continuity, back to Sinai, – while at the same time securing for mind itself that speculative freedom to explore and test propositions that thought requires. When I argued that the Bavli was systematic and therefore not traditional, I set aside the form of the document in favor of an account of its structure and inner cogency of mind.

---

[15]Robin Horton, "African Traditional Thought and Western Science," *Africa* 1967, 37:50-71, 155-187. William Scott Green kindly drew my attention to the stimulating thought of Horton. I read with much appreciation also the important critique of Hans H. Penner, "Rationality and Religion: Problems in the Comparison of Modes of Thought," *Journal of the American Academy of Religion* 1986, 54:645-672. See also *Modes of Thought. Essays on Thinking in Western and Non-Western Societies*, ed. by Robin Horton and Ruth Finnegan (London, 1973: Faber & Faber), where a number of important essays on Horton's article, as well as Horton's response, are collected. The issue on which Horton's essay focuses, the points in common and the contrasts between African traditional thought and Western science, is not pertinent here. I make no judgment on the matter, since my treatment of science ends in the period in which science still formed part of philosophy, and that is long before the advent of experimental science and the development of science as an autonomous realm of intellect.

But the form does create a powerful effect and define thought, and the form – connections imputed, conclusions declared in the context of received writings – imparted its imprint upon intellect as well. The balance, order, proportion, sense of composition of the whole – these definitive traits of the mind of Judaism worked exceedingly well, so long as they worked, in holding together the *two* requirements of mind: freedom to speculate, responsibility to compose and construct for age succeeding age – therefore (in the mythic framework) from eternity to the end of time.

But philosophy and therefore also natural philosophy demanded what the mind of the Judaism of the Dual Torah could not – and can never – concede. And that was the datum that the quest for unity in diversity, simplicity in complexity, order in disorder, and regularity in anomaly, engaged only humanity's mind, but not God's too. All Judaisms, including especially the normative one of the Dual Torah, knew to search for unity, simplicity, order, regularity, and therefore explanation, because to begin with God created the world as unified, simple, orderly, regular, and therefore subject and susceptible to explanation. The premise that one might go in quest for systematic knowledge derived for the Judaism of the Dual Torah from the Torah, which recorded, for humanity to know, God's work in making the world and in forming Israel for the sanctification of the here and now and the salvation of the world at the end of time. Philosophy began with not knowledge but search for knowledge, and the mind of Judaism began with a quest made possible, to begin with, by the character of the human mind, made, as it was, "in our image, after our likeness."

Judaism therefore could not, on its own, generate philosophy, not because issues of a propositional character intervened, or even because modes of thought vastly differed, but for one simple reason.

It was, and is, that philosophy ended where Judaism began.

The Judaism of the Dual Torah could not deny the knowledge that to begin with the mind of Judaism encompassed. The upshot is simple. What philosophy sought – unity, simplicity, order, regularity – is that very destination at which the quest of the mind of the Judaism of the Dual Torah commenced. What the one wanted the other knew it had. And in consequence what the mind of the Judaism was meant to make possible was therefore a different search altogether from the philosophical and the scientific, which was, and is, that search for God whose being formed the unity, the simplicity, the order, the regularity, to which, in the mythic language of faith, sanctification in the world and salvation at the end of time referred. For sanctification spoke of all things bearing each its rightful name, the correct ordering of all reality in the natural world, and salvation addressed the right and true ordering, thus ending of all reality in the world of society, therefore of history. The one can have yielded scientific proposition, the other teleological proposition, and, in the context of the Torah, each did. But the mind of Judaism accomplished its tasks in its way, using its language, in response to the logics self-evident in its circumstance and perception of the world. For the task of a quest for the explanation of how things intersected and made sense drew the mind of Judaism into the Torah, record of God's plan and program for the world. And that has made all the difference. And, if I may conclude as a believing Jew, it still can make all the difference, *it still can.*

7

Why Does Judaism Have an Economics?

The Inaugural Saul Reinfeld Lecture in Judaic Studies at Connecticut College, New London, Connecticut, on Wednesday, April 13, 1988

Let me begin with a simple piece of evidence that the ancient sages of Judaism recognized cycles of abundance and scarcity, if they did not call them business cycles. Sages most certainly understood the principles of market economics as they affected the market mechanism and manipulated those principles to achieve their own goals, as the following story indicates:

> A pair of birds in Jerusalem went up in price to a gold denar.
>
> Said Rabban Simeon b. Gamaliel, "By this sanctuary! I shall not rest tonight until they shall be sold at silver denars."
>
> He entered the court and taught, "The woman who is subject to five confirmed miscarriages or five confirmed fluxes brings only a single offering, and she eats animal sacrifices, and the rest of the offerings do not remain as an obligation for her."
>
> And pairs of birds stood on that very day at a quarter-denar each, [one hundredth of the former price, the demand having been drastically reduced].
>
> (M. Keritot 1:7K-Q)

The story shows that sages recognized the affect upon prices of diminished demand and were prepared to intervene in the market. Now to the more general question at hand: what is an economics, and does Judaism have one, and, if so, why?

An economics is a theory about the rational disposition of scarce resources. The key word is "rational," of course, since what is reasonable in one setting or culture is incomprehensible in another, and in due course I shall explain the rational of the economics of Judaism. But so far as a social entity knows how and why scarce resources are assigned to, or end up in the hands of, one person, rather than some other, or one institution or class or other social organization, rather than some other, that social entity has an economics. A religion, such as Judaism (defined presently), need not have an economics, and most religions do not have an economic theory at all. Christianity prior to the Middle Ages, for example, had no economics, even though it had by then developed a rich and complex politics. And sayings relevant to an economics, answering questions concerning the definition of wealth, property, production and the unit of production, ownership, the determination of price and value and the like, – sayings relevant to economics in general may take shape within a religion, without that religion's setting forth an economics at all. For opinions on this and that, sayings about mercy to the poor, recommendations of right action, fairness, honesty, and the like – all these components of economics do not by themselves add up to an economics.

Only a sustained and systematic, internally coherent theory that over all and in an encompassing way explains why this, not that, defines market in relationship to ownership, production in relationship to price, above all, constitutes an economics. In the case of a religion, moreover, the presence of a theory on wealth and ownership, production and consumption, requires explanation. What we want to know, in particular, is what a particular religion wishes to express through its statements within the realm of economics, and why it is through economics in particular that the religion finds it necessary to make those statements. When, therefore, I ask, why does Judaism have an economics? I mean to answer that particular question: why does Judaism make its statement, in part, by discussing in a systematic and cogent way and within an encompassing theory the matter of the rational disposition of scarce resources?

Economics from Aristotle to Quesnay and Riqueti, in the eighteenth century, dealt with not the science of wealth but rather "the management of the social household, first the city, then the state."[1] Economics disembedded from politics developed only in the eighteenth century. Prior to that time, it formed a principal part of the study of

---

[1] Elizabeth Fox-Genovese, *The Origins of Physiocracy. Economic Revolution and Social Order in Eighteenth-Century France* (Ithaca and London: Cornell University Press), p. 9. See also Karl Polanyi, *The Lifelihood of Man*. Edited by Harry W. Pearson (New York, San Francisco, and London, 1977: Academic Press), p. 7.

political economy. That is to say, economics formed a component of the larger sociopolitical order and dealt with the organization and management of the household (*oikos*). The city (*polis*) was conceived as comprising a set of households. Political economy, therefore, presented the theory of the construction of society, the village, town, or city, out of households, a neat and orderly, intensely classical and, of course, utterly fictive conception. One part of that larger political economy confronted issues of the household and its definition as the principal unit of economic production, the market and its function within the larger political structure, and the nature and definition of wealth. And the reason that one important Judaism had an economics was that that Judaism proposed to tell the Jews how to build an ideal society, a holy society, and in order to make its statement, that Judaism appealed to the correct, hence, the rational distribution of scarce resources: to distributive, rather than to market, economics, as we shall see. It was only through appeal to ancient principles of distributive economics, resting on the Temple, priesthood, and cult, that the Judaism at hand found it possible to say what it wished to say in politic economy.

I. The Economics of Judaism
Which Judaism? Which Economics?

The Judaism the economics of which is under study is the one that rested on the myth of Moses' receiving the Torah at Sinai in two media, written and oral. The written one corresponded to the Hebrew Bible or Old Testament. The oral one was ultimately written down by the sages of Judaism in late antiquity, beginning with the composition of the Mishnah, the Mishnah, a utopian system expressed in the form of a law code, closed at ca. A.D. 200. The initial statement of that Judaism is represented by the Mishnah. The Judaism of the Dual Torah, bearing the adjectives normative, talmudic, rabbinic, classical, and the like, unfolded through the exegesis of the two Torahs, written and oral, Scripture and Mishnah, through the first seven centuries of the Common Era (=A.D.) and yielded as its authoritative document the Talmud of Babylonia or Bavli. But only the initial and fundamental document of that Judaism forms the object of study here. My purpose here is to describe the economics of (a) Judaism in the context of in systemic context, to offer an account of economics in the foundation document of the canon of the Judaism of the Dual Torah.

When we place the economics, or, more really, the political economics of the Mishnah into the context of Greco-Roman economic thought, we gain a clearer picture of the power of economics to serve in the expression and detailed exposition of a utopian design for society.

For, as Robert Lekachman states, "We see the economics of Plato and Aristotle somewhat differently when we realize that what they were discussing above all was the good life, the just state, and the happy man."[2] They sought a unified science of society. And that serves as a suitable definition, also, for the program of the framers of the Mishnah. The authorship of the Mishnah covered every important problem that any treatise on economics, covering not only the rules of household management covered in an *oikonomikos*, but also the law of money-making, found it necessary to discuss, and on that basis, I claim to describe in some modest detail what I conceive to have been the economics of Judaism as the Mishnah's authorship defined Judaism and as the ancient world understood the science of economics, or, in its context, political economy. But let me start from the beginning, and that means, turn to the familiar definition of our subject.

The Mishnah, the initial statement of the Judaism of the Dual Torah, not only encompasses but integrates economics within its larger system. That particular Judaism, indeed, makes its statement, also, through the exquisite details of rules and regulations governing the householder, the market, and wealth. The Mishnah's remarkably successful capacity to make its systemic statement, also, through the concerns of economics, its capacity to accomplish the detailed exegesis of economics within its larger social vision and system – these lack a significant counterpart in the generality of philosophy and theology in ancient times. Only in Aristotle do we find a great system builder who encompassed, within his systemic statement, economic theory. Plato forms no important counterpart, and, as to Christianity, down to the end of late antiquity, in the seventh century, economics as a matter of theory enjoyed no position whatsoever. In theologies of Christianity, for one example, we find slight interest in, or use of, theories on the household, markets, and wealth, in the framing of the Christian statement, which bears no judgment that we may identify as a statement upon, or of, economics. Only when we turn to Aristotle do we find a counterpart to the truly remarkable accomplishment of the authorship of the Mishnah in engaging economics in the service of its larger systemic statement. Indeed, as the Mishnah's authorship's power of the extraordinarily detailed exegesis of economics as a systemic component becomes clear to us, we shall conclude that, among the social theorists of antiquity, the framers of the Mishnah take first

---

[2]Robert Lekachman, *History of Economic Ideas* (New York, 1959: Harper & Bros.), p. 4.

Why Does Judaism Have an Economics? 123

place in the sophistication and profundity of their thought within political economy.³

But the fact that both Aristotle and the authorship of the Mishnah appealed to economic theory in spelling out their ideas by itself does not require us to bring into juxtaposition, for purposes of comparison and contrast, the economic thought of the two writings, Aristotle's and the mishnaic sages'. What requires that work is the simple fact that the Mishnah came forth in the age of the Second Sophistic, and, in diverse ways, adheres to the attitudes and agenda of that movement.⁴ Not only so, but when we do read Aristotle's thought on economic theory, we find clear and detailed propositions in common between him and our authorship. But there is yet a third reason. Both Aristotle and the sages of the Mishnah thought deeply and sustainedly about economic issues. The power of economics as framed by Aristotle, the only economic theorist of antiquity worthy of the name was to develop the relationship between the economy to society as a whole.⁵ And the framers of the Mishnah did precisely that: they incorporated issues of economics, even at a profound theoretical level, into the system of society as a whole, as they proposed to construct society. That is why to paraphrase Polanyi's judgment of Aristotle, the authorship of the Mishnah will be seen as attacking the problem of man's livelihood within a system of sanctification of a holy people with a radicalism of which no later religious thinkers about utopias were capable. None has ever penetrated deeper into the material organization of man's life under the aspect of God's rule. In effect, they posed, in all its breadth, the question of the critical, indeed definitive place occupied by the economy in society under God's rule. That is what we shall see in the remarkable statement, within an even more subtle idiom, of the economics of Judaism as the framers of the Mishnah defined that economics.

Just as through economics, Aristotle made the larger point that animated his system as a whole, so through economics did the framers of the Mishnah. The theory of both, moreover, falls into the same classification of economic theory, namely, the theory of distributive economics, familiar in the Near and Middle East from Sumerian times down to, but not including, the age of Aristotle himself. Before proceeding, let me define market and distributive economics since these form the two economic theories at issue in antiquity, and, among them,

---

³That considerable claim of mine forms the *leitmotif* of this lecture.
⁴This is a topic that in future work I shall treat in its own terms, but we do have to take note of the fact even now.
⁵Polanyi, op. cit., "Aristotle Discovers the Economy," p. 79.

the far more ancient, the distributive, shaped the economic thought of the two important systems of antiquity that made their statement, also, through economics, those of Aristotle and the Mishnah. In market economics merchants transfer goods from place to place in response to the working of the market mechanism, which is expressed in price. In distributive economics, by contrast, traders move goods from point to point in response to political commands. In market economics, merchants make the market work by calculations of profit and loss. In distributive economics, there is no risk of loss on a transaction.[6] In market economics, money forms an arbitrary measure of value, a unit of account. In distributive economics, money gives way to barter and bears only intrinsic value, as do the goods for which it is exchanged. It is understood as "something that people accept not for its inherent value in use but because of what it will buy."[7] The idea of money requires the transaction to be complete in the exchange not of goods but of coins. The alternative is the barter transaction, in which, in theory at least, the exchange takes place when goods change hands. Clearly, therefore, in the Mishnah's conception of the market and of wealth, distributive, not market, economics shapes details of all transactions. In distributive economics money is an instrument of direct exchange between buyers and sellers, not the basic resource in the process of production and distribution that it is in market economics.

II. The Distributive Economics of the Judaism of the Dual Torah

That distributive mode of economics, rationalized within theology and also fully realized in the detail of law, will not have astonished the framers of social systems from ancient Sumerian times, three thousand years before the time of the Mishnah, onward. For from the beginning of recorded time, temples or governments imposed the economics of distribution, and market economics, where feasible at all, competed with the economics of politics, organization, and administration. From remote antiquity onward, a market economy coexisted with a distributive economy.[8] Distributive economic theory

---

[6]Davisson and Harper, *European Economic History*, p. 130.
[7]Ibid., p. 131.
[8]See Morris Silver, *Economic Structures of the Ancient Near East* (London and Sydney: Croom Helm, 1985), and J. Wansbrough's review of that book in *Bulletin of the London School of Oriental and African Studies* 1987: 50-361-2. In this and prior studies Silver has successfully refuted the thesis of Polanyi that "there were not and could not be circumstances conducive to a market economy" (Wansbrough, p. 362). But the distinction between distributive and market economics has no bearing whatsoever upon whether or not, in remote antiquity, there was no such thing as a market in an economic sense, as Polanyi

characteristic of ancient temples and governments, which served as the storage points for an economy conceived to be self-supporting and self-sustaining, involved something other than a simultaneous exchange of legally recognized rights in property and its use; one party gave up scarce goods, the other party did not do so, but received those goods for other than market considerations. Free disposition of property, in distributive economics, found limitations in rules of an other-than-market character, for example, taboos with no bearing upon the rational utilization of resources and individual decisions on the disposition of assets.

If, for example, the private person who possesses property may not sell that property to anyone of his choice, or may not sell it permanently, then the possessor of the property does not exercise fully free choice in response to market conditions.[9] The reason is that he cannot gain the optimum price for the land at a given moment, set by considerations of supply and demand for land or (more really) for the produce of land of a particular character. Another, a co-owner, in addition to the householder in possession of a piece of property, has a say. The decisions of that other owner are not governed solely (or at all) by market considerations. In the case of temple communities or god-kings, land ownership and control fall into the hands of an entity other than the private person, whether we call it the temple, priesthood, the government, the gild, or even the poor(!). Then, with private property and its use placed under limitations and constraints of an other-than-market origin, market trading is not possible: "While there could be a considerable development of governmental status distribution and some marginal barter, there could not develop a price-making market."[10] Private property in land, not merely in control of production, was required for the formation of a market economics in the conditions of antiquity, when ownership of production derived from ownership of land.

A further mark of the distributive economy is that transactions take the form of commodities of real value, that is, barter, and not of

---

maintained. My argument focuses only upon economic theory. But, as is clear, I take for granted that Silver and those he represents have established as fact the coexistence of market and distributive economics, such as I claim to discern, also, in the system of the Mishnah.

[9] Presently we shall note the integral relationship of a theory of ownership of property, specifically, a conception of property being private, and a theory of market economics. A mark of a distributive economics will be systemic intervention into not only the rationing (distribution) of resources but also of the means of production.

[10] Davisson and Harper, op. cit., p. 125.

symbolic value, that is, money. In ancient Mesopotamia, with its distributive economics, while silver was the medium of exchange, it was used in ingots and required weighing at each transfer.[11] That conception dominates in the Mishnah. Finally, in distributive economics, profit is a subordinate consideration, and, in the hands of so sophisticated a mind as Aristotle's and as the Mishnah's authorship's, profit is treated as unnatural. Competing with market economics in the Mishnah is a fully developed and amply instantiated, if never articulated, distributive economics. The Mishnah's authorship took over the economics of the Priestly Code, itself a restatement, in the idiom of the Israelite priesthood, of the distributive economics of temples and kings beginning with the Sumerians and Egyptians and coming down to the Greeks. Market economics was an innovation, its economics not fully understood, at the time of the Priestly Code, and, for reasons of their own, the framers of the Mishnah fully adopted and exhaustively spelled out that distributive economics, even while setting forth a plan for the economic life of "Israel" in a market economy.

That old and well-established theory of economics, in the received Scriptures, is accurately represented by the Priestly Code, spelled out in the rules of the biblical books of Leviticus and Numbers, upon which the Mishnah's authorship drew very heavily. The economic program of the Mishnah, as a matter of fact, derived its values and also its details from the Priestly Code and other priestly writings within the pentateuchal mosaic. Indeed, at point after point, that authorship clearly intended merely to spin out details of the rules set forth in Scripture in general, and, in economic issues such as the rational use of scarce resources, the Priestly Code in particular. The Priestly Code assigned portions of the crop to the priesthood and Levites as well as to the caste comprising the poor; it intervened in the market processes affecting real estate by insisting that land could not be permanently alienated but reverted to its "original" ownership every fifty years; it treated some produce as unmarketable even though it was entirely fit; it exacted for the Temple a share of the crop; it imposed regulations on the labor force that were not shaped by market considerations but by religious taboos, for example, days on which work might not be performed, or might be performed only in a diminished capacity.

In these and numerous other details, the Priestly Code stated in the Israelite-priestly idiom and in matters of detail the long-established principles of distributive economics and so conformed to thousands of

---

[11] A. Leo Oppenheim, *Ancient Mesopotamia. Portrait of a Dead Civilization* (Chicago & London, 1972: The University of Chicago Press), p. 87.

years of that distributive economics that treated private property as stipulative and merely conditional and the market as subordinate and subject to close political supervision. Market economics came into being in Greece in the very period – the sixth century B.C. – in which the Priestly Code was composed. Aristotle theorized about an economics entirely beyond anyone's ken and stated as principle the values of an economics (and a social system, too) long since transcended. Market economics, moreover, had been conveyed in practice to the Middle East a century and a half or so later by Alexander. By the time of the Mishnah, seven centuries after the Pentateuch was closed, market economics was well-established as the economics of the world economy in which, as a matter of fact, the land of Israel and Israel, that is, the Jews of Palestine, had been fully incorporated. Theories of fixed value, distribution of scarce resources by appeal to other than the rationality of the market – these represented anachronisms. But, as the Mishnah's sages' prohibition against profit, which they called "usury" and their odd conception of a true value inherent in a commodity shows us, the framers of the Mishnah developed a dual economics, partly market, partly distributive. That is the fact that permits us to treat as matters of economic theory a range of rules that, in market economics, can have no point of entry whatsoever.

Only when we have grasped the general terms within which those concrete rules are worked out shall we understand the mixed economics characteristic of the Judaism of the Mishnah. A distributive economics, we now realize full well, is one that substitutes for the market as the price-fixing mechanism for the distribution of goods the instrumentality of the state or some other central organization, in the case of Scripture's economics in the Priestly Code of ca. A.D. 500, the Temple. In such an economics, in the words of Davisson and Harper,

Such an organization will involve people's giving and receiving, producing and consuming, according to their status.[12] Substituting for the market as a rationing device, the distributive economy dealt with "the actual things that are distributed," while in markets, "purchases and sales are usually made for money, not directly for other commodities or services."[13]

The definition of market economics calls to our attention the contrary traits of distributive economics, in particular, the intervention of authority other than the market in controlling both production and distribution of scarce goods. In the case of the Mishnah, the Temple requires the recognition of the status of certain individual participants

---

[12]Davisson and Harper, op. cit., p. 115.
[13]Ibid., p. 123.

– in addition to the householder – in the transaction of distributing the material goods of the economy, in particular, portions of the crop. Priests, Levites, and the poor have a claim on the crop independent of their role in the production of the crop, for example, in labor, in landownership, in investment of seed and the like. Not only so, but the market is not the sole point of transfer of value. For material goods of the economy are directed to the Temple – so in the theory of the Mishnah – without any regard for the working of the market. When it comes to the claim of the Temple and priesthood upon the productive economy, there is no consideration of the exchange of material value for material value, let alone of the intervention of considerations of supply and demand, the worth of the goods as against the worth of the services supplied by the Temple, and the like.[14] Davisson and Harper state of the market, "Even politically powerful interests and corporations must agree to accept the market decisions whether or not the outcome of a particular market transaction favors a person of high status."[15] But in the Mishnah, that simply is not so. And, we shall further observe, the Temple taboos imposed upon the productive economy considerations of a nonmarket, nonproductive character, in consequence of which the maximization of productivity forms only one among several competing considerations, and not the most important one, in the planning of production.

This brings us to the fundamental and necessary trait of market economics, private property. Davisson and Harper further state,

> Private ownership of property...is an essential condition of the market, but its existence does not guarantee that a market will exist or that contractual exchanges will occur [that can reach a conclusion with a simultaneous exchange of legally recognized rights in property and its use]. To be sure, in the absence of private property in the ancient Near East and early medieval Europe, we find a distributive economic order. Is there, then, some relation of cause and effect between private property and the operation of a market? It seems that insofar as there is monolithic ownership and control of property (as in the Sumerian temple communities or with the god-king pharaoh of Egypt) there can be no development of a market. Where private property was so limited, there could be no market trading. While there could be a considerable development of governmental status distribution

---

[14]True, the ideology of the Priestly Code insisted that payment of the Temple taxes insured that God would "bless" the country with ample harvests, large herds, big families, and the like. But these factors in shaping of public opinion, therefore of considerations of demand, on their own do not – and cannot – fall into the classification of economic facts.

[15]Davisson and Harper, op. cit., p. 123.

and some marginal barter, there could not develop a price-making market.[16]

That statement again draws our attention to the datum of the Mishnah, which informs, by the way, its economics as well: that God owns the land and that the household holds the land in joint tenancy with God. Private ownership does not extend to the land at all.[17] That simple fact imposes upon the Mishnah's economic theory the principles of distributive economics, even while the framers of that theory address a world of market economics. It accounts for the mixed economics – market, distributive – of the Mishnah. Not only so, but as we just noted, the mortal owner-partner with God in the management of the household is not free to make decisions based solely on maximizing productivity; other considerations as to the use of land, as much as to the disposition of the crop, intervened.

Both Aristotle and the framers of the Mishnah addressed economic theory not only within the framework of distributive economics. They also acknowledged the facts of market economics, even while reaffirming (each party in its own terms and context) the higher (Aristotle: "natural," thus more natural, Mishnah authorship: "holy" and hence holier) value associated with distributive economics. For Aristotle, therefore, the criterion of correct economic action derived from a larger concern to uncover natural, as against unnatural, ways of conducting affairs, and for the sages of the Mishnah, the counterpart criterion appealed to the theology of the Priestly Code, with its conception of the magical character of the land the Jews held as their own, which they called (and still call) "the land of Israel." This land was subject to particular requirements, because God owned this land in particular and through the Temple and the priesthood constituted the joint-owner, along with the Israelite householder, of every acre.

III. Why Does Judaism Have an Economics?

The Mishnah is a document of political economy, in which the two critical classifications are the village, *polis*, and the household, *oikos*. Since, however, the Mishnah's framers conceived of the world as God's possession and handiwork, theirs was the design of a university in which God's and humanity's realms flowed together. Their statement

---

[16]Ibid., pp. 124-125

[17]But God does not lay claim to joint ownership of other goods and services of the economy, apart from the land and its produce, with the result that private ownership of the commercial and manufacturing economy assuredly prevailed, one of the reasons I refer to the Mishnah's economic theory as a mixed one.

bears comparison, therefore, to Plato's *Republic* and Aristotle's *Politics* as a utopian program (*Staatsroman*) of a society as a political entity, encompassing, also, its economics; but pertinent to the comparison also is Augustine's conception of a city of God and a city of man. In the Mishnah we find thinkers attempting, in acute detail, to think through how God and humanity form a single *polis* and a single *oikos*, a shared political economy, one village and one household on earth as it is in heaven.[18]

The Mishnah's sages placed economics, both market and distributive, in the center of their system, devoting two of their six divisions to it (the first and the fourth, for distributive and market economics, respectively), and succeeded in making their statement through economics in a sustained and detailed way far beyond the merely generalizing manner in which Aristotle did. And no one in antiquity came near Aristotle, as I said. It was with remarkable success that the sages of Judaism presented an economics wholly coordinated in a systemic way with a politics. The framers of the Mishnah joined together the premises of two distinct economic theories, market economics. And these two distinct theories, moreover, coexisted on the foundations of an economics of reciprocity, joining heaven to earth.[19]

---

[18] That is why I conceive the more profound inquiry to address the politics of Judaism, as the Mishnah presents that politics: the city of God which is the city of humanity, unlike the distinct cities conceived by Augustine. The matter is neatly expressed in numerous specific rules. See for example Roger Brooks, *Support for the Poor in the Mishnaic Law of Agriculture: Tractate Peah* (Chico, 1983: Scholars Press for Brown Judaic Studies), p. 49 to Mishnah-tractate Peah 1:4-5: "The Mishnah's framers regard the Land as the exclusive property of God. When Israelite farmers claim it as their own and grow food on it, they must pay for using God's earth. Householders thus must leave a portion of the yield unharvested as *peah* and give this food over to God's chosen representatives, the poor. The underlying theory is that householders are tenant farmers who pay taxes to their landlord, God." In this concrete way the interpenetration of the realms of God and humanity is expressed. That conception of the household and the village made up of households, the *oikos* and the *polis*, yields not only an economics, but also a politics. And the politics is the foundation for the economics, as we shall repeatedly observe.

[19] But it seems to me not productive to pursue as an issue of theoretical economics the notion of an exchange between heaven and earth, that is, between God and Israel. That conception leads us deep into territory beyond the substance of economics, into intangibles that we cannot grasp, measure, or weigh. Accordingly, I leave out of this account any notion of an economics of reciprocity and deal only with (re)distribution and market exchange. I also omit reference to "householding" as too vague; no one imagines that Israel's economy in its land was a subsistence economy, certainly not at any point, from the sixth century B.C. forward, covered by the pentateuchal law codes or their successors. So I see no point of interest in householding, because it is

The conception of God's enjoying standing and power within the domain of economic life formed not a theological but an economic fact, on the basis of which decisions on the allocation of scarce resources and on the nature of wealth and ownership were reached and carried out in law. That simple fact constitutes the single indicative trait of the Judaism of the Mishnah, its power to translate theological conviction into exquisitely detailed rules for everyday life. Let me spell out how, in economics, the sages of the Mishnah made their theological statement.

IV. The Distributive Economics of Judaism and the Theology of Judaism

The economic data with which the Mishnah's framers made their statement came to them from the Priestly Code. On the face of matters, therefore, the authorship of the document appealed to an economic theory that derived from an ancient age (we would say it was seven hundred years old, back to ca. 500 B.C., but they would say it was fourteen hundred years old, back to Sinai, which would bear a date of ca. 1200 B.C.). The truly anachronistic character of the Mishnah's distributive economics[20] becomes clear, however, when we realize that by the fourth century B.C., the Middle East received and used the legacy of Greece, brought by Alexander, in which a type of private property, prerequisite to the development of the market and available for the free use of the holder of that property independent of the priesthood or other government intervention, had developed.[21] For the theory of the Mishnah both the market and the distributive systems form one system and represent two components of one system. So we deal with a single theory, holding together two distinct economics. What we shall now see is how the distributive component of the Mishnah's economic theory reshapes the three principal categories that have occupied our attention, the household, the market, and wealth. But we

---

irrelevant, nor can I cope with "reciprocity," because it is a category covering economic relations between units that are not this-worldly (to put it mildly).

[20] For an account of archaizing tendency of the Second Sophistic in general, that is to say, the age of philosophy in which the Mishnah's authors did their work, see E. L. Bowie, "Greeks and Their Past in the Second Sophistic," in M. I. Finley, ed., *Studies in Ancient Society* (London and Boston, 1974: Routledge & Kegan Paul), pp. 166-209. Bowie shows that "the archaism of language and style known as Atticism is only part of a wider tendency, a tendency that prevails in literature not only in style but also in choice of theme and treatment, and that equally affects other areas of cultural activity." I shall address this matter more systematically in my coming study of the Mishnah in the context of the philosophy of the Second Sophistic.

[21] Davisson and Harper, p. 125.

ask, first of all, why the system of the Mishnah appealed to economics to begin with, and the answer to that question comes to us from theology, not economics. What the Mishnah's authorship wished to say, we shall now see, they could express only by utilizing the principal categories of economics under study here.

At the center of the Mishnah's economics is the disposition of resources with unremitting regard to the status of recipients in the transaction. In no way does the economics of Judaism in its initial statement conform to the definition of market economics just now cited. Our task therefore is how to understand in detail the foundation of the principles of distribution that define the theory of economics within the larger system of the Mishnah. In this way we grasp how profoundly the economics of the system has been shaped by the larger systemic statement and message.[22] The Mishnah's distributive economics derives from the theory that the Temple and its scheduled castes on earth exercise God's claim to the ownership of the holy land. It is, in fact, a theology that comes to expression in the details of material transactions. The theology derives from the conviction expressed in the Psalm, "The earth is the Lord's." That conviction is a statement of ownership in a literal sense. God owns the earth. But the particular earth that God owns is the land of Israel, and, within that land, the particular earth is land in the land of Israel that is owned by an Israelite. With that Israelite, a land-owner in the land of Israel, God is co-owner.

From that theological principle, spun out of the notion that when Israelites occupy the land that God has given to the Israelites, namely, the land of Israel, that land is transformed, and so too are the principles of ownership and distribution of the land, all else flows. The economics of the Judaism rests upon the theory of the ownership of a designated piece of real estate, ownership that is shared between God and partners of a certain genus of humanity whose occupancy of that designated piece of real estate, but no other, affects the character of the dirt in question. The theology consists in an account of what happens when ground of a certain locale is subject to the residency and ownership of persons of a certain genus of humanity. The generative

---

[22]Whether or not other economic theories express broader systemic values or are simply disembedded from systems and structures is not at issue in this account. It seems to me clear that all expositions of Aristotle's economics find it possible to show the coherence of his economics with his larger systemic, philosophical concerns. But why Aristotelian economics, read in light of Scripture, much like the economics of the Judaism of the Mishnah, formed out of the marriage of Aristotle and Scripture, should have served Latin Christianity so long (and so well) as it did, I do not know.

conception of the theology involves a theory of the affect – the enchantment and transformation – that results from the intersection of "being Israel:" land, people, individual person alike. But let us turn directly to the economics of it all.

Since God owns the land of Israel, God – represented by, or embodied through, the Temple and priesthood and other scheduled castes – joins each householder who also owns land in the land of Israel as an active partner, indeed, as senior partner, in possession of the landed domain. God not only demands a share of the crop, hence comprises a householder. God also dictates rules and conditions concerning production, therefore controls the householder's utilization of the means of production. Furthermore, it goes without saying, God additionally has provided as a lasting inheritance to Israel, the people, the enduring wealth of the country, which is to remain stable and stationary and not to change hands in such wise that one grows richer, the other poorer. Every detail of the distributive economics therefore restates that single point: *the earth is the Lord's*. That explains why the householder is partner of the Lord in ownership of the land, so that the Lord takes his share of the crop at the exact moment at which the householder asserts his ownership of his portion.[23]

But the ongoing partnership between God and Israel in the sanctification and possession of the land is not a narrowly secular arrangement. Both parties share in the process of the sanctification of the land, which accounts for, and justifies, Israel's very possession of the land. The Israelite landowner has a particular role in effecting the sanctification of the land, in that, land is holy and subject to the rules of God only when the Israelite landowner owns land in the land of Israel. Once more, land located elsewhere owned by Israelites, and land

---

[23]It is not only at the exact moment, but, as a matter of fact, in response to the householder's own decision and intention that God takes an interest in the crop. Before the householder exercises his ownership of the land through disposing of the crop, God does not exercise his ownership, except passively, by dictating the conduct of the means of production. What this means is that, within the anthropology of the mishnaic system, God responds to man's emotions, attitudes, and intentions, and so reveals what I believe we may call anthropopathism. The conception of God as emotionally consubstantial with man therefore is embedded, even, in the economics. In this connection, Abraham J. Heschel, *The Prophets* (Philadelphia: Jewish Publication Society of America) explores the anthropological theology of prophetic writings along the same lines. But I know no study of the emotional correspondences between God and man other than my *Incarnation of God. The Character of Divinity in Formative Judaism* (Philadelphia, 1988: Fortress Press), in which the matter plays no central role.

located in the land of Israel but not owned by Israelites, has no material relationship to the processes of sanctification, in utilization and in the disposition of the products of the land, that are at the heart of the distributive economics at hand. That fact is demonstrated by the conception about the character of the land, and of God's relationship to it, that the longer Israel has lived in the land of Israel, the holier that part of the land. Israel's dwelling in the land makes it holy. "Areas in which Israelites have lived for longer periods of time are holier and are subject to more rigorous restrictions,"[24] than those in which Israel has lived for a shorter period. The laws of the sabbatical year apply more strictly to the territories in which Israel lived before and after 586. Areas occupied only before but not after, or vice versa, are subject to fewer restrictions. This has an important implication for the nature of God's ownership of the land. Newman comments, "In Leviticus the land is sanctified by God alone, who dwells in it and who has given it to Israel, his people. The Mishnah's framers by contrast, claim that Israelites also play an active part in sanctifying the land."[25] Accordingly, in the Mishnah's system, the partnership of Israel, represented by the householder, with God in ownership of the land affects the very character of the land itself, making it different from other land, imparting to it the status of sanctification through the presence of the two sources of sanctification, God and the Israelite, the Israelite householder in particular.

That explains why, in the case of the conception of ownership of wealth set forth by the authorship of the Mishnah, a conception informed by the rules of Leviticus, God's joint ownership and tenancy with the farmer imposed a dual economics, the one, a distributive economic order, the other, a market system pure and simple. The one partner, God, had no strong interest in the market system; the other partner, the householder, was assumed to have only such an interest in the rational utilization and increase of scarce resources, land and crops, herds and chattels. God's share was to be distributed in accord with God's rules, the farmer keeping the rest. That is what I mean by a mixed system, one partner framing policy in line with a system of distributive economics, the other in market economics. The authorship of the Mishnah thus effected and realized in a systematic way rules governing land use, placement of diverse types of crops, rights of ownership, alongside provision of part of the crop to those whom God had designated as recipients of his share of the produce. That explains

---

[24]Louis E. Newman, *The Sanctity of the Seventh Year: A Study of Mishnah-Tractate Shebiit* (Chico, 1983: Scholars Press for Brown Judaic Studies), p. 19.
[25]Ibid., p. 19.

why that authorship could not imagine a market economy at all, and why the administered market (which, as we noted, is no market at all) in which government – priests' government – supposedly distributed status and sustained economic relationships of barter took the place of the market. What falls into the system of sanctification is what grows from the land through the householder's own labor ("cultivated"), is useful to the householder for sustaining life ("food"). God owns the land, the householder is the sharecropper, and the wealth of the householder therefore is the land that God allows for the householder's share and use. Wealth consists of land and what land produces, crops and cattle, as well as a large labor force, comprising the children of a growing population.

At the end we have to listen not only to what the authorship of the Mishnah says, but also to what it does not treat. What are the scarce resources that the economics of Judaism ignores? The economics of the system expresses in tacit omissions a judgment concerning the dimensions of the economy that to begin with falls subject to the enchantment of sanctification expressed in glorious triviality by our authorship. For matching the explicit rules are the authorship's ominous silences. Its land-centeredness permits its economics to have no bearing not only upon the economy comprising Jews who were not householders, but also Jews who lived overseas. The Mishnah's distributive economics is for the "Israel" of "the land of Israel" to which the Mishnah speaks. There is no address to the economics of "Israel" outside of the land. For distributive economics governs only agricultural produce of the land of Israel, and, it follows, market economics, everything else, and everywhere else. No wonder, then, that the framers of the Talmud of Babylonia, addressing, as they did, Jews who did not live on holy or sanctified dirt, took no interest whatsoever in the Mishnah-tractates upon which we have focused here, the ones that state in rich detail the theory of a distributive economics of God as owner, scheduled caste as surrogate, Temple as focus, and enlandisement as rationale, for an utterly fictive system.

Strictly speaking, the economics of the Mishnah is not an economics at all. The reason is that in the Mishnah's system, economics is embedded in an encompassing structure, to which economic considerations are subordinated, forming merely instrumental components of a statement made not in response to, but merely through, economics. And economics can emerge as an autonomous and governing theory only when disembedded from politics and society.[26] Economic

---

[26]That interest in whether or not economics is "embedded" or "disembedded" explains, once more, why I have tried to avoid those components of Polanyi's

institutions, such as the market, the wage system, a theory of private ownership, and the like, in no way can have served the system of the Mishnah, not because in their moral or ethical value they proved less, or more, suitable than competing institutions, such as the sacerdotal system of production and distribution, a theory of divine-human joint tenancy, and a system made up of both wages for labor and also fees for correct genealogy, that the Mishnah's framers adopted. Economics viewed in its own terms cannot have served the system of the Mishnah because the system-builders viewed nothing in its own terms, but all things in the framework of the social system they proposed to construct. I earlier observed that Christian theologians for the first seven centuries simply ignored economics, having no theory to contribute to economic thought and no sustained interest in the subject. But when we realize the character and function of economics in the system of the Mishnah, we realize that the same reason accounts for the presence of an economics as for its absence.

V. Conclusion

Not all Judaic religious systems – statements of a worldview and a way of life addressed to a well-defined social entity – have made judgments upon precisely those issues that conventionally comprise economics.[27] The priestly code did. We look in vain, in the counterpart

---

interpretation that have come under interesting criticism. I find especially suggestive the comments of Sally Humphreys, "Thus, what disturbed the philosophers of the fourth century was not, as Polanyi thought, an increase in profit-making on price differentials, but the disembedding or structural differentiation of the economy, leading to the application of 'economic' criteria and standards of behavior in a wide range of situations recognized as economic above all by the fact that money was involved; the old civic virtues of generosity and self-sufficiency were being replaced by the market attitudes of the traders." See Sally C. Humphreys, "History, Economics, and Anthropology: The Work of Karl Polanyi," *History & Theory* 1969, 8:165-212, p. 211. Note also Otto Erb, *Wirtschaft und Gesellschaft im Denken der hellenischen Antike* (Berlin, 1939), cited by her. Humphreys asks an interesting question: "Would a decrease in the importance of market institutions in a society which had reached this level of differentiation produce a revival of the attitudes whose loss Aristotle and Polanyi deplored? In the Roman Empire the state increasingly had to take over the functions of the market system in order to ensure an adequate supply and distribution of food to the city population. This change was accompanied by an increase in private redistribution....The process of bureaucratization of the economy and the rise under the influence of Christianity of new attitudes to economic matters has never really been studied."

[27]See Barry Gordon, "Biblical and Early Judeo-Christian Thought: Genesis to Augustine," in S. Todd Lowry, ed., *Pre-Classical Economic Thought. From the*

rules of a priestly community, the Essenes at Qumran, for an interest in the same questions. The authorship of the Priestly Code concerned itself with distributive economics, true value, the reversion of property to its "original" owner, and other fundamental conceptions that everything belonged in place, and that there was a given order that constituted the right arrangement and disposition of material wealth. So too, as we shall see, did the authorship of the Mishnah. But I find slight equivalent interest in the law codes of the Essenes of Qumran in these same matters, and there is no counterpart to the sustained and detailed attention to them accorded by the authorship of the Mishnah. For the whole of antiquity, we recognize, Christian theologians and jurisprudents (after Constantine) managed to say practically nothing

---

Greeks to the Scottish Enlightenment (Boston, Dordrecht, Lancaster: Kluwer Academic Publishers), pp. 43-67, and the commentary by Roman A. Ohrenstein, "Some Socioeconomic Aspects of Judaic Thought," *ibid.*, pp. 68-76. Note also the following items, among many:

R. Barraclough, *Economic Structures in the Bible* (Canberra, 1980: Zadok Centre).

Roland de Vaux, *Ancient Israel* (London, 1978: Darton, Longman and Todd).

Barry Gordon, *Economic Analysis before Adam Smith: Hesiod to Lessius* (London, 1975: MacMillan).

Idem., "Lending at Interest: Some Jewish, Greek, and Christian Approaches, 800 B.C.– A.D.. 100," *History of Political Economy*, 1982. 14:406-26.

Frederick C. Grant, The Economic Background of the Gospels (New York, 1973: Russell and Russell) (Repr. of 1926 ed.).

B. J. Meislin and M. L. Cohen, "Backgrounds of the Biblical Law against Usury," *Comparative Studies in Society and History*, 1963-4. p. 6.

Ben Nelson, *The Idea of Usury* (Chicago and London, 1969: University of Chicago Press).

E. Neufeld, "Socio-Economic Background of Yobel and Shemitta," *Rivista degli studi orientali*, 1958, 33-53, 124.

Robert North, *Sociology of the Biblical Jubilee* (Rome, 1954: Pontifical Biblical Institute).

Roman A. Ohrenstein, "Economic Thought in Talmudic Literature in the Light of Modern Economics," *American Journal of Economics and Sociology*, 1968. 27:185-96.

Idem., "Economic Self-Interest and Social Progress in Talmudic Literature," *American Journal of Economics and Sociology*, 1970. 29:59-70.

Idem., "Economic Aspects of Organized Religion in Perspective: The Early Phase," *The Nassau Review*, 1970, 27-43.

Idem., "Economic Analysis in Talmudic Literature: Some Ancient Studies of Value," *American Journal of Economics and Sociology*, 1979. 38.

Idem., "Some Studies of Value in Talmudic Literature in the Light of Modern Economics," *The Nassau Review*, 1981. 4:48-70.

Morris Silver, *Prophets and Markets: The Political Economy of Ancient Israel* (Boston, 1983: Kluwer-Nijhoff).

J. Viner, "The Economic Doctrines of the Christian Fathers," *History of Political Economy*, 1978: 10:9-45.

about matters of economic theory. Only with the advent of Aristotle in the life of the Christian intellect in the West do we find a counterpart interest to that of the authorship of the Mishnah. That authorship made a choice, and we can explain why this, not that, when we realize that the requirements of the system of the Mishnah encompasses, also, the task of framing an economic theory as a medium for the statement of the system's main points concerning sanctification.

What I have shown is that the Mishnah is a document of political economy, in which the two critical classifications are the village, *polis*, and the household, *oikos*. Since, however, the Mishnah's framers conceived of the world as God's possession and handiwork, theirs was the design of a universe in which the God's and humanity's realms flowed together. The result is a distributive economics, familiar from most ancient times onward, but a distributive economics that, in the same system, coexisted with a kind of market economics.[28]

The Mishnah's sages placed economics, both market (for civil transactions) and distributive (for sacred transactions, for example, with scheduled castes and the Temple), in the center of their system, devoting two of their six divisions to it (the first and the fourth, for the distributive and the market economics, respectively), and succeeded in making their statement through economics in a sustained and detailed way far beyond the manner in which Aristotle did. And no one in antiquity came near Aristotle, as I said. It was with remarkable success that the sages of Judaism presented an economics wholly coordinated in a systemic way with a politics. In this proposed kind of study of religion and economics, therefore, we find ourselves on the border between sociology and economics, following how the sociology of economics – and therefore this kind of inquiry concerning religious materials places us squarely into the middle of discourse on political economy. Compared to the work of Plato and Aristotle, the Mishnah's system presents the single most successful political economy accomplished in antiquity.

---

[28] I explain this matter in my *Economics of Judaism. The Initial Statement* (in press).

Appendix

Jews in Economies and the Economics of Judaism
The Case of Salo W. Baron

The economics of Judaism, as the economics of the Jews, is hardly an unexplored field of inquiry.[29] Indeed, any study of pertinent topics, whether of the Jews' economics or of the Jews' own economy, of the Jews in economic life or of the economics of Judaism, takes its place in a long, if somewhat irregular and uneven, line of works on the subject. The most important and best known statement on the economics of Judaism purports to account, by appeal to the economics of Judaism and the economic behavior of Jews, for the origins of modern capitalism. Werner Sombart, *The Jews and Modern Capitalism*,[30] in 1911 set the issues of the economics of Judaism within a racist framework, maintaining that Jews exhibited an aptitude for modern capitalism, and that aptitude derives in part from the Jewish religion, in part from the Jews' national characteristics. Jewish intellectuality, teleological mode of thought, energy, mobility, adaptability, Jews' affinity for liberalism and capitalism – all of these accounted for the role of Jews in the creation of the economics of capitalism, which dominated. Sombart appealed, in particular, to the anthropology of the Jew, maintaining that the Jews comprise a distinct anthropological group. Jewish qualities persist throughout their history: "constancy in the attitude of the Jews to the peoples among whom they dwelt, hatred of the Jews, Jewish elasticity." "The economic activities of the Jew also show a remarkable constancy." Sombart even found the knowledge of economics among the rabbis of the Talmud to be remarkable. In the end Sombart appealed to the fact that the Jews constitute a "Southern people transplanted

---

[29]For an introduction to the economic study of talmudic literature, see Roman A. Ohrenstein, "Economic Thought in Talmudic Literature in the Light of Modern Economics," *The American Journal of Economics and Sociology*, 1968, 27:185-96, who cites earlier writings on the subject, cf. p. 185, n. 3. Ohrenstein's "Economic Self-Interest and Social Progress in Talmudic Literature: A Further Study of Ancient Economic Thought and its Modern Significance," *American Journal of Economics and Sociology*, 1970, 29:59-70, typifies the perfectly dreadful work in hand in that field. I do not here treat Tamari's work on Jewish ethics vis-à-vis economics, because that seems to me a methodologically still more primitive work than any under discussion here.

[30]The edition I consulted is Werner Sombart, *The Jews and Modern Capitalism*. With a new introduction by Samuel Z. Klausner. Translated by M. Epstein (New Brunswick and London, 1982: Transaction Books).

among Northern peoples." The Jews exhibited a nomadic spirit through their history. Sombart contrasted "the cold North and the warm South" and held that "Jewish characteristics are due to a peculiar environment." So he appealed to what he found to be the correlation between Jewish intellectuality and desert life, Jewish adaptability and nomad life, and wrote about "Jewish energy and their Southern origin," "'Sylvanism' and Feudalism compared with 'Saharaism' and Capitalism," and ended, of course, with the theme of the Jews and money and the Jews and the Ghetto.

The romantic and racist view of the Jews as a single continuing people with innate characteristics which scientific scholarship can identify and explain of course formed the premise for Sombart's particular interest, in the economic characteristics of the Jew and the relationship of this racial trait to the Jews' origin in the desert. While thoroughly discredited, these views have nonetheless generated a long sequence of books on Jews' economic behavior. Today people continue to conceive "Jewish economic history" as a cogent subject that follows not only synchronic and determinate, but also diachronic and indeterminate lines and dimensions. Such books have taken and now take as the generative category the Jews' constituting a distinct economy, or their formation of a social unit of internally consistent economic action and therefore thought, the possibility of describing, analyzing, and interpreting the Jews within the science of economics. But that category and its premise themselves still await definition and demonstration, and these to this day are yet lacking. Consequently, while a considerable literature on "the Jews' economic history" takes for granted that there is a single, economically cogent group, the Jews, which has had a single ("an") economic history, and which, therefore, forms a distinctive unit of economic action and thought, the foundations for that literature remain somewhat infirm.[31]

The conception of Jews' having an economic history, part of the larger, indeed encompassing, notion of the Jews' have had a single history as a people, one people, has outlived the demise of the racist rendition of the matter by Sombart. But what happens when we take seriously the problems of conception and method that render fictive and merely imposed a diachronic history of the Jews, unitary, harmonious,

---

[31]I hasten to state at the outset that Jews' role in diverse economies, so far as that role is distinctive, surely permits us to appeal as an independent variable to the fact that certain economic actors are Jews. But what trait or quality about those actors as Jews explains the distinctive traits of Jews as a group – if any does – requires careful analysis in a comparative framework, e.g., Jews as a distinct component of a variety of economies. None of these entirely valid and intellectually rigorous inquires is under discussion here.

and continuous, and when we realize that the secondary and derivative conception of a diachronic economics of the Jews is equally dubious? Whether or not it is racist, that unitary conception of the Jews as a single, distinctive, ongoing historical entity, a social group forming also a cogent unit of economic action, is surely romantic. Whatever the salubrious ideological consequences, such an economics bypasses every fundamental question of definition and method. If the Jews do not form a distinct economy, then how can we speak of the Jews in particular in an account of economic history? If, moreover, the Jews do not form a distinct component of a larger economy, then what do we learn about economics when we know that (some) Jews do this, others, that? And if Jews, in a given place and circumstance, constitute a distinct economic unit within a larger economy, then how study Jews' economic action out of the larger economic context which they help define and of which they form a component? The upshot of these questions is simple: how shall we address those questions concerning rational action with regard to scarcity that do, after all, draw our attention when we contemplate, among other entities, the social entities that Jews have formed, and now form, in the world? And this brings us to the work of Salo W. Baron in social and economic history of the Jews, since in Baron's definition of the matter we are able to see precisely how this kind of study should not be done – and why.

Salo W. Baron[32] claims to know about economic trends among Jews in the second, third, and fourth centuries. As evidence he cites episodic statements of rabbis, as in the following:

> In those days R. Simon ben Laqish coined that portentous homily which, for generations after, was to be quoted in endless variations: "'You shall not cut yourselves,' this means you shall not divide yourselves into separate groups...." Before the battle for ethnic-religious survival, the inner class struggle receded.
>
> Age-old antagonisms, to be sure, did not disappear overnight. The conflict between the scholarly class and "the people of the land" continued for several generations....
>
> Class differences as such likewise receded into the background as the extremes of wealth and poverty were leveled down by the unrelenting pressure of Roman exploitation. Rarely do we now hear

---

[32]*A Social and Religious History of the Jews* (New York, 1952: Columbia University Press) II. *Ancient Times*, Part II, pp. 241-260. Compare my "Why No Science in Judaism?" in *From Description to Conviction* (Atlanta, 1987: Scholars Press for Brown Judaic Studies), on the counterpart problems of intellect exhibited by Saul Lieberman, Baron's contemporary. I place the matter into a still broader context in: *Paradigms in Passage: Patterns of Change in the Contemporary Study of Judaism*. Lanham, 1988: University Press of America. Studies in Judaism Series.

descriptions of such reckless display of wealth as characterized the generation of Martha, daughter of Boethos, before the fall of Jerusalem. Even the consciously exaggerated reports of the wealth of the patriarchal house in the days of Judah I fell far short of what we know about the conspicuous consumption of the Herodian court and aristocracy.[33]

It would be difficult to find a better example of overinterpretation of evidence to begin with irrelevant to the point than Baron's concluding sentence of the opening paragraph of this abstract. Not having shown that there was an inner class struggle or even spelled out what he means by class struggle, how he knows the category applies, let alone the evidence for social stratification on which such judgments rest, Baron leaps into his explanation for why the class struggle receded. That is not the only evidence of what can only be regarded as indifference to critical issues characteristic of writing on Jews' economies, but it is probative. The rest of the passage shows how on the basis of no sustained argument whatsoever, Baron invokes a variety of categories of economic history and analysis of his time, for example, conspicuous consumption, class struggle ("inner" presumably different from "outer"), and on and on.

When discussing economic policies, which draw us closer to the subject of this book, Baron presents a discussion some may deem fatuous.[34] Precisely how he frames the issues of economic theory will show why:

> Economic Policies: Here too we may observe the tremendous influence of talmudic legislation upon Jewish economy.

The premise that there was (a) Jewish economy, and that talmudic legislation affected economic action, is simply unsubstantiated. How Baron knows that people did what rabbis said they should, or that Jews formed an economy in which people could make decisions in accord with sages' instructions, he does not say. The premise of all that follows, then, is vacant. More to the point of our interest in matters of economic theory, we turn to Baron's program of discourse on what he has called "policies:"

> The rabbis constantly tried to maintain interclass equilibrium. They did not denounce riches, as some early Christians did, but they emphasized the merely relative value of great fortunes....The persistent accentuation of collective economic responsibility made the Jewish system of public welfare highly effective. While there was

---

[33]Baron, op. cit., p. 241.
[34]Ibid., pp. 251-255.

much poverty among the Jews, the community, through its numerous charitable institutions, took more or less adequate care of the needy.

Man's right, as well as duty, to earn a living and his freedom of disposing of property were safeguarded by rabbinic law and ethics only in so far as they did not conflict with the common weal....

Private ownership, too, was hedged with many legal restrictions and moral injunctions in favor of over-all communal control....

Rabbinic law also extended unusual protection to neighbors....

Nor did the individual enjoy complete mastery over testamentary dispositions....

Apart from favoring discriminatory treatment of apostates, who were supposed to be dead to their families, the rabbis evinced great concern for the claims of minor children to support from their fathers' estate....

In a period of economic scarcity social interest demanded also communal control over wasteful practices even with one's own possessions....

How this mélange of this and that – something akin to economic policy, some odd observations on public priority over private interest that sounds suspiciously contemporary (to 1952), counsel about not throwing away bread crumbs – adds up to "economic policies" I cannot say. But the data deserve a still closer scrutiny, since Baron represents the state of economic analysis of Judaism and so exemplifies precisely the problem I propose to solve in a different way. Here is his "man's right" paragraph:

Man's right, as well as duty, to earn a living and his freedom of disposing of property were safeguarded by rabbinic law and ethics only in so far as they did not conflict with the common weal. Extremists like R. Simon ben Yohai insisted that the biblical injunction, "This book of the law shall not depart out of thy mouth, but thou shalt meditate therein day and night," postulated wholehearted devotion to the study of Torah at the expense of all economic endeavors. But R. Ishmael effectively countered by quoting the equally scriptural blessing, "That thou mayest gather in thy corn and thy wine and thine oil." Two centuries later, the Babylonian Abbaye, who had started as a poor man and through hard labor and night work in the fields had amassed some wealth, observed tersely, "Many have followed the way of R. Ishmael and succeeded; others did as R. Simeon ben Yohai and failed." Sheer romanticism induced their compeer, R. Judah bar Ila'i, to contend that in olden times people had made the study of the law a full-time occupation, and devoted only little effort to earning a living, and hence had proved successful in both....R. Simeon ben Yohai himself conceded, however, that day and night meditation had been possible only to a generation living on Mannah or to priestly recipients of heave-offerings....In practice the rabbis could at best secure, as we shall see, certain economic privileges for a minority of students, relying upon the overwhelming majority of the population to supply society's needs to economically productive work.

From the right to earn a living being limited by the common weal, we jump to study of the Torah as the alternative to productive labor. That move of Baron's I cannot myself claim to interpret. I see no connection between the balance between "freedom of disposing of property" and "conflict with the common weal," on the one side, and " the issue of work as against study, on the other. The rest of the discussion concerns only that latter matter, and the paragraph falls to pieces by the end in a sequence of unconnected sayings joined by a pseudo-narrative ("two centuries later...") and an equally meretricious pretense of sustained argument "...himself conceded"), all resting on the belief that the sayings assigned to various sages really were said by them.

This reading by Baron of how "the Jews'" policies and behavior in economics are to be studied should not be set aside as idiosyncratic. The obvious flaws of historical method, the clear limitations in even so simple a matter as the competent construction of a paragraph – these should not obscure the fact that Baron's construction of the Jewish economy and Jewish economic policy is representative and not at all idiosyncratic. The received conception first of all imputes to the Jews a single economic history, which can be traced diachronically. Proof lies in works in both English and Hebrew. Take for example the book entitled, *Economic History of the Jews*, assigned to Salo W. Baron, Arcadius Kahan, and others, edited by Nachum Gross.[35] Baron wrote Chapters One through Seven, Kahan, Eight through Ten, of Part One, "general survey," and the titles of these sequential chapters follow: "the first temple period, exile and restoration, the second temple period, the talmudic era, the Muslim Middle Ages, medieval Christendom, economic doctrines, the early modern period, the transition period, the modern period." That, I contend, is a program of diachronic economic history. These chapters can have been composed and presented in the sequence before us only if the author assumed that a single group, with a continuous, linear history, formed also a cogent and distinct economic entity, with its own, continuous, linear, economic history.

"Economic doctrines" as Baron expounds them are amply familiar to us: bits and pieces of this and that. The remainder of the book covers these topics: agriculture, industry, services. Each part is subdivided, for example, under services: "banking and bankers, brokers, contractors, court Jews, department stores, Jewish autonomous finances, market days

---

[35] New York, 1975: Schocken.

Why Does Judaism Have an Economics? 145

and fairs, mintmasters and moneyers, moneylending, peddling, secondhand goods, slave trade, spice trade, stock exchanges." Here again, we may be sure, data on department stores derive from one time and place, those on slave trade, from another. But laid forth sequentially, the chapter titles indicate a conception of a single unitary and continuous economic history, in which any fact concerning any Jew at any time or place connects with any fact concerning any other Jew at any other time or place, the whole forming a cogent economy. Nor should work in Hebrew be expected to exhibit a more critical definition of what is subject to discourse. The same Nachum Gross edited *Jews in Economic Life. Collected Essays In Memory of Arkadius Kahan (1920-1982)*.[36] Here is the portrait of a field, as sequential essays outline that field:

> The Economic Activities of the Jews
>
> The Cardinal Elements of the Economy of Palestine during the Herodian Period
>
> The Economy of Jewish Communities in the Golan in the Mishnah and Talmud Period
>
> The Itinerant Peddler in Roman Palestine
>
> The German Economy in the 13th-14th Centuries: The Framework and Conditions for the Economic Activity of the Jews
>
> On the Participation of Jewish Businessmen in the Production and Marketing of Salt in Sixteenth Century Poland and Lithuania
>
> Economic Activities of Jews in the Caribbean in Colonial Times
>
> Jewish Guilds in Turkey in the Sixteenth to Nineteenth Centuries

and on and on. Nor do I exaggerate the utter confusion generated by the conception of "the Jews" as an economic entity, continuous from beginning to the present. The juxtaposition of these two papers seems to me to make the point rather sharply:

> Jewish Population and Occupations in Sherifian Morocco
>
> On the Economic Activities of the Moldavian Jews in the second half of the 18th and the first half of the 19th centuries

---

[36]Jerusalem, 1985: The Zalman Shazar Center for the Furtherance of the Study of Jewish History.

There is no need to ask what one thing has to do with the other. We just take for granted that Jews are Jews wherever they lived, whenever they thrived, and whatever Jews' occupations were in Sherifian Morocco bears a self-evident relationship to whatever Moldavian Jews did for a living half a world and a whole civilization distant. Having cited the juxtaposition of titles, with justified confidence I simply rest my case.

8

How We Understand Our Traditions: Is Judaism a Traditional Religion?

Conference Address, Seton Hall University
December 3, 1989

A synonym for religion is tradition, as "Jewish tradition" or "the tradition of Judaism," and the counterpart in Roman Catholic discourse is familiar. We call religions "traditions" when we wish to allege that the religious tradition bears the fundament of truth, intact and unchanging, from some authoritative point in the past, for example, revelation.[1] The word "tradition" therefore bears a heavy burden of meaning in both Judaic and Roman Catholic religious discourse, for it defines a taxon, as useful as "religion" itself, for the differentiating adjective that defines us: Judaic serves to modify "tradition" as fittingly as it modifies "religion," indeed tradition is the preferred taxon rather than religion, since, in the rather secular and positivist framework of Jewish community life, "tradition" is less threatening than "religion." "Roman Catholic" tradition" and "Roman Catholic religion," if not interchangeable, then are at least difficult to differentiate.

Why is it so important for both the pious to allege that their religions are "traditions"? In both cases the word "tradition" serves as

---

[1] I acknowledge the quite separate analysis of the traditionality of religion in Wilfred Cantwell Smith's great work, *Meaning and End of Religion*, where he calls upon us to refer to "religious traditions." But the context is not theological, but religions-historical and analytical, and my remarks here in no way contradict his, in my view entirely valid, arguments.

an apologetic and validation for the faith. For it carries within itself the claim that there is a single starting point for all the diverse phenomena of the faith, and, moreover, what we believe has been handed on from that single starting point by the founding and the founder, whether Moses, whether Jesus, and the call to realize and hand on this same fundament of truth that has been received and preserved in the truthful tradition of the Torah, on our side, or the Church, on yours, for believers is difficult to evade. These are very powerful validations of the faith: its authenticity, contemporary diversity being dismissed as inauthentic *ab origine*, its veracity, contemporary doctrine being affirmed as authentic *ab origine*.

The claim of changeless traditionality is still more important in the Christian context. For in the polemical part of the apologetic task, Roman Catholic Christianity appealed to the tradition faithfully preserved by the Church, inclusive of Scripture itself, in response to the Protestant Reformation and its call, *sola scriptura*. On the Judaic side, the appeal to "tradition" as against "modernity," evading the issue of religiosity as against secularity, is meant to justify preserving age-old ways, even when we do not really believe in them – hence the call to nostalgia and sentimentality in Fiddler on the Roof's "Tradition." In these three ways, then, as taxon, as apologetic claim to truth, and as apologetic response to contrary opinion, the appeal to tradition has served both the Roman Catholic and Judaic religious systems and continues to form the foundation stone for the religious life of synagogue and church alike.

But I think in framing in terms of tradition our conceptions of what it is that we affirm, our religion and its way of life and worldview and account of who and what we are as a social entity, we err. This is for several reasons. First, we err because we commit into the hands of scholarship matters of faith that we know are not settled by historical fact at all. So we are disingenuous. The category "tradition" after all imposes upon us not only the possibility of demonstrating the truth of the faith, but also the necessity of proving the facticity of the faith, and that is quite another matter. Accordingly, New Testament scholarship is asked to tell us about "the historical Jesus," and the response, for a century and three quarters, has proved monumentally irrelevant to the faith, except among the doubters. Second, we err because we classify the faith not in its acutely contemporary framework, where it is real and joyful, but in its received and imposed framework, where it is a burden out of the past. Tradition is a sour metaphor, since as a category it imposes the claim of a dead past upon the living present. Yet our religions live because they live in us and through us and for us. The great Catholic theologian and novelist,

Andrew M. Greeley, has written a score of novels to demonstrate for all to see that Catholics truly love being Catholic, they love the sacraments, the love the Church, they love everything about themselves. Such people do not have to be told, Do it because that's the way it's been done. And they would not listen if that were the only because.

But there is a third reason that the metaphor of traditionality does not work. It is that, when we speak of tradition, it is no longer traditional; it is now something that we can distinguish from ourselves, something we can examine, evaluate; it is an inheritance not of attitudes and convictions as to what we know is true, but a legacy to be sifted and sorted out, defended and apologized for. That conception of tradition as something of which we are conscious contradicts the simple fact that when we know we're traditional, we aren't. The word "tradition" describes how things have been done and are done; if we wish to speak of how things ought to be done (which may be the same way in which they have been done) then we require a different word altogether.

For we know a tradition flourishes when we cannot discern tradition at all, only self-evidence that this is how things are done and how they should be done. We know that a tradition has become something else when we define, identify, and defend something we do in the name of tradition: how things have always been, therefore how they should always be. For the claim of traditionality is not merely (of necessity) post facto, it is, alas, post mortem. Cultural continuity comes to the surface only when the chain has broken, allowing us to look backward, aware that we make observations on something distinct from ourselves and our circumstances. Then we see the links of the chain – broken links, broken chain. When we are part of the iron bonds of a valid, vital tradition, we do what we do because it is right, and the apologetic claim that this is what always was and therefore lays claim upon us and our future proves not merely irrelevant but incomprehensible.

But there is another sense to the word "tradition," and that sense may prove useful to reflection on what it is that the Torah and the Church have sustained: what shall we call the faith, how shall we classify it? "Tradition" may refer to "truth [thought] received," hence to the way in which revealed truth is transmitted. The word also may speak of "thought in process of formation," truth that results from a spell of agglutination and long-term sedimentary formation. A system can, and, in the case of Judaism, always is, traditional in that other sense: truth revealed and faithfully nurtured and handed on. That is to say, a system may lay claim to the status of traditionality when its framers say that what they teach derives from a remote past, revelation at Sinai for example, transmitted faithfully from that point onward. And I find that a compelling idea, an evocative metaphor.

That other sense of tradition, the apologetic sense that the "traditional" teachings derive from a long process of a sedimentary order, accumulation and conglomeration, tradition by contrast serves us very poorly; the cost of apologetic is too high. For when we are told that we do what they always did, the upshot is that we must continue to do what they always did. In that sense, a traditional religion cannot invite into the process of religious living in the here and now the participation of the very present generation, and a religious system aborning cannot derive from a process of tradition, even though it can, and ordinarily does, make use of "traditions," truths received from the past. Tradition in the apologetic sense suppresses tradition in the formative sense.

And, as a matter of fact, representing Judaism as a traditional religion in the sense that it began at some one point, continued unchanged and intact from that point, and today must be preserved just as received in its sole authentic form, is not only false as to fact, but also destructive as to faith. The Judaism of the Dual Torah, which is normative and authentic in its various forms, does not begin at some one point, in some one book for instance; it accommodated change, remaining never intact, but always unimpaired. Accordingly, in a descriptive-historical, literary and factual sense, the Judaism of the Dual Torah, the Judaism under discussion here, is in no way a traditional religion, because it was and now is a traditional religion in the other sense I offered: a tradition always in the making, a reworking, in age succeeding age, of the received truths of eternity.

In so framing matters, I contrast thought received as truth transmitted through a process of tradition against thought derived from active rationality. To repeat the two senses of the word: the word "tradition" may be understood to refer to a fixed and unchanging essence deriving from an indeterminate past, a truth bearing its own stigmata of authority, for example, from God at Sinai. Then when we say, "Judaism is a traditional religion," we make a theological statement. We mean to say, Judaism – the Judaism of the Dual Torah – receives and hands on that fundament of truth, Torah, that God revealed to Moses at Sinai. That meaning of "tradition" as received, transmitted truth, then bears consequences for the canon as well. Each canonical document then – as in the case of the Judaism of the Dual Torah – in proportion and measure constitutes a partial statement of that complete tradition.

But the sense of the word "tradition" as the process that describes how ideas have come into being is secular, for it constitutes the statement of what is claimed as a historical fact. And, I argue, when we invoke the concept of tradition in defense of the faith, it is a secular apologia for religion. Specifically, in this historical, scholarly, and secular sense, "tradition" is supposed to refer to a corpus of materials that derive from and form out of prior sources. That is an allegation as to facts, and facts have no bearing upon faith, any more than does faith upon facts. This sense of "tradition" refers not to content – "tradition" from Sinai, that is, "received truth" – but rather to the matter of process. Specifically, this other sense of the word *tradition* speaks of an incremental and linear process that step by step transmits out of the past statements and wordings that bear authority and are subject to study, refinement, preservation and transmission. In that sense, tradition is supposed to describe a process. That constitutes a literary and a historical – not a theological – judgment. When people allege that the Judaism of the Dual Torah (or, in common parlance, simply "Judaism") is a traditional religion, they ordinarily conceive that they make an historical and consequently also a literary statement, but – in the realm of facts and scholarly – what is, as a matter of fact, not a theological, statement at all. That is why I ask whether, as a matter of historical fact and literary evidence, Judaism is a traditional religion. And my answer is, as to process, Judaism is profoundly untraditional, as to content, Judaism is indeed deeply traditional. The truth comes to us from Sinai through generations of study of the Torah. But the process of the truth of the Torah is a process in which each generation renews the whole.

Let me unpack the distinction that I mean to offer. When people speak of "tradition as process" they refer to the formative history of a piece of writing, specifically, an incremental and linear process that step by step transmits out of the past an essential and unchanging fundament of truth preserved in writing, by stages, with what one generation has contributed covered by the increment of the next in a sedimentary process, producing a literature that, because of its traditional history as the outcome of a linear and stage by stage process, exercises authority over future generations and therefore is nurtured for the future. In that sense, tradition is supposed to describe a process or a chain of transmission of received materials, refined and corrected but handed on not only unimpaired, but essentially intact. The opening sentence of tractate Avot, "Moses received Torah from Sinai and handed it on to Joshua," bears the implication of such a literary process. The second meaning of tradition bears not upon process but upon content and structure. People sometimes use the word tradition to mean a fixed and unchanging essence deriving from an indeterminate past, a truth bearing its own seal of authority, for example, from God at Sinai.

The two meanings of the word, the one theological and systemic, the other historical and factual, cannot both apply to a single religious system. A traditional religion in *process* cannot constitute a tradition in *content*. The reason is simple. So far as a process of tradition takes over the formation of a cogent and sustained statement of truth, such as tradition-as-content presents, considerations extraneous to rational inquiry, decided, not demonstrated facts take over and divert the inexorable processes of applied reason from their natural and logically necessary course. So considerations of tradition as truth override considerations of tradition as process – or are themselves overridden.

And the opposite is also the case. Where a cogent statement – tradition as truth – forms the object of discourse, syllogistic argument and the syntax of sustained thought dominate, obliterating the marks of a sedimentary order of formation in favor of the single and final, systematic one. So far as an authorship proposes to present an account of a system, it will pay slight attention to preserving the indicators of the origins of the detritus of historical tradition, of which, as a matter of fact, the systemic statement itself may well be composed. The threads of the tapestry serve the artist's vision; the artist does not weave so that the threads show up one by one. The weavers make ample use of available yarn. But they weave their own tapestry of thought. And it is their vision and not the character of the threads in hand that dictate the proportions and message of the tapestry. In that same way, so far as processes of thought of a sustained and rigorous character yield writing that makes a single, cogent statement, tradition and system cannot form a compatible unit. Where in the formation of a systemic statement reason governs, it reigns supreme and alone, revising the received materials and, through its own powerful and rigorous logic, restating into a compelling statement the entirety of the prior heritage of information and thought.

Now when I represent Judaism as traditional as to truth but not as to process, I contrast thought that develops or unfolds through a process of tradition against thought derived from active rationality. How shall we know whether that description of Judaism accords with the facts? I answer by appeal to the character of Judaism's classical statement, which is the Talmud of Babylonia or the Bavli. Along with Scripture, that is the authoritative and comprehensive statement of Judaism, so I ask: does what is the most rigorously rational and compelling statement of applied reason known to me, which is the Talmud of Babylonia or Bavli, constitute a tradition and derive from a process of traditional formulation and transmission of an intellectual heritage, facts and thought alike? Or does that document make a statement of its own, cogent and defined within the requirements of an inner logic, proportion, and structure, imposing that essentially autonomous vision upon whatever materials its authorship has received from the past? We know the answer because of an already completed sequence of simple tests, which concern the framing of the program of inquiry and the character of the sustained discourse of the Bavli.

Specifically, I can show that in literary terms the Bavli is not traditional, formed out of the increment of received materials, the form of the reception of which governs, but – in the sense now implied – systemic, that is, again in literary terms orderly, systematic, laid out in a proportion and order dictated by the inner logic of a topic or generative problem and – and therefore – authoritative by reason of its own rigorous judgment of issues of rationality and compelling logic. I therefore offer a reasonable hypothesis resting on facts of literature.

This brings us back to the two meanings of the same word, tradition. True, they coexist. But they are incompatible. For the first of the two – tradition as the statement of literary and historical facts – places a document, the Bavli for instance, within an ongoing, determinate historical process, the latter – tradition as received truth, as the story of how a timeless truth has come down to us – speaks of a single statement at the end of an indeterminate and undefined process, which can encompass revelation of a one-time sort. As I said, I use only the first of the two meanings. When, therefore, I ask whether or not Judaism is a traditional religion, answering the question by finding out whether or not the Bavli is a traditional document, I want to know one thing. It is whether the present literary character of the Bavli suggests to us that the document emerges from a sedimentary process of tradition in the sense just now specified: an incremental, linear development, step by step, of law and theology from one generation to the next, coming to expression in documents arrayed in sequence, first to last. The alternative is that the Bavli originates as a cogent and proportioned statement through a process we may compare – continuing our geological metaphor – to the way in which igneous rock takes shape: through a grand eruption, all at once, then coalescence and solidification essentially forthwith. Either the Bavli will emerge in a series of layers, or it will appear to have formed suddenly, in a work of supererogatory and imposed rationality, all at once, perfect in its ultimate logic and structure.

When I maintain that the Bavli is not a traditional document and therefore Judaism, as to process, is not a traditional religion, I issue a judgment as to its character viewed as literature in relationship to prior extant writings. Everyone of course must concur that, in a theological sense, the Bavli is a profoundly traditional document, laying forth in its authorship's terms and language the nature of the Judaic tradition, that is, Judaism, as that authorship wishes to read the tradition and have it read. But this second sense will not recur in the pages that follow.

When I ask whether or not the documents of the Judaism of the Dual Torah exhibit shared traits of logic, rhetoric, or topic that justify imputing to them not merely points of intersection or connection but continuities and commonalities, I do not ask an invented question. It is a position maintained by a sizable sector of those who revere the Torah and interpret it today. I shall show that, as a statement of the continuities of a traditional character, deriving from a long and incremental process of handing on materials from generation to generation and – more to the point – document to document – that position contradicts the evidence of the Bavli, which, we must remember, constitutes the single most authoritative canonical writing of Judaism. What I claim is a simple proposition. The Judaism of the Dual Torah knows not traditions to be recited and reviewed but merely sources,[2] to be honored always but to be used only when pertinent to a quite independent program of thought.

That is to say, to go over the first definition of tradition with which I commenced, the components of the Torah of that Judaism do not contribute equally and jointly to a single comprehensive statement, handed on from generation to generation and from book to book, all of them sources forming a tradition that constitutes the Torah. Each has a particular message and make a distinctive statement. Obviously, all fit together into a common statement, the Torah or Judaism. That fundamental theological conviction defines Judaism and cannot – and should not – give way before the mere testimony of literary evidence. But it is the fact that whatever traits join the whole of the rabbinic corpus together into the single Torah of Moses our Rabbi, revealed by God to Moses at Sinai, they are not literary traits of tradition.

In literary terms, the various rabbinic documents commonly (and, from a theological perspective, quite correctly) are commonly represented as not merely autonomous and individual statements, or even connected here and there through shared passages, but in fact as continuous and interrelated developments, one out of its predecessor, in a long line of canonical writings (to Sinai). The Talmud of Babylonia, or Bavli, takes pride of place – in this picture of "the rabbinic tradition" – as the final and complete statement of that incremental, linear

---

[2] And I should imagine that, when work on the traditions used by the Bavli's authorship makes solid progress, we shall have good reason to say the same of the Bavli's authorship's approach to traditions as much as to sources.

tradition, and so is ubiquitously described as "the tradition," par excellence. Vis-à-vis its sources, the Bavli represents an essentially autonomous, fresh, and original statement of its own. How so? Its authorship does not take over, rework, and repeat what it has received out of prior writings but makes its own statement, on its own program, in its own terms, and for its own purposes.

Every test I can devise for describing the relationship between the authorship of the Bavli and the prior and extant writings of the movement of which that authorship forms the climax and conclusion yields a single result. The authorship at hand does not pursue anyone else's program, except only that of the Mishnah. It does not receive and refine writings concluded elsewhere. It takes over a substantial heritage and reworks the whole into its own sustained and internally cogent statement – and that forms not the outcome of a process of sedimentary tradition but the opposite: systematic statement of a cogent and logical order, made up in its authorship's rhetoric, attaining comprehensibility through the syntax of its authorship's logic, reviewing a received topical program in terms of the problematic and interests defined by its authorship's larger purposes and proposed message. Any samples of the Bavli you take will constitute either a composite of sustained, essentially syllogistic discourse, in which case forming the whole and comprehensive statement of a system, or the increment of exegetical accumulation, in which case constituting restatements, with minor improvements, of a continuous tradition.

True, the authorship of the Bavli drew upon a sizable corpus of materials indeterminate character and substance, which we assuredly do classify as traditions handed on from their predecessors. Hence the authorship of the Bavli made use of both sources, completed documents, and also traditions, transmitted sayings and stories, ordinarily of modest proportions, not subjected to ultimate redaction. But the authorship of the Bavli did whatever it wished with these materials to carry out its own program and to make its own prevailing statement. These received materials, undeniably formulated and transmitted in a process of tradition, have been so reworked and revised by the penultimate and ultimate authorship that their original character does not define the syntax of argument and the processes of syllogistic discourse, except by way of supplying facts for someone else's case. Whether or not we can still discern traces of received statements, even in wordings that point to an origin other than with our authorship, is beside the point. Proof of my case does not derive from the failure or success of scholars to identify the passages of the Bavli that antedate the penultimate or ultimate work of composition.

In its final literary context defined by the documents or sources we can identify, the Bavli emerges as anything but the seal of "tradition" in the familiar sense. For it is not based on distinct and completed sources handed on from time immemorial, subserviently cited and glossed by its own authorship, and it does not focus upon the systematic representation of the materials of prior documents, faithfully copied and rehearsed and represented. We have, of course, to exclude the Mishnah, but this fundamental document is treated by the authorship of the Bavli in a wholly independent spirit. The upshot is that the Bavli does not derive from a process of tradition in the first sense stated above, although, as a faithful and practicing Jew, I believe that the Bavli truly constitutes "tradition" in that second, theological sense to which I referred: a new statement of its own making and a fresh address to issues of its own choosing.

But the literary character of the process that created the Bavli is irrelevant to the demonstration of that theological proposition, which derives its proof from the entire history of Judaism from the Bavli onward. Viewed as literature, the Bavli is not a traditional document at all. It is not the result of an incremental and linear process; it does not review and restate what others have already said; its authorship does not regard itself as bound to the program and issues received from prior ages. The Bavli constitutes a systemic and not a traditional statement. True, the Bavli encompassed also extant and prior documents. But it made of these diverse writings a statement – a tradition in that other sense – formed out of prior sources, that is (from the system's perspective) a single, whole, homogeneous, cogent and (therefore) authoritative statement.

The Bavli cannot be shown systematically and generally to continue the program and inquiry of predecessors. Therefore with the Bavli a new tradition got underway, but the Bavli does not derive from, and state, a prior tradition in the sense just now spelled out. For in few ways does the Bavli give evidence of taking its place within such a process of tradition, and we cannot appeal to the document to demonstrate that the authorship of the Bavli represented itself as traditional and its work as authoritative on that account? The appeal of the authorship of the Bavli is to the ineluctable verity of well-applied logic, practical reason tested and retested against the facts, whether deriving from prior authorities, or emerging from examples and decisions of leading contemporary authorities. True enough, the Bavli contains ample selections from available writings. The authorship of the Bavli leaves no doubt that it makes extensive use of extant materials, sayings, and stories.

For example, the authorship of the Bavli invokes verses of Scripture. It further takes as its task the elucidation of the received code, the Mishnah. More to the point, frequent citations of materials now found in the Tosefta as well as allusions to sayings framed in Tannaite Hebrew and attributed to Tannaite authority – marked, for instance, by TN' – time and again alert us to extensive reference, by our authorship, to a prior corpus of materials. Not only so, but contemporary scholarship has closely read both brief sayings and also extended discourses in light of two or three or more versions and come to the conclusion that a later generation has taken up and made use of available materials.[3] Most striking of all, our authorship claims in virtually every line to come at the end of a chain of tradition, since the bulk of the generative sayings – those that form the foundation for sustained inquiry and dialectical discourse – is assigned to named authorities clearly understood to stand prior to the work of the ultimate redactors. Even if we preserve a certain reluctance to take at face value all of these attributions to prior authorities, we have to take full account of the authorship's insistence upon its own traditionality. In all of these ways, the authorship of the Bavli assuredly stands in a line of tradition, taking over and reworking received materials, restating viewpoints that originate in prior ages. And that fact makes all the more striking the fundamental autonomy of discourse displayed by the document at the end. So let us serve as interlocutors for the great authorship at hand and present some pointed questions to the Bavli's formers and framers.

Were we therefore to enter into conversation with the penultimate and ultimate authorship of the Bavli, the first thing we should want to know is simple: what have you made up? And what have you simply repeated out of a long-continuing heritage of formulation and transmission? And why should we believe you? The authorship then would be hard put to demonstrate in detail that its fundamental work of literary selection and ordering, its basic choices on sustained and logical discourse, its essential statement upon the topics it has selected

---

[3]I present a sizable sample of these prior exercises in source criticism in the volumes edited by me, *The Formation of the Babylonian Talmud. Studies on the Achievements of Late Nineteenth and Twentieth Century Historical and Literary-Critical Research* (Leiden: E. J. Brill, 1970) and *The Modern Study of the Mishnah* (Leiden: E. J. Brill, 1973). These two volumes cover the more important contemporary figures, with special attention to David Weiss Halivni. The only figure omitted did his important work afterward, Shamma Friedman, and, as I noted earlier, to a sample of his work I devoted a seminar, the papers of which were then published in William Scott Green, ed., *Law as Literature, Semeia* XX (Chico: Scholars Press, 1984).

– that anything important in their document derives from long generations past.

Should they say, "Look at the treatment of the Mishnah," we should answer, "But did you continue the Yerushalmi's program or did you make up your own?" And in the total candor we rightly impute to that remarkable authorship, the Bavli's compositors would say, "It is our own – demonstrably so."

And if we were to say, "To what completed documents have you resorted for a ready-made program?" our *soi-disant* traditionalists would direct our attention to Tosefta, their obvious (and sole) candidate. And, if they were to do so, we should open the Tosefta's treatment of, or counterpart to, a given chapter of the Mishnah and look in vain for a systematic, orderly, and encompassing discourse, dictated by the order and plan of the Tosefta, out of which our authorship has composed a sizable and sustained statement.

True, we readily recognize that the Tosefta's materials play their role. But seeing the Tosefta in its terms, noting how slight a portion of a given Tosefta chapter the Mishnah's authorship has found accessible and urgent, we should dismiss out of hand any claim that the Bavli's fundamental structure and plan encompasses systematic and orderly exposition of the Tosefta's structure and plan for a given Mishnah chapter. The opposite is the case.[4] Tosefta makes its contribution unsystematically and episodically, where and when the authorship of the Bavli, for its reasons (not always obvious to us) has permitted the Tosefta to do so. That is hardly the mark of traditionality, subservience to a received text, such as the counterpart treatment of the Mishnah by the Bavli's authorship – a treatment that is orderly, routine, complete, and systematic – indicates.

And when, finally, we ask our authorship to state its policy in regard to Scripture and inquire whether or not a sustained and ongoing tradition of exegesis of Scripture has framed discourse, the reply will prove quite simple. "We looked for what we wanted to seek, and we found it."

These four loci at which boundaries may have merged, and intersections turned into commonalities, therefore mark walled and

---

[4]Rabbi Yaakov Elman's study of the impact of Tosefta Pisha upon Bavli Pesahim has shown beyond all doubt the fact that there is no systematic and orderly plan of Tosefta citation and exegesis at the foundations of the Bavli's inquiry into the matter. Quite to the contrary, reference to the Tosefta's materials on the same topic turns out to be casual, episodic, and unpredictable. The sustained research behind his oral report, at the Society of Biblical Literature meeting in Atlanta on November 24, 1986, of this matter will in due course be published in this series.

sealed borders. A received heritage of sayings and stories may have joined our authorship to its teachers and their teachers – but not to that larger community of sustained learning that stands behind the entirety of the writings received as authoritative, or even a sizable proportion of those writings. The presence, in the ultimate statement of the Bavli, of sayings imputed to prior figures – back to Scripture, back to Sinai – testifies only to the workings of a canon of taste and judgment to begin with defined and accepted as definitive by those who defined it: the authorship at hand itself. The availability, to our authorship, of a systematic exegesis of the same Mishnah chapter has not made self-evident to our authorship the work of continuation and completion of a prior approach.

Quite to the contrary, we deal with an authorship of amazingly independent mind, working independently and in an essentially original way on materials on which others have handed on a quite persuasive and cogent statement. Tosefta on the one side, Scripture and a heritage of conventional reading thereof on the other – neither has defined the program of our document or determined the terms in which it would make its statement, though both, in a subordinated position and in a paltry limited measure, are given some sort of a say. The Bavli is connected to a variety of prior writings but continuous with none of them. And the Bavli formed the model of the sense in which traditionality pertains: after the fact, as truth, not before the fact, as process.

Viewing the documents exemplified by the Bavli from the angle of their intrinsic traits, we find no pervasive continuities, no single community of texts. I see not only an absence of a collectivity, but a failure even of sustained imitation of later texts by earlier ones.[5] Indeed I am struck by the independence of mind and the originality of authorships that pretend to receive and transmit, but in fact imagine and invent.[6] The received position will not find satisfaction in the modest points of intersection and overlap that we have noted in our

---

[5] The matter of imitation I take up in a separate, and very preliminary study, *From Tradition to Imitation*.

[6] True, individual texts do relate to other individual texts, either in a sustained dialectical relationship, as in the case of Mishnah and its continuator-exegeses, or in a taxonomic relationship of connection, as in the case of Sifra and Sifré to Numbers and of Genesis Rabbah and Leviticus Rabbah, or in an episodic and anecdotal relationship, as in the case of documents that make use of sayings or stories in common. (The connection between these sayings or stories that occur in two or more documents scarcely requires analysis in the present context; what we have is simply diverse versions of given units of discourse.)

survey of the sample of the Bavli. In fact, overall, there is no community of texts existence of which is proven by intrinsic traits.[7]

If I had to specify a single aesthetic tension confronting any of our authorships, it is to establish a claim of continuity while doing pretty much anything someone wanted to do. The Mishnah's authorship rejected that matter altogether, ignoring the inherited conventions of language as Scripture dictated the characteristics of Hebrew, ignoring the topical program of Scripture's legal codes for its own program (absorbing the received one to be sure), ignoring the entire structure of authority based on pseudepigraphic authorship characteristic of Scripture ("Moses" as author of Deuteronomy, for instance). No imitation here! Nor any in Tosefta. And even the Bavli at the end yielded a fundamental structure utterly original, independent of that of the Yerushalmi, as I have shown elsewhere.[8] Let me state the upshot for systemic analysis very simply: We err when we seek to demonstrate that a system recapitulates its texts.

That is what leads us to impute to texts intrinsic traits of order, cogency, and unity. It is, further, what provokes us to postulate connection, rather than demonstrating it. The source of error flows from treating as literary facts what are, in fact, judgments of theology, that is, the reification of faith, the transformation of convictions of culture into facts of literature and – it must follow – a theory of hermeneutics. The fact is that the system not only does not recapitulate its texts, it selects and orders them, imputes to them as a whole cogency that their original authorships have not expressed in and through the parts, expresses through them its deepest logic, and – quite by the way – also dictates for them the appropriate and operative hermeneutics. The canon (so to speak) does not just happen after the fact, in the aftermath of the texts that make it up. The canon is the event that creates of

---

[7]To state the proposition in negative terms, let me point to a few simple facts. A community of texts should exhibit traits of sharing, even of imitation. But the authorship of the Tosefta does not imitate the Mishnah; that of Leviticus Rabbah does not imitate that of the Sifra; and on and on. There are paramount and definitive points of originality in every document, including the Bavli. In fact, we now realize, a criterion for an adequate theory of the intrinsic connections among the documents of the rabbinic canon must derive not from the issue of originality but of imitation. Let us ask ourselves just where and how the diverse components of the Mishnah, Tosefta, and Bavli imitate one another – and where and how they do not. When we rapidly survey the Bavli, we see few marks of imitation, and a vast corpus of indications of total independence, one document from the other, and thus of essential originality.

[8]*Judaism: The Classic Statement. The Evidence of the Bavli* (Chicago: University of Chicago Press, 1986), and compare *The Talmud of the Land of Israel*. 35. Introduction. Taxonomy (Chicago: University of Chicago Press, 1984).

How We Understand Our Traditions

documents holy texts before the fact: the canon is the fact. The system – the final and complete statement – does not recapitulate the extant texts. The antecedent texts – when used at all – are so read as to recapitulate the system. The system comes before the texts and defines the canon.

We once more revert to the first of the two meanings of the word tradition. The Bavli in relationship to its sources is simply not a traditional document, in the plain sense that most of what it says in a cogent and coherent way expresses the well-crafted statement and viewpoint of its authorship – that alone. Excluding, of course, the Mishnah, to which the Bavli devotes its sustained and systematic attention, little of what our authorship says derives cogency and force from a received statement, and most does not. The premise of all learning of an independent order is that the Bavli's authorship has imputed to the Mishnah those meanings that that authorship, on the foundations of its own critical judgment and formidable power of logical reasoning in a dialectical movement, itself chose to impute. That reading of the Mishnah became the substance and center of tradition, that is, the ultimate statement, out of late antiquity, of the Judaism of the Dual Torah. We do not know that that reading triumphed because of the persuasive power of applied reason, rationality, cogent discourse resting on acute reasoning that together comprise the hermeneutics of the Bavli. But in an ideal world, that purely intellectual achievement would have accounted for its success. In any event, the Bavli's authorship's cogent, rigorously rational reading of the received heritage has demonstrably emerged not from a long process of formulation and transmission of received traditions, in each generation lovingly tended, refined and polished, and handed on essentially as received. Indeed, to revert to the opening question of the preface, I should doubt that it could have, for the literary evidence we have examined hardly suggests that a system of applied reason and sustained, rigorously rational inquiry can coexist with a process of tradition. The thought processes of tradition and those of system building scarcely cohere. Where applied reason prevails, the one – tradition – feeds the other – the system – materials for sustained reconstruction.

How things are in theory I cannot say. But in fact the Bavli's statement has given us the system that the Bavli's penultimate and ultimate authorship worked out. This statement accords with the choices dictated by that authorship's sense of order and proportion, priority and importance, and it is generated by the problematic found by that authorship to be acute and urgent and compelling. When confronting the exegesis of the Mishnah, which is its indicative trait and definitive task, the authorship of the Bavli does not continue and complete the work of antecedents. Quite to the contrary, that authorship made its statement essentially independent of its counterpart and earlier document.

So the Judaism of the Dual Torah that appeals for its ultimate encyclopaedic statement of law and theology to the Bavli – really is the making of the authorship of the Bavli, not principally the accumulation, in the Bavli, of the sifted-over detritus of prior authorships. The upshot as to theory may be stated very simply, and in a way to be tested in the study of the history of other religions as well: the system not only is not traditional, but, in age succeeding age, the system – the Torah – begins exactly where and when it ends. In the example of the Judaism of the Dual Torah come to full expression in the Bavli, such tradition as the authorship at hand has received ends when the system that receives that tradition begins. The inexorable logic and order, proportion and syllogistic reasoning that sustain tradition as truth must govern supreme and alone, revising the received materials and restating into a compelling statement, in reason's own encompassing, powerful and rigorous logic, the entirety of the prior heritage of information and thought. That restatement is the Bavli in its day, and the many and diverse traditions of Judaism that come to full realization in our day.

The way to read tradition as content is as a reasoned and systematic statement of a system. The reading then is defined by the rules of general intelligibility, the laws of reasoned and syllogistic discourse about rules and principles. The way to read tradition as process is as a traditional and sedimentary document. That reading lies through the ad hoc and episodic display of instances and examples, layers of meaning and eccentricities of confluence, intersection, and congruence. That is why, for my part I maintain that tradition as content and tradition as process cannot share a single crown. Moreover, the formative documents of Judaism demonstrate that Judaism constitutes not a traditional but a systemic religious statement, with a hermeneutics of order, proportion, above all, reasoned context, to tell us how to read each document. We cannot read these writings in accord with two incompatible hermeneutical programs, and, for reasons amply stated, I argue in favor of the philosophical and systemic, rather than the agglutinative and traditional, hermeneutics. The reason is that the character of the principal source of the Judaism of the Dual Torah, the Bavli, requires a systemic, not an associative, hermeneutics.

I conclude by affirming for the Bavli and therefore for Judaism the theological sense of the word *tradition:* a fixed and unchanging essence deriving from an indeterminate past, a truth bearing its own marks of authority, from God at Sinai. Because of its compelling and, in terms now defined, secular demonstration of the reasoned and rational character of all of created existence, the authorship of the Bavli created what assuredly became a profoundly traditional and, again in defined terms, religious and theological document, laying forth in its authorship's terms and language the complete and authoritative statement of the Torah, oral and written, that is the world-creating statement, made by Judaism, of that reasoned and orderly world that God had by rule created and by rule now sustains, world without end until by God's will and reasoned rule, the Messiah comes – an eternity of perfect rationality.

9

Are Jews "Religious"?

The First Avram Endowment Lecture, Brooklyn, 1987
Brooklyn Heights Synagogue

This lecture reviews a part of the argument of
From Words to Worlds:
Enchantment and Transformation in Judaism
(New York, 1987: Basic Books)

Copyright 1987 by Jacob Neusner
All rights reserved.

I. What Do We Mean by "Being Religious" in Judaism?

The criterion for "being religious" in the Judaism of the Dual Torah is being holy, and the instrumentality of sanctification is joining the words, "...who has sanctified us by the commandments and commanded us to...," to the appropriate actions. Jews are "religious" – that is, undergo sanctification and enter into the realm of sanctity, as holy "Israel" – any number of times in a day, for sanctification takes place – or can take place – at any moment and under any circumstance. It happens when in deed and word the Jew – "Israel" in the here and now – takes everyday and ordinary experiences and transforms them through prayer and rite into metaphors for the sacred. Sanctification is an act of enchantment through rite, that makes of us humanity, in the here and now, "in our image, after our likeness." And that happens very often and in many ways, and in things we do, and in things we do not do.

Enchantment works through celebration and story, acting in a way other than the ordinary so as to act out a story that tells me I am something other – and more – than I thought I was. Commemorating and celebrating, exemplifying through gesture, denoting and expressing through deed and word, enchantment transforms the individual and the group, both me and us. It tells us I am not where I am but somewhere else, I am not when I think I am but in another time altogether, and I am not who I am but someone else. I am not myself alone: I stand for much else, more than I imagined. Enchantment appeals to individual and to emotion, to collectivity and shared attitudes and feelings alike. That is why when we survey the occasions for enchantment and transformation, we speak of both the I and the we. Enchantment moreover so changes us as a group as to tell us we are someone else than we thought we were, we are living not merely now but in another moment entirely, and that we are not only ourselves but a wholly other entity: more than we thought we were, much more. We represent in the here and now a much larger us. That is what happens when the Jew says, "...who has sanctified us by the commandments and commanded us...."

For Jews enchantment does take place, and therefore Jews indeed are religious. Since any Judaic system differs from all non-Judaic religious systems, Jews' patterns of religiosity do not conform to those familiar to Protestant and Catholic and Orthodox Christianity. The Day of Atonement, the Passover seder, the marriage ceremony, the burial rite, these and other celebrations of the home and family moreover mark the lives of the vast majority of Jewish Americans and Canadians, West Europeans, Brazilians and Argentinians, Australians and South Africans. Engagement with the political issues of Jewish corporate life, typified by work in behalf of Soviet Jewry and concern with the State of Israel, encompasses the same, vast majority. The concern engages vivid energies, deep emotions. The one set of rites derives, as I shall explain, from the Judaism of the Dual Torah, the other from the Judaism of Holocaust and Redemption. So American and other diaspora Jews not only are deeply religious, but they sustain in their lives of active piety two distinct, if in some ways intertwined, Judaic systems, or Judaisms.

These two Judaisms, each with its symbolic system and appeal to a story of who "we" are and what on that account "we" must do, coexist side by side in the lives of the middle range consensus of Jewry. I speak in particular of Jews who live both integrated and segregated lives: strangers entirely at home in the nations of the West. They want to be Jewish, but also something else – indeed, many other things, and so they are. And yet, in the torn but mended hearts of Jews of Reform, Conservative, middle-range Orthodox, Reconstructionist, or for that matter Humanist commitment, whether those Jews are members of synagogues or unaffiliated with synagogues, these two Judaisms evoke profound and life-transforming affections – attitudes and emotions. The one serves home and family, the other the corporate community. A simple statement of their ubiquity suffices to prove the powerful influence of the Judaism of the Dual Torah. Nearly all Jews attend Passover seders, either joining family, or forming family for the occasion. When one Jew marries another Jew, it is virtually unheard of for them to have a civil, not a Judaic religious marriage. That rite too derives from the Judaism of the Dual Torah. The indicator for the other Judaism, the Judaism of Holocaust and Redemption, proves equally one-sided: deep concern for the State of Israel, profound response to the tale of the destruction of European Jewry from 1933 to 1945. When we discern their power and influence and understand how they work, we shall see how and why Jewish Americans and Canadians, West Europeans, Brazilians and Argentinians, Australians and South Africans, in varying ways to be sure, constitute a singular people on earth.

In answering the question of whether or not American Jews are religious, I obviously do not invoke as my sole criterion of religiosity Orthodoxy in its essentially segregated expression such as is so familiar here in Brooklyn. Indeed, I do not even deal with that small segment of the Jewish American world that finds its way to the synagogue twice a day, that study the Torah morning and night, that live out their lives wholly within the Judaism of the Dual Torah and entirely within the circles of the faithful. That sector of Jewry, self-segregated and rightly self-assured, raises no questions about religiosity and it of course is religious. It indeed is pious in the profound and rich sense of the Judaism of the Dual Torah. Synagogues of that sector of Jewry, mostly Orthodox, are crowded on weekdays and require two or three or more worship-services on Sabbaths. Nor do those Jews (in the main) remain aloof from the appeal of Holocaust and Redemption. For those Jews, Judaism encompasses the whole of life and commitment, however, and both the private and the familial, and also the civic and the public, life of Jewry join in a single entity, defined within the Torah in two parts, oral and written, which God handed over to Moses at Mount Sinai. The bulk of Jewish Americans, even here in Brooklyn, not to mention Canadians, West Europeans, Latin Americans, South Africans, and Australians do not live within the disciplines of the Torah and do not live entirely segregated lives. While in North America, most of those nonobservant (in the Orthodox sense) also do not affiliate with the Orthodox community, in Western Europe and the European communities of South Africa and Australia, they do; but the picture does not change. Jews integrated into the values and civilization of the West have produced a twin-Judaism, the one for the home, the other for the Judaic polity and the life of public discourse, and it is that dual – family, civic – Judaism that shapes and defines the lives of nearly all Jews of the West, those who are not fully observant in the Orthodox definition of observance. No study has suggested that the observant Orthodox encompass by any consequential indicator so much as 10% of the Jews of North America, surveyed en masse, though in a few major cities, such as New York City or London, the percentage is perhaps double.

II. Words into Worlds

In maintaining that American Jews are profoundly religious because they respond to the enchantment of Judaism(s) and are transformed by the wonder of the two distinct systems at hand, I propose three propositions in succession.

The first is that words have power. Rightly spoken with proper intentionality, coming from the heart, words bring forth worlds, through enchantment turning the everyday into something remarkable. That is, through the enchantment of its rite, Judaism changes us Jews from what we were into something else, something more, something other than our ordinary selves. The enchantment takes place in heart and soul and mind, comes to expression in deed turned into gesture. A commonplace deed may be to light a candle. A gesture is to kindle a flame to inaugurate the Sabbath. A deed is to eat a cracker. A gesture is to raise a piece of unleavened bread – a cracker of a certain kind – and to announce that it is the bread that our ancestors ate when they hastily left Egypt – and then to eat the cracker. Enchantment reaches fulfillment in the transformation of the here and now of the everyday into the then and there of life with the living God. Enchantment engages the given of our lives and transforms that into a gift.

But, second, not all words work. Only some words of Judaism so work as to make worlds of meaning, that that takes place only in a very particular circumstance. That is, in the Judaism that thrives in America and Canada, Western Europe and Latin America, South Africa and Australia, when words speak to the individual and to the family. Lacking the experience of religion lived in corporate community, people find it difficult to enter into, let alone transform, those social worlds of Judaism that transcend the private life. People appeal, when at home, to one set of rites and their accompanying myths – stories explaining the truth, and they respond, when in community, to another set of rites and myths, telling a different story altogether. The private life and home are changed by rite into holy places. The shared life of the community, lived with other Jews, is not commonly changed by words deriving from the same origin. But the life of the corporate community too is transformed into heightened being, made to refer to experience and value not materially present. When worlds speak of me, my life and my family, they transform; when they speak of us, all Israel, all together, in the language of the holy, the same words fall away unheard. But other words, not deriving from the Dual Torah, written and oral, that constitutes God's revelation to Israel, the Jewish people, invoke, evoke, provoke, transform. Those other words do change us, as profoundly and as completely, as do the words of the rites of the Dual Torah. The same tears come, but the music is different.

And, third, another set of words do work for those same Jews, words that make a different world from the one formed of imaginary Israel in the family of Abraham, Isaac, and Jacob. Those other words form a separate Judaism from the one evoked for individual and family on those rites of passage nearly universally observed. The corporate community unchanged by the words of one Judaism comes into being through the power of the words of a different Judaism. I identify that other Judaism and explain why in the context of the religious life of Jewries throughout the free world, where Jews are free to practice any Judaism of their choice or none, the nature of religion in general leads to the formation of the two Judaisms, one for the private life of home and family, the other for the political life of the community and its public policy, that today flourish. So I claim to explain why this, not that, in the life of one of today's genuinely vital religions, Judaism in North America and Latin America, Western Europe, South Africa and Australia.

Two vast Jewries lie beyond my claim to understanding. The one, in the Soviet Empire, to us is locked away and inaccessible. The other, in the State of Israel, lives out an existence in political, therefore also social and cultural, facts utterly unlike those of us in the diaspora or Golah (exile). I cannot pretend to understand and explain what Judaisms work, or do not work, how they change and how they do not affect, the Jews of those vast communities. The Judaisms at work in the State of Israel and in the Jewry of the Soviet Empire demand description, analysis, and explanation too. But, while I believe the questions I ask pertain, I cannot pretend to explain what I do not understand.[1]

---

[1] I see nothing much in common between the civil religion of American Judaism and the civil religion of the State of Israel, and there is nothing compelling that links the version of Orthodox Judaism that predominates – itself in diverse expressions – in the State of Israel and the Judaisms of the diaspora. A segment of American Orthodoxy alone enters into relationships with the Israeli counterpart. No other Judaic expression in America and Canada attempts to do so. I do not pretend to know anything at all about Israeli Judaism and cannot attempt to describe, analyze, and interpret its system(s).

The social world of the synagogue, the concrete realm of worship, presents a different picture from the widespread, popular observance of rites of home and family. The power of theological expression contained within synagogue worship proves deeply affecting on some occasions, for example, the New Year and Day of Atonement, which address the life of the individual, but also important on others, Sabbaths and weekdays. The Judaism for individual, home, and family brings Jews to synagogues on some days, not on others, and that explains why that power of liturgy that the synagogue possesses exercises so little charm for Jews that the synagogues stand empty most of the year. The synagogues turn words into a world of meaning, specifically, on those occasions on which the words address the self. Bare, empty, silent, the synagogues (except only those of a sector of Orthodoxy, the self-segregated one living out life only among other Jews) work no wonders when, from day to day and on Sabbaths and festivals, they speak to the us of all Israel as a corporate community. "Israel" as the holy society that God has loved listens to different words from those of the synagogue, responding to a different Judaism from the Judaism of the synagogue liturgy.[2]

III. Two Judaisms, Two Kinds of Religious Living

Since two Judaisms flourish in the vast middle-range of the socially integrated Jewries of the West, one for home and family, one for the shared life of the corporate community, we have now to describe each one. The first of the two Judaisms flourishes in the synagogue, as I said, and the second, in the streets. The one is private, the other public, the one personal and familial, the other civic and communal.

The Judaism found compelling in the private life derives from the Judaism of the Dual Torah, oral and written, that took shape in late antiquity, the first seven centuries of the Common Era, and reached its definitive statement in the Talmud of Babylonia. That Judaism not only flourished as the normative and paramount system into the nineteenth century, but now, on the eve of the twenty-first, continues to impart shape and structure to the ongoing life of the synagogue, its liturgy, its holy days and festivals, its theology, its way of life and worldview. This Judaism is familiar from the life of the synagogue and requires no systematic description.

What has been written on the subject thus far has not proved illuminating for the questions that seem to me important.
[2]But I think that, for reasons I shall spell out in the closing chapter, through the arts we may cast that spell once more that allows words to form not only worlds, but one world encompassing all Israel in the here and now.

The second Judaism came on the scene only in the aftermath of World War II and the rise of the State of Israel. I call it the "Judaism of Holocaust and Redemption,"[3] because it is a Judaic system that invokes, as its generative worldview, the catastrophe of the destruction by Germany of most of the Jews of Europe between 1933 and 1945 and the creation, three years afterward, of the State of Israel. This Judaism is deeply particular to the Jewish community and does require a brief description.

This Judaism has its way of life, its religious duties, its public celebrations. It is communal, stressing public policy and practical action. It involves political issues, for example, policy toward the State of Israel, government assistance in helping Soviet Jews gain freedom, and, in the homelands of the Jewish Americans or Canadians or Britons or French, matters of local politics as well. Let me spell out the worldview and way of life of that other Judaism, one with power to transform civic and public affairs in Jewry as much as the Judaism of the Dual Torah enchants and changes the personal and familial ones. In politics, history, in society, Jews in North America respond to the Judaism of the Holocaust and Redemption in such a way as to imagine they are someone else, living somewhere else, at another time and circumstance. That vision transforms families into an Israel, a community. The somewhere else is Poland in 1944 and also the earthly Jerusalem in 1967 or now (so long as we are not there, except for a week in a luxury hotel), and the vision turns them from reasonably secure citizens of America or Canada into insecure refugees finding hope and life in the land, and State, of Israel. Public events commemorate, so that "we" were there in "Auschwitz," which stands for all of the centers for the murder of Jews, and "we" share, too, in the everyday life of that faraway place in which we do not live but should, the State of Israel. That transformation of time and of place, no less than the recasting accomplished by the Passover seder or the rite of *berit milah* or the *huppah*, turns people into something other than what they are in the here and now.

The issues of this public Judaism, the civil religion of North American Jewry (and not theirs alone), are perceived to be political. But the power of that Judaism to turn things into something other than what they seem, to teach lessons that change the everyday into the remarkable – that power works no less wonderfully than does the power of the other Judaism to make me Adam or one of the Israel that

---

[3]More than a decade ago I first heard that phrase from Professor David Blumenthal, Emory University, when we were colleagues at Brown University. I believe it was his invention, a fitting name indeed for the phenomenon at hand.

crossed the Red Sea. The lessons of the two Judaisms, of course, are not the same. The Judaism of the Dual Torah teaches about the sanctification of the everyday in the road toward the salvation of the holy people. The Judaism of Holocaust and Redemption tells me that the everyday – the here and the now of home and family – ends not in a new Eden but in a cloud of gas; that salvation lies today, if I will it, but not here and not now. And it teaches me not only not to trouble to sanctify, but also not even to trust, the present circumstance.

The Judaism of Holocaust and Redemption supplies the words that make another world of this one. Those words moreover, change the assembly of like-minded individuals into occasions for the celebration of the group and the commemoration of its shared memories. Not only so, but events defined, meetings called, moments identified as distinctive and holy, by that Judaism of Holocaust and Redemption mark the public calendar and draw people from home and family to collectivity and community – those events, and, except for specified reasons, not the occasions of the sacred calendar of the synagogue, that is, the life of Israel as defined by the Torah. Just as in the USA religions address the realm of individuals and families but a civil religion – Thanksgiving, the Fourth of July, the rites of politics – defines public discourse on matters of value and ultimate concern, so the Judaism of the Dual Torah forms the counterpart to Christianity, and the Judaism of Holocaust and Redemption, as I said, constitutes Jewry's civil religion.

The power of the Judaism of the Holocaust and Redemption to frame Jews' public policy – for many to the exclusion of the Judaism of the Dual Torah – may be shown very simply. The Holocaust formed the question, Redemption in the form of the creation of the State of Israel, the answer, for all universally appealing Jewish public activity and discourse. Synagogues except for specified occasions appeal to a few, but activities that express the competing Judaism appeal to nearly everybody. That is to say, nearly all American Jews identify with the State of Israel and regard its welfare as more than a secular good, but a metaphysical necessity: the other chapter of the Holocaust. Nearly all American Jews are not only supporters of the State of Israel. They also regard their own "being Jewish" as inextricably bound up with the meaning they impute to the Jewish state.[4] In many ways these Jews

---

[4] That is not to suggest American Judaism constitutes a version of Zionism. Zionism maintains that Jews who do not live in the Jewish state are in exile. There is no escaping that simple allegation, which must call into question that facile affirmation of Zionism central to American Judaism. Zionism further declares that Jews who do not live in the State of Israel must aspire to migrate

every day of their lives relive the terror-filled years in which European Jews were wiped out – *and every day they do something about it.* It is as if people spent their lives trying to live out a cosmic myth, and, through rites of expiation and regeneration, accomplished the goal of purification and renewal. Access to the life of feeling and experience, to the way of life that made one distinctive without leaving the person terribly different from everybody else – emerged in the Judaic system of Holocaust and Redemption. The Judaism of Holocaust and Redemption presents an immediately accessible message, cast in extreme emotions of terror and triumph, its round of endless activity demanding only spare time. That Judaism realizes in a poignant way the conflicting demands of Jewish Americans to be intensely Jewish, but only once in a while, providing a means of expressing difference in public and in politics while not exacting much of a cost in meaningful everyday difference from others.

This brings me back to my principal theory. What works enchantment works because it refers to experience we have had, and what rite does not transform fails because it has no field for its magnetic magic. Some words evoke worlds, others do not, because some words refer to worlds we know, others speak of things we cannot recognize or identify. The individual in family understands life as metaphor. The family as part of community within the realm of religion does not. Corporate Israel exists in other dimensions, but not in the religious one. "Israel" forms a metaphor for a social entity – of a particular order. But if our experience of being "Israel" does not correspond to the prevailing metaphor, expressed by its rites and prayers, then those rites and prayers will not change us. Then rites and prayers that evoke a different experience of "being Israel" will prove effective. Now to the coexistence of the two Judaisms, can I explain

---

to that nation or, at the very least, raise their children as potential emigrants. On that position American Judaism chokes. Zionism moreover holds that all Jews must concede, indeed affirm, the centrality of Jerusalem, and of the State of Israel, in the life of Jews throughout the world. Zionism draws the necessary consequence that Jews who live outside of the State of Israel are in significant ways less "good Jews" than the ones who live there. Now all of these positions, commonplace in Israeli Zionism and certainly accepted, in benign verbal formulations to be sure, by American Jews, contradict the simple facts of the situation of American Jews and their Judaism. First, they do not think that they are in exile. Their Judaism makes no concession on that point. Second, they do not have the remotest thought of emigrating from America to the State of Israel. That is so even though in ceremonial occasions they may not protest when Israelis declare that to be their duty. Third, that they may similarly make a ritual obeisance carries the corollary of the peripherality of the diaspora in general, and of the mighty community of American Jews in particular.

which one works when it does, and does not work when it fails? My theory is simple.

Words work when the imagination makes them work; in our minds we make and therefore remake our world. Those words that in their primary propositions do retain powerful appeal address a circumstance that makes them welcome. The words that leave us Jews in general untouched and make no difference in shaping our world do not. *Words enchant in one setting, bore in another, because of their circumstance in which they are recited and the context in life's experience in which they are heard, not because of their propositions.*

The premise of prayer in the synagogue is simple. Public prayer is something we do together because it is our task. It is our task because we constitute corporate Israel and say our prayers as a community or a social entity. Synagogue prayers then create that social entity, that Israel, just as other prayers at life's passages call into being the world of Eden or through recalling Egypt and Exodus express a certain resentment. But if we undertake the obligations we accept on our own volition and at our own option, not out of obligation at all, then words of public worship will create no worlds. If prayer is what changes the *me* into the *us*, and prayer is something we accomplish together because we have to, whether or not we feel it, then prayer will or will not evoke a world I know, depending on my social experience. Specifically, if I to begin with know no community beyond myself and my family, then words that evoke a corporate community will refer to a world I cannot imagine. Words that speak to my home and family will address a world I know – and therefore can reimagine in response to the right words.

Now, Jews' understanding religion as essentially private and personal, this is a generation of home and family, to which supernatural collectivities such as holy Israel, a corporate community before God, have little appeal. Experiences in life that everyone has, such as hunger and satisfaction, having a baby, feeling different, or getting married undergo transformation because, to begin with, they refer to facts of life that are very real to us. But to what shared experience does public worship appeal, beyond an obligation to say the prayers? The testimony of the boring, bare, empty synagogues from day to day and Sabbath to Sabbath says, none. God lives for Israel – but not there. The fault lies not with the synagogue, surely not with the rabbi, who gives his or her life for Judaism, but with this-worldly Israel's social premise. What turns individuals and families into something larger than themselves, changing the *is* into a *what if* of a shared, social metaphor? It is a provocative question, which precipitates a self-evidently valid answer.

The passage through life makes me wonder about love and marriage, birth and family, aging, death. Life in society presents to me questions about who I am in relation to others like me in "being Jewish" or not like me. To answer those questions, I plausibly invoke enchantment, pretending to be something different from, more than what I seem to be. The *is* becomes an *as if* when the everyday demands it. Shall I then conclude that no experience shared beyond self and family links Jew to Jew into *an* Israel? Nothing could be more wrong. Jews form a variety of *Israels* – but nothing in their experience today evokes for them that Israel that, within the economy of the sacred, stands before God. The reason is that, for Jews as for others in American and Canadian societies, religion is personal. What forms families into communities are experiences of a different order altogether. They therefore invoke a different set of metaphors from those they conceive to be religious. To these other metaphors – those that interpret corporate experience in what are deemed appropriate, therefore essentially political, terms – we now turn.

IV. Permissible Difference and the Two Judaisms of America

I see two fundamental reasons for the present state of affairs, which finds the religion, Judaism, intensely affective in the private life and remarkably irrelevant to the public. The one reason is the prevailing attitude toward religion and its correct realm; the other is the Jews' reading of their experience of the twentieth century, which has defined as the paramount mode of interpreting social experience a paradigm other than that deriving from the life of that Israel that is the holy people of mind and imagination, therefore also of sanctification and salvation. Let me explain what I mean by the first of the two, the definition of the proper place of religion in public and political life.

When we ask why the bifurcation between the personal and the familial, subjected to the Judaism of the Dual Torah, perceived as religion, and the public and civic, governed by the Judaism of Holocaust and Redemption, perceived as politics, we first of all turn outward. For the explanation lies in the definition of permissible difference in North America and the place of religion in that difference. Specifically, in North American society, defined as it is by Protestant conceptions, it is permissible to be different in religion, and religion is a matter of what is personal and private. Hence Judaism as a religion encompasses what is personal and familial. The Jews as a political entity then put forth a separate system, one that concerns not religion, which is not supposed to intervene in political action, but public policy.

Judaism in public policy produces political action in favor of the State of Israel, or Soviet Jewry, or other important matters of the corporate community. Judaism in private affects the individual and the family and is not supposed to play a role in politics at all. That pattern conforms to the Protestant model of religion, and the Jews have accomplished conformity to it by the formation of two Judaisms. A consideration of the Protestant pattern, which separates not the institutions of Church from the activities of the state, but the entire public polity from the inner life, will show us how to make sense of the presence of the two Judaisms of North America.

Here in Protestant North America people commonly see religion as something personal and private; prayer, for example, therefore speaks for the individual. No wonder, then, that those enchanted words and gestures that, for their part, Jews adopt transform the inner life, recognize life's transitions, and turn them into rites of passage. It is part of a larger prejudice that religion and rite speak to the heart of the particular person. What can be changed by rite, then, is first of all personal and private, not social, not an issue of culture, not affective in politics, not part of the public interest. What people do when they respond to religion, therefore, affects an interior world – a world with little bearing on the realities of public discourse: what – in general terms – should we do about nuclear weapons or in terms of Judaism how we should organize and imagine society. The transformations of religion do not involve the world, or even of the self as representative of other selves, but mainly the individual at the most unique and unrepresentative. If God speaks to me in particular, then the message, by definition, is mine – not someone else's. Religion, the totality of these private messages (within the present theory) therefore does not make itself available for communication in public discourse, and that by definition too. Religion plays no public role. It is a matter not of public activity but of what people happen to believe or do in private, a matter mainly of the heart.

The Judaism of the Dual Torah forms the counterpart to religion in the Protestant model, affecting home and family and private life. The Judaism of Holocaust and Redemption presents the counterpart to religion in the civil framework, making an impact upon public life and policy within the distinctive Jewish community of North America. The relationships between the two Judaisms prove parlous and uneven, since the Judaism of home and family takes second place in public life of Jewry – and public life is where the action takes place in that community. Not only so, but the Judaism of the Dual Torah makes powerful demands on the devotee, for example requiring him or her to frame emotions within a received model of attitudes and appropriate

Are Jews Religious? 177

feelings. The Judaism of Holocaust and Redemption, by contrast, provides ready access to emotional or political encounters, easily available to all – by definition. The immediately accessible experiences of politics predominate. The repertoire of human experience in the Judaism of the Dual Torah, by contrast, presents as human options the opposite of the immediate. In that Judaism Jews receive and use the heritage of human experience captured, as in amber, in the words of the Dual Torah. That is why, in public life, Jews focus such imaginative energies as they generate upon "the Holocaust," and they center their eschatological fantasies on the "beginning of our redemption" in the State of Israel. Two competing Judaisms, the one that works at home, the other in public, therefore coexist on an unequal basis, because the one appeals to easily imagined experience, the other to the power of will to translate and transform the here and the now into something other.

V. Experience, Imagination and the Divided Heart of Jewry

The Judaism of Holocaust and Redemption speaks of exclusion and bigotry, hatred and contempt – experiences we do not have to imagine for ourselves – and therefore asks us to imagine ourselves in gas chambers. All of us have known (though many suppress the knowledge) exclusion. No Jew can imagine himself or herself to be utterly like "everyone else," because the beginning of being a Jew is, by definition, to be different because one is a Jew – whatever the difference may mean. Accordingly, the Judaism of Holocaust and Redemption addresses an experience that is common and – by definition – accessible to all Jews. The Judaism of the Dual Torah speaks of God and humanity in God's likeness, after God's image. It calls up the experience of exile and redemption, appealing to corners of experience that, for us as we are, prove empty. The Judaism of the Dual Torah demands sensibility, intellect, understanding; it asks us to build bridges from who we are to what the Torah tells us we may become. Not everyone musters the inner energy to imagine, and many do not. No wonder, then, that the Judaism of Holocaust and Redemption enjoys priority over the Judaism of the Dual Torah – except in those corners of life, in those private moments of intense personal experience, at which the Torah, and only the Torah, serves to tell us what is happening to us. The competition, as I said, is unequal, because the one Judaism reaches into that sore surface of life of being Jewish, that is, being different by reason of being Jewish, while the other plumbs the depths of our being human in God's image – not the same thing at all.

And yet –

And yet – if I may make my judgment explicit – the Judaism of the Holocaust and Redemption, with its focus upon the out-there of public policy and its present paramountcy, offers as a world nightmares made of words. Its choice of formative experiences, its repertoire of worthwhile human events – these impose upon Jews two devilish enchantments. First, the message of Holocaust and Redemption is that difference is not destiny but disaster – if one trusts the gentiles. Second, the media of Holocaust and Redemption, political action, letters to public figures, pilgrimages to grisly places – leave the inner life untouched but distorted. Being Jewish in that Judaism generates fear and distrust of the other, but it does not compensate by an appeal to worth and dignity for the self. The Judaism of Holocaust and Redemption leaves the life of individual and family untouched and unchanged. But people live at home and in family. Consequently, the Judaism of Holocaust and Redemption in ignoring the private life makes trivial the differences that separate Jew from gentile. People may live a private life of utter neutrality, untouched by the demands of the faith, while working out a public life of acute segregation. The Judaism of Holocaust and Redemption turns on its head the wise policy of the reformers and enlightened of the early nineteenth century: a Jew at home, a citizen out there. Now it is an undifferentiated American at home, a Jew in the public polity.

The Judaism of the Dual Torah, for its part, proves equally insufficient. Its address in here, to the self and family to the near exclusion of the world beyond leaves awry its fundamental mythic structure, which appeals to history and the end of time, to sanctification and the worth of difference. Viewed whole, each of its components at the passage of life and the passing of one's own life – the disposition of birth, marriage, aging, for example, the encounter with difference – makes sense only in that larger context of public policy. Separating the private and familial from the public and communal distorts the Judaism of the Dual Torah. Ignoring the individual and the deeply felt reality of the home leaves the Judaism of Holocaust and Redemption strangely vacant, in the end a babble of tear-producing, but unfelt, words, a manipulation of emotions for a transient moment. The Judaism of the Holocaust and Redemption is romantic. The Judaism of the Dual Torah accomplishes the permanent wedding of Israel, the Jewish people, to God. The one is for hotels, the other for the home. But both Judaisms speak to our heart – the divided heart today. It is time for mending.

10

Liturgy in Contemporary Society: Why Some Rites Retain Power in the Case of Judaism

Lecture, Pontifical Anselm University
Thursday, January 13, 1989

The power of liturgy, including sacrament and prayer, forms the generative reality of Roman Catholic Christianity, which has from the very founding of the Eucharist discovered the life of the faith in the sacraments as the Church has handed on those sacraments, and then, only then, in the declaration of faith through theology, or in the realization of faith through institutions of culture and politics. First came the liturgy, then the story, and long afterward, the theology. My question in this context, which is, why some rites retain power and others do not, will perhaps present a dissonance. Do not all rites retain their supernatural force? From God's perspective they do. But from a worldly angle of vision, matters are otherwise. We Americans know that some rites retain enormous power over popular imagination and behavior, and, alas, others do not. A simple census of the number of Christians in Church on Christmas or Easter tells us that for vast numbers attending Church, worship on those occasions carries greater weight than doing so on any other occasion.

I mean to raise a question concerning liturgy, therefore, that is not liturgical, but that helps us understand the power of liturgy in the world as we know it. It is in terms of Judaic religious life and practice today that I shall frame and answer my question – why this, not that. That is to say, why is it that some liturgies bear enormous power, and others find themselves neglected? The reason is not that Judaic religious life is weaker or stronger than the Roman Catholic or the

Buddhist or the Muslim or the Protestant or Orthodox Christian. Nor is the reason that that life is attenuated. The simple reason is that the Jews live in a variety of worlds, Western here in Europe and in the USA, Middle Eastern in the State of Israel. They form a bridge from one form of modern life to another. They furthermore are sufficiently familiar so that people can draw conclusions and generalizations from their particular case. But they are sufficiently different so that people can compare and contrast that case with others of a more numerous or representative sector of contemporary life. So we ask ourselves, in a general way, are there liturgies that enjoy greater popular adherence than others, and if so, what are they?

The answer to that question depends upon recognition that not one but two Judaisms flourish in the West, and the liturgies of each reach deep into the hearts of Jews. The one Judaism is for home and family life, and it is the received Judaism of the Dual Torah, written and oral, or one of that Judaism's continuators. The other Judaism is for public and corporate life, and it is the civil religion of a different Judaism altogether, one that I call the Judaism of Holocaust and Redemption. So, in point of fact, there are two Judaisms that flourish in the vast middle range of the socially integrated Jewries of the West, one for home and family, one for the shared life of the corporate community. Each of these two Judaisms answers an urgent question, but the question for the one is not the same as the one addressed by the other.

The Judaism found compelling in the private life derives from the Judaism of the Dual Torah, oral and written, that took shape in late antiquity, the first seven centuries of the Common Era, and reached its definitive statement in the Talmud of Babylonia. That Judaism not only flourished as the normative and paramount system into the nineteenth century, but now, on the eve of the twenty-first, continues to impart shape and structure to the ongoing life of the synagogue, its liturgy, its holy days and festivals, its theology, its way of life and worldview.

The second Judaism – the Judaism of Holocaust and Redemption, strongly identified with the rise of the State of Israel – came on the scene only in the aftermath of World War II and the rise of the State of Israel. I call it the "Judaism of Holocaust and Redemption," because it is a Judaic system that invokes, as its generative worldview, the catastrophe of the destruction by Germany of most of the Jews of Europe between 1933 and 1945 and the creation, three years afterward, of the State of Israel. This Judaism too has its way of life, its religious duties, its public celebrations. It is communal, stressing public policy and practical action. It involves political issues, for example, policy toward the State of Israel, government assistance in helping Soviet

Jews gain freedom, and, in the homelands of the Jewish Americans or Canadians or Britons or French, matters of local politics as well.

The first of the two Judaisms flourishes in the synagogue, as I said, and the second, in the streets. The one is private, the other public, the one personal and familial, the other civic and communal. That other Judaism exercises the power to transform civic and public affairs in Jewry as much as the Judaism of the Dual Torah enchants and changes the personal and familial ones. In politics and history, in society, Jews in Europe and North America respond to the Judaism of the Holocaust and Redemption in such a way as to imagine they are someone else, living somewhere else, at another time and circumstance. That vision transforms families into an Israel, a community.

Let me now spell out one among the many rites of the individual and the family that liturgically evokes profound response among Jews. It is the Days of Awe, the New Year or Rosh Hashshanah, and the Day of Atonement, or Yom Hakkipurim. These days are nearly universally observed by Jews throughout the world. They are days of profound religious feeling and spirit; there is nothing national or particular about them; their themes are individual and also universal.

Called in America "the holy holy days," the Days of Awe, ten momentous days from Rosh Hashshanah, the New Year, through Yom Kippur, the Day of Atonement, fill the synagogues to overflowing. Bare empty space on Sabbaths and festivals, the synagogues on the Days of Awe set the stage for mob scenes. And that fact presents a puzzle. Clearly, Judaism does work its enchantment and transforms some moments – some, but not others. Since there are plenty of empty seats on the Sabbath between the New Year and the Day of Atonement, as on all other Sabbaths, it is not the season alone. The point is that the same Judaism, invoking the same symbolic system and mythic structure, in some instances transforms but in others changes nothing. If people respond to one rite and not another, we ask what makes one rite compelling, another irrelevant. To understand the way worlds come from words, we have to explain both what works and what does not.

We listen first to the answer, then recover the question, of the rite. It is the question that the rite answers that provides a key to the treasury of the spirit contained within that rite. Only having taken up the contents of the liturgy may we seek an explanation in the larger context of contemporary Judaism and so explain why this, not that. The same theory that tells us why people respond to one liturgy has also to explain why they do not respond to some other. When we can explain why this, not that, we shall have reached the end of our inquiry into the transformation that the received Judaism can, and cannot, accomplish. So to ask the question: what basic theory, framed in the heart and soul of the religious life of Judaism, will explain the popularity of the Passover seder, which nearly everyone does, and the neglect of the Sabbath, which nearly no one does, and what moves people on Rosh Hashshanah but not on The Festival of Sukkot, following soon afterward?

First, let us listen with some care to the answers of the Days of Awe, for through these we shall find it possible to state the questions, from which, in our further step outward, we shall reach that larger social context that frames the whole. The New Year, *Rosh Hoshshanah,* and the Day of Atonement, *Yom Kippur,* together mark days of solemn penitence at the start of the autumn festival season. These in the prayers said on the occasion are solemn times. The words of the liturgy, specifically, create a world of personal introspection, individual judgment. The turning of the year marks a time of looking backward. It is melancholy, like the falling leaves, but hopeful: even as with the pennant and the series' losers: next year is another season.

The answer of the Days of Awe concerns life and death, which take mythic form in affirmations of God's rule and judgment. The words create a world aborning, the old now gone, the new just now arriving. The New Year, Rosh Hashshanah, celebrates the creation of the world: *Today the world was born.* The time of new beginnings also marks endings: *On the New Year the decree is issued: Who will live and who will die?* At the New Year – so the words state – humanity is inscribed for life or death in the heavenly books for the coming year, and on the Day of Atonement the books are sealed. The world comes out to hear these words. The season is rich in celebration. The synagogues on that day are filled – whether with penitents or people who merely wish to be there hardly matters. The New Year is a day of remembrance on which the deeds of all creatures are reviewed. The principal themes of the words invoke creation, and God's rule over creation, revelation, and God's rule in the Torah for the created world, and redemption, God's ultimate plan for the world.

On the birthday of the world God made, God asserts his sovereignty, as in the New Year Prayer:

> Our God and God of our Fathers, Rule over the whole world in Your honor...and appear in Your glorious might to all those who dwell in the civilization of Your world, so that everything made will know that You made it, and every creature discern that You have created him, so that all in whose nostrils is breath may say, "The Lord, the God of Israel is king, and His kingdom extends over all."

Liturgical words concerning divine sovereignty, divine memory, and divine disclosure correspond to creation, revelation, and redemption. Sovereignty is established by creation of the world. Judgment depends upon law: "From the beginning You made this, Your purpose known." And therefore, since people have been told what God requires of them, they are judged:

> On this day sentence is passed upon countries, which to the sword and which to peace, which to famine and which to plenty, and each creature is judged today for life or death. Who is not judged on this day? For the remembrance of every creature comes before You, each man's deeds and destiny, words and way.

These are strong words for people to hear. As life unfolds and people grow reflective, the Days of Awe seize the imagination: I live, I die, sooner or later it comes to all. The call for inner contemplation implicit in the mythic words elicits deep response.

The most personal, solemn, and moving of the Days of Awe is the Day of Atonement, *Yom Kippur*, the Sabbath of Sabbaths. It is marked by fasting and continuous prayer. On it, the Jew makes confession:

> Our God and God of our fathers, may our prayer come before You. Do not hide yourself from our supplication, for we are not so arrogant or stiff-necked as to say before You....We are righteous and have not sinned. But we have sinned.
>
> We are guilt laden, we have been faithless, we have robbed....
>
> We have committed iniquity, caused unrighteousness, have been presumptuous...
>
> We have counseled evil, scoffed, revolted, blasphemed....

The Hebrew confession is built upon an alphabetical acrostic, as if by making certain every letter is represented, God, who knows human secrets, will combine them into appropriate words. The very alphabet bears witness against us before God. Prayers to be spoken by the congregation are all in the plural: "For the sin which we have sinned against You with the utterance of the lips....For the sin which we have sinned before You openly and secretly...." The community takes upon itself responsibility for what is done in it. All Israel is part of one community, one body, and all are responsible for the acts of each. The sins confessed are mostly against society, against one's fellowmen; few pertain to ritual laws. At the end comes a final word:

> O my God, before I was formed, I was nothing. Now that I have been formed, it is as though I had not been formed, for I am dust in my life, more so after death. Behold I am before You like a vessel filled with shame and confusion. May it be Your will...that I may no more sin, and forgive the sins I have already committed in Your abundant compassion.

While much of the liturgy speaks of "we," the individual focus dominates, beginning to end.

The Days of Awe speak to the heart of the individual, telling a story of judgment and atonement. So the individual Jew stands before God: possessing no merits, yet hopeful of God's love and compassion. If that is the answer, can there be any doubt about the question? The power of the Days of Awe derives from the sentiments and emotions aroused by the theme of those days: what is happening to me? Where am I going? Moments of introspection and reflection serve as guideposts in people's lives. That is why people treasure such moments and respond to the opportunities that define them. The themes of the Days of Awe stated in mythic terms address the human condition, and the message penetrates to the core of human concerns about life and death, the year past, the year beyond, the wrongs and the sins and the remissions and atonement. People nearly universally respond to the liturgy of sin and confession, atonement and forgiveness. But the same people on the next Sabbath rarely find their way to that same synagogue that they crowded on the Days of Awe.

The issue of the power of one liturgy, not some other, derives neither from faith or doubt. The same people who pray the words I have quoted neglect other words of equal power within Judaism. If the issue is not that the more reasonable is the more practiced, then what explains the power of some words and not others? In my view, the issue is the question and the answer – people will believe all sorts of things if they want to, and deny the end of their nose if they do not want to. The rites of the actually practiced Judaism, denoted by the words that create worlds, have in common a single trait: it is their focus on the individual, inclusive of the family. The rites of the Judaism that for the generality of Jewry do not work to make worlds exhibit this common trait: they speak to a whole society, or to civilization, to nation or people. The corporate community, doing things together and all at once, conducts worship as service. The corporate community celebrates and commemorates events in the world of creation, revelation, and redemption. Sabbaths and festivals focus upon the corporate life of Israel, a social entity. The words that people say on these occasions do not speak to many Jews. The individual rites of passage, celebrating family, such as circumcision, marriage, and the rites that focus upon the individual and his or her existence, such as the Days of Awe, retain enormous power to move people.

The liturgies of the Sabbath and festivals are neglected. Why is that so? Because they present powerful answers to questions people do not want to ask in the synagogue, but do ask elsewhere. Why this, not that? I point to the message contained in the rites that speak to the subjectivity and individuality of circumstance, lay stress on the private person, recognize and accord priority to the autonomous and autocephalic individual. What people find personally relevant they accept; for them, the words evoke meaning and make worlds. The rites that speak to the community out there beyond family, to the corporate existence of people who see themselves as part of a social entity beyond, scarcely resonate. The context therefore accounts for the difference and even for variations. Jews live one by one, family by family. Words that speak to that individuality work wonders. Jews do not form a corporate community but only families. Words that address the commonality of Israel not as the congregation of individual Jews but as a community bound by law to do some things together, fall unheard, mere magic, not wonder working at all.

To state the upshot in secular terms, the fundamental condition of "being Jewish" so far as people identify "being Jewish" with the receive Judaism of the Dual Torah in the West is that it involves individual and family, *but imparts in social experience no knowledge of what it means to live in corporate community.* People cannot appeal to experience of a life in Israel and as Israel, an entire social entity, so as to validate the issues resolved by the rites of the corporate community, the Sabbath, for example, and the synagogue. The questions of community not asked, not felt, not understood, the answers in rite give information no one needs or can use.

Now that we have begun to form a theory of where and why words work and do not work, we confront the single most puzzling fact in contemporary Judaism. It is the contrast between the vivid and encompassing life of the faith in families, and the decadent state of the synagogue in its critical function, which is the offering up of prayer day by day and on Sabbaths and festivals. The simple fact that families covering nearly the whole of American Israel celebrate the Passover banquet seder but only paltry numbers then assemble the next morning in synagogue worship states the question. The fact that nearly all Jews bury their deceased in accord with the rites of Judaism (whether Reform or Orthodox) underlines the question. Why the one, not the other?

The reason is simple. Public worship rests upon the experience of the corporate community, which is responsible *in the aggregate* for offering up prayers. But so far as Jews as a whole confess to a common experience of the world, it bears no relationship to worship or the responsibilities of divine service. So, once more, what we see is the transformation of Judaism into an exercise, by choice, of home and family, rather than an expression, out of duty imposed from above and beyond, of the corporate community, Israel God's people. People who do not in their ordinary life experience the commonality of community also do not, in their cultic life, conceive that a task awaits for which all bear responsibility and to which the personal attitudes and feelings of the individual prove immaterial.

The conception of prayer characteristic of the Judaism of the Dual Torah that took shape in the first six centuries of the Common Era and predominated from then to now derives from the Temple and its priesthood and offerings. Prayer, that Judaism held, continues the offerings of the altar to God. Now the priesthood in the book of Leviticus represented those offerings in a very particular way, and that representation predominates in the Mishnah, ca. 200, and its exegetical continuations in the Tosefta, the Talmud of the Land of Israel, and the Talmud of Babylonia, ca. 300-600. In these definitive documents, the priestly conception of the Temple cult shaped the synagogue activity of prayer. That conception treated the offerings of the altar in the Temple in Jerusalem (the "tent of meeting" of the books of Exodus, Leviticus, and Numbers) as responses to God's command: This you shall do. The language is simple: "The Lord spoke to Moses saying, 'Speak to the children of Israel and say to them....'" The command addressed the community as a whole through the priesthood.

People with no knowledge of a religious life lived out in corporate society, who see religion as, if not utterly personal, then fundamentally familial, can hardly expect themselves to recognize obligations to offer up, as a group, the recitation of certain words. The issue is not that offering up unfelt words taxes the imagination, while offering up compelling words makes sense. The same social experience that tells us why the vast majority of Jews form families to observe the Passover banquet rite explains why they do not ordinarily participate in public worship in the synagogue. Their social experience informs them that under the aspect of eternity to be a Jew is to be part of a family, but tells them little in the aspect of their inner life about corporate responsibilities as a community.

So let me give my answer to the question, why this, not that. Some liturgies change us, others do not, because some words refer to worlds we know, others speak of things we cannot recognize or identify. The individual in family understands life as metaphor. The family as part of community within the realm of religion does not. Corporate Israel exists in other dimensions, but not in the religious one. Consequently, the synagogue, which has served the very specific purpose of divine service to God through both the provision of public worship as is required of the community and the study of the Torah in public as is also demanded of the community, both changes and decays. It changes into a community center, flourishing (where it does) in those aspects of its program to which the holy words scarcely reach. It decays in that the service of the heart becomes lip service, words passively mumbled in suppression of utter incredulity.

Now, Jews' understanding religion as essentially private and personal, this is a generation of home and family, to which supernatural collectivities such as holy Israel, a corporate community before God, have little appeal. Experiences in life that everyone has, such as hunger and satisfaction, having a baby, feeling different, or getting married undergo transformation because, to begin with, they refer to facts of life that are very real to us. But to what shared experience does public worship appeal, beyond an obligation to say the prayers? For Jews as for others in American and European Protestant societies, religion is personal. What forms families into communities are experiences of a different order altogether. They therefore invoke a different set of metaphors from those they conceive to be religious. To these other metaphors interpret corporate experience in what are deemed appropriate, therefore essentially political, terms. And their liturgies play a powerful role as well. But it is a different set of liturgies, deriving from a different Judaism, from the one that speaks of God's revelation to Moses at Mount Sinai.

Jews form a corporate community and share a substantial range of social experience. But that shared social experience in politics also takes form in transformations of the given into a gift, so that the *is* of the everyday polity shades into the *as if* of another time and place, as much as in the transformation by the Judaism of the Dual Torah of the passage of the individual through the cycle of life. The social experience forms the premise of the religious life. But the Jews' social experience of polity and community does not match the religious experience of home and family. Hence the religious side to things conforms to the boundaries of family, and the public experience of politics, economics, and society that Jews share comes to expression in quite different ways altogether.

The other Judaism, the one of Holocaust and Redemption rather than Eden, Sinai, and the World to Come, is political in its themes and character, myth and rites. The worldview of the Judaism of Holocaust and Redemption evokes political, historical events – the destruction of the Jews in Europe, the creation of the state of Israel, two events of a wholly political character. It treats these events as unique, just as the Judaism of the Dual Torah treats Eden and Adam's fall, Sinai, and the coming redemption, as unique. It finds in these events the ultimate meaning of the life of the Jews together as Israel and it therefore defines an Israel for itself – the State of Israel in particular – just as the Judaism of the Dual Torah finds in Eden, Sinai, and the world to come the meaning of the life of Israel and so defines for itself an Israel too:

the holy Israel, the social entity different in its very essence from all other social entities. That other Judaism, the Judaism of Holocaust and Redemption, addresses the issues of politics and public policy that Jews take up in their collective social activity. But it too has its rites and even its liturgies.

When we ask why the bifurcation between the personal and the familial, subjected to the Judaism of the Dual Torah, perceived as religion, and the public and civic, governed by the Judaism of Holocaust and Redemption, perceived as politics, we turn outward. For the explanation lies in the definition of permissible difference in North America and the place of religion in that difference. Specifically, in North American society, defined as it is by Protestant conceptions, it is permissible to be different in religion, and religion is a matter of what is personal and private. Hence Judaism as a religion encompasses what is personal and familial. The Jews as a political entity then put forth a separate system, one that concerns not religion, which is not supposed to intervene in political action, but public policy. Judaism in public policy produces political action in favor of the State of Israel, or Soviet Jewry, or other important matters of the corporate community.

Judaism in private affects the individual and the family and is not supposed to play a role in politics at all. That pattern conforms to the Protestant model of religion, and the Jews have accomplished conformity to it by the formation of two Judaisms. A consideration of the Protestant pattern, which separates not the institutions of Church from the activities of the state, but the entire public polity from the inner life, will show us how to make sense of the presence of the two Judaisms of North America and in much of Europe as well. I see the reason in a simple misunderstanding of the nature of religion. In Protestant North America people commonly see religion as something personal and private, prayer, for example, therefore speaks for the individual. No wonder, then, that those enchanted words and gestures that, for their part, Jews adopt transform the inner life, recognize life's transitions and turn them into rites of passage. It is part of a larger prejudice that religion and rite speak to the heart of the particular person. What can be changed by rite, then, is first of all personal and private, not social, not an issue of culture, not affective in politics, not part of the public interest.

Liturgy is an act not of sociology but of faith. Still, we who carry out the liturgy live in society and form our religious imagination in the crucible of the here and the now. It is no wonder, then, that, for contemporary Judaism, a religion that is personal and familiar should compete with a religion that is public and corporate. For, in the life of Jews as of Christians and Muslims and Buddhists and others, that is how we receive and live life in this day. Since the life of society is marked by difference, all of us have to find space within our lives for being of more than a single order. And our social experience comes prior to our religious vocation. True, in religion, God made the world. But the religious community – in this case, Israel, the holy people of God – is what consecrates the world. The words of religion – liturgies – do not make religion. Religious people make religion. And, like the builders of the tower of Babel, all they have for mortar is slime.

Part Two
LECTURES ON JUDAISM IN HISTORY

11

Politics and Theology in Talmudic Babylonia

The Rudolph Lecture
Syracuse University, 1969[1]

I

Common to both politics and religion is the question, 'Why should I...?" The predicate contains diverse conclusions: Why should I pay taxes? Why should I obey the law? Why should I believe in God? Why should I keep the Sabbath? Why should I serve in the army? Why should I wait for the Messiah? But in both realms of human society, the claim is made that normative, not merely descriptive, statements may be made *and* enforced. That is to say, one *must* love one's neighbor, one *must* uphold the Constitution.

It is, therefore, quite natural that politicians have made use of religious emotions, myths, and institutions to provide either normative, prescriptive legitimacy for their enterprise, as in the case of societies in which church and state are united, or to gain for political institutions and symbols the charisma forthcoming from religious associations or sentiments, as in the case of societies which separate church and state. "I pledge allegiance," a political action, depends upon "under God," a religious assertion which lends a sanctity the flag otherwise cannot claim.

---

[1]The analysis of Babylonian Jewish politics and theology that follows is based upon my *History of the Jews in Babylonia* (Leiden: E. J. Brill, Studia Post-biblica), I. *The Parthian Period* (1965, 1969); II. *The Early Sasanian Period* (1966); III. *From Shapur I to Shapur II* (1968); IV. *The Age of Shapur II* (1969); V. *Later Sasanian Times* (1970).

If this is obvious, it is equally clear that religious institutions and elites have rarely enjoyed sufficient security to eschew the support of political institutions, including the coercive, this-worldly power to be derived from them. So far as religious institutions have wanted something from people – obedience to a moral code, submission to a set of ritual taboos, confession of a theological creed – those institutions have seldom failed to make use of political means to achieve the works of the spirit. It is, therefore, a reciprocally useful relationship. Both parties need, as I said, to move men, better yet, to provoke men to move themselves through patriotism or through conscience, to conform to the needs of the state or society, on the one hand, or to the imperatives of the divinity and his agencies on the other. Each party contributes – the one worldly force, the other legitimacy "under God" to that force. Both rely upon myth, upon a statement of ultimate reality in highly symbolic form. Whether it is the myth of the state or the myth of the holy nation, the myth of the God, or of the true meaning of meaningless, shapeless events, hardly matters. Since both politics and theology speak of ultimate concerns and make normative demands, they share common convictions of meaning or truth based upon all-embracing myth. This is, I think, why they seem so similar not only in function, but also in structure.

These observations of self-evident facts may lend perspective to the detailed examination of a specific historical example of the complex relationships between church and state – the conflict between two claims of legitimacy in Jewish Babylonia in late antiquity. The specific example has special interest, for in Babylonian Jewry in the first five centuries A.D. it was by no means clear which was church and which was state. All parties expressed their politics in theological terms, and none was divorced from political life. Within Jewry two claims of legitimacy, two justifications of authority, two definitions of the meaning of Israel's history and the way to its salvation competed, on unequal terms to be sure. If in the West church was church and state was state, and people generally knew which was which, in the ancient community of Babylonia such distinctions were hardly so clear.

II

Modern Judaism contains within itself two major theories of authority and legitimacy – Orthodox and Reform. If we approach the past without careful recognition of how we imagine it on the basis of contemporary ideas, we shall distort it more than need be. We begin, therefore, with a brief review of regnant theories of authority in contemporary Judaism.

Legitimacy in Orthodoxy now derives from the latest decisions of the Torah sages. Such sages are men not only pious and learned but also widely accepted as pious and learned, a status partly achieved, but even more conferred, by others. The Torah sages are presumed both to know and to embody the will of God as revealed in the Oral and Written Revelation of Sinai. The Oral Torah is believed to have been handed down from Moses to the prophets, then through various media to the rabbis of the Talmud who put it into writing in talmudic and cognate literature. Afterward others came along to study and apply the law, an endless chain from Sinai to today. For Orthodoxy, therefore, the authority of the law derives from revelation at Sinai. Its practical operation is in the hands not of merely anybody who knows the law, but of the sage who qualifies himself through discipleship in the rabbinical schools and circles, through piety, through the approval of those who have gone before.

When reformer of Judaism sought to achieve changes in the traditional modes of life and thought, they could hardly hope to work within the established patterns of legitimacy, for these were so structured as to prevent articulated, recognized change. Innovation was absolutely prohibited, unless justifiable in terms of tradition. Those in charge of the tradition were selected by a process guaranteeing that innovators would gain entry with difficulty, if at all. New principles of authority and of legitimacy therefore had to be found, or change would connote disintegration. Properly justified, change could be shown to signify the will of God, not merely the outcome of expediency, convenience, or other base motives. Whether in fact the things reformers sought to excise and introduce "really" represented matters of convenience – conformity to a world Jewish men badly wanted to enter – is of no interest here. We must take it for granted that while ordinary folk may have had slight concern for the theological bases for change, they greatly wanted another way. But the elite, the intellectual virtuosi, needed justification; they had to satisfy themselves that they were serving not merely their ordinary human needs or their social aspirations, but the one true God.

Three sorts of theories presented themselves, explored within Reform and Conservative Judaism in Europe and America. The first was the appeal to reason, which meant "common sense." The second was the appeal to the will, to the social reality, of "Catholic Israel," in Schechter's infelicitous term; that is to say, the way the people, universal Israel, do things must be regarded as legitimate, for the "Tradition," often hypostatized, is borne by the community, and the community's way and the traditional *halakhah* – law, or way – cannot be thought to diverge. Social mores were thus raised to the level of normative truth; customs became commandments; ordinary, routine habits not merely achieved, but conferred legitimacy. Change proved acceptable because it had happened.

The third was to appeal to the "golden age" of the faith, to return to the true moment when revelation came forth whole, to measure all things by the heavenly model revealed "in that perfect time." Historians of religion will, of course, recognize what lies before us, namely, a peculiarly modern, postarchaic, and therefore all the more ironic, exemplum of the myth of the eternal return. Reformers in Judaism followed the excellent precedent of reforms in Christianity, based upon the way Jesus had really wanted things or upon the life of the early church. If only we can conform to the reality of that time, we shall achieve not merely "reform," but rather the true state of the tradition. What has happened since, the accretions of time, the conglomerations of profane, often regrettable history – these can be wiped away, cut off in a clean stroke. We can once more achieve true faith, and when we do, final redemption cannot be long postponed. The new messianism produced legitimacy for reform, but only incidentally, for its profound direction was clear: the New Jerusalem. If change was now justified and seemed not merely proper according to social requirement, but called for the will of God properly understood, that was a happy by-product. In 1875 Isaac Mayer Wise, founder of American Reform Judaism, predicted that by 1900 Reform Judaism would be the religion of the greater part of mankind. So grand a vision of the world, so keen a sense of introducing the eschaton, lent remarkable consequence to changes of trivialities.

The golden age was, of course, the age of the prophets, and the part of the prophetic message found truly godly was the part Jews found both reasonable and personally germane: the ethical teachings. Prophetic apocalypse was regarded as inauthentic, unless, as we saw, the prophets were still alive. The demand for justice and lovingkindness, the return to the ethically centered faith of old, a faith without ritualism and with little ritual, without legalism and with only the law of love (which meant, more or less, to do pretty much as you liked, within the limits of the moral apothegmas whose ambiguity no one then articulated) this demand, this proposed return constituted a new theory of legitimacy, a new norm for authenticity, thus a new basis for authority in Judaism. The demand for justice and mercy, moreover, conformed to the needs of European Jewry. Jews were Europe's Negroes, and Germany was their Mississippi or New York. It was only natural to suppose God's primary requirement was to do justice, love mercy, and walk humbly with God, for these were both the opposite of the traits of profane society, and the most necessary requirements for decent life for Jews themselves. God wanted what they required, and had so stated to the prophets; now, by conforming to that imperative, Jews might work not only for themselves, but for the Lord.[2]

III

The competing claims of normative authority, of legitimacy in modern Judaism, serve to set into perspective the religious politics of talmudic Babylonia, for as in the recent past, so in remote times, two fundamentally different theories of authority and legitimacy presented themselves to Jewry. Like those of modern Judaism, both were based upon myth, but the myths were different, if interrelated.

Our frame of reference is Babylonian Jewry in Iranian times, that is, under the Parthian (ca. 240 B.C. to A.D. 226), and Sasanian (A.D. 226-640) dynasties. The community, perhaps half a million people, consisted of the descendants of the Judeans exiled in the early sixth century B.C. Of its culture before the first century A.D. we know practically nothing. We may take it for granted that the Jews revered Jahweh, the Temple in Jerusalem, and the Mosaic law. The community must have possessed its own authoritative traditions on what God expected of them, and those traditions would have consisted of the Law and ad hoc interpretations, presumably by local priests and other sages, of its laws and theology. For the rest, we have no evidence other than the Talmud's anachronistic attribution of a fully articulated rabbinic tradition to Babylonian Jewry from earliest days. Such an attribution presupposes that Moses did indeed receive both an Oral and a Written Torah at Sinai, and that the oral tradition was brought, along with the written one, by the exiles. But we can hardly presuppose the historical part of the Torah myth of rabbinic Judaism and then describe Babylonian Jewry as the rabbis later on would like it to have been from the beginning. In fact, our primary evidence, the Babylonian Talmud, was edited in the sixth century A.D., and its useful data on Babylonian Jewry pertain to the second century A.D. and afterward.

The Babylonian Talmud was, moreover, produced by the rabbis in their academies. Their viewpoint, their records, their interpretation of events predominate to the exclusion of all else. Men in antiquity did not preserve literature they believed to be false. They either allowed it to fall into oblivion, or they revised it to conform to their own ideas of what was right and wrong, of what was worth preserving. The only knowledge independent of a tendentious historical tradition reaching

---

[2]See my "From Theology to Ideology: The Transmutations of Judaism in Modern Times" in *Churches and States. The Religious Institution and Modernization*, ed. K. H. Silvert (New York, 1967), pp. 13-51).

us from antiquity derives from archaeology. But if the texts are equivocal, the stones are silent. (In any case, apart from the Dura synagogue and the magical bowls, we have no pertinent archaeological materials.[3])

It is important to stress the Talmud's limitations as a historical source at the outset, for, as we shall quickly see, its viewpoint on the state of Jewish politics in Babylonia is one-sided indeed. As a historical record, it is approximately comparable to the faculty minutes of Harvard and Yale Universities, the record of some Supreme Court decisions, and the pious "lives" by Parson Weems. On such a basis, our knowledge of American history would not be abundant. What, moreover, should we know of American politics if we had only the platforms of the Democratic National Conventions? And how should we conceive the politics of the Republican Party on the basis of what the Democrats say in their campaign literature?

Two known competing political viewpoints were those of the Babylonian rabbis, represented in the Babylonian Talmud, on the one hand, and of the exilarch, *resh galuta*, recognized by the Iranian government as ruler of the Jewish community, on the other. Of the latter, we know, as I said, only what the rabbis reported. We have no exilarchic account of Babylonian Jewish history. We do not know, except by indirection, how he explained his politics, how he justified his rule, how he won assent from Jewry.

IV

My notion of the rabbis' political theory derives at the outset from a strange story in the Babylonian Talmud (b. Gittin 62a). The story concerns a rabbinical master of the second half of the third century, Geniva, a troublemaker who was finally put to death by the exilarch of the day, Mar 'Uqba:

> R. Huna and R. Hisda were sitting, when Geniva happened by. One said to the other, "Let us arise before him, for he is a master of Torah."
>
> The other said, "Shall we arise before a man of division?"
>
> Meanwhile he came, and said to them, "Peace be unto you, Kings, peace be unto you, Kings."
>
> They said to him, "How do you know that rabbis are called *kings?*"
>
> He said to them, "As it is said, *By me, kings rule*" [Prov. 8:15, referring to wisdom].

---

[3]See my "Archaeology and the Jews of Babylonia." in *Near Eastern Archaeology in the Twentieth Century*, edited by J. A. Sanders (New York, 1970), pp. 331-47.

Politics and Theology in Talmudic Babylonia 199

> "And how do you know that a double greeting is given to kings?"
>
> "As Rav Judah said in the name of Rav, 'How do you know that a double greeting is given to the king? As it is said, *Then the spirit came upon Amasai who was chief of the thirty* [I Chron. 12:18, continuing 'Peace, peace be upon you']."
>
> They said to him, "Would you care for a bite with us?" He replied,....

The story of his trial and execution is as follows (b. Gittin 7a):

> Mar 'Uqba sent to R. Eleazar [ben Pedat], "Men are opposing me, and it is in my power to hand them over to the government. What is to be done?
>
> He drew a line and wrote to him, "*I said, I will take heed to my ways, that I sin not with my tongue, I will keep a curb upon my mouth while the wicked is before me* [Ps. 39:2], that is, even though the wicked is against me, I shall guard my mouth with a muzzle."
>
> Again he said to him, "They are greatly troubling me, and I cannot overcome them."
>
> He replied, "*Resign thyself unto the Lord and wait patiently for him* [Ps. 37:7], that is, wait for the Lord and he will bring them down prostrate before you. Arise early and stay late in the academy, and they will perish of themselves." The matter had scarcely left the mouth of R. Eleazar when they placed Geniva in a collar.[4]

The difficulty Geniva gave the exilarch Mar 'Uqba had something to do with the relationship between the rabbi and the exilarch. Geniva and his party had said or done something the exilarch found extremely irritating, which led the latter, who had no capital jurisdiction over the Jews, to hand him over to the Iranian government. To support its functionary's authority, the Persian regime would properly see to matters.

Since the bulk of Geniva's reported sayings are quite standard rabbinical traditions, it is only the passage on the "double greeting" which provides a hint of what it was he might have done, so to irritate Mar 'Uqba. We may suppose that he had publicly declared something the academic rabbis kept to themselves, namely, that the exilarch, who judged cases according to Persian law, who derived his authority not from knowledge of the rabbinical traditions, but from the support of a heathen government, who collaborated in the affairs of that government – that such a one was not really qualified to administer Jewry's affairs, but that the *rabbis,* who were kings, ought to rule. Such a threat to the exilarch position could have elicited one response only – to put the troublemaker out of the way. Before that

---

[4]That is, he was imprisoned and was being brought out for execution.

time, the exilarch would have encouraged rabbis to keep their distance from Geniva, despite his obvious mastery of Rav's traditions. Indeed, R. Huna, who was Rav's chief student apart from Rav Judah, and R. Hisda, who was Mar 'Uqba's teacher, were well aware of the dangers of associating with the "man of division." Their respect for his learning was tempered by their hesitation to have anything at all to do with him. Geniva for his part responded by quoting traditions deriving from Rav, which they quite obviously did not know. By stressing their being "kings" he meant to point out the egregious quality of the relationship: they should not serve one lesser than themselves. They were rabbis, therefore kings, and Scripture had said so.

V

The viewpoint of the exilarch appears from a saying of one of his rabbinical adherents, Nahman b. Jacob, who lived at the same time as Geniva. He stated (in b. Sanhedrin 98b): "If [the messiah] is among the living, he is such a one as I, as it is said, *And their nobles shall be of themselves and their governors shall proceed from the midst of them* [Jer. 30:21]."

As part of the exilarch, R. Nahman saw himself in an extraordinary light. Jeremiah refers to the time of the Messiah when the fortunes of Jacob will be restored. The restoration would be signified by the Jews' once again governing themselves. So R. Nahman implied that the rule of the exilarchate certified, and might in time mark the fulfillment of that particular messianic promise. Such a saying reflects the political theology of the exilarch. Being both scion of David and recognized governor of the Jews, the exilarch represented fulfillment of the prophetic hopes for the restoration of a Jewish monarch of the Davidic line. Hence his rule was legitimate and should be obeyed. R. Nahman's citation of Jeremiah provides one of our few glimpses into the way the exilarch explained his rule to the Jews. It shows not merely Persian approval and support, but a wholly proper basis in Jewish geneology and history provided the theoretical foundation of his power. By contrast, not Davidic overlordship, but obedience to the Torah, the rabbis held, would signify the advent of messianic rule.

The Davidic origins of the exilarch were first referred to in the time of Judah the Prince, patriarch of Palestinian Jewry at the end of the second century A.D. Judah asked R. Hiyya, a Babylonian who was probably related to the exilarch (in b. Horayot 11b):

> Rabbi [Judah the Prince] inquired of R. Hiyya, "Is one like myself to bring a hegoat [as a sin-offering of a ruler, according to Lev. 4:23]?
>
> "You have your rival in Babylonia," he replied.

"The kings of Israel and the kings of the house of David," he objected, "bring sacrifices independently of one another."

"There," Hiyya replied, "they were not subordinate to one another. Here is [in Palestine] we are subordinate to them [in Babylonia]."

T. Safra taught thus: Rabbi inquired of R. Hiyya, "Is one like me to bring a hegoat?"

"There is the sceptre, here is only the law giver, as it was taught, *The sceptre shall not depart from Judah*, refers to the Exilarch in Babylonia who rules Israel with the sceptre, *nor the ruler's staff between his feet* [Gen. 49:10] refers to the grandchildren of Hillel who teach the Torah to Israel in Public."

The reference to Gen. 49:10, *The sceptre shall not depart from Judah*, is striking, for it shows that the Davidic claim was tied to the exercise of political authority. So far as the Palestinians were concerned, the exilarch's claim was taken as fact.

VI

The rabbis believed that, along with the Written Torah, God had revealed to Moses at Mount Sinai an oral, unwritten Torah, which had been preserved and handed on from prophets to sages, and finally to rabbis. Israel's life was to be shaped by divine revelation. The rabbis alone knew the full configuration of the will of God. Their claim to rule rested upon that conviction. It thus clashed with the consequence, phrased in equally theological terms, drawn by the exilarch from the belief that he was qualified to rule because he was descended from the seed of David. Moreover, rabbinic political authority ran counter to the widespread conviction of Jews that anyone holding political power over them had better be able to claim Davidic ancestry. The rabbis, by contrast, authenticated *their* claim not only by their teaching of Torah, but also by their knowledge of the secrets of creation, including the names of God by which miracles may be produced, the mysteries of astrology, medicine, and practical magic, as well as by their day-to-day conduct as a class of religious virtuosi and illuminati. They eagerly recruited students for their schools who would join with them in the task of studying the "whole Torah," and go forth afterward to exemplify, and, where feasible, enforce its teaching among the ordinary people. They were seeking totally to reform the life of Israel to conform to the Torah as they taught it. They believed that when Israel would live according to the will of "their father in heaven," then no nation or race could rule over them, but the Anointed of God would do so. History as a succession of pagan empires would come to an end. Israel would live in peace in its own land. An endless age of prosperity on account of Israel's reconciliation with God would follow. So the issues were not inconsiderable.

"How do you know that rabbis are called kings?" The reply is, "Scripture says, 'By me kings rule'." Such was not the view of the exilarch, who wanted it to be believed that he ruled because he was an heir of David, and indeed exercised more direct control of the Jewish community than the Palestinian patriarch. It is worth quoting the entire passage to which Geniva made reference:

> By me kings rule,
>   and rulers decree what is just;
> By me princes rule,
>   and nobles govern the earth.

This passage was part of a key prooftext for the rabbinical schools, for in it, "Torah," which they believed they alone properly expounded, is described as the beginning of the works of creation, as the foundation for right politics and the sole source of righteousness, justice, knowledge. Torah came before creation, and provided the design for the world. The chapter (Prov. 8:34-6) closes,

> Happy is the man who listen to me
>   watching daily at my gates,
>   waiting beside my doors.
> For he who finds me finds life,
> and obtains favor from the Lord;
> But he who misses me injures himself;
>   all who hate me love death.

It was far more than a matter of power politics. When the rabbis read a reference to the gates and doors of Torah, they knew what it meant, namely, the gates of *their* academies, and none other.

The crux of the matter was, as had been stated, how was redemption to be gained? The rabbis believed it was through a legal reformation of Israel. The exilarch and his relative thought differently, for R. Nahman supposed that their Davidic connection ought to prove sufficient in time to produce a messiah, even in their own day, if God willed it. Redemption would proceed from the academies, or it would come from the Davidites, but the two were mutually exclusive: "All who hate me love death." The exilarchs were seen by their enemies to "hate me," namely, "Torah." Beyond the concrete issues of the day, the question of redemption smouldered in the shadows, lending eschatological significance to a politics which was, from our perspective, concerned with trivialities. "Torah" was central in the redemptive process; a legal reformation would effect "Torah" and so bring about the Messiah's coming. Had the exilarch subordinated himself to the academies and accepted their direction – as the academicians later said he did – the potential conflict between the conflicting legacies might never have been realized.

But the exilarch had a powerful claim too. He was of David's seed, and from him, or one of his relatives, would come the Messiah. That claim was probably far older and better established in the mind of Babylonian Jewry than the rabbis', and for far better reasons. The exilarch had no reason to subordinate himself to the academy, and he had very good reason not to.

VII

Which was church, and which was state? From the rabbis' perspective, it is clear that the exilarch was a merely political figure, by they were endowed with the sanctity deriving from Torah, revelation. So they would, in modern terms, have called themselves "the church," and the exilarch was "the state." And – "by me, kings rule." But the exilarch's viewpoint could not have conformed to theirs. So far as he was concerned, his rule was as the surrogate of the Messiah, indeed the best assurance that the Messiah would one day come – and would come from his own household. Israel was not rejected of God so long as she governed herself, and the exilarch's present rule was therefore proof of the continued validity of the covenant, of the enduring messianic hope. The sceptre had *not* departed from Judah. The exilarch was *not* a secular authority. He claimed to descend from David, to be the link between the rule of David in the ideal past and the rule of David in the ideal future. The Torah-myth thus came into conflict with the Messiah-myth as the exilarch expounded it.

Nor can we say that the exilarch, a "merely political figure," was alone in making use of a religious myth for political purposes. The rabbis too sought to control political institutions – the courts and administrative agencies of Babylonian Jewry. They wanted to make use of those political institutions for religious purposes, that is, to coerce ordinary Jews to conform to the Torah as they taught it. Theirs was, therefore, a partially political aspiration.

In truth, both parties claimed to be "the church" *and therefore to be the state also.* No distinction was recognized between politics and religion. If one ruled, it was because God wanted him to do so. If another obeyed, he obeyed heaven, revelation, not merely the arbitrary fiat of a temporarily powerful individual. Society should be governed by God's law; on this, everyone agreed. The only issue was, who knows that law? And who is the one to interpret and apply it? Political argument was phrased in theoretical language, and only by accepting the claim of one party and rejecting that of the other are we able to describe one as "the church," the other as "the state."

Political theory obviously was subsumed under the eschatological, messianic issue: how is Israel to be saved? The rabbis' answer was phrased by R. Papa toward the end of the fourth century. He said, "When the high-handed disappear from Israel, then the Magi will cease [among the Iranians]. When the judges cease to exist in Israel, the *gezirpati* [gendarmes] will cease to exist [among the Iranians]."[5] R. Papa's saying was based upon Zephaniah 3:15, *The Lord has taken away the judgments against you, he has cast out your enemies. The King of Israel, the Lord, is in your midst, you shall fear evil no more.* Zephaniah's statement is in the prophetic present: these things come about, the Messiah is here. R. Papa transformed an unconditional promise into a conditional one: only when the one happens will the other come about.

We do not, by contrast, know the exilarch's answer. He certainly expected that some day the Lord would send the Messiah, raising him up out of the house of the exilarch, related as it was to the Davidic family. I suspect that theory, a commonplace one, represented the older political view of Babylonian, as well as Palestinian, Jewry. Redemption would come in God's own time, through David's descendant. Anyone who presumed to exercise political authority over Jews had best begin with a claim to derive from the Davidic household. We know that Davidic ancestry was alleged in fact by practically every important Jewish figure in the political life of the late antiquity, including the Hasmoneans, Jesus, the Hillelite family in Palestine, the exilarch – even Herod!

In Iranian culture, it was similarly conventional to claim to be an heir of the Achemenids. The Parthians did so, not at the outset of their rule, but only when they found that military superiority no longer could sustain the Arsacid throne. Then, in the first century, they announced they were descended from the Achemenids.[6] The Sasanians likewise stated from the very outset they were heirs of the Achemenids. They held the Parthians were illegitimate. The Sasanians were the

---

[5]Babylonian Talmud, Sanhedrin 98a.
[6]See my "Parthian Political Ideology," *Iranica Antiqua* III, i: 40-59; Jósef Wolski, "The Decay of the Iranian Empire of the Seleucids and the Chronology of Parthian Beginnings," *Berytus* XII, i (1956-57); 35-52; his critique of Elias J. Bickerman's "Notes on Seleucid and Parthian Chronology," *Berytus* VIII, ii (1944): 79-83. On the Sasanians, Richard N. Frye, *Heritage of Persia* (New York, 1963), pp. 198ff. The *Kar Namak* of Ardashit, among other sources, states that Sasan was a shepherd, descendant of the Achemenids. On the Davidic claim in general, Y. Liver, *Toledot Bet David* (Jerusalem, 1959).

restorers of the ancient, rightful dynasty of Iran. In fact, therefore, the claim to be descended from a remote, glorious emperor was a widespread political convention in the time. What was strikingly unconventional was the rabbis' Torah myth and its political expression.

It apparently was not enough for anyone to claim to rule because he had power, because he was wise, because custom dictated it. Jewish politics revolved around the messianic issue. Others could obey because it was expedient or merely necessary, but Jews would listen only to the Messiah's surrogate, obey only the word of God. In the humblest details of daily conduct they sought significance of a grand, metahistorical dimension. Ruling no state like other states, Jewry entered a fantasy world in which what they did control was believed to possess far greater significance, despite its worldly triviality, than even the deeds of great and impressive empires held by others: "Others are ruled by the court of Ctesiphon, by the king of kings. We obey the king of kings of kings, the Holy One." The debate centered, therefore, on what obedience to God entailed, as I said, whether God's will was contained in the Torah of the rabbis or whether it was expressed through the rule of the exilarch, the scion of David. Theology imposed itself on politics because, I imagine, theology was all the Jews had left to render their politics worthwhile.

VIII

The two parties were not originally in conflict with one another. On the contrary, the exilarch probably fostered the growth of the rabbinical movement in Babylonia, and did so with good reason.

The exilarchate began to function effectively in the second half of the first century. Whether it was older than that – dating back to the time of Jehoiachin at the beginning of the sixth century B.C., as was commonly believed – we cannot say. But the only concrete information we have about the politics of first-century A.D. Babylonian Jewry omits all reference to an exilarch, even while discussing important matters in which an exilarch, if there was one, would have been involved. During the time of troubles of the first half of the first century, when one Parthian pretender after another seized the throne, Babylonia, like the rest of the Parthian empire, enjoyed no secure government at all. Josephus tells the story of two Jewish brothers, Anilai and Asinai, who in the chaotic times seized power in central Babylonia, ruling not only the Jewish communities but the whole area.[7] They set up their own government which lasted for nearly two decades.

---

[7] Antiquities XVIII, 310-79.

The time of troubles began to abate with the rise of Vologases I. While the indecisive struggle between Parthia and Rome, ending in about 65 A.D., may have weakened his government, it appears that a number of constructive efforts must have curbed the power of the nobles and established a secure frontier with both Rome and Armenia (Roman preoccupation in Palestine from 66-73 was a factor), for Vologases I achieved something unknown in Parthia for more than half a century: he held power through several decades and avoided both foreign disasters and internal strife. His foundation of Vologasia, near Seleucia-Ctesiphon, doubtless greatly assisted the expansion of the silk trade with the east, on the one hand, and Palmyra on the other, and the increasingly profitable trade probably provided new financial resources for the throne.

If the story of the Jewish "baronry" in and around Nehardea is historical (and there is no reason to doubt it), then the central government must have had to give considerable attention to the government of this numerous ethnic minority. The very position of the great areas of Jewish settlement required it, for the Jews formed a large segment of the settled population around the winter capital of Ctesiphon, the Greek city of Seleucia, and the new emporium at Vologasia. The Jewish population surrounding the heart of the empire must be suitably governed. From the events of ca. A.D. 20-36, it must have been clear to the reforming administration that Jews in Babylonia were not adequately governed.

What choices were open to the Arsacid authorities? They could, of course, ignore the problem, and allow events to take their course in the Jewish territories and settlements. This was manifestly unsatisfactory. They could, second, attempt to include the government of the Jewish ethnic groups within the territorial sovereignties of other places. The Jews about Seleucia could have been under the Greek authorities of that city (as doubtless those *in* the city itself were). But this course of action would have been unsatisfactory for three reasons. First, the Greek cities were not the regime's most loyal adherents. Second, the Jews and Greeks got on no better, according to Josephus's narrative, than they did in Alexandria. Third, the Jewish settlements were too extensive for incorporation into surrounding political units, while at the same time they were not sufficiently compact or concentrated to form a separate unit (this appears from the Greek massacre of Jews after the fall of the Asinai-Anilai barony). An ideal solution would have been the establishment among the Jews in Babylonia of an *ethnic* authority of their own, like that which probably existed after the destruction of the first temple in Babylonian and in Achemenid times.

If such an authority could develop and win the loyalty of the Jewish population to the Arsacid regime, then the Parthian government would accomplish three useful purposes. First, it would assure an effective government in the Jewish villages and towns and over Jewish minorities in the Greek and Iranian settlements. Second, it would secure the peace of strategically vital territories near the capital. Third, in time it might make use of the authority so constituted for its foreign policy, by exploiting the Jewish authority's connections with Jews in Roman Palestine. There is every evidence that some Jews in Palestine and throughout the upper Mesopotamian valley did act in a manner favorable to Parthian interests at a number of crucial points in the second century, particularly in the time of Trajan's invasion in 116-18, the war against Antoninus Pius and Marcus Aurelius in 161-65, and against Sevus Alexander in 193-200. It would have been very much in the interest of the Parthian government, in its period of reorganization under Vologases I and afterward, to found, or to encourage and support the foundation of, a Jewish ethnarch, exilarch, in Babylonia.

A further factor likely played a part in Parthian consideration of the Jews' administration. The destruction of the Temple in Jerusalem in 70 posed a serious problem to the Parthian government. In former times, Babylonian Jewry, like that in other parts of the diaspora, was loyal to the Temple. Pilgrims went up to Jerusalem, and Temple collections of a half-*sheqel* were gathered regularly in Nehardea, in the south, and in Nisibis, in the north, and forwarded in armed caravans to the Temple. The Temple authorities, for their part, sent letters to Babylonia, as did the pharisaic party, to advise the Jews on matters of calendric regulation and other religious issues. After the destruction, the authority of the Temple was assumed by the remnants of the pharisaic party at Yavneh, where, with Roman approval, the powers formerly exercised by the Temple administration became vested in R. Yohanan ben Zakkai and R. Gamaliel II after him. The Parthians enjoyed the services of an excellent intelligence bureau, and must have known that the Palestinian Jewish authority would no longer be exercised by quasi-independent officials, but would be very closely supervised by the Romans.

If the Parthians had been willing to allow a limited, and on the whole politically neutral, authority to be exerted from the Jerusalem Temple over their subjects, they would never permit such authority to be exerted by a Roman functionary. Quite to the contrary, just as the Romans sought to mobilize Jewish support and to use Jewish officials for their own purposes, so the Parthians exploited the fact that within their hereditary enemy's territories flourished a large religious-ethnic group with strong ties across the Euphrates and a deep sense of grievance against Rome. They always tried to foment unrest among minority groups within the Roman Empire. The Romans, for their part, were keenly aware of the danger of leaving substantial ethnic groups to straddle their borders; for this reason they invaded Britain and attempted to retain Armenia in the preceding century and a half. They were, moreover, deeply concerned about Jewish public opinion in Parthia, and therefore hired Josephus to convey their view of war guilt to the Jews across the Euphrates.

Although the evidence that the exilarchate was actually created at this time is slight, it ought not to be ignored. first, Josephus's narrative contains no hint of an indigenous Jewish authority in Jewish areas of Babylonia before A.D. 40. On the contrary, the silence of Josephus on this point is made very striking indeed by his testimony about how the Jews actually *were* governed at this time, namely, by Asinai and Anilai. If there *was* an exilarch between A.D. 20 and 40, there is no evidence that that fact mattered in the slightest. He certainly did not exert any authority or affect events in any way.

There is, however, some evidence that after 70 A.D. an exilarchic line was founded. This evidence appears in the list of exilarchs of the *Seder 'Olam Zuta*. Among those from the time of the first destruction of Jerusalem to 70 A.D., the *Seder 'Olam Zuta* preserves no names or traditions worth taking seriously, and one may conclude that its eighth-century author had no reliable information on the subject. But its list after 70 includes names that are attested in other sources. The text gives the names as follows:

> And at this time Shemaiah died. And there arose after him Shekhenaiah his son, who is the tenth generation of Jehoiachin the King at the time of the destruction of the Second Temple....Shekheniah died and Hezekiah his son arose, Hezekiah died and was buried in the land of Israel in the valley of Arabella in the east of the city. 'Aqov his son arose. 'Aqov died and Nahum his son arose after him. There were sages with him, their names being Rav Huna and Rav Hiunena, Rav Matennah and Rav Hananel. Nahum died. After him arose Yohanan his brother, son of 'Aqov. His sage was Rav Hananel. Yohana died. After him arose Shefet his son. Shefet died. 'Anan his son arose. When 'Anan died Nathan remained in his mother's womb. He is Nathan of Zuzita, *Rosh Golah* [exilarch]. Nathan died. After him arose Rav Huna his son. Rav and Samuel were his sages.[8]

---

[8]See W. Bacher, "Exilarch," *Jewish Encyclopedia* V: 288-93; Felix Lazarus, *Die Häuper der Vertriebenen*, in *Jahrbücher für jüdische Geschichte*, 1890; S.W. Baron, *The Jewish Community* (Philadelphia, 1942), I, 68-69, 145-50, 173-86, 192-93, III, 12, n. 12. The list of exilarchs before 70 is obvious a *midrash* of some kind

Since Rav and Samuel date from the end of the Arsacid period, we may conclude that the above list covers the period from ca. 70 A.D. to ca. 226. Without examining the list in detail, we may suggest that at least some of the names on it, particularly Nahum and Huna, find support in earlier sources, and that the tradition recorded in *Seder 'Olam Zuta* may well imply the beginning of sound information on an actual institution sometime in the latter half of the first century.

The exilarchate in Parthian Babylonia, like the patriarchate in Roman Palestine, was the most convenient means to manage a potentially useful ethnic group's affairs at home and to exploit its connection abroad. It was, as I said, most certainly a way of annulling whatever influence Jewish functionaries of Rome might exert over Babylonian Jewry, by providing an alternate, home-born authority, supported and closely supervised by the government. Both the exilarch and patriarch were backed up by imperial troops, R. Judah having a detachment of Goths at his command, the exilarch an armed retinue, and both eventually achieved great spiritual influence over their respective Jewish communities. Both were created in part because of the destruction of Jerusalem: the patriarchate as a means of governing internal Jewish affairs in which the Romans had no special interest and at the same time of keeping the peace in Palestine; the exilarchate to do the same in Babylonia. At the same time both were intended to prevent aliens from influencing Jews under their control, and themselves to exert malevolent influence across the frontier where possible.

In the second century, the exilarchate developed into a powerful instrument of government with its agents enjoying the perquisites of the Iranian nobility. It inflicted the death penalty and governed the Jews by its own lights, enforcing its judgment with military force when it

---

on I Chronicles 3. But the names afterward begin to make sense. Jacob Liver, *Toledot Bet David*, pp. vi, viii, 141-47, and 28-46, discusses the uselessness of the earlier traditions, but he does not reject those relating to the period after A.D. 70. On the contrary, he holds (p. 44) that the data on the two or three generations before Rav Huna are of some value. He notes (p. 147) that the Davidic claim was a post-factum effort to legitimize authority held already, parallel to the Achemenid claim of the Arsacids. If so, the claim would have been advanced ca. 50-150 A.D., for by the time of R. Judah the prince and R. Hiyya it is spoken of with great respect. This was approximately the same time that the Arsacids themselves were publicizing their Achemenid genealogy. Baron holds that the failure of Josephus to mention this office is not conclusive, as it affords at best an *argumentum e silentio*. But Josephus is not silent at all about the inner life of the Jewish community in Babylonia at this period. See also S. Funk, *Die Juden in Babylonien* (Vienna, 1910), I: 31-41; Y. I. Halevy, *Dorot Ha Rishonim*, II: 246-52. Lazarus discusses the phrase about the scholars at the side of the exilarch, pp. 16-17. It is likely to be an echo of a later polemic.

chose. If the several Jewish revolts against Rome, at times highly propitious from the Parthian viewpoint, were in fact instigated by its agents, and if the support given to the Arsacid throne in the crisis of Trajan's invasion was, in a measure, the result of exilarchic influence, then the Parthians must have judged the exilarch to be a great success indeed. By the end of the second century, the exilarch R. Huna was regarded with a mixture of respect and apprehension in Palestine, where his claim to Davidic ancestry in the male line, superior to R. Judah's allegedly in the female line, was recognized. Among the Jews and Parthians alike, the exilarchate played a major political and administrative role.

IX

The Babylonian Jews' first contact with the pharisaic-rabbinic movement *may* have antedated the Bar Kokhba War by a century, but the movement first established its characteristic institution, the rabbinical academy, during the war. Refugee sages, fleeing the terrible struggle and its aftermath, settled in Babylonia. The school of R. Ishmael probably remained. What is of interest to us is the exilarch's relationship to the rabbis. It is clear that Nathan, son of the exilarch, was sent to school under rabbinical auspices, and later continued his studies in the Palestinian schools as well. Several other Babylonians in the Palestinian schools, including R. Hiyya and his sons and his nephew Rav, were probably related to the exilarch. The evidence thus points to the existence of a few Tannaim *from* Babylonia, and a few others *in* Babylonia, in the second century. Generally those who lived *in* Babylonia were colleagues or disciples of R. 'Aqiba and R. Ishmael before the Bar Kokhba War. Those who came *from* Babylonia were normally exilarchic relatives. When law teachers came to Babylonia, the exilarch must have provided the means for conducting law schools, just as he had sent his son, and was to send his relatives later, to study in the Palestinian schools of the same sort.

The development of tannaitic Judaism in Babylonia, therefore, was probably encouraged by the exilarch in his effort to secure well-trained officials. How shall we account for the prorabbinical sentiment of the exilarch? I suggest that the exilarch must have had to contend with other Jewish authorities, such as powerful local figures like Anilai and Asinai. These potentially dangerous competitors for the rule of Jewry were seen to be "assimilated" to Parthian culture. Babylonian Jewish officials such as Arda, Arta, and Pil-y Barish[9] were "Parthian" in many ways, though very good lawyers. They were upper-class Jews who possessed wealth and influence, much as did the exilarch himself. One good way of circumventing their influence over the ordinary Jews, who could have had much less contact with Parthian politics, court life, and, therefore, general culture, would have been to present the exilarch himself as the protagonist of the ancient tradition of Moses against the Iranized Jewish elite competing with him for power.

The ancient tradition of Moses was pretty much what one wanted it to be. But how to establish such a public "image"? How better than to associate oneself with the Palestinian rabbis, whose prestige had been rising ever since the destruction of the Temple, and who could send disciplined, learned, and charismatic rabbis to serve the exilarch, build his administration, and bolster his claim? Those rabbis, alleging themselves knowledgeable in the Mosaic law and accredited with wonderful powers over nature, were believed to be holy men. They thus could lend prestige to the peculiar political claim of the exilarch.[10] Against such holy men, what could local strong men, powerful upper-class leaders offer? If, as I have suggested, the exilarchate was a relatively new institution, and if the Parthian government, which created it, was unable because of the terrible invasions and unsettled domestic conditions of the second century to provide necessary support, then the exilarch would have had his hands full simply establishing his preeminence over other, older kinds of local Jewish authorities. The Palestinian rabbis, as well as those Babylonians who might be trained by them, provided a ready and inviting means of setting up an effective and "legitimate" administration.

The rabbis thus served to enhance the legitimacy of the exilarchate, by providing stronger theological foundations for the exilarch's political power and by attesting to the validity of his claim to be descended from David. Their learning, holiness, and magical powers won the assent of ordinary people to their legal and exegetical doctrines. They were useful to the exilarch, for they could give him what he lacked, both a means of influencing the ordinary people and a source of administrative talent and local leadership. For their part,

---

[9]These are "Parthianized" Jewish officials who made trouble for Palestinian rabbis in mid-second century Babylonia, see b. Gittin 14a-b; Neusner, *History*, Vol. I, 2nd ed., pp. 94-97.
[10]On the rabbis as holy men, see my "The Phenomenon of the Rabbi in Late Antiquity," *Numen* XVI, i (1969): 1-20; and "The Ritual of 'Being a Rabbi' in Later Sasanian Times," *Numen* XVII (1970): 1-18.

the rabbis were prepared to collaborate with any political leader who would give them power over Jewry to achieve their religious program. Together the rabbis and exilarch might outweigh the competing, centrifugal forces constituted by older, local grandees of various sorts and in various places.

By the turn of the third century, the tannaitic movement in Babylonia included a few local authorities, such as the father of Samuel in Nehardea, and a larger number of trained and authorized representatives. It hardly dominated Babylonian Jewish life and posed no threat whatever to the exilarch, who made use of Tannaim for his purposes and was probably glad to have more of them. The exilarch must have provided the chief source of financial support for the schools and of employment for their graduates. He was equally eager to accept the credentials of Palestine-trained rabbis, and to authorize newcomers to serve in his system of courts as lawyers, judges, and communal administrators.

The exilarch, moreover, was particularly anxious to employ men who who apply in Babylonia the newly promulgated Mishnah just now issued in Palestine by the patriarch, Judah the Prince. Whatever old traditions and ad hoc decisions existed in Babylonia, the new Mishnah, based upon a viable and supple exegetical method, organized according to logical categories, and, most important, advertised as the very will of God revealed along with the Written Torah by God to Moses at Mount Sinai and transmitted from that time to the present by faithful prophets, sages, and rabbis, had an irresistible appeal. Still a relatively new institution, the exilarchate must have been glad to associate with itself and its administration so grand a prestige as accrued to the Mishnah in the minds of those who accepted the pharisaic-rabbinical claim.

Among these were the exilarch's own son, his relatives, and others close to him. He, too, was therefore probably a believer. The exilarch claimed to be of the seed of David. How better to win the loyalty and conformity of ordinary people than to couple that claim with the equally impressive one: "In the Jewish courts we at least apply not merely the scattered, though hoary, traditions of our forefathers of the *golah*, but the whole revelation of Sinai itself." In the decades after the revelation and promulgation of the Mishnah by the patriarch in Palestine, the exilarch gladly accepted its authority, and therefore hired men who would apply it – under *exilarchic* auspices to be sure. The tannaitic movement, small and possessing little influence and authority in Babylonia to begin with, received the enthusiastic backing of the exilarch, who had earlier sent representatives to the Palestinian schools. Whatever other schools there were must have either ceased to exist or have begun to teach the Mishnah and its accompanying traditions, exegetical methods, and rules.

The Tannaim responded in kind by ruling that it was only with the authorization of the exilarch that one might judge cases in Jewish Babylonia. "Authorization" in rabbinic discourse meant actual bureaucratic appointment by the exilarch, and so an alliance was forged between the rabbinate, needing political support, and the exilarch, requiring prestigious and qualified functionaries.

One recalls the parallel policy of the Safavids of the sixteenth and seventeenth centuries. Coming to power as sectarian enthusiasts, the Safavids assembled doctors of the Shi'ite law from their places of refuge in the Moslem world in the time of Ismail Safavi (ca. A.D. 1500). As W. H. McNeill describes it:

> Not surprisingly, it proved easier for the court and the Shi'a doctors to agree upon what should be suppressed than upon details of positive doctrine. The shahs were reluctant to surrender any of their prerogative, even to men of religion; and Shi'a purists found it hard to forgive the remaining imperfections of even the most sympathetic regime....Acquiring a reputation for miraculous powers and familiarity with God's will, these Shi'a doctors attained great influence over the people at large, until their opinions came to constitute a fairly effective check upon the actions of the shah himself.[11]

It would be difficult to find a better analogy to what was about to happen in Jewish Babylonia. The exilarch assembled, encouraged, and gave great powers to the doctors of pharisaic-rabbinic law, which was, according to the rabbis, to be the only law of Judaism. The learning, charisma, and magical powers of the rabbis rendered them ever more influential over ordinary people, so that by the beginning of the fourth century, the exilarch found himself with a diminishing range of powers and options, ever more narrowly hemmed in by rabbinical influence, which was, by nature, inimical to his.

X

The practical conflict between the exilarch and rabbis may best be described in terms of an issue debated in the early fourth century: Do rabbis pay taxes?

The exilarch imposed taxes, divided them among Jews of various towns and groups, collected, and transmitted them to the state on specified occasions. It would hardly enhance his authority if he could not impose his will upon everyone, including the rabbis. Choosing to make the payment of the poll tax the decisive issue, the rabbis

---

[11] *The Rise of the West* (New York, 1965), p. 679.

asserted that they were not like other Jews, but formed a special class, which should not be subjected either to the authority of the exilarch or to the control of the state. It was the rabbis who raised the issue for reasons of their own. For his part, the exilarch saw no reason to change the status quo of two centuries' standing.

Why did rabbis choose just this time to claim they did not have to pay taxes? In part, the reason was that they were convinced they had no other correct course, and in part the time seemed promising. From Shapur I's death in 273 to the end of the minority of Shapur II in about 325, the central government was distracted by, among other things, disastrous foreign wars, the suppression of the Manichaens, dynastic struggles every few years, and finally the centrifugal effects of the weak regency. When Shapur II came to power, his attention was drawn to international and military issues. The Sasanian government in his time never paid the Jews much attention, so long as the revenues were forthcoming, and nothing subversive happened. Both conditions were met. The rabbis' subversion was not directed at the Sasanian government. So long as the full quota of head taxes was paid, it hardly mattered to the state who actually paid them or who did not. Greater affairs of state must have occupied not only Shapur, who certainly was not consulted on trivialities such as these, but also the ministers of Ctesiphon. The Jewish question was a local matter without much consequence, Had they seen otherwise, the ministers of Shapur would have been perfectly well prepared to investigate antigovernment activity and punish those they thought guilty. The same satraps and Mobads who tortured the Christian monks and nuns, priests, bishops, and laity of Babylonia and Adiabene for not paying taxes were quite capable of persecuting the rabbis, if not the Jews as a group, had they thought it useful to the security of the state. They did nothing of the sort and I suppose they saw no reason to. Once the great persecution against the Christians began, moreover, the exilarch could hardly have called for aid to those whose capacities for bloody mischief now stood fully revealed. Had he asked for state aid in suppressing the rabbinate as a class, he would have embittered the ordinary Jews against himself, and the record of rabbinical martyrdoms, accompanied by the conventional miracles done by both heavenly messengers and earthly saints, would have rendered him totally distasteful to common folk. Under normal circumstances ordinary people might have supported him, but not in a time of the martyrdom of a few particularly holy men. It seems to me, therefore, that the exilarch at first was unwilling, and then quite unable, to enlist the powers of the state. And the state, unknowing and uninterested, paid attention to quite different matters. Still, in such a circumstance it was a chancy thing. The rabbis took that chance.[12]

The exilarch was perfectly well prepared to grant unusual favors to the rabbis as an estate. They had special privileges at court; they were given advantages in marketing their produce. The exilarch was quoted as instructing Rava to see whether a certain man, claiming rabbinical status and therefore privilege, was really a scholar. If so, Rava was to reserve a market privilege for him, so that he might sell his produce before others.[13] Since the rabbis staffed exilarchic courts, it was certainly advantageous to protect them.

The rabbis' claim to be exempt from the poll tax, or *karga*,[14] was quite another matter. The exilarch could not exempt rabbis from the poll tax, for he would have had to make up the deficit himself. One of the principal guarantees of continued peace for the Jewish community was the efficient collection of taxes, which was the responsibility of the exilarch. All he could do was to shift the burden of taxes to others, so that the rabbis' share would devolve upon ordinary Jews. He naturally was not ready to do so, and I do not think ordinary people would have wanted him to. The tax rates were so high that poor people struggled to find the money to pay them. References abound to people's selling their property, or themselves into slavery, to raise the necessary money. The state was not prepared to compromise, for on its part it simply could not afford to do so. War was necessary to protect its territory, including first and foremost Babylonia itself. Armies cost money. Everyone must help pay, particularly those who lived in so rich and fertile a region. Moreover, those living closest to the capital were least able to evade the taxes. So the exilarch could hardly accede to the rabbis' demand. The Persians would not allow it; the ordinary Jews could not afford it.

The rabbis' claim of tax exemption was phrased in comments upon Scripture. They were certain that from most ancient times, rabbis were not supposed to pay taxes, and it would be a transgression of scriptural precedent if they now did so. Rava held that King Asa was punished simply because he imposed forced labor (*'ngry'*) on the sages of his day, citing the following Scripture, "Then King Asa made a proclamation to all Judah; *none* was exempted" (I Kings 15:22).[15]

---

[12]On the control of the schools, Neusner, *History*, Vol. IV, pp. 91-100, 119-24.
[13]B. Bava Batra 22a.
[14]See George Widengren, "The Status of the Jews in the Sasanian Empire," *Iranica Antiqua* I (1961): 149-53.
[15]B. Sotah 10a.

Rava's comment was merely a warning. A more positive claim was made by R. Nahman b. Isaac (b. Bava Batra 8A):

> R. Nahman b. R. Hisda applied the head tax to the sages.
>
> R. Nahman b. Isaac said to him, "You have transgressed against the teaching of the Torah, the Prophets, and the Writings. Against the Torah, as it is written, *Although he loves the people, all his saints are in your hand...* [Deut. 33:3].
>
> "Against the Prophets, as it is written, *Even when they study* [lit.: give] *among the nations, now I shall gather them, and a few of them shall be free from the burden of king and princes* [Hosea 8:10].
>
> ['Ulla said, this verse is said in the Aramaic language, 'If they all study, now I shall gather them, and if a few of them study, they shall be free from the burden of king and princes.']
>
> "Against the writings, as it is written, *It shall not be lawful to impose upon them [priests and Levites] minda, belo, and halakh* [Ezra 7:24], and Rav Judah explained, '*Minda* means the portion of the king, *belo* is the poll tax, and *halakh* is the *'annona'*.'"

The several Scriptures are not of equal weight. The passage in Deuteronomy suggests that "his saints," who, the rabbis thought, were rabbis, were in God's hand. Therefore, they do not require the protection of walls or armies and should not have to pay for them. Likewise Rav Judah had said that everyone must contribute to the building of doors for the town gates except rabbis, who do not require protection.[16]

The meaning of the passage in Hosea is quite clear: when the Jews study the Torah among the gentiles (i.e., in Babylonia), a few should not have to pay taxes, and these, quite obviously, are the rabbis, 'Ulla's comment changes the eschatological sense of the verse, but the prooftext is clear as it stands. The citation from Ezra explicitly states that priests do not have to pay the "portion of the king" or the poll tax. What was not made explicit, because everyone in the schools knew it, is that the rabbis believed they had inherited the rights and privileges of the priesthood, since study of Torah was not equivalent to the priestly offerings in Temple times. Therefore, according to Artaxerxes' order reported by Ezra, rabbis do not have to pay the head tax. This was quite explicit in Scripture, and beyond question. Even the Iranian government should not impose the poll tax on them, they supposed. The following saying of Rava is extraordinary (b. Nedarim 62b):

> Rava said, "It is permitted for a rabbinical disciple to say, 'I will not pay the poll tax,' as it is written, *It shall not be lawful to impose minda,*

---

[16] B. Bava Batra 8a.

belo, or halakh [Ezra 7:24], and Rav Judah said, '*Minda* is the king's portion, *belo* is the poll tax, and *halakh* is the corvée'."

Rava moreover stated, "A rabbinical disciple is permitted to say, 'I am a servant of fire and do not pay the poll tax'." What is the reason? It is only said in order to drive away a lion.

Rava's remarkable saying that a rabbinical disciple may lie to evade the poll tax, and even deny that he is a Jew, tells us nothing about what would have happened had he done so. The tax collectors in the Jewish community were Jews, not Iranians. What Rava has in mind is a Jew's telling the Jewish collector that he is an apostate. There may be an implied threat, that "if you do not leave me alone, I shall become a servant of fire." I doubt that Rava imagined a rabbinical disciple would so assert before a Mobad, who knew full well how to assess such a claim. His thought was that it is so wrong to collect the poll tax from rabbis, that the disciples may perjure themselves and even pretend to commit overt apostasy. It is a very strong assertion, so extreme that I can hardly imagine anyone's attributing it to Rava had he not actually said it.

XI

We do not know what the exilarch said or did, for rabbinical sources, which are the only sources we have, do not tell us. If Torah, Prophecy, and Writings are brought to testify, and public apostasy theoretically was permitted to a rabbinical discipline, one can hardly suppose that rabbis were not under pressure. The greater likelihood is that they paid their tax but resisted as powerfully as they could through their most effective weapons, namely, ascription of their tax exemption to Moses, Hosea, and Artaxerxes, and publicly announcing permission to evade the taxes even by committing the worst sin they could think of.[17] I can only conclude that the exilarch exerted such pressure because he both had and wanted to. The vehemence of the rabbis' traditions on the subject must be interpreted as evidence of his success.

We do not know whether R. Nahman b. Isaac actually managed to intimidate R. Nahman b. R. Hisda, or, as I said, whether *any* young rabbinical disciples in fact lied to the tax collectors. We do know Shapur's police executed Christian tax resisters. Since we have absolutely no evidence of "martyrdom" among the rabbinate on account

---

[17]Confessing "fire worship" would have been see by ordinary people as public apostasy. Since the rabbis had long insisted a Jew should die rather than commit murder, sexual crimes, or public apostasy, this must have been the worst sin the rabbis could imagine for such a situation.

of nonpayment of taxes, I feel sure there was none. The rabbis protested, but they must have paid. To the exilarch, that would have been all that really mattered. But the rabbis would have been embittered because they not only lost money which would have bothered the poorer ones, but also were forced to transgress their religious convictions about their own rights and privileges. Their view of the sanctity of the rabbinate is clear. They were the "saints" in God's hand. It was a sin for them to pay the poll tax, and it was a greater sin still for the exilarch – heir of David and Asa – to force them to do so. Asa had been punished for imposing the corvée upon the rabbis. What they hoped would happen to the exilarch in the time to come, one may only imagine.

The exilarch had publicly to respond to the criticism and disloyalty of hostile elements in the rabbinate. I should suppose his response would have taken the form of propaganda no less venomous than the rabbis'. He would have stressed, to begin with, the fact that he was descended from the house of David, for that was the foundation of his politics. He would, moreover, have alluded to the cost to others of the rabbinical tax exemptions. Not only would the rabbis not pay their fair share of the rising imposts, but some of them even solicited funds, quite separate from those accruing to the Jewish government, for the support of schools which the exilarch in any case paid for. The rabbis wanted to establish a second Jewish government, which the Persians would never allow. "In these troubled times, when Christians are giving evidence of what happens to minority communities that fall afoul of the state, it will not pay to solicit Persian hostility!" The condition of the Jews themselves provides the best testimony to the soundness of exilarchic rule. "Consider the fact that others are persecuted. Jews are secure. Chaos reigned everywhere, but at home, order, or as much order as responsible government can bring when faced with such dissident, provocative elements." Hostility must have been directed against the rabbis on account of their indifference to the condition of Jewish slaves.[18] The exilarch could therefore have concluded his message by asking, "How many wish to enslave themselves to pay heavier taxes so that rabbis may now enjoy the full benefit of their private, fantastic, and self-serving scriptural exegesis? Not all rabbis, to be sure, but only a minority of them are guilty of such intended subversion. Most of them," the exilarch would have concluded, "remain loyal to the house of David and its living representative." So the exilarch.

Three centuries earlier, Yohanan ben Zakkai, a pharisaic leader, excluded from the bastions of power and displeased with the Temple's

---

[18]Neusner, *History*, Vol. III, pp. 24-29.

administration of its holy office, had found a suitable polemic in the words of Qohelet 4:18, *Guard your foot when you go to the house of God and be ready to hearken....* He said that it was better to listen to the words of the wise than to offer the sacrifices of fools,[19] meaning the ancient priesthood. Now his words found an echo in the saying attributed to Rava (b. Berakhot 23a):

> *And be ready to listen.* Rava said, "Be ready to listen to the words of the sages, for if they sin, they bring an offering and carry out penance. *It is better than when fools give.* Do not be like fools who sin and bring an offering, but do not do penance."

Rava stressed that even sages may sin, but if they do, they repent and seek reconciliation with God. We do not know, of course, of any polemic, such as I have imagined, directed by the exilarch against rabbis. Rava's exegesis is quite outside of a historical context. Yet it would have been an evocative and appropriate response to such an indictment as the exilarch might lodged against his opposition.

XII

The history of the conflict between the exilarch and the rabbi did not end in the middle of the fourth century. During the next fifty years, the exilarch was able to reassert complete control over the rabbinical schools. As the same time, however, he made certain that his functionaries and heirs received an excellent rabbinical education. So he capitulated, in effect, by becoming a rabbi himself – as is the case of Huna b. Nathan. But he also made certain that the schools where Jews became rabbis remained under his very close supervision. We can therefore designate no true victor. The rabbis rabbinized the exilarchate. The exilarch in the end exercised substantial control over the rabbinate. And all suffered in the common disaster during the reign of Peroz, when both leading rabbis and the exilarch believed the Messiah would come in 468 – four hundred years after the destruction of Jerusalem – and foolishly acted upon the consequences of that belief. Jewish government was wiped out. But that is another story.[20] It was an ironic denouement. The rabbis followed the exilarch's messianism and endorsed it. If, therefore, the exilarch was "rabbinized," the rabbis

---

[19] See my *Life of Rabban Yohanan ben Zakkai* (Leiden, 1962), pp. 44-45.
[20] See Neusner, *History*, Vol. V, 95-105. See Markham J. Geller, "Jesus' Theurgic Powers: Parallels in the Talmud and Incantation Bowls," *Journal of Jewish Studies* XXVIII, 2 (1977): 141-55. Geller contributes nothing new and seems to think he is the first to discover these altogether familiar materials, an unfortunate example of slovenly perusal of the available scholarly literature.

were "messianized." The two theories were united; the two parties perished together.

Jewish theories of legitimacy, authority, and politics took one form after another over the next sixteen centuries. Yet whatever the guise, the Messiah myth and the Torah myth recurred again and again as if the presence of the one imposed upon the opposition the necessity of espousing the alternative. So the eschatolgical emphasis of Reform Judaism a century ago came into conflict with the stress of Orthodoxy on the tradition and its authority deriving from Sinai. What are the equivalent theories today? Where shall we find the contemporary Torah myth, the living Messiah myth? These questions, too, require study, perhaps a few centuries from now when the dust has settled.

12

History and Purity in First-Century Judaism

On the occasion of the celebration of the five-hundredth anniversary of the University of Tübingen, 1977[1]

Purity in Stasis: The Foundations of the Mishnaic System of Cleanness

When we reduce to their most fundamental propositions the sayings in Mishnah-Tosefta attributed to the document's earliest-named authorities or those serving as presuppositions to such sayings, we come upon a complete system of uncleanness.[2] Each principal component of such a system – a definition first, of the sources of uncleanness; second, of the circumstances, or places, or times at which uncleanness is affective; and third, of the modes by which uncleanness is removed and purification attained – is in place by the turn of the first century A.D. This mishnaic[3] system, I shall now explain, is in exquisite stasis, resting upon eternally recurrent natural forces, and, at its essence, is

---

[1] This paper was read as a lecture at the Protestant Theological Faculty of the University of Tübingen on the occasion of the celebration of the 500th anniversary of that university. I express my thanks for the cordial hospitality and friendship accorded to me by members of both the Protestant and the Catholic faculties and for the honor of the invitation to speak on the celebration of the jubilee.

[2] This work is done in detail in my *History of the Mishnaic law of Purity*, vol. 22, *The Mishnaic System of Uncleanness: Its Content and History* (Leiden, 1977). A few of the results of the study, as they pertain to the first century A.D., are summarized here.

[3] I refer to the system as *mishnaic* because it is ultimately preserved, with complications and expansions, in Mishnah. There is reason to claim the system to be pharsaic in origin.

221

above the realm of historical event and action. What is unclean is abnormal and disruptive of the economy of nature, and what is clean is normal and constitutive of the economy and the wholeness of nature. The hermeneutic route to that conception is to be located, to begin with, in the way in which what is unclean is restored to a condition of cleanness. It is restored through the activity of nature – unimpeded by human intervention in removing the uncleanness – through the natural force of water collected in its original state. Accordingly, if to be clean is normal, then it is that state of normality which is restored by natural processes themselves. It follows from the exegetical fulcrum of purification that to be unclean is abnormal and is the result of unnatural processes. The first of these is death, which disturbs the house of life by releasing, in quest of a new house, corpse uncleanness, to be defined as that which is released by death. Corpse uncleanness may be contained in a tent, which is a small enclosed space, or, as we see in later strata, in a broken utensil. Once corpse uncleanness finds that new home, its capacity for contamination ends. The second are menstrual blood, flux of blood outside of the menstrual cycle, and a flow from the penis outside of the normal reproductive process. Here too the source of the uncleanness, in the case of the Zabah and the Zab, most certainly is constituted by that which functions contrary to nature or which disrupts what is deemed to be the normal course of nature. The bed and the table are to be so preserved as to remain within the normal lines of the natural economy. It follows that cleanness of the table is to be attained and protected, with regard to both the food which is consumed thereon and to the utensils used in preparing and serving it. The former is defined, of course, along lines of what is acceptable to the cult. The latter matter is developed out of pertinent passages of Scripture and these verses are interpreted in such a way as to serve the system as a whole. Specifically, what is ordinary, useful, distinctive to a given purpose, and normal is deemed susceptible to uncleanness and must therefore be kept apart from those things which, for their own reasons, are deemed extraordinary and abnormal. If such an object then is made unclean, it must be restored to cleanness through natural processes. Food and drink, by contrast, fall outside of the system of purification; no provision is made for them.

The system takes shape, therefore, through the confluence and contrast of opposites perpetually moving from the one side to the other – from the clean to the unclean, from the unclean to the clean. It is remarkably stable and unchanging. Death happens constantly. Water flows regularly from heaven to earth. The source of menstrual uncleanness is as regular as the rain. And the similar uncleanness of the Zab and Zabah through analogy attains regularity through that same source. Meals happen day by day, and if, for the Israelite within the system, the table is a regular resort, so too is the bed. The system therefore creates an unchanging rhythm of its own. It is based on recurrent natural sources of uncleanness and perpetual sources of cleanness, and it focuses upon the loci of ordinary life in which people, whatever else they do, invariably and always are going to be engaged: nourishment and reproduction – *the sustenance of life and the creation of life.*

There is scarcely room for history, which above all is disruptive and disintegrative. Only when the symbolic perfection of the cult's perpetuity is shattered by events will a place have to be made for history. But at that point the cultic system, including uncleanness, is made subordinate to some other system and no longer serves as the principal focus and pivot of the system. Then uncleanness and all that goes with it become conditions for the expression of some further, now deeper, ontology, rather than the a priori ontological and mythopoeic reality. History, in the form of perceived disruption of the Temple. whether through destruction and cessation of the cult at Jerusalem or through the conviction of the cult's desecration by its own practitioners, transforms what is primary and uncontingent into something contingent and secondary. Some systemic element in the available symbolic repertoire other than Temple and cult, for instance, Land and People, comes to the center. The Essenes of Qumran, seeing themselves as the new Temple, accomplish a subtle shift in that their community locates itself at the center, from which the cultic metaphor flows. They are not merely *like* the Temple. Since uncleanness can effect exclusion from the community, that community itself forms the metaphorical crux. The real, this-wordly cult, including conditions for this conduct in cleanness, moves to the periphery. Then the focus of the lines of structure shifts. Uncleanness will be made to bear other meanings (for example, societal ones) and will be forced to define something other than the terms of exclusion from the concrete holy Temple. In this regard the shift comes even at Qumran, for there cleanness is definitive of admission to the commune; uncleanness, of exclusion.[4] When we ask about the role of history in the system of uncleanness at the foundation of the mishnaic law, this fact will assume importance.

---

[4]The point here is that if one disobeys the social regulations of the Essene community at Qumran, he is declared effectively unclean and excluded from the right to touch the pure things of the community. It follows that the community is now deemed *equivalent* to the cult, not merely *like* the cult (see my *Idea of Purity in Ancient Judaism* [Leiden, 1973], pp. 53-54, 67-68, 80-82).

The argument, that at the core of the system is the conviction that what is normal is clean and what is abnormal or disruptive is unclean, is powerfully supported by the convictions of the Priestly Code on why Israel should keep clean and normally is clean. It is because the opposite of *unclean* is *holy*. Israel's natural condition, pertinent to the three dimensions of life – Land, people, and cult – is holiness. God's people is to be like God in order to have ultimate access to him. Accordingly, it is what causes Israel to cease to be holy, in the present context uncleanness, which is abnormal, and, to state the reverse, what is abnormal is unclean. Cleanness thus is a this-worldly expression of the mythic conception of the holiness and the set-apartness of all three – people, Land, and cult. By keeping oneself apart from what affects and afflicts other lands, peoples, and cults ("the Canaanites who were here before you"), the Israelite attains that separateness which is expressive of holiness and reaches the holiness which is definitive also of the natural condition of Israel. The processes of nature correspond to those of supernature, restoring in this world the datum to which this world corresponds. The disruptive sources of uncleanness – unclean foods and dead creeping things, persons who depart from their natural condition in sexual and reproductive organs (or, later on, in their skin condition and physical appearance), and the corpse – all of these affect Israel and necessitate restorative natural processes.

Purity Now and at the End:
The Essenes' Telelogical Interpretation of Purity

What is the place of the system of cleanness in the larger structure of which it is part? For the Essene community at Qumran the answer is not difficult to find. The community treated cleanness as vital at its chief group activity, the meal, because it saw itself as a sacred community assembled at a meal, the cleanness of which both expressed the holiness of the group and replicated the holiness of the Temple. Of still greater interest, cleanness is a precondition of participation in the eschatological war which loomed on the community's horizon and for which it proposed to prepare carefully, in part through perpetual cultic cleanness. After the war the soldiers were to restore their status of cleanness and that of the Jerusalem Temple, presumably because of the contamination of the corpses they would make in battle. It follows that cleanness is understood as a precondition of holiness; and holiness, of the messianic eschaton. Cleanness for the Essenes therefore constitutes not an abiding status, a permanent process outside of history.

It is a necessary step in the historical process itself; the condition of the eschatological war which leads to the end of history.[5]

The Essene community at Qumran, after all, conceived that a world historical event had already intruded into the realm of cleanness. Jerusalem and its Temple were hopelessly contaminated at the hands of willfully unclean people, people who had sexual relations in the Temple or the city and thereby contaminated both.[6] Accordingly, the eternal and recurrent system of cleanness *already* had been disrupted. That is, in part, why the Essene community found it necessary at a given point in time to establish a realm of holiness, and therefore of cleanness, on its own and outside of the Temple. But the original breaking of the system out of its eternal cycle once and for all time introduced into the system a historical-eschatological concern. Cleanness now is not natural to Israel but only to that segment of Israel assembled in the community. Cleanness is to be restored through the activity of that saving, pure, and purifying remnant. Provisional for now, cleanness will be made permanent only at the end of time and the conclusion of history.

The endless cycle, once removed from the eternity of the holy Temple which had been desecrated, could be restored to its perfect cyclicality only when history itself could for all time be brought to a final conclusion by the anointed Messiah and the holy warriors, at which time the holiness and cleanness of the Temple would be restored. Cleanness is a precondition of the end of days, which at the table of Qumran can be foreshadowed and adumbrated. But cleanness also, for its perfection, now depends upon the coming of the end of days. It is, therefore, an accident of history, not an element of a system essentially immune to history. Once historicized, cleanness and the system of which it is part never cease to be, not subjects and actors, but objects of social and metaphysical reality. Perfection once was and once more can be attained. But those for whom the Temple had been desecrated and was as good as destroyed conceived that what should not be subject to the vagaries of historical disaster indeed had been destroyed. It is only

---

[5] As we note in a moment, this same notion (without the concept of an eschatological war) is attributed to Pinhas b. Yair (M. Sot. 9:15). But the saying stands all by itself. I cannot find anyone else who shares his notion that cleanness leads to sanctification which leads onward and upward in the salvific ladder. As I shall point out below, one of the exceedingly difficult problems is that we have no clear notion of the role of cleanness in the eschatological theory of Pharisaism, nor, indeed, do we have a reliable picture of that theory to begin with.

[6] My sometime colleague, Yigael Yadin, phrases this matter felicitously in saying that to the Essenes the events of A.D. 70 took place long before 70.

through the introduction, into historical processes, of the sacred community that cleanness would regain the perfect locus it had lost. In the meantime, cleanness would, at best, contingently serve as a precondition of the end and as a definition of the commune aiming at the end. The unarticulated system of the Essenes, remarkably congruent in its skeletal characteristics to that of the earliest sages of Mishnah, therefore locates cleanness within the scheme of history in the interim and not as essential to an eternally recurring cycle in an unchanging natural economy.

The mishnaic system at its origins, by contrast, hardly leaves space for change. Its cogency and capacity to function as a system depend upon the opposite of change. We refer once more to the way in which uncleanness is removed, for that is the path into the center of the system. The system itself exhibits two fixed and static dimensions which correspond to and complement one another: nature and supernature. Omitted from the system is what is not natural but man-made. The intervention of man interrupts the process of purification and renders water incapable of effecting uncleanness. By definition, water drawn by man is unsuitable. Thus, the one point when human intervention is possible is the point which explicitly secures human exclusion from the system. Man of course does not bring about the uncleanness of the sources of uncleanness. But what the mishnaic system at the outset chooses to say about that matter is insufficiently distinctive to produce a contrary expectation. Man is the locus of uncleanness. The ways in which human beings sustain and create life define the foci and the loci of the system. But in these matters, too, human intervention is secondary. Man cannot clean food but must choose clean food and protect its cleanness. Human beings must refrain from sexual relations at certain times. Their unnatural condition with respect to their sexual organs makes them vehicles for the imposition of uncleanness on objects they use in ordinary life – beds and chairs. That means everywhere they stand or sit or lie can be made unclean by them. But, as I said, the one point at which human volition enters the system, the choice to remove uncleanness permits no role whatsoever to the human being. A person can enter the system by inadvertence. A person cannot leave it by conscious creation of means of purification. That pair of opposites is excluded.

If human action is systematically excluded, what about the complex of human actions which constitutes history? Obviously, human beings may desecrate not only themselves, but their tables and beds, and the cult and Temple as well. But, for the Pharisees, the Temple has not been desecrated. Everything we know about them suggests that, to the contrary, the cult is as it always was from the moment God ordained it: a locus of sanctity, a place of cleanness. So far as the cult defines the being of Israel, so long as the enduring conduct of its affairs in cleanness and holiness shapes the fundamental ontological situation of Israel, Israel – Land, cult, and people alike – is beyond history. Or, to put it differently, while things happen, history does not. The first destruction and the subsequent restoration of the Temple testify to the permanence of that system of permanent normality of which the center is the cult, the setting is the Land, the actors are the priests and people – all of them holy and set apart, above all, from history.

We simply do not know the place in history assigned to cleanness by the framers of the mishnaic system. It is clear from the Essenes' thought on the subject that cleanness defines the group, on the one side, and sets the precondition of the groups' eschatological program, on the other. The evidence in our hands leaves not a hint at an equivalent conception in the earliest stratum of Mishnah.[7] If, to be sure, we identify the Pharisees with the framers of Mishnah, then we may expect to find a concern for the condition of the state and for the conduct of its affairs. For to begin with, the Pharisees are represented as a political party. It would and should follow that the replication of cultic cleanness at the table should bear deep meaning for the larger anticipation of the group for the conduct of affairs. For system are one and comprehensive, and it is not possible to suppose that all that characterizes Pharisees before 70 is an interest in tithing and purity law. The Gospels' picture is of a group engaged in political activities not only in eating clean meals. Josephus' account of the earlier Pharisees is equally explicit on their politics. Accordingly, cleanness may constitute, as Pinhas b. Yair says (M. Sot. 9:15), a way station on the path to the Messianic kingdom prior to and a condition for holiness. None of this is to be gainsaid.

To ask further about the role of history in the Mishnah's primitive system of uncleanness, we return to our observation that, for the Essenes, the lines of structure delineated by uncleanness shift, along with the point of centrality, the locus of the system's interest. At the Essene community of Qumran uncleanness served to exclude and cleanness to include, therefore defining the periphery of the commune. Cleanness performed a social and sectarian function. The center from which lines of structure go forth is reached by following those lines back to the locus defined by them. It thereby becomes clear that cult is replaced at the center by society, the Essene society in particular. The cult of Jerusalem has been rejected at one specific time. From that moment what happens

---

[7]To be sure, cleanness defines those who may eat together, which seems to be a fairly essential characteristic of the self-definition of Pharisaism.

perpetually is made contingent upon what has happened at some point. Ontological reality now is defined not in eternal, recurrent, and unchanging patterns of being. Once something has happened, then happenings, events of the life of the commune, disrupt the old eternal patterns. The community itself perceives just that and focuses its attention on what is to come in the eschaton. It follows that the vehicle, the locus, of meaning is that one thing which moves from the old mode of permanence to the new: the community itself, which in the interim, is all there is to bear the burden of the sacred. That is why, I think, the focus of uncleanness shifts from cult which is reduced to a mere metaphor, to community which is served by, and also generative of, the said metaphor.

The Two Systems Compared

If this is a sound observation, then what do we learn about Mishnah's equivalent focus of uncleanness and the point of origin of lines of structure signified thereby in the context of history? What place is there for transience and historical movement in the earliest system of uncleanness contained within Mishnah? The answer to the question of who is excluded by uncleanness and included by cleanness must lie in exactly the same datum as has just now come under discussion. What is permitted and prohibited? We begin with the negative observation that, while in IQS one is unclean who violates the norms of the community, in early and late mishnaic law one is unclean who is made unclean only and solely by those sources of uncleanness specified in Scripture or generated by analogy to those of Scripture. The contrast of the Essene community yields the fact that the mishnaic system at its foundations presents no element of a societal revision of the locus of uncleanness, for there is none in the definition of the sources of uncleanness. The locus remains in the cult, where it was, but the periphery is extended to include the table. Keeping clean does not define one's membership in a sect, so far as Mishnah is concerned. The very tight adherence in Mishnah's fundamental stratum to Scripture and its explicit rules, both by interpreting them literally (as was done at Qumran) and by exegetically expanding them by analogy – treating the table like the table of the Lord in the Temple and the bed like the bed which in Canaanite times polluted the land, shows that no shift whatsoever had taken place in the point from which the lines of structure, delineated by uncleanness, go forth. The Temple is uncontingent. The extension of the Temple's rules outside is secondary and contingent. The bed and table depend for meaning and significance upon the cult. Life is to be created and sustained in accord with the rules definitive of the world which is the center of life: the holy altar. Nothing has effected a shift in focus, from the enduring, real Temple of Jerusalem, either exclusively or even primarily to the community which keeps the cleanness laws and defines itself in terms of those laws. What is prohibited by uncleanness is entry into the Temple and analogous commensality at any table, anywhere. What is permitted is nurture and creation of human life everywhere. Israel remains whole, and uncleanness and cleanness do not effect social differentiation within it. If the law is not made to define a sect but to establish the rules by which common actions may be carried out, then for those who shape the world (in part) through the system under examination, nothing has happened to reshape the locus of the rules and disrupt their linear relationship to their enduring center. To state matters bluntly: for the mishnaic system history has not (yet) happened.

The cult ordained by God goes on above, not through, time. For the mishnaic system at its origins, no shift has taken place in the patterns of the lines of structure. The table and the bed are at the periphery and conduct at the one and in the other depends, as it always has, on the model by which rules of conduct are framed. Since the Temple in all its holiness endures, no other locus comes into view. The community formed by those who keep the laws in just the right way is not distinct from the world of those who do not, and indeed does not constitute a community at all, Israel remains Israel in all its full, old sense. The Land is wholly holy, not only that part of it consecrated by the life of the holy community thereon. Nothing has changed in the age-old ontology which defines being and discovers reality in order, permanence, recurrence, and the eternal, enduring passage of time. The sacrifice still marks and differentiates the days and months and seasons and links them into a larger pattern. Time's passage depends upon it. The cult still stands at the pivot, the spatial center of the Land, still forms the nexus between heaven and earth. The people, the whole people, still performs regular and holy actions through the priesthood which is at its center. Those who then eat their meals as if they are priests know they are not priests but aspire to the priestly sanctity. They do not claim to be the new priests or the only true and right ones.

If, as seems clear, nothing has changed, then the reason is that nothing has happened. It follows that cleanness is not a condition of the eschaton, and uncleanness is not a function of history. Cleanness is attained now where it always has been attained and uncleanness now is definitive of the locus of cleanness as it has always defined the locus of cleanness. The Temple remains, depriving of consequence what happens around and outside it. If we are unable to discern either a place for history in the uncleanness law, or a role in history for that law, the reason is apt to be that there is none.

Yet it is not wholly accurate to say that nothing has happened. True, nothing has happened to deprive the Temple of its mythopoeic power and central, pivotal position. But something must have happened to draw a small group of people to the conclusions that the sanctity of the Temple is to be extended beyond its walls, on the one hand, and that the locus of the sanctity is to be their table and bed by analogy to the cult, on the other. Obviously what could have happened is that someone responded to the Priestly Code by coming to such a conclusion, which, if not innate, at least is defensible within the exegesis of Leviticus 11-15 and 18. But that too seems unlikely simply because significant shifts have taken place and important conceptions have come to the fore, giving expression for instance to modes of purification on which the Priestly Code is ambiguous. At some point the enduring character of the Temple evoked a conception of replicating the Temple's modes of sanctification in and among Israel's Land and People, just as, at some point, the unsatisfactory character of the Temple and its priesthood provoked the group which settled at Qumran to come to the same conclusion but to effect that conclusion in a diametrically opposite way. Accordingly, the structurally and systemically analogous character of the ideas on uncleanness of the two groups – the Essene community at Qumran and the people who stand at the threshold of the development of mishnaic law – demand the conclusion that, as for Qumran so for Mishnah, there has been an event or a personality of immense consequence. But in the latter case, that is all that we know, and it is, as I have said, only by comparison to the former.

If this theory of the character of the earliest stratum of mishnaic thought on cleanness is sound, then over the next century from the beginning of the mishnaic system before the first century A.D. we should find development of the given laws but no essentially new viewpoints. The generative analogy cannot shift. Creative intellectual forces can only take up and build upon what has been laid down at the outset. The point at which we should anticipate (but do not observe) major developments will be after the destruction of the Temple. Then the Pharisees' continuators in the time of Yavneh will enter into the situation of the Essenes in the age of the Temple.

I have carefully avoided specifying the time at which the mishnaic system originated, claiming only that it is prior to the turn of the first century. It is equally important to avoid claiming to know the sort of group within which the system began. Only with grave reservations have we alluded to the Pharisees as the point of origination or even as the sect which principally stands behind the system transmitted through successive generations to the authorities of 70 and afterward. Still, I think we may specify two facts about that group within which the system as a whole takes shape.

First, like the Essene community at Qumran, the group behind Mishnah surely included a sizable number of priests. Mishnah's fundamental concerns and emphases, while different from those of the Priestly Code, fall wholly within the code's conception of what lies at the core of Israelite ontology. Moreover, the subtle and complex development of scriptural rules on transfer of uncleanness (e.g., *midras* and *maddaf*) has to have been undertaken somewhat earlier. It is likely that priests in the Temple will have had occasion to do the work more than any other group. The availability of such technical terms as *midras* surely suggests that prior to the systemic construction in which these terms and concepts are given their place, the concepts themselves had been worked out. Whether or not the group consisted mainly, or even exclusively, of priests we do not know. The probability is that it encompassed ordinary Israelites pretending to be wanting to live life as priests. But that is less clear than that it was composed of knowledgeable and experienced people, who had a clear notion of cultic law and knew how to apply it.

Second, unlike the group at Qumran, the people whose thought supplies the foundation of Mishnah's legal development did not deem the Temple to be desecrated. They probably did not regard their table as the surrogate for the Temple, but only as a locus *analogous* to its altar. The otherness of the metaphor is preserved. The table is *like* the altar. It is not conceived either *as* a new altar, or as *equivalent* in sanctity to the old one. These two simple and indubitable facts, upon which we have reflected at length, seem to me to yield a picture of a group different in social definition from the Essenes, with a different set of concerns, to be sure expressed in terms of cleanness similar to those of the Essenes, and with a different conception of the central ontological issues of cleanness and of holiness. For them the Temple stood for an ideal to be realized outside its precincts. The cult presented a transcendent aspiration to be attained beyond its gates. Accordingly, the conceptions of the Priestly Code are grasped in all of their philosophical profundity and religious depth and explored at new heights of meaning. Whether priests or lay people, whether gathered out of the common life or located within it, the people whose conceptions stand behind and generate the mishnaic system of uncleanness pursue the sanctification of Israelite life, and set for themselves the goal of sanctifying profane things and purifying unclean ones. Scripture demands the distinction between holy and unclean.

Mishnah begins with the profound conviction that that distinction is to be made so that it may be overcome. To begin with, it asserts that the common is to be surpassed, the profane to be transcended, the unclean to be made sacred.

Purity After 70: Early Rabbinism and the Mishnaic System of Uncleanness

After 70, the unfolding of the system proceeds without significant variation or change and follows the lines already laid out in the period before 70. Let us dwell upon the points of continuity which are many and impressive. The development of the rules on the uncleanness of menstrual blood, the Zab, and corpse uncleanness is wholly predictable on the basis of what has gone before. The principal conceptual traits carry forward established themes. For example, if we have in hand an interest in resolving matters of doubt, then, in Yavneh, further types of doubts will be investigated. Once we know that a valid birth is not accompanied by unclean blood, we ask about the definition of valid births. Yavnean rulings of corpse contamination dwell upon secondary and derivative issues. In important areas of the law the system goes ahead in a remarkably predictable path, clearly moving forward, past the destruction of the Temple, along lines laid down long before. What happens when a system, revolving about a symbolic center and perceived as a metaphorical construction, loses its concrete point of comparison, the center to which everything is deemed peripheral and comparable? What happens to the modes of thought – thinking through analogy and contrast – which give conceptual form and force to the system? The clear answer to the latter question in the case of the mishnaic law of purities is that the modes of thought persist. New inquiries may be raised, but the ways of working them out in conceptual detail already are known and predictable; analogical and contrastive thinking about the known illuminates the unknown.

If, for example, we consider an important innovation in the law, we find ourselves able to interpret it without reference to the impact of the Temple's destruction. It would have come about had the Temple remained standing, and this is demonstratable. I refer to the innovation of Aqiba in introducing into the process of declaring "leprosy" clean or unclean an authority unknown in Scripture, namely, not a priest but a sage, who is "expert in them and in their names." The sage knows the facts of the character of the *nega'* and *ṣara'at* and therefore can be relied upon to rule which is clean and which is unclean. The introduction into the system of a whole corpus of law on a source of uncleanness cannot, to be sure, be credited to the need to make a place for the sages, authorities not of the priestly caste. Scripture itself is clear on *nega' ṣara'at* as a source of major uncleanness.

The Essene community at Qumran as well as the nascent Christian community likewise make provisions for the participation of a nonpriest in the system. After himself healing a leper, Jesus tells the man, "Go, show yourself to the priest" (Matt. 8:1-4, Mark 1:40-44, Luke 5:12-14). Likewise CD 13:5-7[8] provides for an informed person to instruct a priest in what to say in connection with blemishes: "But if there be a judgment regarding the law of blemishes, then the priest shall come and stand in the camp, and the overseer shall instruct him in the exact meaning of the Law. Even if he [the priest] be an imbecile, it is he who shall lock him up; for theirs is the judgment." Accordingly, provision for the role of the informed person is an aspect of the working out of relationships between the commune and the established priesthood and Temple, and in no way is the destruction of the Temple a particular and causative factor in the consideration of the problem. The sage does not heal, of course, but has the knowledge to recognize symptoms of healing or uncleanness. The role of each sort of authority is particular to the system of which he forms a part.

Perfection and Implausibility

The destruction of the Temple cannot be presented as the principal cause of the several important shifts in the mishnaic system of uncleanness which took place in the Yavnean period.[9] The lines of development in many important components of the system are continuous with the character of the law before 70. Whether or not the Temple was destroyed, it was inevitable that these areas would develop within the as-yet unanswered questions – the logical tensions implicit in their earliest structure. The provision of a place for the sage in the determination of uncleanness formerly reserved for the priest does not depend of the event of 70, since exactly the same consideration is revealed in CD. Any system, not only Mishnah's in which an authority other than the priest stands at the center must at some point take up the problem of how said authority related to the priest in decisions reserved by Scripture to the priesthood. The answer in CD and in Negaim is to treat the priest as an indispensable idiot, preserving for him a formal role while treating that role as a decidedly secondary formality. The profound thought of Makhshirin and Kelim on the role of man in inaugurating the working of the system responds to the

---

[8]C. Rabin, *The Zadokite Documents* (Oxford, 1958), p. 62.
[9]Yavnean period, from Yavneh, the location of the rabbinic group after 70.

conception of Miqvaot of the role of nature in bringing the process to a conclusion and restoring the economy of nature. Internal systemic considerations, imbedded in the logic of the law, account even for the transformation of what had been an undifferentiated metaphor into a fact. A single continuum now joins the table at home to the altar.[10] Cleanness of the domestic table is not merely *like* cleanness of the Temple altar but stands in a single concrete line which ascends from the former, via the cleanness of the priest's heave-offering, to the latter. What formerly was compared to something else now is placed into material relationship with that other thing.

Yet the fact remains that the Temple *was* destroyed. The legal developments under examination are given in the names of Yavneans and stand in a direct line either with rulings given in the names of authorities before 70 or with suppositions taken for granted and not subjected to controversy after 70. The evidence, both in its silence and in its full expression, strongly suggests that it was after 70 in particular that these interesting developments of the system did take place. Whether or not they would have occurred if the calamity did not happen of course is not subject to inquiry. As I have argued, they are implicit in the antecedent system and susceptible of discovery without regard to external events. Even though the role for the authority other than the priest is defined by the Essenes at a different time and in other circumstances from the age and context of the calamity of 70, even though the system itself invites consideration of the role of human agency and intent in its commencement, and even though the deep thought on levels of sanctification is invited by the ambiguities of the very metaphor upon which the system is founded, the facts are what they are.

It follows that, while we cannot ask how the destruction of the Temple affected the mishnaic system of uncleanness, we do ask how the development of the system after 70 is congruent with the effects of the Temple's destruction. The answer is obvious. First, the destruction radically revises the institutional context for the priestly government of surviving Israel. New sorts of leaders emerge, one of which is the sage, qualified because he is expert "in them and in their names." Negaim testifies to that fact and to the further and still more important fact that Aqiba in particular proposes to investigate the

---

[10] I refer to the development of the notion of removes of uncleanness, first, second, third, corresponding to levels of sanctification of food, ordinary food, heave-offering, and Holy Things, for example, as exemplified at M. Tohorot 2:3-7. It would carry us far afield to lay out the sources on this complex matter. The point which is relevant is as given.

deep implications of the rise of the sage for a law to the working of which the priest is essential. The catastrophe raises the question of whether or not people bear responsibility for what has happened. If they do, they take on a heavy burden of guilt. If they do not, however, they face an equally paralyzing fact: their own powerlessness to shape their fate. The issue is resolved by stress upon the responsibility of Israel for its own fate, a painful conclusion made ineluctable by the whole of the scriptural heritage of Leviticus, Deuteronomy, and the prophetic literature. But Scripture is clear that those who have brought disaster by their deeds also can overcome it. Reversion to the right way will produce inexorable redemption. If people are not helpless, then their deeds and their intentions matter very much. The catastrophe provides an occasion for reflection on the interplay between action and intention, in the established supposition that what people propose to do and actually do are their own responsibility. And, as we have seen, the central issue – the fate and focus of the sacred – is faced head-on.

The mishnaic system of uncleanness at Yavneh contains within itself developments remarkably congruent to the institutional, psychological, and metaphysical crisis precipitated by the destruction of the Temple. Its message is clear. The sages will lead Israel to the restoration of the world destroyed by Israel's own deeds. They will do so through the reformation of attitudes and motives, which will lead to right action with the result that, even now, the remnants of holiness may be protected from the power of uncleanness. The holy priesthood and people, which endure and which are all that endure after the cultic holocaust of 70, form the last, if diminished, sanctuary of the sacred. In domestic life, at table, the processes of life are nurtured and so shaped as to preserve and express that remnant of the sacred which remains in this world. The net result of the Yavnean stage is the law's unfolding is that history – the world-shattering events of the day – is kept at a distance from the center of life. The system of sustaining life shaped essentially within an ahistorical, indeed antihistorical, ontology goes forward in its own path, a way above history.

Yet the facts of history are otherwise. The people as a whole can hardly be said to have accepted the ahistorical ontology framed by the sages and in part expressed by the system of uncleanness. They followed the path of Bar Kokhba and took the road to war once more. When three generations had passed after the destruction and the historical occasion for restoration through historical – political and military – action came to fulfillment, the great war of 132-35 broke forth. A view of being in which people were seen to be moving toward some point within time, the fulfillment and the end of history as it was known, clearly shaped the ontological consciousness of Israel after 70 just as had been the case in the decades before 70. So if to the sages of our system, history and the end of history were essentially beside the point and pivot, the construction of a world of cyclic eternities being the purpose and center, and the conduct of humble things like eating and drinking the paramount and decisive focus of the sacred, others saw things differently. To those who hoped and therefore fought, life had some other meanings entirely.

The second war proved still more calamitous than the first. In 70 the Temple was lost and in 135, even access to the city. In 70 the people, though suffering grievous losses, endured more or less intact. In 135 the land of Judah, surely the holiest part of the holy Land, evidently lost the bulk of its Jewish population. Temple, Land, people – all were gone in the forms in which they had been known. In the generation following the calamity of Bar Kokhba, what would be the affect upon the system of uncleanness?

The answer is predictable: there would be no affect whatsoever. The system would go on pretty much as before, generating its second- and third-level questions as if nothing had happened. For a brief, unreal twilight, the old pretense of a life beyond history and a system untouched by dynamics of time and change would be attempted. The result, in the history of the mishnaic system of uncleanness, would be the hour of systemic fulfillment, the moment of the richest conceptual, dialectical achievement, a bright and brilliant time in which 200 (or more) years of thought would come to ultimate incandescence. And, at the end, Our Holy Rabbi (Judah the Patriarch) would capture the light in permanent utensils of unbreakable language. But pretense that nothing had happened, or could happen, does not make history. Things *had* happened. The system of uncleanness, unfolding beyond time and change, now complete and whole in flawless intellectual and literary structures, is set aside at the time of its perfection. The system which had denied an end time and constructed a world without end itself would fall into desuetude. History would give it its place on the crowded shelf of unused utensils, each containing its true, but implausible truths.[11]

---

[11]See my "History and Structure," *Journal of the American Academy of Religion* 45, no. 2 (1977): 161-92.

13

The Talmud as History

The Allan Bronfman Lecture, Shaar Hashomayim Synagogue, Montreal, November 8, 1978

The Hill Professor's Lecture, University of Minnesota, Minneapolis and St. Paul, November 15, 1978

Plenary Lecture in honor of the tenth anniversary of the founding of the Association for Jewish Studies, Boston, December 17, 1978.

Printed in Method and Meaning in Ancient Judaism
(Missoula, 1979: Scholars Press for Brown Judaic Studies) 1:41-58.

I

Enduring works of the intellect last because they speak to minds beyond limits of space and boundaries of time. The mark of greatness is the vision and will to transcend all frontiers and address an age one can scarcely imagine. But what is heard beyond the bounds of space and time is not always, and perhaps not ever, what the original mind meant to say. Like a diamond, which reveals a different light to the eyes of each of those who see it, these lasting works of mind, whether in art or music, philosophy or literature, religion or science, enjoy a diverse reception. People hear what they are capable of perceiving. One generation reads Shakespeare in light of one set of issues and another, in light of a different set. The history of the reception of the thought of Socrates is shaped by Plato and of that of Plato, by Aristotle. As Harold Cherniss points out, Aristotle's criticism of pre-Socratic philosophy, of Plato, and of the Academy is complicated by Aristotle. For he attributes to Plato a theory which is not in Plato's writings (1935, 1944, 1945). On this basis, Cherniss (1934:ix) accepts the possibility that "Aristotle was capable of setting down something other than the objective truth when he had occasion to write about his predecessors."[1] The discovery of that possibility, however, had to await the coming of Harold Cherniss, twenty-three hundred years after Aristotle. The reason for the delay explains much about the consciousness and culture of the West in the intervening centuries. So it is self-evident that the great intellectual accomplishments of humanity, the ones which endure for centuries, not only transcend the limits of time and space,[2] they also overcome the barriers of their own composition: the mind of the maker, the world to which the maker spoke and which, to begin with, received the work and accepted (or rejected) it. This is so for the diverse collections of the Hebrew Scriptures, for Plato, for the traditions of Chinese and Indian philosophy and Christian theology, and for that document distinctive to the inner life of the Jewish people for nearly two millennia, the Talmud.

A history of the study of the Talmud, from the Talmud's formative period in the first and second centuries of the common era down to the present day would provide insight into the intellectual history of Judaism, of which the Talmud is the principal component. It also would

---

[1] Compare my *History of the Mishnaic Law of Purities* (1977, XVII:202-220) on the Houses of Shammai and Hillel as represented by second-century authorities such as Meir, Judah, Simeon, and their contemporaries. I am able to show that attributed to the ancient Houses are positions on issues moot after Bar Kokhba's War, and that the opinions assigned to the Houses by the second-century authorities are suspiciously similar to those held by the second-century masters. The second-century figures play an active part in the formation of the "tradition" of the Houses. Since the same authorities give in their own names what they also state in the names of the Houses, there can be little doubt that the attributions to the Houses are, in fact, invented and fictitious. This is especially likely because the authorities of the period after 70, which intervenes between the Houses and their epigones, are remarkably ignorant of the principles espoused by the Houses and even of the basic issues debated by them. A gap of over a century in a continuous tradition is curious.

[2] See S.C. Humphreys (1975). She states:

> One of the factors influencing the intellectual to adopt a transcendental perspective appears to be the need to make his work comprehensible to an audience widely extended in space and continuing indefinitely into posterity. How far is our own appreciative response to these works – and especially to the rationalism of the Greek philosophers – due to the authors' deliberate intention of transcending limitations of social structure and temporal horizons? How far is this successful transcendence due to content and how far to form, to the structuring of the communication in such a way that it contains within itself enough information to make it immediately comprehensible? Is this a common quality of rational discourse and of "classic" works of art?

give us important facts about the sociology of the Jewish people, the character of its religious life in diverse dimensions, the nature of the educational and cultural institutions which express and shape that life. The reason is that the conditions of society define the things society wants to know. The shape of the program of study of the inherited monuments of culture is governed by the people who propose to carry out that program and the interests of the people who are supposed to contemplate the results of the work.

To take one very current example, Christopher Lasch explains the reason that The University of Chicago became the great center for sociology which it did – the place in which, for a long time, the issues of sociology were defined – and also the reason that sociology done in Chicago took up the very questions asked:

> The presence in other departments of the university of such important thinkers as Veblen, John Dewey, and Mead; the enterprise of Jane Addams...and other settlement workers in accumulating empirical data on urban life and insights into its pathology; the many-sided intellectual awakening known as the "Chicago renaissance"; the existence of the city itself as a laboratory of industrial conditions – all these made Chicago almost inevitably a center of sociological studies. Nor is it surprising that those studies addressed themselves especially to the sociology of urban life. From the perspective of Chicago, which had grown from a frontier settlement to a huge industrial metropolis in less than a century, completely rebuilding itself after the fire of 1871, rapid urbanization loomed as the central fact of modern society....Accordingly, the city should be studied as a total environment that gave rise to a distinctive way of life (1977:33-34).

I quote Lasch at length because he provides a model for two propositions. First of all, he shows that the conditions of society generate the data to be examined by the intellectuals. Second, he indicates that the character of the studies carried out by them is defined by those same conditions. Sociology took up the questions of society and family, in the place in which the work was done, by the people by whom the work was done, specifically because the context defined both what was to be studied and who should do the work.

If then we ask how the Talmud was studied, we transform a question of intellectual method, superficially a formal question about traits of logic and inquiry. We find ourselves asking about the world in which Jews lived, the values they brought to the Talmud, and the reasons that moved them to open its pages to begin with. So, as I said, when we contemplate the study of the Talmud, we find ourselves examining the history of the inner life of the Jewish people and, self-evidently, the intellectual history of Judaism.

I argue this proposition with some care so that my basic perspective on historical interest in the Talmud will be clearly defined. The questions I wish to answer are these:

First, why was the Talmud studied as a historical document?

Second, what was the intellectual program of the people who originally decided that the Talmud should be studied as a historical document?

Third, why is the Talmud studied today, in a very considerable measure, as a historical document?

Fourth, what is the intellectual program of the people who today do the work?

Persuasive answers to these four questions will give us a clearer notion of the work we do and a firmer definition of the work to be done in the future. So when we speak of the Talmud as history, we address ourselves to questions of acutely contemporary character and cultural consequence.

II

The beginnings of the study of the Talmud as history, like the beginnings of nearly all of the methods and ideas of the "Jewish humanities," lie in nineteenth-century Germany. Ismar Schorsch (1975:48) points out that the definition of the modern debate about the Talmud, in mostly historical terms, was supplied in a single decade, the 1850s. Four books were published in less than ten years, which defined the way the work would be done for the next one hundred years. These are Leopold Zunz's publication of Nahman Krochmal's *Moreh nebukhe hazzeman* ("guide to the perplexed of our times"), 1851; Heinrich Graetz's fourth volume of his *History of the Jews from the Earliest Times to the Present*, which is devoted to the talmudic period, 1853; Geiger's *Urschrift und Uebersetzungen der Bibel*, 1857; and Zechariah Frankel's *Darkhe hammishnah* ("ways of the Mishnah"), 1859.[3] These four volumes place the Talmud into the very center of the debates on the reform of Judaism and address the critical issues of the debate: the divine mandate of rabbinic Judaism (Schorsch, 1975:48).[4]

The talmudic period defines the arena of the struggle over reform because the Reform theologians made it so. They had proposed that by

---

[3]I pay little attention to Geiger in what follows because his work had little influence on the course of talmudic historiography. The main lines of research followed from Frankel, for biography, and Graetz, for narrative history.

[4]*Ibid*. Historical study also served as an instrument in the attack on talmudic tradition and defense of Reform Judaism in Poland in the same period. See Biderman (1976:19-44).

exposing the historical origins of the Talmud and of the rabbinic form of Judaism, they might "undermine the divine mandate of rabbinic Judaism" (Schorsch, 1975:48). As Schorsch points out, Geiger's work indicates the highwater mark of the attack on rabbinic Judaism through historical study.[5] Krochmal, Graetz, and Frankel present a sympathetic and favorable assessment. In so doing, however, they adopt the fundamental supposition of the Reformers: the Talmud can and should be studied historically. They concede that there is a history to the period in which the Talmud comes forth. The Talmud itself is a work of men in history.

The method of Graetz and of Frankel, therefore, is essentially biographical. One third of Frankel's book is devoted to biographies of personalities mentioned in the Talmud. What he does is collect the laws given in the name of a particular man and states that he appears in such and such tractates, and the like. His card file is neatly divided but yields no more than what is filed in it (Gereboff, 1973:59-75).[6] What is important is not what he proves but, as I said, what he implicitly concedes, which is that the Mishnah and the rest of the rabbinic literature are the work of men. Graetz likewise stresses the matter of great men. As Schorsch characterizes his work:

> Graetz tried valiantly to portray the disembodied rabbis of the Mishnah and Talmud as vibrant men, each with his own style and philosophy and personal frailties, who collectively resisted the disintegrating forces of their age....In the wake of national disaster, creative leadership forged new religious institutions to preserve and invigorate the bonds of unity....He defended talmudic literature as a great national achievement of untold importance to the subsequent survival of the Jews (1975:48).

---

[5]*Ibid.*

[6]Gereboff concludes as follows:

For Frankel Rabbi was the organizer and the law-giver. He compiled the Mishnah in its final form, employing a systematic approach. The Mishnah was a work of art; everything was "necessary" and in its place. All these claims are merely asserted. Frankel gives citations from Mishnaic and Amoraic sources, never demonstrating how the citations prove his contentions. Frankel applied his theory of positive-historical Judaism, which depicted Jewish life as a process combining the lasting values from the past with human intelligence in order to face the present and the future, to the formation of the Mishnah. The Mishnah was the product of human intelligence and divine inspiration. Using their intelligence, later generations took what they had received from the past and added to it. Nothing was ever removed. Frankel's work has little lasting value. He was, however, the first to analyze the Mishnah critically and historically; and this was his importance.

Now why, in the doing of history, the biographies of great men should be deemed the principal work is clear: the historians of the day in general wrote biographies. History was collective biography. Their conception of what made things happen is tied to the theory of the great man in history, the great man as the maker of history. The associated theory was of history as the story of politics, thus of what great men did. Whether or not the Jewish historians of the "talmudic period" do well, moderately well, or poorly, the sort of history people did in general I cannot say. The important point is that the beginnings of the approach to the Talmud as history meant biography.

What was unimportant to Graetz, Frankel, and Krochmal was a range of questions of historical method already thoroughly defined and worked out elsewhere. So the work of talmudic history was methodologically obsolete by the standards of its own age. These questions had to do with the reliability of sources. Specifically, in both classical and biblical studies, long before the mid-nineteenth century a thorough-going skepticism had replaced the gullibility of earlier centuries. Alongside the historicistic frame of mind shaped in the aftermath of the Romantic movement, there was an enduring critical spirit, formed in the Enlightenment and not to be eradicated later on. This critical spirit approached the historical allegations of ancient texts with a measure of skepticism. So for biblical studies, in particular, the history of ancient Israel no longer followed the paths of the biblical narrative, from Abraham onward. In the work of writing lives of Jesus, the contradictions among the several gospels, the duplications of materials, the changes from one gospel to the next between one saying and story and another version of the same saying and story, the difficulty in establishing a biographical framework for the life of Jesus – all of these and similar, devastating problems had attracted attention. The result was a close analysis of the character of the sources as literature, for example, the recognition – before the nineteenth century – that the Pentateuch consists of at least three main strands: JE, D, and P. It was well known that behind the synoptic Gospels is a source (called Q, for Quelle) containing materials assigned to Jesus, upon which the three evangelists drew but reshaped for their respective purposes. The conception that merely because an ancient storyteller says someone said or did something does not mean he really said or did it goes back before the Enlightenment. After all, the beginnings of modern biblical studies surely reach into the mind of Spinoza. He was not the only truly critical intellect in the field before Voltaire. But as a powerful, socially rooted frame of mind, historical-critical and literary-critical work on the ancient Scriptures is the attainment of the late eighteenth and nineteenth centuries. And for the founders of talmudic history, Graetz, Frankel, and Krochmal, what had happened in biblical and other ancient historical studies was either not known or not found to be useful. And it was not used.

No German biographer of Jesus by the 1850s could have represented his life and thought by a mere paraphrase and harmony of the Gospels, in the way in which Graetz and Frankel and their successors down to the mid-twentieth century would paraphrase and string together talmudic tales about rabbis, and call the result "history" and biography. Nor was it commonplace, by the end of the nineteenth century, completely to ignore the redactional and literary traits of documents entirely, let alone their historical and social provenance. Whatever was given to a rabbi, in any document, of any place or time, was forthwith believed to provide evidence of what that rabbi really said and did in the time in which he lived. Even Christian "fundamentalism" approaches the biblical literature with greater shame than this!

III

Now why these people did what they chose to do is no more important than why they refrained from doing what they chose not to do. Just as they chose to face the traditionalists with the claim that the Talmud was historical, so they chose to turn their backs on the critical scholarship of their own day with that very same claim that the Talmud was historical. I think the apologetic reason is self-evident and requires no amplification. We may now answer our first two questions. The Talmud was first studied as a historical document because, in the war for the reform of Judaism, history was the preferred weapon. The Talmud was the target of opportunity. The traditionalists trivialized the weapon, maintaining that history was essentially beside the point of the Talmud: "The historians can tell us what clothes Rabh wore, and what he ate for breakfast. The Talmudists can report what he said." But, it goes without saying, polemical arguments such as these, no less than the ones of the Reformers, were important only to the people who made them up.

The weapon of history in the nineteenth century was ultimate in the struggle for the intellect of Jewry. And the intellectuals, trained as they were in the philosophical works of the day, deeply learned in Kant and Hegel, made abundant use of the ultimate weapon. The Reformers similarly chose the field of battle, declaring the Hebrew Scriptures to be sacred and outside the war. They insisted that what was to be reformed was the shape of Judaism imparted by the Talmud, specifically, and preserved in their own day by the rabbis whose qualification consisted in learning in the Talmud and approval by those knowledgeable therein.

But the shape of the subject and its results, paradoxically, also reveal the mind of the traditionalist Reformers, Graetz and Frankel. Their intellectual program consisted of turning the Talmud, studied historically, into a weapon against the specific proposals and conceptions of the Reformers. And for the next hundred years, with only one important additional area of study, the history of the "talmudic period" would be the story of rabbis, paraphrases of talmudic and midrashic units strung together with strings of homilies – where they were strung together at all.

This additional area of study need not detain us for long, for what is done in it is essentially what is done in biography. I refer to the study of what was called "talmudic theology" or "talmudic thought" or "rabbinic theology." In English the pioneering work is Solomon Schechter's *Studies in Judaism,* three volumes beginning in essays in the Jewish Quarterly Review, 1894 through 1896. The next important work in English is George F. Moore's *Judaism,* published in 1927, then C. G. Montefiore's and H. Loewe's *Rabbinic Anthology,* 1938, and Ephraim Urbach's *The Sages. Their Concepts and Beliefs,* in Hebrew in 1969 and English in 1975. There were parallel works in German as well.[7] In all of these works the operative method is the same as in biography, but the definitive category shifts to theology. Each work takes up a given theological category and gathers sayings relevant to it. The paraphrase of the sayings constitutes the scholarly statement. Urbach correctly defines the work which was not done: "the history of the beliefs and concepts of the Sages against the background of the reality of their times and environment" (1975:5). The use of evidence for the theological character of talmudic Judaism is just as gullible and credulous as it is for biographies of talmudic rabbis. What is attributed to a given rabbi really was said by him. What he is said to have done he really did. No critical perspective is brought to the facts of the Talmud. And the Talmud always supplies the facts, all the facts, and nothing but the facts.

We need not dwell on the historical study of the Talmud for theological purposes, therefore, because the methods were no different from those taken to be essentially sound for the study of the Talmud for biographical purposes. And these two purposes – biography and theology – define the character of nearly all of the historical work done in talmudic literature for the century from the decade of

---

[7]These are briefly summarized and criticized by Urbach (1975:1-18).

foundation onward. Graetz set the style for such history as was attempted; Frankel for biography. The greatest achievements of the next hundred years – I think of the names of Buechler and Alon, for example[8] – in no way revised the methods and procedures or criticized the fundamental suppositions laid forth in Graetz and Frankel. When we realize the conceptual and methodological history of biblical studies in that same century, when we gaze upon the stars which rose and the stars which fell, when we remember the fads and admire the lasting progress, we realize that the Talmud as history is a world in which the clock started in 1850 and stopped in 1860. That of course is an exaggeration. Even those who could find no better methods and suppositions than those used for a hundred years could at least propose better questions. A clearly historical, developmental purpose is announced, though not realized, for example, by Urbach, when he says:

> The work of the sages is to be viewed as a protracted process aimed at the realization of the Torah and the ideals of the prophets in the reality and framework of their time. (1975:17).

Now while this is a clearly apologetic and theological proposal, it does make a place for the notion of change and development, that is, a genuinely – not merely a superficially – historical proposal.

At the end let me quote Schorsch's (1975:61-62) judgment of Graetz, which forms a devastating epitaph to the whole enterprise of talmudic history from the 1850s to the 1950s:

> Above all, Graetz remained committed to the rejuvenation of his people. His faith in God's guiding presence throughout Jewish history, as witnessed by two earlier instances of national recovery, assured him of the future. His own work, he hoped, would contribute to the revival of Jewish consciousness. He succeeded beyond measure. As a young man, Graetz had once failed to acquire a rabbinic pulpit because he was unable to complete the delivery of his sermon. There is more than a touch of irony in the remarkable fact that the reception accorded to Graetz's history by Jews around the world made him the greatest Jewish preacher of the nineteenth century.

IV

The second century of the historical study of the Talmud and related literature is marked by the asking of those questions ignored in the first: What if not everything in the Talmud happened as it is narrated? What if the attribution of a saying to a given rabbi does not

---

[8]See A. Buechler (1906, 1912, 1928) and G. Alon (1957-58). Alon's lecture notes were published as *Toledot hayyehudim be'eres yisra'el betequfat hammishnah vehattalmud* (1954-55). These are uneven, and most of the work on ancient history is seriously out of date.

mean that the rabbi really said what he is supposed to have said? Then what sorts of historical work are we able to do? What sorts can we no longer undertake?

At the outset let me specify the answers to my third and fourth questions, raised earlier: What is the intellectual program of the people who today do the work? Why is the Talmud studied today as a historical document?

Answering these questions requires attention to the character of the people who do the work. These are all university people. Talmudic history may be taught in some Jewish theological institutions – not in Yeshivas at all – but no books or articles in talmudic history emerge from these schools. The books and articles in this field over the past twenty years have been written by university professors in America, Canada, Europe and the State of Israel. The reason this particular aspect of talmudic studies is important to professors in diaspora-universities should be made clear.

Among those engaged in the teaching of the "Jewish humanities," the Talmud is a particularly important document. It is distinctively Jewish. The Hebrew Scriptures are not; they are a splendid literature and a self-evidently important one. Much of the medieval philosophical and mystical literature is of very special interest. The Talmud, by contrast, speaks of the formative years of Judaism as we know it; and it addresses itself, also, to the centuries in which the two other religions of the West (Christianity, for the earlier phases of the Talmud, and Islam, for the very last phases) were taking shape. Consequently, there is a genuine interest in talmudic learning among a wide audience of scholars and students. It is natural, therefore, for people in the setting of secular universities to turn to talmudic studies as a distinctively Jewish, important, and welcomed topic.

But what people in universities want to know has little to do with the ritualistic repetition of hagiography. They are not apt to sit still very long for edifying tales of ancient rabbis (or other sorts of holy men either). There is a contemporary program of research, a set of questions which just now appear urgent and pressing, as much as the issues of the reform of Judaism through historicism appeared urgent and pressing a century ago.

Of still greater importance for the present part of the argument, there is a considerable and shared program of criticism, historical, literary, anthropological and philosophical, as well as *religionsgeschichtlich*. This program is naturally attractive. One question which to New Testament scholars seems unavoidable is how to tell what, if anything, Jesus really said among the sayings attributed to him, and what Jesus really did among the deeds assigned to him.

The Talmud as History

There is no way that what is perceived as "fundamentalism" will find a serious hearing in the study of Judaism when that same attitude of mind is found irrelevant in the study of Christianity of the same place and nearly the same time. It follows, as I indicated at the outset, that the pressing problems of this second century of talmudic studies for historical purposes are not, Did Rabbi X really say what is attributed to him? but, What do we know if we do not know that Rabbi X really said what is attributed to him? What sort of historical work can we do if we cannot do what Frankel, Graetz, and Krochmal thought we could do?

V

Since the contribution of the nineteenth and early twentieth century historians in the talmudic area was to biography, let me now report the results of a considerable scholarly program of the past nearly two decades. I refer, specifically, to the study of the lives and thought of the rabbis – "Tannaim" – who are supposed to have flourished between the destruction of the Second Temple in 70 and the advent of Bar Kokhba in 132 and who are therefore associated with the period, if not the locus, of Yavneh. My *Life of Yohanan ben Zakkai* (1962) marks the end of an old epoch in methodology, and my *Development of a Legend: Studies on the Traditions concerning Yohanan ben Zakkai* (1970) signals the beginning of the new one in this area of study. A series of studies and dissertations has been successfully accomplished. These have repeatedly produced a few significant results.

First, in the study of the traditions attributed to, and stories told about, the earlier rabbis, we have to take account of three wholly distinct types of material which seem to have no influence upon, or connection with, one another. These are legal, exegetical, and "biographical."

The legal materials attributed to all of the rabbis of Yavneh occur in the earliest rabbinic documents, Mishnah and Tosefta. In general they unfold, where the history can be assessed, in a disciplined and orderly way. As I showed in *Eliezer ben Hyrcanus,* what is attributed to Eliezer ben Hyrcanus in the names of his immediate disciples and contemporaries will unfold and be subject to development in later strata, literary or attributive. But it will never then be contradicted. Moreover, pericopae bearing evidence of later origination in documents after Mishnah, or bearing attestations of authorities of the third and fourth century, fall nearly wholly within the thematic framework established by materials bearing names of earlier attestations or occurring in Mishnah. This means that in the area of legal sayings there was no tendency promiscuously and without clear warrant to attribute to Eliezer whatever people wanted. On the contrary, there seems to have been a rather disciplined effort to amplify and augment materials assigned to him solely within the conceptions and principles already established in his name. This is a sign that the unfolding of the legal tradition in the three of four hundred years after the turn of the second century was governed by attention to what is said in the name of the earlier authorities and will not be characterized by attribution to an early authority of an idea first invented later on, for instance, for the purpose of securing for that new idea the prestige of the name of the revered and ancient master.

When, by contrast, we come to exegetical materials, that is, sayings on the meaning of scriptural verses given in the name of Yavnean authorities, we find it simply impossible to relate what is said on Scripture to what is said on law. Time and again, the students of the traditions assigned to Yavnean rabbis have been stymied by the problem of how to relate the exegetical to the legal corpus. What they find in Genesis Rabbah or Leviticus Rabbah, the earliest complications of exegetical sayings, and what they find in Mishnah and in Tosefta, or even in the two Talmuds, are simply without apparent relevance to one another. Nor are the exegetical materials themselves susceptible to the sort of study of development and disciplined amplification referred to in connection with the legal ones. In the exegetical compilations, Eliezer, Ishmael, Tarfon, and Gamaliel simply supply names to which exegeses are assigned without (as-yet-perceived) rhyme or reason. The exception will be reference in the legal exegetical compilations, particularly Sifra and Sifré, to legal rulings of Mishnah-Tosefta, in which case the point is to demonstrate that said rulings derive from exegesis, not from reason. These self-evidently are secondary to, and dependent upon, Mishnah-Tosefta and in no way change the picture.[9]

As to "biographical" materials, by which are meant sayings or stories in which a rabbi's name is mentioned, these are of two kinds. In the first, a rabbi's name is used without any clear claim that a particular individual and his intellectual or moral traits come under discussion. There will be set sequences of names, for example, Eliezer, Joshua, Gamaliel, Aqiba. But what is said about, or done with, those names bears no relationship whatever to biography, that is, to what a particular individual said or did. In the second, a particular rabbi's name is used in a clearly homiletical story, for example, how Tarfon

---

[9]Compare my *History of the Mishnaic Law of Purities*. VII. Negaim. Sifra (1975:1-12, 211-30).

The Talmud as History

tended to his mother's needs. Even if we were to believe all of the stories presented to us as "biographical," we should have very little biography for the earlier rabbis. The reason is that the homilies all together add up to no effort, even casual and unsystematic, to record what a given authority really said or did through a significant part of his lifetime. The blatant homiletical purpose precludes nineteenth century biography in these "biographical" materials.

A further insuperable barrier to biography is the absence of a generally accessible framework of biography for individual rabbis. There is no effort to report the outlines of a single authority's career, beginning to end. Because of that fact, even if all the sayings could be shown really to have been said by the rabbi in whose mouth they are set, and all the deeds really to have been done by him, we still should not have a hope of writing the sort of biography which Graetz and Frankel and their successors proposed to do. Their failure was apparent even at the outset: they really had nothing much to say and, when the sermons came to an end, so did their biographies.[10]

Since the three kinds of materials given in the name of a particular rabbi bear virtually no internal interrelationships, on the one hand, they must be used for purposes other than the composition of biographies. For even if we concentrate on the legal sayings, inclusive of the stories of various types, whether precedents or illustrations, we come to insuperable problems. These are generated by the documents in which said sayings occur. If we were to propose to describe a given authority's legal ideas, that is, his religious philosophy expressed through concrete teachings on the conduct of ordinary life, we should want to begin with some evidence that what a given authority is supposed to have said really has been said by him. Otherwise, our account of his legal ideas is really not intellectual biography at all. But when we approach the diverse documents of the law, we find that the sayings attributed to all authorities are given in highly patterned and stereotyped language, so that it is hardly possible to claim that, to begin with, we have in our hands anything like *ipsissima verba*. We may have access to what an authority thought. That has yet to be demonstrated, and I think it is beyond proof. But we rarely can show, and therefore do not know, that what he thought has been preserved in the words in which he expressed his thought.

We often can demonstrate the opposite. For Mishnah and Tosefta are documents formulated in the processes of redaction. What the redactors have done to create Mishnah, in particular, is to revise the whole of the received corpus into the language and redactional

---

[10] I owe this point to Morton Smith.

constructions of their own preference.[11] I am inclined to think that, prior to the time of "Our Holy Rabbi," Judah the Patriarch, materials were collected along the lines of a single authority's name, or of a single formal pattern, or of a single principle of law affecting diverse topics of law. But Rabbi's preference clearly is to group materials not in the name of a given authority, form, or abstract principle, but, essentially, topically, even though the sherds and remnants of materials brought together along other lines do remain in our hands. It follows, in any event, that while what is attributed to a given authority may or may not derive from him or his circle of disciples, we have no hope of presenting sizable bodies of sayings in the exact words spoken by a given authority.

VI

Since these are the facts, it must be concluded that the effort to recover the biographies of individual rabbis of the late first and early second centuries is not feasible. It seems to me that the same conclusion holds for the rabbis who lived in the later second century, since the literary facts pertinent to Aqiba apply without much variation to Judah, Simeon, Meir, or Yosé. The state of the question of the rabbis of the third and fourth century is apt to be shaped by the nature of the quite different processes of literary formulation and transmission which produced the Talmud in which their materials in the main are preserved, on the one side, and those same processes which yield the midrashic compilations, on the other. These have not been critically assessed in detail, so we cannot yet come to conclusions on the promise of rabbinic biography for the "Amoraic" period.

We hardly are justified, however, to conclude that we learn nothing about earlier rabbinic Judaism from the study of the sayings and stories assigned to its founding generations. On the contrary, once we ask the correct questions, we find we learn much worth knowing. In the study of the history and character of the traditions in the names of Yavneans, for example, we learn what it was important to say about those authorities in the times in which those responsible for the later compilations did their work. We notice, first of all, that in the third and fourth and later centuries, the telling of stories about earlier rabbis was deemed an important part of the work of tradition-making and handing on the tannaitic corpus. Men who, in their own day and for a century thereafter, are important, for example, in Mishnah-Tosefta,

---

[11]This is demonstrated at some length and systematically in my *History of the Mishnaic Law of Purities*. XXI. The Redaction and Formulation of the Order of Purities in Mishnah and Tosefta (1977:Chap. VII).

The Talmud as History

principally in connection with opinions in their names on mooted topics of Mishnah-Tosefta, now, in the strata of the Talmuds and in the midrashic compilations require yet another treatment entirely. They must be turned into paragons of virtue and exemplars of the values of the growing rabbinic movement. Long after their legal traditions had come to closure, their "biographies" continue to grow in response to a self-evident need to expand the modes by which rabbinic tradition would express itself and preserve and impart its teachings. The histories of the traditions of the several authorities of Yavneh prove beyond doubt that it is in the third and fourth centuries that the telling of stories about rabbis of the first and second centuries, the making up of homilies about their deeds, and the provision of a more human visage for the ancient authorities became important to rabbinic circles of both Palestine and Babylonia.

It furthermore should not be supposed that the attribution of sayings to authorities of the late first and second centuries bears no consequences for the study of the history of earlier rabbinic Judaism. The contrary is the case. For we are able to devise a method by which we may test part of what is alleged in those attributions, which is that the saying belongs at a given point in the history of rabbinic legal thinking, and not later. If to Aqiba is assigned a saying which in conception and logic is prior to one attributed to Judah or Meir, of the next generation, and which furthermore appears to generate the conception attributed to Judah or Meir, then we may fairly conclude that to the time of Aqiba belongs the conception of the saying given in his name. That sort of conclusion may not appear so satisfying, but upon that basis a fairly firm and solid history of the law and its religious and philosophical conceptions is to be worked out.

That kind of history in no way depends upon whether or not Aqiba really said what is attributed to him, but only whether we are able to find evidence that what is assigned to Aqiba or any other Yavnean is prior in conception or principle to what is assigned to Judah or Meir or any other Ushan after Bar Kokhba. Upon that basis a history of the unfolding of the law is to be founded. The consequent history of ideas further may be correlated with the great events of the age to which, it would seem reasonable, rabbis' thinking upon any important question necessarily responded, for instance, the Temple's destruction or Bar Kokhba's catastrophe. Once the history of the law is worked out for the Mishnah-Tosefta, we should have a fair picture of the foundations of the earlier stages of rabbinic Judaism. These in turn will delineate the work which must follow.

VII

A sign of a field of study in flux is the incapacity of scholars to find common grounds for disagreement. At the present time the Talmud is read as history in two completely different ways. Those who do it one way cannot communicate with those who do it in the other way. For example, those who maintain the established theory of the character of the talmudic sayings and stories as facts of history, pure and simple, will present to those who do not the following arguments: 1) the rabbis were scrupulous about the truth; 2) facts incorrectly reported were challenged; 3) the holy rabbis of the Talmud surely would not lie. To these assertions, a master of the contrary viewpoint – that talmudic stories, like biblical ones, have to be read in a critical spirit – will reply with such words as "sometimes" and "probably." That is, the rabbis sometimes were scrupulous about the truth. Facts sometimes were challenged when reported incorrectly. The holy rabbis of the Talmud probably would not lie. But, this master will add, "Rabbinic literature is full of obviously contradictory and grossly false statements. Contradictory reports stand unchallenged as often as they are corrected. The rabbinic literature contains innumerable nonsensical and obviously incredible statements." So, this master concludes, "If the rabbis were so scrupulous and painstaking as you pretend, how do you account for the enormous mass of claptrap they handed down?"[12]

Clearly, an argument phrased in the language of piety provokes the language of antipiety, as well it should. But it appears to me that the argument is poorly phrased when the "veracity" of "the rabbis" is made the issue. What really requires attention is the identification of the things we shall concur to regard as facts and the questions to which these facts are claimed to be relevant. An Israeli graduate student (of American origin) who attended a conference at which issues such as those under discussion here were raised made the following comment:

> I am used to historians who argue with one another by showing that the hypothesis suggested by competitors is either contradicted by some known datum or necessarily involved or extravagant to explain the known data, as a simpler hypothesis would equally do. That is, everyone assumes that the few known data, which by themselves do not give us an understandable picture, are the surviving fragments of

---

[12] I here paraphrase a correspondence between a distinguished American scholar and an equally accomplished Israeli one about the veracity of talmudic stories about rabbis and attributions of sayings to rabbis. Language in quotation marks is drawn from the actual correspondence. I am not free to reveal the names of the participants. The argument did take place in precisely the terms in which I represent it.

a 'building' which once stood. The historian's job is to suggest what the building looked like.

Now this conception of the writing of history confuses history with mathematics. It is, indeed, a conception possible only for a graduate student who has heard lectures but given none, read and criticized many books but not yet formulated even his own thesis topic.[13]

But the insight that no longer is there any agreement whatever on what constitutes facts and how facts are discovered and defined is significant. I think it is entirely sound and accurate, not only for the conference on which the student comments, but also for the state of the field of the Talmud as history. That is why the sort of discourse about "the holy rabbis' not telling lies" is possible. For, as I think is clear from the perspective of historical studies, we are not entirely sure what we mean by the truth. That is why we cannot say what is an untruth. We in the humanities do our work in an age of powerful, conflicting currents of thought. There is little argument on fundamental issues of method and theories of knowledge. It is no wonder that the character of the work done in this first quarter of the second century of the study of the Talmud as history should appear to be diverse and lacking a common core of consensus and concurrence. Since that is so of society at large, why should it not be so of scholarship?

Works Consulted

Alon, Gedelia

1954-1955 *Toledot hayyehudim be'eres yisra'el betequpat hammishnah vehattalmud.* 2 vols. Tel Aviv.

1957-58 *Mehqarim betoledot yisra'el.* 2 vols. Tel Aviv. Trans. Israel Abrahams: *Jews, Judaism and the Classical World. Studies in Jewish History in the Times of the Second Temple and Talmud.* Jerusalem, 1977.

Biderman, Israel M.

1976 Mayer Balaban. *Historian of Polish Jewry.* New York.

Boyce, Mary

1975 *A History of Zoroastrianism.* Leiden: E.J. Brill.

---

[13][The graduate student is now a junior faculty member at the Hebrew University of Jerusalem. Where else!]

Cherniss, Harold
1935　　*Aristotle's Criticism of PreSocratic Philosophy.* New York: Octagon.
1944　　*Aristotle's Criticism of Plato and the Academy.* New York.
1945　　*The Riddle of the Early Academy.* Berkeley and Los Angeles: University of California Press.

Gereboff, Joel
1973　　"The Pioneer: Zechariah Frankel." pp. 59-75 in *The Modern Study of the Mishnah.* Ed. J. Neusner. Leiden: E.J. Brill.
1979　　*Tarfon.* Brown Judaic Studies. Missoula: Scholars Press.

Ginzberg, Louis
1955　　"The Significance of the Halachah for Jewish History." *On Jewish Lore and Law.* Philadelphia: The Jewish Publication Society of America (orig. 1929).

Green, William S.
1977　　*Men and Institutions in Earlier Rabbinic Judaism.* Brown Judaic Studies. Missoula: Scholars Press.
1978　　"What's in a Name? – The Problematic of Rabbinic 'Biography.'" pp. 77-96 in *Approaches to Ancient Judaism.* Missoula: Scholars Press.
1979　　*Joshua ben Hananiah.* Leiden: E.J. Brill.

Kadushin, Max
1964　　*Worship and Ethics. A Study in Rabbinic Judaism.* Evanston: Northwestern University Press.

Kanter, Shamai
1979　　*Gamaliel of Yavneh.* Brown Judaic Studies. Missoula: Scholars Press.

Lasch, Christopher
1977　　*Haven in a Heartless World. The Family Besieged.* New York: Basic Books.

Moore, George Foot
1921　　"Christian Writers on Judaism." *Harvard Theological Review* 14:197-254.

1927 *Judaism.* 3 vols. Cambridge: Harvard University Press.

Neusner, Jacob

1962 *A Life of Yohanan ben Zakkai. Ca. 1–80 C.E.* Leiden: E.J. Brill.

1965-70 *A History of the Jews in Babylonia.* 5 vols. Leiden: E.J. Brill.

1970a *Development of a Legend: Studies on the Traditions Concerning Yohanan ben Zakkai.* Leiden: E.J. Brill.

1970b *Formation of the Babylonian Talmud: Studies on the Achievements of Late Nineteenth and Twentieth Century Historical and Literary-Critical Research.* Leiden: E.J. Brill.

1971 *The Rabbinic Traditions about the Pharisees before 70.* 3 vols. Leiden: E.J. Brill.

1973a *Eliezer ben Hyrcanus. The Tradition and the Man.* 2 vols. Leiden: E.J. Brill.

1973b *The Idea of Purity in Ancient Judaism.* Leiden: E.J. Brill.

1973c *Invitation to the Talmud. A Teaching Book.* New York: Harper & Row.

1973d *Modern Study of the Mishnah.* Leiden: E.J. Brill.

1974-77 *A History of the Mishnaic Law of Purities.* 22 vols. Leiden: E.J. Brill.

Porton, Gary

1976 *The Traditions of Rabbi Ishmael.* 4 vols. Leiden: E.J. Brill.

Primus, Charles

1977 *Aqiba's Contribution to the Law of Zera'im.* Leiden: E.J. Brill.

Saldarini, Anthony J.

1976 "Review: History of the Mishnaic Law of Purities I-III." *Journal of Biblical Literature* 95/1:151.

Sandmel, Samuel

1978 *Judaism and Christian Beginnings.* New York: Oxford University Press.

Sarason, Richard S.

1979 *A History of the Mishnaic Law of Agriculture. Demai.* Leiden: E.J. Brill.

Schechter, Solomon

1970 *Studies in Judaism.* 3 vols. Paterson, N.J.: Atheneum.

Scholem, Gershom

1960 *Jewish Gnosticism, Merkabah Mysticism, and Talmud Tradition.* Based on the Israel Goldstein Lectures, Delivered at the Jewish Theological Seminary of America. New York: Jewish Theological Seminary of America.

Schorsch, Ismar

1975 Heinrich Graetz. *The Structure of Jewish History and Other Essays.* New York: Jewish Theological Seminary of America.

Smallwood, Marytx

1976 *The Jews under Roman Rule.* Leiden: E.J. Brill.

Smith, Jonathan Z.

1978 *Map is Not Territory. Studies in the History of Religions. Studies in Judaism in Late Antiquity.* Leiden: E.J. Brill.

Smith, Morton

1963 "A Comparison of Early Christian and Early Rabbinic Tradition." *Journal of Biblical Literature* 82:169-76.

1968 "Historical Method in the Study of Religion." *History and Theory. Studies in the Philosophy of History*, Beiheft 8. *On Method in the History of Religions.* Ed. James S. Helfer. Middletown: Wesleyan University Press.

Zahavy, Tzvee

1977 *The Traditions of Eleazar ben Azariah.* Brown Judaic Studies, Missoula: Scholars Press.

14

New Perspectives on Babylonian Jewry in the Tannaitic Age

*Perspectives in Jewish Learning Series,
The Spertus College of Judaica, 1964*

Babylonian Jewry has long held the interest of Jews in other lands and ages. From hoary antiquity, it made its mark on Judaism. Jeremiah addressed an oracle to Babylonia; two of the greatest literary prophets, Ezekiel and Second Isaiah, prophesied there. From Babylonia in Persian times came the spiritual and material resources for the rebuilding of the land of Israel and the return to Zion. Seven centuries later, Babylonian Jewry began the great enterprise of transforming the Mishnah of R. Judah the Prince into the constitution for the life of a varied and vigorous people in a land greatly different from that for which the lawbook was originally designed; and that enterprise resulted, within three hundred years, in the production of the Babylonian Talmud, which is one of the greatest literary, legal, and moral achievements of the mind of man. From the close of the talmudic period for more than five hundred years Babylonia remained the center of world Jewry, as from its academies went forth instruction, and the word of the Lord from its religious leaders. In the second century C.E., R. Hananiah the nephew of R. Joshua was ridiculed for acting as if he expected that from Babylonia would Torah go forth, and the word of the Lord from Nehar Pekod. If this was once supremely ironic ridicule, in later ages it became a fact.

Yet shadow covers much of Jewish history in Babylonia, for while we have an impressive record in the Hebrew Scriptures and in the Babylonian Talmud and afterward, for the period from the time of Ezra, 440 B.C., to R. Judah the Prince, ca. 200 C.E., we have almost no direct evidence of what was happening in the Jewish community which so very soon after R. Judah's death (ca. 220 C.E.) was to blossom forth in a myriad of ways, and the legacy of which from that time to the present illuminates Jewish history. Proof of the paucity of our knowledge is that fact that Rashi and the Tosafists debate (Bab. Talmud Gittin 6a, 'Eruvin 28a, Bava Qamma 80a) whether the Oral Torah existed before the return of Rav to Babylonia ca. 220 C.E. or not, Rashi holding that it did not, the Tosafists holding that it did, and both contending on the basis of an ahistorical, scholastic inquiry unsupported by historical study of sources. Modern scholarship engaged in the debate in the same sterile terms. Simon Dubnow and J. H. Weiss held that Rav indeed "brought the Torah" to Babylonia because before his time it was absent. Dubnow states outright: "In Babylonia at the time of Rav and Samuel, there were neither great sages nor academies." Dubnow and Weiss simply did not inquire very deeply into the available literature, for if they had, they could not have made such statements.

To my knowledge, the first modern scholar to devote himself to a critical, systematic historical study of Babylonian Jewry in the period from Ezra to Rav was Nahman Zvi Getzav, who published, in Warsaw in 1878, a book entitled, *By the Waters of Babylonia*. I have never seen a citation to Getzav's book and discovered it only accidentally. After I had completed my own work, and had sent it to the press, I found and read Getzav's book, and to my pleasure, found that every major methodological advance I believed I had made had, in fact, been utilized by this unknown writer.

It is reassuring indeed to know that one is not an orphan – even after the fact. Two further scholars made lasting, and irreplaceable contributions to our knowledge of Babylonian Jewish history in the Tannaitic age and afterward, I.Y. Halevi, in *Dorot HaRishonim* (vol. Ic) and II Ze'ev Yavetz in *Sefer Toldot* Yisrael. Yavetz was writing an essentially popular history, but because of his sound training in traditional literature and the seriousness with which he attempted to utilize this literature, he had the merit, which I do not believe Weiss and Dubnow had, of making a very careful, detailed study of tannaitic and early Amoraic literature, and prepared on that basis a thoroughly systematic, and, if apologetic, reasonably rich account of the subject. The real foundation of our knowledge is to be found, however, in Halevi's work. Halevi has been neglected where he is not ridiculed. Yet his work must be the basis for all research into talmudic history because of the penetrating reason, historical understanding and, usually thorough and meticulous character of his inquiry. One may readily understand why superficial students have not paid much attention to

Halevi. He writes in a very difficult style; he conducts a vigorous polemic, so that one not infrequently loses touch with his argument in the maze of his pugnacious and fiery denunciation of one scholarly hypothesis after another. His work consists mainly of a collection and deep analysis of relevant sources, so that in the end, the reader must himself recover whatever history Halevi makes available. It is, nonetheless, well worth trying.

Numerous scholars have, of course, made substantial contributions to limited aspects of Babylonian Jewish history in the period under study, for example, N. Brüll on Adiabene (in *Jahrbücher für Jüdische und Literatur*, K, 1874, pp. 58-86) and Felix Lazarus on the exilarch (in the same place, X, 1890, pp. 1-183). Furthermore, talmudic scholars, who have elucidated literary, legal, and philological questions, but who have ignored historical ones, have made possible whatever historical understanding we may be able to achieve, these are too numerous to mention. In my book, a very full bibliography of all useful work is provided. Here I want to emphasize only the specifically *historical* studies, of which, as I said, only Halevi and Yavetz are significant. On the later period, one would have to consider also S. Funk, *Die Juden in Babylonien* (Berlin, 1902), and Jacob Obermeyer, *Die Landschaft Babylonien im Zeitalter des Talmuds und des Gaonats* (Frankfurt a/M., 1929), to name only two of the most important works, as well as that of the living scholars, G. Widengren, M. Ber, and H. Mantel. Nor is it possible here to cite the substantial contributions of the Iranists to our subject.

Apart from Getzav, however, no one has brought to the subject an interest in the external history and culture, mainly that of the Parthians. In the pages that follow, I shall lay stress on the interrelationships between Parthian and Jewish history in Babylonia, because I believe these to have been a predominate theme in that history.

II

Nahman Zvi Getzav opens his book by expressing his astonishment that in the dark hour of exile, the Psalmist *had* to take an oath to keep thoughts of Jerusalem in his heart over his chiefest joy. "But in such a time, when his heart was full of sorrow and his eyes were a fountain of tears...should there come to his mind the very thought of rejoicing and happiness....In the hour of anger and bitterness, how would it enter his mind to think of a happy occasion at all?" Getzav remarks, therefore, about the wonderful capacity of the Psalmist to sustain a thought of hope for future prosperity in the strange land, and to perceive that in time, when he would be at home on soil no longer alien, such an oath would indeed find its test. H. L. Ginzberg likewise pointed out that conditions in Babylonia must have proved prosperous indeed, for Ezekiel had to invent a new *mizvah*, the commandment to pine away in the strange land, lest the point and purpose of the punishment of exile be lost. Basing his teaching on Leviticus 26:39, "And those of you that are left shall pine away in your enemies' hands because of their iniquity, and also because of the iniquities of their fathers shall they pine away." Ezekiel taught (24:21-3) that even on the occasion of death, one should not mourn, but he should pine away and groan. If there was one *mizvah*, however, which the exiles kept faithfully it was that of Jeremiah (29:5-8): "Build houses and live in them, plant gardens and eat their produce....Seek the welfare of the city where I have sent you into exile and pray to the Lord on its behalf, for in its welfare you will find yours." It was exactly this that they did.

Jewry was able to take root in Babylonia and to flourish, as it was clear to Ezekiel and to Jeremiah that they would flourish, in part because they had come to the richest and most productive part of what became the Persian empire. The land was rich and well-watered. An ancient canal system ensured a proper distribution of water, and rich land was available for the farmer. Moreover, Babylonia served the economy of antiquity as a crossroads of many trading routes. One city after another grew up at the confluence of these routes, extending eastward to India and to China, on the one hand, and westward, and north, across the fertile crescent, and, during the first and second centuries, straight out across the desert via Palmyra as well, precisely because for geographical reasons the routes met in central Babylonia and nowhere else. Thus if Babylon flourished as a center of world trade, so did Seleucia, Vologasia, Ctesiphon, and Bagdad later on all within a few miles of one another. Until the discovery of sea routes from Egypt to India, and, later on, from Europe to India and the Far East, Babylonia enjoyed the benefits of its situation as a natural and necessary emporium for international commerce, and prospered above other regions less favorably situated. Furthermore, if economic conditions were favorable, political conditions fostered even more the development of a stable, generally peaceful communal life. First of all, Babylonia was ruled by a succession of world empires, each of which was eager to establish its capital (or one of its capitals) there. The Persians, the Seleucids, the Parthians, and the Persians again, in succession, sought the peace of the region as eagerly as did its inhabitants, because of its strategic location on the crossroad not only of trade but also, quite obviously, of routes of communication. Thus though the Achemids came from or based their power in Persis, the Seleucids

Syria, the Parthians Parthia, and the Sasanians Persis again, all established a major center of military and political power in Babylonia. The ethnic constitution of the region, finally, favored the continued existence of a minority group such as the Jews. The Jews were only one of many peoples and varying cultural groups which made their home in the region. For more than twenty centuries, Babylonia was settled territory, and one conqueror after another left a cultural and demographic deposit in the land, so that by the time the Jews reached there, no one group dominated, apart from the native Babylonians who after a brief time no longer had the political power to enforce their religious and cultural convictions on a newly arrived group. (Nor did they try to do so when they could.)

These favorable conditions continued to prevail during what we call the tannaitic period. This period dates, conventionally, from 10 to 220 C.E.; the former date is that generally given to the death of Hillel, the latter, to that of Judah the Prince. Since the Parthians reached Babylonia ca. 140 B.C.E., and firmly established their hold on the region only twenty years later, my study of the pre-Amoraic period begins with 140, but we shall focus our attention on the first and second centuries C.E. simply because these centuries have yielded far more information than the preceding 150 years.

III

When the Parthians broke out of the Iranian plateau onto the low lands of the Mesopotamian valley, they inherited the government of a land of many peoples, who formed a mosaic of ethnic groups in Babylonia as a kind of living palimpsest. Of these, the oldest and best established was the Babylonian-Akkadian civilization, which continued to pursue its ancient forms, pray to the old gods, and make astronomical observations in the old way, into the first century C.E. Recent scholarship, as exemplified, for example, in the current researches of Professor Baruch Levine, among others, has demonstrated significant Babylonian influence on talmudic law and philology. Given the long period of symbiosis and the continuing interaction between Jewish and Akkadian civilization, one should expect to find substantial evidence of such influence. During the tannaitic period, Babylon itself gradually lost population, as trade was shifted elsewhere by the Parthians (as by the Seleucids beforetime), and by the second century C.E. the city was mostly ruined, being visited by Jewish "tourists" who were shown the ruins of the place and who pronounced blessings to him "who destroyed the palace of the wicked Nebuchadnezzar" (Bab. Talmud Berakhoth 57b).

Greeks formed a more vigorous cultural group in the region. Their settlement had been encouraged under the Seleucids, and very large numbers lived mainly in the cities and engaged in trade and urban commerce and in government employment. Seleucia on the Tigris, the largest city of the region, was Greek, as were many other centers of population. They maintained schools and academies, theaters, and other traditional cultural institutions. The Parthians, moreover, adopted the culture of their Greek subjects. They used Greek on their coins; preserved Seleucid political institutions and forms, and cultivated Hellenistic literature at their court. Thus the Jews regarded the Parthians as "Greeks." For example, Rav told R. Kahana (Bab. Talmud Bava Qamma 117a) "Until now, the Greeks, who did not take much notice of bloodshed were [here and ruled but] now the Persians who are particular regarding bloodshed are here and they will certainly cry murder." (Rav's opinion reveals also the wide degree of self-government allowed to the Jews by their neighbors, but mainly engaged by their inherited tradition. The Greek cities governed themselves, and the Arsacid chancellery at Ctesiphon, like the polis at Sus and Seleucia, followed Hellenistic forms and employed a large number of Greeks. Moreover, the Greeks cultivated their philosophy in academies in Babylonia, and metaphysicians, astronomers, naturalists, historians, geographers, and physicians worked there.

Babylonian Jews had every opportunity to acquire a knowledge of Greek culture, for they lived in large numbers in Seleucia, Charax Spasinu, and other cities. Jewry in Dura certainly acquired substantial knowledge not only of the Greek language, but also of other aspects of Greek culture. Nonetheless, by and large, the Jews, like the Greeks, Babylonians, other Semitic groups, and the Parthians, formed a separate cultural-ethnic group, influenced by their neighbors, but mainly engaged by their inherited tradition. Between the fifth and the second C. B.C.E. we have very little information about them. Josephus reports that Jews fought in the army of Alexander, but refused to assist in the restoration of the ruined temple of Bel at Babylon. The Persian *shah-an-shah* Artaxerxes Ochus earlier had transported a large number of Jews to Hyrcania, ca. 340 B.C.E., possibly on account of a revolt. At any event, the Seleucids won the loyalty of Babylonian Jewry, just as the Romans won that of the occidental diaspora. Antiochus the Great, for example, sent two thousand Jewish families from Mesopotamia and Babylonia to Lydia and Phrygia, in Asia Minor, to help pacify the country. We learn in II Maccabees 8:20 that Jews cooperated in the defense of Babylonia alongside the Macedonians, though we do not know when or against which invader. Like the Jews in Alexandria, Babylonian Jewry was loyal to the imperial power and favored by it. As a minority, they depended upon its protection, and could at the same time be made a mainstay of the imperial regime. Thus at the time of the Maccabean war against the Seleucids, Babylonian Jewry remained quiescent, just as the diaspora communities of Alexandria, Cyrenaica, Antioch, and Cyprus kept the peace during the war against Rome of 66-73, though they rebelled violently when their own interests were seriously threatened by Trajan's Mesopotamian and Babylonian campaign of 114.

We do not know anything at all about the demography of Babylonia or Mesopotamia in this region and have no way to assess, even approximately, the number of Jews. We do know, however, that Jews lived throughout the areas, from Adiabene, and Armenia in the north to the Persian Gulf, from the Mygdonius-Khabur system, tributary of the Euphrates, at Nisibis to Media in the east, (and perhaps further east than Media) and of course, flourished in large numbers in central Babylonia, near the great city of Seleucia and across the whole stretch drained by the Royal Canal. One may venture a guess that the Jews were fewer in numbers than the indigenous Babylonians, and surely no more numerous, probably less so, than the Greeks and, taken as a whole, the smaller Semitic ethnic groups. But while these groups were mainly concentrated, either in cities or in specific satrapies, the Jews probably formed a minority in many cities of the Euphrates valley and throughout the western satrapies of Parthia, and some were in the east as well, in Afghanistan and India, though we do not know when they got there, and a majority in many towns and villages in central Babylonia as well.

Of Babylonia's many conquerors, the Parthians least affected the life of the settled peoples. The culture of the area was not significantly influenced by northern Iranian elements during the Parthian period, though one should qualify that judgment by noting that the Iranian loan words in the Talmud are mainly of Parthian, and not Sasanian, origin, according to S. Telegdi, and by examining in close detail the discussion of Geo Widengren on Jewish-Parthian cultural contacts (*Supplements to Vetus Testament* IV, Leiden, 1957, pp. 197-242, and see the same author's *Iranian-Semitic Cultural Relationships*, Cologne, 1958 and his "Status of Jews in the Iranian Empire," *Iranica Antiqua*, I 1961, pp. 117-162). The Parthians were not greatly concerned with the cultural or religious affairs of the conquered lands. They had no interest in changing the language or affecting local government. They made every effort to conciliate various groups in their empire. When they founded new cities for Iranian settlement, they were careful to preserve the rights of older ones and avoided imposing upon commercial centers the inconvenience of military colonies. The Parthians were a military aristocracy and chose to rule not directly but through various kinds of authorities, Greeks for the Greeks, Jews for the Jews, Armenians for the Armenians, to each of whom they maintained a feudal relationship. Their vast empire stretched from the Oxus River to the Persian Gulf, from the Euphrates to the Punjab. It never evolved toward a powerful central government under a monarch who held virtual monopoly of real power, unlike Rome. On the contrary the monarch, who was called "the king of kings" was that in fact as well as in name. The Parthians prized a heroic life, their days were spent in the chase, in banquet, in noble exploits of arms. Their name in modern Persian is *pahlavan*, which means hero, brave man. And so they were. Their religion, like many other aspects of their culture, is barely known to us today. It was within the Iranian religious idiom, in which there were many subdivisions and even aberrations. Their dominant influence was that of the Magi.

Modern scholars have called the Parthians, in the classical tradition, a "mere herd of a people" and viewed them as a kind of interim state, between Achemenid and Sasanid empires, whose culture was a kind of decadent, orientalized Hellenism. In a word, they were regarded as nomadic barbarians. This was the Greek and Roman view of Parthia, and until recent archaeological discoveries were properly interpreted by Rostovtzeff, Tarn, Wolski, and others, the same view prevailed in modern times. S. Krauss, for example, states that "of course the uncultivated Parthians could exercise no religious influence upon the Jews." Whether or not this was so remains to be demonstrated. Certainly the influence of Iranian ideas, images, and myths upon Judaism in this period was powerful and it is difficult to explain it as the legacy of the Achemenids. In any case, when one reflects upon the wide and mediating influence of Parthian art and architecture, one ceases to regard the Parthians as a mere herd of a people. They filled moreover a major political and geographical role in the Middle East, not only reuniting most of the Achemenid empire, but also holding the Euphrates frontier against Rome, with brief intervals, for centuries. The Seleucids never broke Parthia, but were broken by them. The Romans at the height of their power could not overcome them. Most important, the Parthians held the eastern and northern frontiers against the waves of nomadic people from the Asian heartland who swept time and again against their borders. Thus they preserved the Middle East as a cradle for civilization against those who ultimately (under the Mongols) were to ravish it. And they did so with the vigorous help of the small peoples of the Euphrates valley whom they tied to their empire by ties of economic and political self-interest. Moreover, in their time, they served as the intermediary for trade and culture between the Occident and China. The Arsacid dynasty held power in the Middle East for more than four and a half centuries, a longer time than any other dynasty ever ruled Iran and its neighboring lands before that time or afterward. To sustain themselves over such a long and turbulent time, the Parthians had to have created a strong and cultured state, possessed a flexible structure of military and political power, and won the vigorous loyalty of disparate and resourceful peoples.

This survey of Jewish history in Parthian Babylonia will deal with economic, political, and cultural, including religious and literary issues. In it I shall state positively some of the hypotheses and conjectures which I have offered in my *History of the Jews in Babylonia, I. The Parthian Period* (E. J. Brill, Leiden, 1964, *Studia Post-biblica* IX). At some point, a historian has the right to state in definite, positive terms what he believes to have happened, even though his belief rests upon conjecture and interpretation to a substantial degree, as does mine concerning a subject for which we have so few sources. Here I shall exercise that right. The serious student will want to turn to the documentation and argumentation of my *History* to evaluate the bases upon which the following statements are made.

IV

For this period, our knowledge of the economic life of Babylonian Jewry is limited. We know from the later literature that large numbers of Jews engaged in agriculture, and have no reason to believe that matters greatly changed with the coming of the Sasanians. Therefore one may presume that in the Parthian period, the agricultural conditions of Jewry were not greatly different from those described, mainly on the basis of Amoraic materials, in J. Newman, *The Agricultural Life of the Jews in Babylonia, 200-500 C.E.* (London, 1932). As we noted above, these conditions were generally prosperous, commensurate with the fertility of the land and abundance of water.

What is especially interesting is the fact that Tannaim born in Babylonia and resident in Palestine and in Babylonia were engaged in the silk trade (some were in other forms of commerce), and were normally wealthy men. This was true of R. Hiyya, and hence of his sons, and his nephews Rav and Rabba b. Hana; of Abba b. Abba the father of Samuel; and of R. Judah b. Bathyra of Nisibis. Further, the Jews of Edessa were engaged in the silk trade, and chief among the Jewish-Christian apostles of the Euphrates valley was Haggai, a silk dealer. Furthermore, Jewish merchants lived in Charax Spasinu, at the head of the Persian Gulf, and traveling merchants were provided with a hostel in the Dura synagogue. One source (Gen. Rabbah 77:2 ed.

Theodor-Albeck p. 910, 1.6) states explicitly that R. Hiyya, R. Simeon the son of R. Judah, and R. Simeon b. Gamaliel traded in silks at Tyre, and another (midrash on Samuel 100:13) that Samuel's father and R. Judah b. Bathyra traded in silks.

Galilee was a center of silk-weaving enterprises. Jews were active in the manufacture and tailoring of silk garments. Babylonian Jews were, moreover, in a particularly advantageous position to trade in silk. The trade routes normally passed through Mesopotamia, as we have noted. The Parthian government took extreme measures to prevent the Romans and Chinese from entering into direct trade relationships, for it profited greatly as intermediary. Thus it was not before 160 A.D. that Rome and China made direct contact, and since the best routes passed through Seleucia on the Tigris, the bulk of the silk trade continued to pass through Parthian hands. Since the chief market for raw silk was the manufacturing regions in the Roman orient, the Parthians found Jewish merchants to be ideal middlemen. They were a loyal group within the empire (of this, more below). They had excellent contacts with Palestine. They could both receive and transship the merchandise without its passing through many hands. Obviously, the Parthian government could make use of the silk merchants for other, political purposes as well.

R. Hiyya and his nephew Rav were related to the exilarchate, though I do not know the exact degree of relationship. If so, then it was through the Jewish exilarch that the Parthian government directed some measure of the trade in silk. The exilarch's agents in Palestine dealt with the patriarch, probably with Roman approval, as the story about the joint business trip of R. Hiyya and the son of R. Judah the Prince suggests. The Roman market included Jewish silk merchants as well. Thus the Jewish traders took advantage of their peculiar political situation, as part of a large group settled on both sides of a fluctuating, contested frontier, and served their respective imperial governments as intermediaries in a trade profitable to each. The Jewish traders imported goods from the Orient to Babylonia, and transhipped them from there through Nisibis, a major way station in the trade between the two empires, where R. Judah b. Bathyra was settled, to Northern Palestine, where the raw wool was spun and woven into cloth and tailored into garments for the Roman market. In the second century C.E. this trade greatly expanded. Some Jews were able to profit. Those, specifically, who maintained connections with both the Palestinian market and the Babylonian suppliers were of particular value to their respective governments, which, in Palestine through the patriarchate, and in Babylonia through the exilarchate, regulated the immensely profitable trade.

The late second century was a time of emigration from Palestine, in the wake of the continuing economic decline brought on by the disastrous war of 132-135. The Tannaim heaped extravagant praise on him who remained in the holy land, precisely because so many did not, and could not. They told stories, for instance (Deut. Sifre 80) of how leading Tannaim, specifically R. Eliezer b. Shamua, R. Judah b. Bathyra, R. Mattia, and others, proposed to emigrate but recalling the verse in Deuteronomy, "And you shall dwell therein," repented their decision and weeping, returned to the land. Yet at the same time, we know of considerable migration from Babylonia to Palestine. Hiyya, Jonathan b. Eliezer, Rav, Rabba b. Hana, Levi b. Sisi, Hanina b. Hama, and others went up to Palestine and participated in the academy and consistory of R. Judah the Prince. How did they support themselves? They generally bought land and lived as absentee-rentiers or engaged in commerce. We know that several of these, particularly Levi b. Sisi and Rav, made repeated trips to Babylonia. Thus the "two houses in Israel" greatly profited from the influence they exerted with their respective governments and from the direct contacts they enjoyed with their opposite numbers abroad.

V

The economic activities of Jewish merchants were only one expression of a centuries-old Parthian-Jewish entente. From the time the Parthian invaders reached Babylonia, to the second quarter of the third century when the Arsacids fell from power, a bond of mutual interest tied the Jews, both in Palestine and in Babylonia, to the Iranians. When Ardavan V died, and Rav lamented (Bab. Talmud 'Avodah Zarah 10b), "The band is broken," the lament was not only for a lost emperor, but also for the end of a dynasty under which the Jews had flourished and in which they had placed great hopes. We have no similar expression from Parthian lips, but since the Jews' rebellion in 66 C.E. had prevented a Roman invasion of Parthian Armenia, since the Jews' fortuitous uprisings in Mesopotamia, Egypt, Lybia, Cyprus, and possibly in Palestine had saved the Parthians in the darkest days of Trajan's invasion, since there were Jews in Palestine who in 150-160 helped to create the unrest desired by the Parthian Shah Ardavan III before his invasion in the next decade, and since some Jews made trouble for the Romans in the troubled decade from 190 to 200 when the Parthians again invaded the Roman Orient, one must assume that the Parthians recognized how useful the Jews could be, and frequently were, in their international affairs. Iran and Israel today maintain cordial political and commercial relations, just as had the Achemenids and the

Jews under Ezra and Nehemiah. One must recognize continuing geopolitical factors which fostered this cooperation from the earlier time to our own day. From the Iranian perspective, Palestine represents one window on the West and a point where allies could be most useful. It is the road to Egypt and adjacent to Syria and Asia Minor. If held by a friendly power, as Artaxerxes made certain it would be, Palestine might serve as a useful focus of Iranian influence. At the same time, it was in the interest of both the Jews and the Iranians to prevent other, stronger powers from occupying the Middle East. Faced with the intrusion of Rome (in antiquity), they could force upon the invader the necessity of fighting a southern front in Palestine and a northern one in upper Mesopotamia and Iranian Armenia as well. When, on the other hand, Armenia became a major power, as it did under Tigranes the Great in the First Century B.C.E., it was to the interest of the Jews, under the Hasmonean Alexander Jannaeus, and the Parthians to make a common cause, as they did. Finally, the Iranians forced the Romans to evacuate Palestine in the time of Herod, and so for the coming centuries they were associated by some Jews with the hope that Rome might be driven out of Palestine. Just as the Maccabees and the Arsacids helped one another, by independent action, to overcome Seleucid power, so some hoped that in days to come, a Jewish ruler might with Iranian help recover Palestine from the Romans. Having no conflicts and much in common, the two peoples benefited one another in antiquity as today.

Another important aspect of Parthian-Jewish relations concerned Babylonia alone. There the Jews required some form of government. We do not know what, if anything, the Parthians devised for them between the conquest of Babylonia in 140-120 B.C.E., and the rise of Vologases I and his reorganization of the empire ca. 70 C.E. It may be that the traditional Jewish authority, in the Persian period in the hands of a Davidic heir, was recognized by them. We know from Josephus' account of the return of Hyrcanus "as their high priest and king," which would suggest, as seems reasonable in any case, that they enjoyed a substantial measure of self-government under Jewish authorities possessing considerable influence and prestige. Our first solid information, however, dates from the first century C.E. Josephus relates the story of two Jewish weavers, Asineus and Anileus (in Hebrew, Ḥasinai and Ḥanilai) who, during the troubled times between 20 and 35 C.E., when Parthian central government collapsed in a welter of conflicting claims for the throne, established a Jewish state, recognized by the weak central authorities, in part of Babylonia around Nehardea. In the same period, the Greek city of Seleucia on the Tigris, not far away, likewise separated itself from the central government, and it is doubtful that stable government existed in the whole region. The brothers eventually fell from power when they overreached their boundaries, and the local Semites, Greeks and Babylonians, with Parthian help, drove "the Jews" into exile in Nehardea and Nisibis, the former strong point in the area, the latter a center of Jewish settlement in northern Mesopotamia. Thus in the first half of the first century anarchy reigned in Babylonia. When Vologases I (51-79) came to power, he sought to curb the power of the nobility, to establish a secure frontier with Rome, to pacify the whole empire, and to encourage stable government and trade. In dealing with the Jews, Vologases constituted a stable ethnic authority, dependent upon the throne and loyal to its interest, which consisted of a Jewish official who claimed Davidic origin (because anyone, even Herod, attempting to rule Jews would best win their respect through such a genealogy, just as Vologases himself put forward a claim to be descended from the Achemenid as a means of reenforcing the charisma of his rule). This ethnarch, who was later called the *resh galuta* (exilarch), exercised authority not over a unitary territory but rather over Jews in a number of places, scattered in communities among other ethnic groups, though M. Ber holds mainly in Babylonia. As a high official within the empire, the *resh galuta* was able to secure the protection of the Jews, and at the same time, to help win their support for the regime. We have seen that he was one means by which the Parthians regularly traded with the Roman Orient. It seems reasonable to suppose that the exilarch helped to mobilize Jewish support for the Parthian empire in times of crisis, for one can hardly regard the fortuitous uprisings of Jews behind the Roman lines in 114-117 and at subsequent periods as totally accidental. Since Parthia was such a highly feudalized state, the provision of an ethnic authority bearing fealty to the throne was perfectly natural, just as an effort to set up a territorial authority would have been inconvenient and probably the source of new unrest among non-Jewish groups.

In the second century, the exilarchate became an effective power. It was very much an amalgam of Jewish and Parthian forms. We know, for one thing, that the father of R. Nathan was a high government official, for when, in ca. 150-155, R. Nathan with R. Meir engaged in a conspiracy to weaken the prestige of R. Simeon b. Gamaliel's patriarchate, R. Simeon referred to the *kamara*, or ceremonial sash, of R. Nathan's father, which had helped him to win a high position within the Palestinian consistory, one may assume, with G. Alon, as the representative of Babylonia Jewry. We know, also, that when R. Hananiah the nephew of R. Joshua intercalated the calendar in Babylonia, an action which, if successful, would weaken the authority of the Palestinian patriarchate in one of its most crucial functions in the diaspora. He was joined by a man, (Ahiah or Nehunyon) who was a local authority. But it should be noted that R. Nathan was among those who told R. Hananiah to desist. Further, when the apostles Yosi b. Kefar and R. Dosetai b. R. Yanna went to Babylonia to collect funds for the Palestinian patriarchate (ca. 150), they reported difficulties with Babylonian Jewish authorities who enjoyed a retinue of horses, possessed great influence with the government so that they might issue sentences of imprisonment and death, and bore Parthian military names and wore Parthian equestrian dress. The names, Arda/Arta and Pil-y Barish, meant "Righteous" and "elephant-rider," respectively, and indicate that the high Jewish officials bore good Parthian names, as did some Jews in Dura Europos.

In the time of R. Judah the Prince the exilarch had achieved great prestige and power. His claim of Davidic origin was widely accepted, for R. Judah himself professed willingness to take second place to the exilarch. The agent of the exilarch in Palestine was, as we have seen, probably R. Hiyya, assisted by his sons and nephews Rav and Rabbah b. Hana. That Hiyya was related to the exilarch and functioned as part of his court is suggested by four facts. First of all, Hiyya and the *resh galuta* of the next generation, Mar Ukban, came from the same place in Babylonia, Kifri, and, they both laid claim to Davidic ancestry. I find it impossible to believe that men who came from the same place and regarded themselves as descended from the same eponymous ancestor did not at the same time recognize a blood relationship. Second Hiyya accompanied the exilarch to the Parthian court on at least one occasion, for he expressed perplexity (Yer. Talmud Berakhoth 2.4) on who sees the king of kings first, the exilarch or the *arkapat* (a government official, whose precise functions are still disputed). Third, Hiyya repeatedly called his nephew Rav "the son of the *PHTY*". The Aramaic title *PHT*, used in Ezra and Daniel, referred in Parthian documents from Nisa to a satrap. Thus Hiyya called his nephew the son of a satrap, and referred to him by a title not only of earlier Aramic usage, but also a living and significant Parthian heterograph. If Frye is correct in regarding *PHT'* as a heterograph for *batesa*, and in proposing an analogy to *bitahs* in both Georgian and Armenian, then the title refers to the representatives of the *shah-an-shah* living at the courts of subkings or vassal kings. Applied to a Jewish authority, the title may indicate that the holder was either direct representative of the *shah-an-shah* among the Jews, or the representative of the throne to the court of the exilarch – I think the former. Fourth, in his relationships with R. Judah, R. Hiyya repeatedly reminded R. Judah about the existence of a "rival" in Babylonia, and R. Judah responded with great anguish, at the same time severely curtailing the rights of R. Hiyya to teach publicly.

In a real sense, the exilarch (called variously R. Huna and R. Anan in the late second century) and R. Judah the Prince did fulfill equivalent functions within the Parthian and Roman empires respectively. Both institutions, the exilarchate and the patriarchate, originated in the same period, namely, at the time of the destruction of the Temple, and both were political efforts to take account of that fact. The Romans had to find a means of governing Jewish Palestine, and had, more important, to assure that the substantial influence of the Palestinian Jewish authority over the diaspora would be exerted to their benefit and not subversively. When the Temple was destroyed, the Pharisees had offered them a useful opportunity: in exchange for the freedom to cultivate their traditions and to govern the inner life of Palestinian Jewry, they would undertake to keep the peace and behave as loyal subjects. In the first sixty years after the destruction of Temple, the Romans supported R. Yohanan ben Zakkai and his successor, R. Gamaliel, and after the disastrous interlude of Bar Kokhba's War, in which the Hillelite house had been thrust aside in favor of revolutionary leaders, the Romans even more vigorously supported the Hillelite scions, R. Simeon b. Gamaliel and R. Judah the Prince, with far more satisfactory results. R. Judah for his part used his consistory to keep the pace in Palestine; for example, in the troubled years of 193-195 he even sent his agents, R. Eleazar b. R. Simeon and R. Ishmael b. R. Yosi to hand over guerillas to the Romans, which both men's fathers, R. Simeon b. Yoḥai and R. Yosi b. Halafta, had gone into hiding to avoid having to do so. The result was that the Jews in Palestine were ruled by loyalist leaders, who exerted their influence in the diaspora in wholly nonpolitical ways. The patriarchate's history finds its parallel in the exilarchate. If I am correct in holding that the exilarchate was founded or reestablished after a period of turmoil, during the reign of Vologases I, probably around 70, then it stands to reason that the destruction of the Temple was a major, though perhaps not decisive, cause. In former times, Babylonian Jewry, like that in the other diaspora communities, was loyal to the Temple. They sent up pilgrims and offerings; the Temple collections were gathered regularly in Nehardea, in the south, and Nisibis in the north, and forwarded in armed caravans to Jerusalem. The Temple authorities for their part sent letters to Babylonia, as did the pharisaic party, to advise them on matters of the calendar and other issues. Afterward, the Parthians, who enjoyed the services of an excellent intelligence bureau, must have known that the Palestinian Jewish authority would no longer be held by quasi-independent officials, but would be very closely supervised by Rome, as was the case. If the Parthians were willing to allow limited, and on the whole politically neutral authority to be exerted from

Jewish Jerusalem, it seems quite unlikely that they would permit a Roman functionary to do the same. On the contrary, just as the Romans sought to mobilize Jewish officials to carry out their purposes, so, quite obviously, the Parthians attempted, and with greater success than Rome as it turned out, to exploit the fact that within their enemy's territories as within their own flourished a large religious-ethnic group with strong ties across the border, and a deep sense of grievance against Rome. The Parthians always tried to foment unrest among minority groups within the Roman empire. The Romans, for their part, were keenly away of the danger of leaving a substantial ethnic group to straddle their borders, and for this reason, for example, invaded Britain and attempted to retain Armenia in the preceding century and a half. (Likewise, the Romans hired Josephus to insure that their view of the guilt for the war of 66-73 and the consequent destruction of the Temple, a catastrophic event in the minds of the diaspora communities, would be well known in the Parthian Empire, and Josephus explicitly directed his remarks to his "co-religionists" across the Euphrates.) It is clear, therefore, that the exilarchate and the patriarchate were parallel institutional devises by which contending empires sought to manage one of the potentially useful ethnic groups within their own, and their enemy's, borders. In both cases, the Jewish authorities enjoyed the support of imperial troops, R. Judah having a detachment of Goths, the exilarch enjoying an armed retinue. In both cases, the Jewish authorities achieved great influence over the local Jewish communities. The end of Arsacid rule might well have struck Rav as a grievous turn in events, for a very close alliance indeed, between the government and the Jewish community, was snapped.

VI

The main reason that Rashi and the Tosafists debated whether the Oral Tradition was cultivated in Babylonian Jewry before the return of Rav is that talmudic literature provides no clear-cut historical evidence on which to come to a positive conclusion. Nonetheless, Halevi's unerring knowledge of the sources led him to conclude that there were such academies and that the Oral Tradition preexisted the establishment by Rav and Samuel of major academies in Sura and Nehardea respectively. (I do not believe Samuel founded the Nehardean academy in any case.) He based his conclusion on the fact that several Tannaim were known to have flourished in Babylonia. We shall consider the facts below.

It is important, first of all, to define the issue carefully. We know that the Oral Tradition was born in the Palestinian schools organized by the scribes and sages from the time of Ezra. We know that the cultivation of this tradition was necessitated by the fact that a fixed, written document, the Torah, came to dominate the life of Jewish Palestine, in various ways and in a number of differing interpretations. Once a written constitution establishes its domination over the cultural and religious life of a society, it becomes necessary to preserve the abiding contemporaneity of such a document by means of continuing, authoritative exegesis, which claims to discover, by disciplined and acceptable hermeneutical devices, the meaning of the document, as it was from of old, for a new and unexpected age. We have no way of knowing what, if anything, developed within Babylonia to parallel this phenomenon in Palestine. Frank Cross, Jr. and others have argued, wholly plausibly in my opinion (see my "Ŝkand Miscellanies," *Iranica Antiqua*, 1964, and Frank Cross, Jr., "The History of the Biblical Text in the Light of Discoveries in the Judean Desert," *Harvard Theological Review*, 57, 4, 1964, pp. 281-300) that Babylonian Jewry produced a biblical-textual tradition quite independently of Palestine.[1] It is certainly reasonable to suppose that the scriptural traditions of Babylonia were of great antiquity, for the Babylonian exiles brought with them great spiritual resources, and, as we have noted, themselves produced both prophets and other kinds of religious authorities. It follows that there were schools and academies for the mixture of these traditions. We know that the Greeks possessed such academies, and that the Iranians, in the Parthian period, likewise cultivated their traditional literature. It has been asserted that the Avesta was written down and redacted for the first time in the first century C.E., and while the matter is subject to much dispute, it is clear, at the very least, that the Magi in Parthian times conducted some kind of schools, as they did in the Sasanian period. (On this, see especially H. W. Bailey, *Zoroastrian Problems in the Ninth Century Books*, Oxford, 1943). Likewise we have references in talmudic literature to both "the laws of the Babylonians" (Gen. R., 33.3, Theodor-Albeck ed., p. 306, 1. 3-7) and to a rule of exegesis "transmitted to us from the captivity" (Esther Rabbah Proem 11, see also Gen. R. 42.3, Bab. Talmud Megillah 10b, etc.). There is absolutely no reason to doubt, therefore, that Babylonian Jews did possess academies and *an* oral tradition by which both scriptural laws and lore were exposited. It is equally likely that such a tradition was indigenous, based upon specifically Babylonian-Jewish traditions, and likely to lay greatest emphasis upon local

---

[1] But the plausibility is entirely for historical reasons, and not for technical ones. I am not qualified to assess Cross' technical argument, which must be evaluated on its own terms by those who are.

matters. Thus, for example, the Dura synagogue apparently devoted the entire western wall to scenes from the life of Ezekiel, which one should expect in a community which regarded Ezekiel as a native prophet. Furthermore, it is likely that the Merkavah tradition was cultivated, again in part because of its peculiarly local venue, in Babylonia. (Evidence on this will be found in pp. 155-160 of my book, and is too extensive to warrant repetition here.) Thus one cannot disagree with Halevi and Yavetz that *an* Oral Tradition flourished in Babylonia. But we have no way whatever, of knowing whether it was exactly the same Oral Tradition, in general or in detail, as in Palestine, and it seems to be entirely unlikely that it was, simply because the potential varieties of biblical exegesis are so vast, even by the hermeneutical principles within a single school of thought, namely Pharisaism, that chances are most remote that people separated from one another by considerable distances and very different conditions of life and thought would by accident reach identical conclusions. One example of the differences between Palestine and Babylonia in a very simple legal matter suffices. When Rav returned to Babylonia he found that the laws of separation of milk and meat then practiced in Palestine were unknown in the part of Babylonia he visited. When Levi b. Sisi visited Nisibis, he was offered the head of a peacock in milk, which he refrained from eating. Babylonian-Mesopotamian exegesis held that while milk and meat may not be mixed, fowl is not meat (it does not enter the category of a "kid in its mother's milk," for fowl do not nourish their children with milk) and hence might be eaten with cheese or milk. A number of explicit references support this statement. It seems therefore unlikely that the Oral Tradition on this particular point was widely accepted in Babylonia. Likewise there is reason to believe that Babylonian Jewry was a great void into which Rav poured out Torah. It was, on the contrary, what it was, and was changed in time by the effective application of the Mishnah and its accompanying traditions.

But it was not the advent of Rav that brought about the change. Palestinian traditions were cultivated in Babylonia from the beginning of the second century, if not before. Rav's coming simply accelerated a process which was well underway, and which by that time was carried on not by isolated teachers only, but within at least two major academies. All of the evidence that Halevi amassed to prove the pre-existence of the Oral Tradition in Babylonia concerned precisely these two academies! Before the second century, we have evidence that some kind of learning flourished in Babylonia. We know the names of Naḥum the Mede (but about him, little else), and Hillel the Babylonian. Hillel is one of the great enigmas of our subject. Some have foolishly asserted that he "really" came from Alexandria, but the bases of such assertions are so flimsy that they reveal more about the lack of historically rigorous thought of those who propose them than about Hillel's origins. He came to Jerusalem, and quickly achieved prominence both in the pharisaic party and in the Temple administration. His teachings were allegedly mainly from Palestinian authorities, for his elevation to power was based upon his ability to cite earlier, recognized Palestinian teachers of the law, in addition to his acute reasoning through scriptural exegesis. (Some have held that in Babylonia, exegesis was mainly through casuistic reasoning, rather than through traditional teachings, because the absence of "*the* Oral Tradition" necessitated the cultivation of the power to reason, but I do not know what to make of such an argument.) Hillel's early career tells us that he came and studied, so presumably he had learned enough in Babylonia to want to come and study. To this extent only may we conclude that Hillel's career indicates the probability of Jewish schools in Babylonia. Since on much firmer grounds we have good reason to accept such a probability, there is not much to be gained in further speculation about Hillel's Babylonian origins.

The first representative of Pharisaism across the Euphrates came as agent not of the pharisaic party but of the Temple administration. He was Judah ben Bathra, who lived in Nisibis, a northern Mesopotamian frontier garrison town frequently disputed by Rome and Parthia before Trajan finally conquered it for Rome. Nisibis was, as we noted earlier, one of the chief collection points for Temple funds. Judah was sent to oversee the transshipment of these funds, which were probably collected mainly in the region around the city itself, including Armenia and Adiabene, where large numbers of the Ten Tribes exiled in the time of the Assyrians continued to live in the places of their resettlement, in the Khabur River valley and its environs. Judah watched out for the interests of the Temple, and on one occasion (Bab. Talmud Pesaḥim 3b) he sent a warning to Jerusalem that a Semitic pagan was about to desecrate the Temple. At the same time, Judah was most certainly a Pharisee. We know this, first, because he is frequently cited in pharisaic literature, where his opinions are taken very seriously, and second, because he offered a proof for the validity of the water-offering (Bab. Talmud Shabbath 103b, Sifre Numbers 150), which was one of the chief points of cultic procedure on which the Sadducees and Pharisees differed. After the destruction, one may suspect that he was in touch with the opponents of R. Yohanan ben Zakkai, the B'ne Bathyra. Since his legal opinions were passed on, he most certainly conducted an academy in Nisibis. A second Tanna in Babylonia was Nehemiah of Bet Deli, a student of Rabban Gamaliel I.

He lived in Nehardea, where he received R. Akiba during his visit to the Parthian empire, and passed on to him a teaching of R. Gamaliel concerning an issue then current in the Palestinian academy. We have no further knowledge of Nehemiah.

Hananiah, the nephew of R. Joshua b. Hananiah, one of the greatest Tannaim in the late first century Yavneh, was sent down to Babylonia because he was placed under the spell of the sorcery of the "*minim* of Capernaum," which presumably means that he was attracted by the teachings of Jewish-Christians. Babylonia at that time did not have a Christian community; its first bishop dates from 300 C.E. On the contrary, in Babylonia and in Nisibis, Christianity was unable to get a foothold before the third century, while already at the beginning of the second century, Adiabene and, a little later on, Edessa had been evangelized. The reason for the substantial delay in the spread of Christianity was that while Nisibis and Babylonia Jewries were under the influence of Tannaim, the communities in Edessa and Adiabene, the latter only recently converted to Judaism, were not, and the Christian interpretation of prophetic literature met with little opposition there. In any case, in Babylonia Hananiah certainly continued to pursue the study of mystical lore of a Gnostic kind, which may have brought him near the "*minim* of Capernaum" in the first place. He was a learned man, who had studied the opinions of many of the leading figures of his uncle's time, and in Babylonia he engaged in teaching and applying the law. In time he became a major authority, and when the Palestinian consistory was dissolved by the Bar Kokhba War, he carried on functions formerly reserved to it, and to Palestine, specifically by intercalating the calendar. When, about 145 C.E., the Palestinians were again able to assert their prerogatives, they sent several messengers, in particular R. Nathan, the son of the exilarch, and R. Isaac, possibly also R. Yosi b. Kefar, a Babylonian, and the grandson of Zechariah b. Kevutal, the last high priest in the Jerusalem Temple, to order him to desist. By an appeal to public opinion the Palestinian agents were able to reestablish the predominance of the Holy Land. Since Hananiah was advised by R. Judah b. Bathyra in Nisbis, and probably also by R. Josiah (in Huzal, see below) to submit, he did so, but not before he had reminded the Palestinians that he was far better qualified than they to calculate the calendar.

The Judah b. Bathyra whom Hananiah consulted was the namesake of the first century Pharisee. He lived also in Nisibis, and was born ca. 90-100 C.E. and died ca. 160-170 C.E. When the Bar Kokhba War broke out, many of the students of R. Akiba were forced to flee the country for having been ordained, contrary to Roman orders, by one of the last of the pre-Bar Kokhba sages, R. Judah b. Bava. They fled, perhaps as a group, to R. Judah b. Bathyra in Nisibis, who sheltered them for a period of at least ten years, before the return of peace and cessation of repression permitted them to come back to Palestine. At Usha they reestablished the patriarchal consistory. Through most of the second century, therefore, a major tannaitic academy flourished in the north. After R. Judah b. Bathyra, the academy was probably headed for a time by R. Eliezer b. Shamua. He taught not only Palestinian refugees, but also native Babylonians, in particular Joseph the Babylonian and Yosi b. Kefar.

Between 135 and 200, the major center of tannaitic learning in Babylonia was at Huzal. Like the Akibans, the students of R. Ishmael had to flee from Palestine because of the Bar Kokhba War. We know the names of only two of R. Ishmael's students, R. Josiah and R. Jonathan. Since R. Josiah was originally a Babylonian, born in Huzal, it was quite natural for him to return home with his colleague. There may have been some kind of an academy in Huzal long before, for R. Josiah gives a law in his father's name (Bab. Talmud Pesahim 54a), which would suggest that an earlier, lesser-known generation of Babylonian Tannaim existed. In any case, R. Josiah was mainly educated in Palestine, though he also studied with R. Judah b. Bathyra in Nisibis. In Huzal, he and his colleagues conducted an academy where they trained the generation of Tannaim to come. These included R. Ahai, R. Josiah's son, a leading Tanna in R. Judah's day, R. Hiyya, Rav, and Issi ben Judah.

R. Jonathan, R. Josiah, and R. Nathan are cited in substantial disproportion in tractates Pisha and Nezikin of the Mekhilta, and R. Josiah is frequently cited in connection with R. Nathan in other places. The disproportion is as follows: Of all the places in Mekhilta where the men are cited, 37 out of 51 are Josiah's, 35 out of 41 of Jonathan's, and 31 out of 62 of Nathan's sayings are found in these two tractates; additionally, of 5 sayings of R. Ahai, four are in the two tractates, and 75 out of 101 of R. Ishmael's are in Pisha and Nezikin. This is a highly abnormal distribution, for a random, relatively equal distribution would have found (approximately) not more than 11 of Josiah's, 9 of Jonathan's, 14 of Nathan's, and 23 of Ishmael's sayings in the designated tractates. Since R. Josiah and R. Jonathan are never cited in post-Bar Kokhba sayings in Palestine and most certainly did not attend the consistory at Usha in 145, it seems most reasonable to suppose that the designated tractates of the Mekhilta took shape originally (though not in their final redaction) at Huzal. Further, since R. Nathan probably spent the war years and a few years afterward in Babylonia, but did return to Palestine, it is clear that the tractates in question were probably based upon exegetical traditions cultivated in

Huẓal between ca. 135 and 150, years in which the three men were in Babylonia together. In any case, the Ishmaelite school transferred its activities to Babylonia, and since sayings of these Tannaim were cited by Samuel and some of his Babylonian contemporaries and students they probably provided at least part of the education of a new generation of Babylonians, who, in addition to indigenous traditions, began after the Bar Kokhba War to have direct access to the Palestinian Oral Tradition.

The contents of the Oral Tradition in Tractates Pisḥa and Nezikin contain no peculiarly Babylonian elements, so far as I can see. What is striking is that the Palestinian teachings were preserved without perceptible change. One infers that much more of the Oral Tradition must likewise have been taught at Huẓal, and that the great body of pharisaic-tannaitic tradition began to provide at this time a central part of the curriculum. It was therefore, on account of the emigration at the time of the Bar Kokhba War that *the* Oral Tradition as we know it to have existed in Palestine reached Babylonia and struck roots there. I do not believe that the pharisaic Oral Tradition flourished in Babylonia before the Bar Kokhba War, though it may have been represented in the persons of one or two Palestinian emigrés (and perhaps also may have been studied by Babylonians who went up to Palestine and returned home, but of these we know absolutely nothing). But it was, as I said, most certainly established not only through individuals, but in permanent academies, by the Akibans in the north and Ishmaelites in the south, as a result of the Bar Kokhba War. Whatever was changed by Rav's coming, one thing did not require his attention, and that was the establishment, for the first time, of rabbinic academies. These were, without any doubt at all, well established and flourishing by this time, and for nearly a century before.

In the next generation, that of R. Judah the Prince in Palestine, the Babylonian tannaitic academies produced a large number of students, some of whom migrated to Palestine. At Huẓal the chief students were R. Aḥai, R. Josiah's son, R. Ḥiyya, Rav, and Issi b. Judah. A group of Tannaim originated in Kifri, including R. Ḥiyya and his sons, and his nephews Rav and Rabba b. Ḥanna. Other figures were Hanina b. Hama, Jonathan b. Eliezer, and the Nehardeans Abba b. Abba the father of Samuel, and Levi b. Sisi. Of these, R. Dosetai may not have been a Babylonian at all, but he made a number of journeys to Babylonia, in the company of R. Yosi b. Kefar, in behalf of R. Aḥai. R. Dosetai's first visit was probably ca. 145 C.E., when he represented the patriarchate against Hananiah's intercalation of the year, and his last was in the time of R. Judah, probably between 170 and 180 C.E. R.

Yosi likewise was sent to collect funds for the patriarchate. Issi of Huzal is another enigmatic figure, for he was known by several names, some of them closely related, as Joseph of Huzal, Joseph the Babylonian (Issi was a diminutive of Joseph), but others of them completely unknown, such as Issi b. Gur Arye, Issi b. Mehallel, Issi b. Akavya, etc. Issi kept a private notebook, which Rav found in the school of R. Hiyya, which was in Tiberias, and both Rav and R. Hiyya cited Issi's teachings. He was therefore an important figure in both countries. [Mordecai Hakoken has held (Sinai XXXIV, 1954, pp. 231-40, 325-34, 407-23) that Issi was a guerrilla leader, and that his variety of names was necessitated by his place in the anti-Roman underground. Hakoken then considers each and every teaching of Issi, and reads each one in the "light" of his basic "insight." It is a possibility. Anything is possible. But whether it is probable that Issi was a "guerrilla leader" or not needs to be seen against the background of the history of the period and requires a measure of support, however, conjectural, from specific evidences of that fact. Hakoken never evaluates the historical usefulness, if any, of the sources he cites, and offers no general reconstruction of the events of the day. While his discussion of Issi's alleged politics is clever, and perhaps offers valuable insight, he has failed to provide propositions in a form which others may critically evaluate. He has given us, rather, a strange "exegetical principle" by which to exposit all the traditions on a difficult and remote Tanna, but history is not written hermeneutically, and Hakoken's suggestion remains merely that.]

R. Hiyya bore a name traditionally associated with Babylonia. According to Samuel Daiches (*The Jews in Babylonia in the Time of Ezra and Nehemiah according to Babylonian Inscriptions*, London, 1910, p. 12) the name Ahiahu was found in a number of Nippur documents. In Dura, likewise, Hiyya was very commonly found in the synagogue graffiti (C. Kraeling, *The Synagogue,* New Haven 1956, p. 272). R. Hiyya came, as we have noted, from Kifri, and was related to the exilarch, who made his court there, and probably represented his commercial, and possibly also political, interests in Palestine as well. Huzal was a center of Benjaminites, and since Hiyya was a Benjaminite (as a Davidide) he may have had some relatives in the town. In any case, he was educated at Huzal, though whether this was under R. Josiah and R. Jonathan seems unlikely, since R. Hiyya outlived R. Judah the Prince (d. ca. 220 C.E.) and would have been born about 150, and attended the Huzal academy about 165-175. He also had some contact with R. Judah b. Bathyra in Nisibis. By the time he reached Palestine he has achieved considerable mastery of the traditions, and was respected for his knowledge not only of Babylonian traditions of law and exegesis, but also of autochthonous medicine. (His nephew Rabba b. Ḥana studied in Palestine with his uncle, and returned to Babylonia before 200, subsequently coming to Palestine at least once.)

Ḥanina b. Ḥama was a student of R. Hamnuna, Scribe of Babylonia, before his migration. Like other Babylonian Tannaim, particularly Nathan, Ḥiyya, and Jonathan b. Eliezer, he acquired some knowledge of medicine, a subject pursued in Babylonia from ancient days. Ḥanina continued to maintain relations with Babylonia. He was the 'typical' Babylonian Tanna: rich, engaged in commerce, trained in medicine, educated partly in Babylonia but mainly in Palestine, regarded as a Babylonian throughout his life, and always in touch with his homeland.

Two of the most important transitional figures were Levi b. Sisi and Abba b. Abba the father of Samuel. Levi may have come from Susa, if his name means anything, and though he spent much of his life in Palestine, he frequently went back and forth, like Yosi b. Kefar, as the agent of the Palestinian consistory, and eventually settled in Nehardea. He studied at R. Judah's academy, probably as a youth, for he lived to ca. 240 C.E. and discussed many issues with Rav and Samuel. he was appointed by R. Judah as a provincial judge in Palestine, but failed in the position. He traveled with Samuel's father, and may, like him, have been in the silk trade. Like him and like R. Ḥiyya and Rav, he pursued esoteric, mystical traditions. Like Ḥiyya, he was believed to have miraculous powers. His friend and colleague, Abba b. Abba, was born and educated in Babylonia. In the silk trade, he visited R. Judah b. Bathyra in Nisibis, presumably before ca. 160/170, and Palestine as well. Since he was born ca. 140 C.E., and was alive in Babylonia when Levi came after 220 C.E., he probably lived to a very old age. In Nehardea he was widely respected. As a rich man and learned in the traditions, he arranged the *'eruv* for the entire town, took charge of the affairs of orphans, and issued legal decrees, including divorces.

The religion of Babylonian Jewry in the tannaitic period is mostly unknown and irrecoverable. We do not have a single source, apart from the designated sections of the Mekhilta, which originated in the first instance in Babylonia. All we have is what may be inferred from Palestinian sources which, in the first place, exhibit no keen interest in abstract theological issues, and, in the second, tell us nothing whatever about Babylonian Judaism. Nonetheless we do know that Ishmaelite teachings were strongly represented. The Huẓal academy certainly transmitted the exegetical viewpoint of the Ishmaelite students. On Deut. 15:10, for one instance we know that the viewpoint attributed to the school of R. Ishmael was expressed by R. Aḥai the son of R. Josiah,

R. Ḥiyya after him, and by R. Naḥam, a student of Samuel more than a half-century later. We know, too, that an indigenous exegetical tradition flourished; though we have only very limited evidences of what it taught, we may be sure that it included considerable attention to the Merkavah chapters of Ezekiel and other mystical lore.

We have general references to Babylonian courts and laws. For example, R. Dosetai b. R. Yannai and R. Yosi b. Kefar reported that the Jewish-Parthian officials who thwarted them constituted a *bet-din shaveh*, a court ready at hand or a court of one mind. the knowledge of that particular court was considerable, for the issue at hand involved whether a quittance had to be given for the legal liability of property handed over to the Palestinian agents. When the Palestinians were unwilling to accept legal responsibility for the property while in transit, the Babylonian Jews applied physical force to recover the goods. Such a legal principle leads us to infer that Babylonian Jews have impressive knowledge of law. Furthermore, Babylonian synagogues preserved their own local customs, for we know that such synagogues existed in Sepphoris and Tiberias, which suggests that Babylonians followed a liturgy somewhat different from that prevailing in Palestine. Likewise, Rav taught R. Ḥiyya "the laws of the Babylonians," during one of the latter's periods of excommunication. R. Sherira Gaon states that there was a Mishnah in Beylonia, entitled "The Mishnah of R. Nathan," which was taught in Babylonian schools before the time of Rav. The definition of the Babylonian tannaitic tradition depends upon close legal and literary analysis of conflicting mishnaic interpretations of Rav and Samuel, for Samuel's opinions (where specially supposed to be traditions, and nor merely interpretations or ad hoc decisions) would provide evidence of the content of the non-Palestinian viewpoint. In any event, no one can doubt that Babylonian Jewry possessed a rich legal tradition, for it was substantially self-governing, and thus must have possessed rich bodies of antecedent decisions to govern its collective social, commercial, and moral life long, long before the return of Rav. This body of law must have been based, as Jewish law normally was, on Scriptures and its interpretation. Just as Palestinian Judaism, in its several modulations, was always scriptural, so was that of Babylonian Judaism. And just as the Scripture was interpreted according to the hermeneutical, and, more broadly, historical and theological viewpoints of those doing the interpreting, so this must have been the case in Babylonia. But I do not believe we shall ever know very much about what those viewpoints consisted of.

Rav's coming has been regarded as marking a decisive turning point in the history of Babylonian Jewish community, and so it was. But it should by now be entirely clear that Rav did not "bring the Torah" to Babylonia, for it had never left. Nor did he bring knowledge of Tannaitic Judaism, for it was present close to a century before his arrival. What he did bring must become clear in a close study of the early Sasanian period of Babylonian Judaism. What he did *not* bring has become abundantly obvious through this survey of the tannaitic sources on the history of Babylonian Jews and Judaism in the Parthian age.

VII

It has become stylish among American Jewish ideologists to compare our community to that of Babylonia. for example, Oscar Janowsky states (in *The American Jew: A Reappraisal*, Philadelphia, 1964, p. 396). "The great centers of Jewish population of the past did not blossom into cultural communities in a few generations. The Jews were in Babylonia in the sixth century B.C.E. but they did not achieve cultural leadership until eight hundred years later. In Spain and in Western Germany, Jews lived in considerable numbers for at least six hundred years before cultural life assumed significant proportions in the tenth century C.E." The comparison between American and Babylonian Jewry seems appropriate because in both cases, these communities flourished alongside that in the land of Israel, in antiquity as in our own time.

Yet is is important to emphasize, if comparisons must be made, what separates American Jewry now from Babylonian Jewry in the second century. The Jews in Babylonia, unlike those in America, never divorced themselves from their tradition, either through apathy or through lack of education. It is simply incorrect to say that they existed without substantial cultural and religious resources for eight hundred years, or to believe that they only began much later to achieve "cultural leadership" (whatever one means by that, for Babylonian Jewry did not "lead" Palestinian Judaism at any point before the fifth century, if then!). Babylonian Jewry always cultivated indigenous traditions. When new and challenging viewpoints were brought there from Palestine, it was the meeting between the old, needing revivification and the new, requiring a new and vigorous host-culture, which produced the impressive outburst of legal, theological, and educational creativity characteristic of the third and fourth century Babylonian Judaism. Without an antecedent tradition, and without a large and cultured population, Babylonian Jewry could never have responded creatively to the challenges of early Sasanian times, both the inner challenges represented by Rav's coming and the advent of the Mishnah, and the external ones embodied in the great mixing of cultures and religions in the time of Shahpur I. Rav did not have to teach the Bible, or the centrality of law and theological concern for the community life. These he found. He had to reorient the community, and when he did so, it was with the cooperation of resident authorities of great prestige, wide influence, and profound learning.

A second striking difference is that of leadership. Babylonian Jewry possessed in the exilarchate a highly developed political authority. It also accepted the leadership of the Tannaim of both Babylonian and Palestinian origin. The extent of their actual authority was probably limited. But their influence and prestige were not. These men were substantial, for they possessed both learning and material wealth. Babylonian Jewish leaders led in meaningful ways. They led the formation of culture and the application of religion. When they stood apart, as they did, from the common culture, they did so in the cause of an uncommon demand upon the lives of their community, and not merely because they possessed greater material wealth than the masses, though they mostly seem to have been wealthy. American Jewry has no exilarch, nor is it clear to me that it needs one. But it also does not have many leaders who are both rich *and* learned, and it is difficult to conceive of an effective communal (as opposed to spiritual) leader who cannot give some material support to his plans. The "Torah" and "Greatness" in a single person which were the attributes not only of R. Judah the Prince, but also of Samuel's father, Samuel and many others, are not commonplace in American Jewry, where important Jews are generally important by reason of wealth alone. The Jews have never taken seriously the leadership of men whose qualifications did not include spiritual gifts and also great learning, who did not participate sincerely and personally in the life of the community and in the activities of religion and piety which the community stood for, and it is not surprising that American Jewry today ignores, or apathetically tolerates, the pretensions of its current generation of "leaders." With rare and noteworthy exceptions, these leaders have nothing at all in common with the kind of men who exerted profound influence in ancient Babylonia.

Furthermore, Babylonian Jewry saw itself in a very different perspective from that which characterizes our community. It regarded itself as the bearer of important truths. It believed that Jewry existed for universally significant reasons. In the economy of the universe, the Jew bore a very special place. Through the Jewish community, men were brought nearer to their Father in Heaven. Through Jewish laws, men were made better human beings. Through Jewish theology men understood better than they could in any other way what reality was about. Babylonian Jews in the third century lived in one of the world's centers of culture in their day. Shapur brought to his court men of advanced learning and science from every part of the civilized world. From Babylonia went forth a new universal religion, that of Mani. In Babylonia an ancient religious tradition, that founded by Zoroaster, rooted itself once again, with the unrelenting conviction that through its cult and teachings God would best be served, the world most accurately explained, and man most assuredly reach salvation. In Babylonia, moreover, Christianity made numerous converts (toward the end of the third century). There also flourished the cults of many gods, believed by men to be of some value in attaining desired ends. In this cosmopolitan, sophisticated, and relativistic universe, not terribly different from ours in the plurality of opinions available to men and in the richness and vitality of its cultural potentialities, the Jews did not respond as they do today. They did not turn away from their own tradition out of embarrassment, out of fear that it could not contribute to the great conversation among many kinds of men which flourished in their day. They did not treat their traditions with indifference, either because of the attractions of other cultures or because of inability to relate their own to affairs of the day, or surely because they would not devote the time and effort needed to achieve significant mastery of their ancient heritage. On the contrary, they took great pride in their own traditions, and if like Samuel and Levi ben Sisi, they sought to learn from those of others (in their case, from Ablat, an Iranian sage), they did so with a full understanding that they had adequate criteria, furnished by their own heritage, of what was true and what was not. So they admired what was good, acquired what was true, including medicine and astronomy, and mostly rejected what was of no consequence, no matter how much stock others put in it, such as astronomy and the various forms of magic and superstition. Above all, they acquired from the interesting world in which they lived a deeper sense for who they themselves were, what they represented in the scheme of things.

For our part, American Jews do not yet have a vivid awareness of how much effort is required to master their own tradition; nor do they have enough respect for themselves and their tradition to devote the necessary effort. They are captivated by the attractions of their cosmopolitan, sophisticated, and relativistic situation, but are unable to find the equilibrium necessary to cope with it with dignity and with a keen sense for what is valuable, and what is not.

It is frequently said that the difference lies in the change in man's spiritual situation. In former times, men of different culture reinforced one another's worldview, while today, the traditional viewpoints of Judaism do not find support, as once they did, in the "outside" world. Of

Babylonia, this is by no means true. The world of the Babylonian pagan, whether Iranian or Greek, did not reaffirm the teachings of Judaism, but on the contrary, challenged them – even within their own terms – by asserting that the way to health, prosperity, and redemption lay through the service of this cult or that cult, or many cults, each of which offered its own very attractive rites for redemption. Up the river about 150 miles from the center of Jewish settlement in Babylonia lay a frontier trading and garrison town called Dura-Europos. In Dura was settled a relatively small and unimportant Jewish community, whose synagogue nestled far away from the great courts and marketplaces of the city, against the outer wall. In Dura, the Roman soldiers held that Mithra was God. The cults of every pagan Semitic deity flourished there. Iranian cults and Greek cults flourished side by side, and doubtless many felt that the truth was one, only seen through a many-faceted prism. On the walls of their synagogue, the Jews wrote an immortal comment on the religions and high cultures they observed around them. As interpreted by Professor Erwin Goodenough in *Jewish Symbols in Greco-Roman Times* (New York 1963, vols. IX-XI), the walls of the synagogue indicate that the Jews had a rich appreciation for the spiritual blessings of each cult, and announced to the world that whatever was good in any of them was to be found first and best in the synagogue, and in the Torah which was at the center of its design. The west wall presented, for example, the scene of the destruction of the gods of the Philistines, before the ark of the Holy One of Israel. These gods were drawn precisely according to the artistic conventions widely familiar to those who frequented pagan shrines. No one could have missed the point. As Goodenough states, "The theme of the synagogue as a whole might be called the celebration of the glory and power of Judaism and its God." The artist of the synagogue did so by copying the "inner shrine of a pagan temple and filling it with images of human beings and Greek and Iranian divinities." And the point of it all was to respond with tenacious and unfailing pride to the challenges of the pagan environment with the ever-new assertion that the Lord, the God of Israel, is the one God, and there is none else.

Until any Jewish community, anywhere and at any age in history, can respond to the challenge of its age by affirming as a community and through the lives of its individual members that the gods of the age are no-gods; but that the Lord, God of Israel, rules and that His dominion is supreme over all, it cannot begin to compare itself to Babylonian Jewry in the tannaitic age, nor begin to hope to achieve what Babylonian Jewry in the Amoraic age created and left as a legacy for all time.

15

From Enemy to Sibling: Rome and Israel in the First Century of Western Civilization

The Bokser Lecture
Queens College, 1986

Rabbi Ben Zion Bokser was my teacher and friend. When I was a student at the Jewish Theological Seminary of America, I was privileged to study homiletics with him, though he in no way bears fault for my incapacity in that area. I remember him very fondly as a kind and patient, also erudite and scholarly man, a model of the rabbi as exemplar of the values of Torah-study. Later on I had the pleasure of receiving as a doctoral student another Rabbi Bokser, now Doctor and Professor Baruch M. Bokser, and I had the joy of observing how the heritage of the father lives on in yet another generation. I have known few people so sympathetic as Ben Zion Bokser, I know all of us rejoice in the many memories of his humanity and learning that we retain and cherish. My thanks to Queens College for the honor of asking me to prepare and deliver a lecture in his memory. I know that, in the *yeshiva shel maalah*, he will find patience to tolerate a lecture, not one word of which the author of *Pharisaic Judaism in Translation* and similar books whose methods accord with the premises of another age, not our own, will have understood or found persuasive. That is the way of learning: an ongoing process. But since, as I shall presently show, my purpose is to reject results, therefore methods, of my own, my tribute to the memory of Ben Zion Bokser will be understood. He knew that, in learning, the verb, learning, is active and continuous and progressive. No conclusion demands defense, but all results require our best efforts. And the way forward is always to reconsider and refine and rethink.

That is what he stood for: learning in the progressive present; always happening in the here and now. So we begin.

I. Rome and Israel
The Methodological Issue

Judaism and Christianity in late antiquity present histories that mirror one another. When Christianity began, Judaism was the dominant tradition in the Holy Land and framed its ideas within a political framework until the early fifth century. Christianity had to work out of its subordinate definitive Judaism. (Elsewhere, of course, Christianity had to work out of its subordinate position as well.) From the time of Constantine onward, matters reversed themselves. Now Christianity predominated in expressing its ideas in political and institutional terms. Judaism, by contrast, had lost its political foundations and faced the task of working out its self-understanding in terms of a world defined by Christianity, now everywhere triumphant and in charge of politics. The important shift came in the early fourth century. When I speak of the West's first century, therefore, I mean the fourth. That was when the West began in the union of Christian religion and Roman rule. Let me now turn to the issue of method to be illustrated in the topic at hand.

The relationships between Rome and Israel in late antiquity, from the destruction of the Temple in A.D. 70 to the Muslim conquest of the Land of Israel in the mid-seventh century, have attracted attention over the years.[1] What is at issue has not always come to the fore. What scholars have done, when approaching the rabbinic writings of the age, is to collect and organize all the sayings on Rome and to treat the resulting composite as "the talmudic," or "the rabbinic" view of Rome. In doing so they have followed the established way in which to investigate the thought of classical Judaism on any given subject. It is to collect pertinent sayings among the diverse documents and to assemble all these sayings into a composite, a portrait, for example, "*the rabbinic view of Rome.*" The composite will divide up the sayings in accord with the logic of the topic at hand. If, for example, we want to know the thought of classical Judaism about God, we collect everything and then divide up the result among such rubrics as God's attributes, God's love, or Providence, or reward and punishment, and the like. Differentiation therefore affects not the documents but the topic. That

---

[1] See, for the systematic work, Shmuel Krauss, *Persia and Rome in Talmud and Midrash* (Jerusalem, 1947, in Hebrew) and, most recently, Mireille Hadas-Lebel, "La fiscalité romaine dans la littérature rabbinque," *Revue des études juives*, 1984, 143:5-29.

is to say, whatever we find, without regard to the document in which the saying or story occurs, joins together with whatever else we find, to form an undifferentiated aggregate, thus to illustrate a given aspect of our topic, thus God's love or Providence, as these topics are treated in a diversity of documents. How then do we organize our data? It is by allowing the topic we study to tell us its divisions, that is to say, the logic of differentiation derives from the topic, not the sources from which we draw sayings about a topic at hand.

My research for a number of years has led me to differentiate among documents and to ask each document to deliver its particular viewpoint to me. When, therefore I wish to trace the history of an idea, it produces the representations of that idea as yielded by documents, read singly and one by one, then in the sequence of their closure.[2] I do not join together everything I find, without regard to its point of origin in a complete compilation of rabbinic sayings. Rather I keep things apart, so that I record what I find in document A, then in document B, and onward through the alphabet. What this yields is a history of the idea at hand as the documents, laid out in their sequence, tell me that history.

Now how shall we test whether the approach just now outlined proves superior to the established one? The answer is to ask what we discover if we do not differentiate among documents, as against what we find when we do. Let me spell this out, and then proceed to an examination of the issue at hand: a particular topic, sources for which are laid forth one way, then investigated and interpreted in two different ways. In the present context, I may not have to plead guilty of excessive criticism of colleagues' scholarship, since both approaches to the description and interpretation of the relationship of Rome and Israel derive from my own work, that is, the one that failed to differentiate among sources, then the one that does effect what I maintain is the required differentiation. In setting forth the positions of Neusner *vs.* Neusner, I shall explain where and how I erred and why I think my revision is correct.

II. Testing the Worth of Differentiation among Documents

Let me begin by asking, how shall we know which approach is better, or even right? The answer to the question derives from a test of

---

[2]For reasons I spell out in my *Religious Study of Judaism. Description, Analysis, Interpretation. First Series* (Atlanta, 1985: Scholars Press for Brown Judaic Studies), I call this "the canonical history of ideas." The matter does not require attention here.

falsification: how can we show, therefore how do we know, whether we are right or wrong. One way of testing the viability of a method is to ask whether it facilitates or impedes the accurate description and analysis of data. Let me spell out this criterion.

My test of the proposed approach of differentiating among documents consists in trying one approach and then its opposite to see the result: a perfectly simple experiment. Our criterion for evaluating results is simple: if we do things in two different ways, in the results of which of the two ways do we see the evidence with greater, in which lesser, perspicacity? That criterion will rapidly improve its entirely objective value. So these are the questions to be raised. If we do not differentiate among documents, then we ask what happens if we do differentiate. If we do differentiate, we ask what happens if we do not. These are simple research experiments, which anyone can replicate. To spell them out also poses no great difficulty. If differentiating yields results we should have missed had we not read the documents one by one, then our category has obscured important points of difference. If not differentiating yields a unity that differentiating has obscured, so that the parts appear, seem all together, to cohere, then the category that has required differentiation has obscured important points in common. How shall we know one way or the other? Do we not invoke a subjective opinion when we conclude that there is, or is not, a unity that differentiation has obscured? I think not. In fact the operative criterion is a matter of fact and does not require subjective judgment. How so? Let me state the objective criterion with emphasis:

[1] If we find that each one of the documents says on its own essentially what all of the documents say together, so that the parts do turn out to be interchangeable, then imposing distinctions suggests differences where there is none. The parts not only add up to the sum of the whole, as in the case of a homogenizing category. Each of the parts replicates the fundamental structure of the whole. In that case, differentiation proves misleading.

[2] If, by contrast, when viewed one by one, our documents in fact do not say the same thing by themselves that all of them say when read together, our category, failing to recognize differences, suggests a unity and a cogency where there is none. The parts may well add up to the sum of the whole, but each of the parts appears to stand by itself and does not replicate the statement to which, as part of a larger whole, it contributes. In that case, not effecting a considerable labor of description of the documents one by one will obscure the

very center and heart of matters: that the documents, components of the whole, are themselves autonomous, though connected (if that can be shown) and also continuous (if that can be shown).

Accordingly, the results of an experiment of differentiation where, up to now, everything has been read as a single harmonious statement, will prove suggestive – an interesting indicator of the effect and usefulness of the category at hand. At the end we shall return to these questions and answer them.

Since, in the case of "the Talmudic view of Rome," we treat all writings produced by all Jews as essentially homologous testimonies to a single encompassing Judaism, we shall now engage in a hitherto-neglected exercise of differentiation. We ask what each source produced by Jews in late antiquity, read by itself, has to say about the subject at hand. How shall we differentiate among the available writings? The simplest route is to follow the lines of distinction imposed by the writings themselves, that is, simply, to read one book at a time, and in the order in which the several books are generally held to have reached closure.

III. The Canonical Principle in Category-Formation

The limns of documents then generate, form, and define our initial system of categories. That is, the document to begin with is what demands description, then analysis by comparison and contrast to other documents, then interpretation as part of the whole canon of which it forms a part.[3] In the case at hand, what we have to do is simply ask the principal documents, one by one, to tell us their picture of the topic at hand, hence, Rome and Israel's relationship to Rome. Each document, it is clear, demands description, analysis, and interpretation, all by itself. Each must be viewed as autonomous of all others. At a later stage, each document also is to be examined for its relationships with other documents that fall into the same classification (whether that classification is simply "Jewish" or still more narrowly and hence usefully defined). Then, at the end, each document is to be allowed to take its place as part of the undifferentiated aggregation of documents that, all together, constitute the evidence of a Judaism, in the case of the rabbinic kind, the canon of the Torah.

---

[3]I hasten to add, I do not take the canon to be a timeless category, as my analysis of the Mishnah and its associates indicates. Quite to the contrary, the canon itself takes shape in stages, and these form interesting categories for study.

Let me spell this out. If a document reaches us within its own framework as a complete book with a beginning, a middle, and an end, we do not commit an error in simple logic by reading that document as it has reached us, that is, as a book itself. If further a document contains materials shared verbatim or in substantial content with other documents of its classification, or if a document explicitly refers to some other writings and their contents, then we have to ask the question of connection. We have to seek the facts of connectedness and ask for the meaning of those connections. In the description of a Judaism, we have to take as our further task the description of the whole out of the undifferentiated testimony of all its parts. For a Judaism does put together a set of once discrete documents and treat them as its canon. So in our setting we do want to know how a number of writings fit together into a single continuous and harmonious statement. In the present setting, only the part of the work is required.

IV. The Outsider in General, Rome in Particular

We come to the topic at hand: Rome and Israel. To begin with we approach the matter from its most abstract angle: Rome as representative of an outsider. The outsider in general represented a danger that took many forms, for the outsider found definition in a variety of ways. He could be an Israelite holding views other than those of sages. A perfectly loyal man, for example, who did not accept the rabbis' remarkable claims in behalf of the sanctity of what they knew, or all of their rules, posed a threat. An outsider could be a woman, simply because, in sages' view, men were normal, women abnormal. It could be a Samaritan, sharing Scripture but reading it differently. It could be a Christian, with the old Scripture and a new one, claimed to complete the old. It could be a Roman, alien and powerful. It could be an Iranian, from the other side of the frontier, or someone still more different than that. So, in all, we may invent a hierarchy of difference, from nearest to farthest away, and we may further postulate not only degrees of difference but also differentiation among the different, and that on a polythetic basis.

Let us now proceed to review four important sources as autonomous components of a larger canon and to ask each of them to speak for itself, all by itself, on the topic at hand. These fall into two groups: the Mishnah (inclusive of tractate Abot) and a document of Mishnah-exegesis, the Tosefta, and two documents of Scripture exegesis, Genesis Rabbah and Leviticus Rabbah. The former testify to the minds of compositors who flourished in the late second and third centuries (before Christianity became the state religion of the Roman empire), the later, the late fourth and fifth centuries (after the establishment of Christianity as imperial cult and faith). We shall parse the ideas at hand as they unfold in these four compilations.[4] Then we shall trace the result, which is the canonical history of the topic at hand. Finally, we shall review the original results and show where and how they erred – and, above all, explain the reason why. In that way we shall carry out an exercise in the testing of a method. That is to say, we ask what happens when we do, and when we do not, differentiate.

V. Differentiating among Documents
1. Rome (Esau, Edom) in the Mishnah and Tractate Abot

If we ask the Mishnah, ca. A.D. 200, its principal view of the world beyond, it answers with a simple principle: the framers of the document insist that the world beyond was essentially undifferentiated. Rome to them proved no more, and no less, important than any other place in that undifferentiated world, and, so far as the epochs of human history were concerned, these emerged solely from within Israel, and, in particular, the history of Israel's cult, as M. Zeb. 14:4-9 lays matters out in terms of the cult's location, and M. R.H. 4:1-4 in terms of the before and after of the destruction.[5] The undifferentiation of the outside world may be conveyed in a simple fact. The entire earth outside of the Land of Israel in the Mishnah's law was held to suffer from contamination by corpses. Hence it was unclean with a severe mode of uncleanness, inaccessible to the holy and life-sustaining processes of the cult. If an Israelite artist were asked to paint a wall-portrait of the world beyond the Land, he would paint the entire wall white, the color

---

[4]Since we cannot demonstrate that what is attributed to authorities within the pages of the documents really was said by them, we also cannot impute to a generation prior to that of redaction any of the ideas expressed in the several documents: what we cannot show, we do not know. And, to the contrary, what we can show, which is what the documents demonstrably speak for the authorship of the final redaction, we do know: the opinions of the ultimate, sometimes also the penultimate, redactors. That is all we know at this time. So, whether or not the Mishnah or Leviticus Rabbah contains ideas held prior to the generation of redaction is not at issue. I claim here to say what the authorship at the end wished to state, in the time and circumstance of redaction. What else these documents contain, to what other ages and authorships they testify – these are separate questions, to be taken up on in their own terms. I have done so for the Mishnah and Tosefta in various works of literary and historical study.

[5]In my *Messiah in Context, Israel's History and Destiny in Formative Judaism* (*Foundations of Judaism*, Vol. II. *Teleology*) (Philadelphia, 1983: Fortress) I dealt at some length with the larger question of the later reimagining of Israel's history. But that is not at issue here.

of death. The outside world, in the imagination of the Mishnah's law, was the realm of death. Among corpses, how are we to make distinctions? We turn then to how the Mishnah and tractate Abot treat Rome, both directly and in the symbolic form of Esau and Edom. Since the system at hand treats all gentiles as essentially the same, Rome, for its part, will not present a theme of special interest. So if my description of the Mishnah's basic mode of differentiation among outsiders proves sound, then Rome should not vastly differ from other outsiders.

As a matter of fact, if we turn to H. Y. Kosovsky, *Thesaurus Mishnae* (Jerusalem, 1956) I, II, IV, and look for Edom, Esau, Ishmael, and Rome, we come away disappointed. "Edom" in the sense of Rome does not occur. The word stands for the Edomites of biblical times (M. Yeb. 8:3) and the territory of Edom (M. Ket. 5:8). Ishmael, who like Edom later stands for Rome, supplies a name of a sage, nothing more. As to Rome itself, the picture is not terribly different. There is a "Roman hyssop" (M. Par. 11:7, M. Neg. 14:6), and Rome occurs as a place name (M. A.Z. 4:7). Otherwise I see not a single passage indicated by Kosovsky in which Rome serves as a topic of interest, and, it goes without saying, in no place does "Rome" stand for an age in human history, let alone the counterpart to and opposite of Israel. Rome is part of the undifferentiated other, the outside world of death beyond. That fact takes on considerable meaning when we turn to the later fourth and fifth century compilations of scriptural exegeses. But first, we turn to the Mishnah's closest companion, the Tosefta.

VI. Differentiating among Documents
2. Rome in the Tosefta

When we come to the Tosefta, a document containing systematic and extensive supplements to the sayings of the Mishnah, we find ourselves entirely within the Mishnah's circle of meanings and values. When, therefore, we ask how the Tosefta's authors incorporate and treat apocalyptic verses of Scripture, as they do, we find that they reduce to astonishingly trivial and local dimensions materials bearing for others world-historical meaning – including symbols later invoked by sages themselves to express the movement and meaning of history. No nation, including Rome, plays a role in the Tosefta's interpretation of biblical passages presenting historical apocalypse, as we now see in the Tosefta's treatment of the apocalyptic vision of Daniel. There we find that history happens in what takes place in the sages' debates – there alone!

From Enemy to Sibling 295

T. Miqvaot
7:11

A. A cow which drank purification-water, and which one slaughtered within twenty-four hours –

B. This was a case, and R. Yosé the Galilean did declare it clean, and R. Aqiba did declare it unclean.

C. R. Tarfon supported R. Yosé the Galilean. R. Simeon ben Nanos supported R. Aqiba.

D. R. Simeon b. Nanos dismissed [the arguments of] R. Tarfon. R. Yosé the Galilean dismissed [the arguments of] R. Simeon b. Nanos.

E. R. Aqiba dismissed [the arguments of] R. Yosé the Galilean.

F. After a time, he [Yosé] found an answer for him [Aqiba].

G. He said to him, "Am I able to reverse myself?"

H. He said to him, "Not anyone [may reverse himself], but you [may do so], for you are Yosé the Galilean."

I. [He said to him,] "I shall say to you: Lo, Scripture states, And they shall be kept for the congregation of the people of Israel for the water for impurity (Num. 19:9).

J. "Just so long as they are kept, lo, they are water for impurity – but not after a cow has drunk them."

K. This was a case, and thirty-two elders voted in Lud and declared it clean.

L. At that time R. Tarfon recited this verse:

M. "I saw the ram goring westward and northward and southward, and all the animals were unable to stand against it, and none afforded protection from its power, and it did just as it liked and grew great (Dan 8:4) –

N. "[This is] R. Aqiba.

O. "As I was considering, behold, a he-goat came from the west across the face of the whole earth, without touching the ground; and the goat had a conspicuous horn between his eyes.

P. "He came to the ram with the two horns, which I had seen standing on the bank of the river, and he ran at him in his mighty wrath. I saw him come close to the ram, and he was enraged against him and struck the ram and broke his two horns' – this is R. Aqiba and R. Simeon b. Nanos.

Q. "And the ram had no power to stand before him' – this is R. Aqiba.

R. "But he cast him down to the ground and trampled upon him' – this is R. Yosé the Galilean.

S. "And there was no one who could rescue the ram from his power' – these are the thirty-two elders who voted in Lud and declared it clean.'"

I cite the passage here only to underline the contrast between the usage at hand and the one we shall find in the late fourth or early fifth century composition.

Since, in a moment, we shall take up writings universally assigned to the later fourth or early fifth century, when Rome had turned definitively Christian, we do well to ask the Tosefta to tell us how it chooses to speak of Christianity. Here too the topic (if it is present at all) turns out to produce a trivial and not a world-historical comment, a fact that in a moment will strike us as significant. To the first-century authority, Tarfon is attributed the angry observation that there were people around who knew the truth of the Torah but rejected it:

Tosefta Shabbat 13:5

> The books of the Evangelists and the books of the minim they do not save from the fire [on the Sabbath]. They are allowed to burn up where they are, they and [even] the references to the Divine Name that are in them....
> Said R. Tarfon, "May I bury my sons if such things come into my hands and I do not burn them, and even the references to the Divine Name which are in them. And if someone was running after me, I should escape into the temple of idoltry, but I should not go into their houses of worship. For idolators do not recognize the Divinity in denying him, but these recognize the Divinity and deny him. About them Scripture states, "Behind the door and the doorpost you have set your symbol for deserting me, you have uncovered your bed' (Is. 57:8)."

This statement has long persuaded scholars that the rabbinic authority recognized the difference between pagans and those minim under discussion, reasonably assumed to be Christian. I see no reason to differ from the established consensus. The upshot is simple: when Christians came under discussion, they appear as a source of exasperation, not as Israel's counterpart and opposite, let alone as ruler of the world and precursor to Israel's final triumph in history. We stand a considerable distance from deep thought about Israel and Rome, Jacob and Esau, this age and the coming one. What we witness is a trivial dispute within the community at hand: heretics who should, but do not, know better. And when we hear that mode of thought, we shall look back with genuine disappointment upon the materials at hand. They in no way consider the world-historical issues that would face Israel, and the reason, I maintain, is that, at the closure, no one imagined what would ultimately take place: the conversion of the empire to Christianity, the triumph of Christianity on the stage of history.

We turn, finally, to the usage of the words Esau, Edom, Ishmael, and Rome, which in just a moment will come to center stage. Relying on H. Y. Kosovsky [here: Chaim Josua Kasowski], *Thesaurus Thosephthae* (Jerusalem, I: 1932; III: 1942; VI: 1961), we find pretty much the same sort of usages, in the same proportions, as the Mishnah has already shown us. Specifically, Edom is a biblical people, T. Yeb. 8:1, Niddah 6:1, Qid. 5:4. Ishmael is a proper name for several sages. Most

From Enemy to Sibling

important, Ishmael never stands for Rome. And Rome itself? We have Todor of Rome (T. Bes. 2:15), Rome as a place where people live, e.g., "I saw it in Rome" (T. Roma 3:8), "I taught this law in Rome" (T. Nid. 7:1, T Miq. 4:7). And that is all.

If we were to propose a thesis on "Rome" and "Christianity" in the Talmud and Midrash based on the evidence at hand, it would not produce many propositions. Rome is a place, and no biblical figures or places prefigure the place of Rome in the history of Israel. That is so even though the authors of the Mishnah and the Tosefta knew full well who had destroyed the Temple and closed off Jerusalem and what these events had meant. Christianity plays no role of consequence; no one takes the matter very seriously. Christians are people who know the truth but deny it: crazies. To state the negative: Rome does not stand for Israel's nemesis and counterpart, Rome did not mark the epoch in the history of the world, Israel did not encompass Rome in Israel's history of humanity, and Rome did not represent one of the four monarchies – the last, the worst, prior to Israel's rule. To invoke a modern category, Rome stood for a perfectly secular matter: a place, where things happened. Rome in no way symbolized anything beyond itself. And Israel's sages did not find they had to take seriously the presence or claims of Christianity.[6]

VII. Differentiating among Documents
3. Rome in Genesis Rabbah

So much for books brought to closure, in the case of the Mishnah, at ca. A.D. 200, and, in the case of the Tosefta, perhaps a hundred years later (no one knows). We come now to the year 400 or so, to the documents produced in the century after such momentous events as, first, the conversion of Constantine to Christianity, second, the catastrophe of Julian's failure in allowing the Temple to be rebuilt, the repression of paganism and its effect on Judaism, the Christianization of the Holy Land, and, it appears, the conversion of sizable numbers of Jews in the Land of Israel to Christianity and the consequent Christianization of Palestine (no longer, in context, the Land of Israel at all). We turn first to Genesis Rabbah, generally assigned to the year 400. What do we find there?

In Genesis Rabbah sages read the book of Genesis as if it portrayed the history of Israel and Rome – Rome in particular. Now Rome plays a role in the biblical narrative, with special reference to the counterpart and opposite of the patriarchs, first Ishmael, then Esau, and, always,

---

[6]The dogma that Christianity never made a difference to Judaism confused me too, as I shall point out presently.

Edom. For that is the single obsession binding sages of the document at hand to common discourse with the text before them. Why Rome in the form it takes in Genesis Rabbah? And how come the obsessive character of sages' disposition of the theme of Rome? Were their picture merely of Rome as tyrant and destroyer of the Temple, we should have no reason to link the text to the problems of the age of redaction and closure. But now it is Rome as Israel's brother, counterpart, and nemesis, Rome as the one thing standing in the way of Israel's and the world's, ultimate salvation. So the stakes are different, and much higher.

Let us begin with a simple example of how ubiquitous is the shadow of Ishmael, Esau, Edom, Rome. Wherever sages reflect on future history, their minds turn to their own day. They found the hour difficult, because Rome, now Christian, claimed that very birthright and blessings that sustained Israel. Wherever in Scripture they turned, sages found comfort in the iteration that the birthright, the blessing, the Torah, and the hope – all belonged to them and to none other. Here is a striking statement of that constant proposition.

LIII:XII

1. A. "[So she said to Abraham, 'Cast out this slave woman with her son, for the son of this slave woman shall not be heir with my son Isaac.'] And the thing was very displeasing to Abraham on account of his son" (Gen. 21:11):

    B. That is in line with this verse: "And shuts his eyes from looking upon evil" (Is. 33:15). [Freedman, p. 471, n 1: He shut his eyes from Ishmael's evil ways and was reluctant to send him away.]

2. A. "But God said to Abraham, 'Be not displeased because of the lad and because of your slave woman; whatever Sarah says to you, do as she tells you, for through Isaac shall your descendants be named'" (Gen. 21:12):

    B. Said R. Yudan bar Shillum, "What is written is not 'Isaac' but 'through Isaac.' [The matter is limited, not through all of Isaac's descendants but only through some of them, thus excluding Esau.]"

3. A. R. Azariah in the name of Bar Hutah, "The use of the B, which stands for two, indicates that he who affirms that there are two worlds will inherit both worlds [this age and the age to come]."

    B. Said R. Yudan bar Shillum, "It is written, 'Remember his marvelous works that he has done, his signs and the judgments of his mouth' (Ps. 105:5). I have given a sign, namely, it is one who gives the appropriate evidence through what he says. Specifically, he who affirms that there are two worlds will be called 'your seed.'

    C. "And he who does not affirm that there are two worlds will not be called 'your seed.'"

No. 1 makes "the matter" refer to Ishmael's misbehavior, not Sarah's proposal, so removing the possibility of disagreement between Abraham and Sarah. Nos. 2 and 3 interpret the limiting particle, "in,"

From Enemy to Sibling 299

that is, *among* the descendants of Isaac will be found Abraham's heirs, but not all the descendents of Isaac will be heirs of Abraham. No. 2 explicitly excludes Esau, that is Rome, and No. 3 makes the matter doctrinal in the context of Israel's inner life. As the several antagonists of Israel stand for Rome in particular, so the traits of Rome, as sages perceived them, characterized the biblical heroes. Esau provided a favorite target. From the womb Israel and Rome contended.

LXIII:VI
1. A. "And all the children struggled together [within her, and she said, 'If it is thus, why do I live?' So she went to inquire of the Lord. And the Lord said to her, 'Two nations are in your womb, and two peoples, born of you shall be divided; the one shall be stronger than the other, and the elder shall serve the younger']" (Gen. 25:22-23):
   B. R. Yohanan and R. Simeon b. Laqish:
   C. R. Yohanan said, "[Because the word, 'struggle,' contains the letters for the word, 'run,'] this one was killing that one and that one was running to kill this one."
   D. R. Simeon b. Laqish: "This one releases the laws given by that one, and that one releases the laws given by this one."
2. A. R. Berekhiah in the name of R. Levi said, "it is so that you should not say it was only after he left his mother's womb that [Esau] contended against [Jacob].
   B. "But even while he was yet in his mother's womb, his fist was stretched forth against him: 'The wicked stretch out their fists [so Freedman] from the womb' (Ps. 58.4)."
3. A. "And the children struggled together within her:"
   B. [Once more referring to the letters of the word "struggled," with special attention to ones that mean, "run,"] they wanted to run within her.
   C. When she went by houses of idolatry, Esau would kick, trying to get out: "The wicked are estranged from the womb" (Ps. 58:4).
   D. When she went by synagogues and study-houses, Jacob would kick, trying to get out: "Before I formed you in the womb, I knew you" (Jer. 1:5)."
4. A. "...and she said, "If it is thus, why do I live?"
   B. R. Haggai in the name of R. Isaac: "'This teaches that our mother, Rebecca, went around to the doors of women and said to them, 'Did you ever have this kind of pain in your life?'"
   C. "[She said to them,] '"If thus:" If this is the pain of having children, would that I had not gotten pregnant.'"
   D. Said R. Huna, "If I am going to produce twelve tribes only through this kind of suffering, would that I had not gotten pregnant."
5. A. It was taught on Tannaite authority in the name of R. Nehemiah, "Rebecca was worthy of having the twelve tribes come forth from her. That is in line with this verse:
   B. "'Two nations are in your womb, and two people, born of you, shall be divided: the one shall be stronger than the other, and the elder shall serve the younger. When her days to be delivered were

		fulfilled, behold, there were twins in her womb. The first came forth red, all his body like a hairy mantle, so they called his name Esau. Afterward his brother came forth....' (Gen. 25:23-24).
	C.	"'Two nations are in your womb:' thus two.
	D.	"'and two peoples:' thus two more, hence four.
	E.	"'...and one shall be stronger than the other:' two more, so six.
	F.	"'...and the elder shall serve the younger:' two more, so eight.
	G.	"'When her days to be delivered were fulfilled, behold, there were twins in her womb:' two more, so ten.
	H.	"The first came forth red:' now eleven.
	I.	"Afterward his brother came forth:' now twelve."
	J.	There are those who say, "Proof derives from this verse: 'It if is thus, why do I live?' Focusing on the word for 'thus,' we note that the two letters of that word bear the numerical value of seven and five respectively, hence, twelve in all."
6.	A.	"So she went to inquire of the Lord:"
	B.	Now were there synagogues and houses of study in those days [that she could go to inquire of the Lord]?
	C.	But is it not the fact that she went only to the study of Eber?
	D.	This serves to teach you that whoever receives an elder is as if he receives the Presence of God.

Nos. 1-3 take for granted that Esau represents Rome, and Jacob, Israel. Consequently the verse underlines the point that there is natural enmity between Israel and Rome. Esau hated Israel even while he was still in the womb. Jacob, for his part, revealed from the womb those virtues that would characterize him later on, eager to serve God as Esau was eager to serve idols. The text invites just this sort of reading. No. 4 and No. 5 relate Rebecca's suffering to the birth of the twelve tribes. No. 6 makes its own point, independent of the rest and tacked on. In the next passage Rome appears as a pig, an important choice for symbolization, as we shall see in Leviticus Rabbah as well:

LXV:I

1.	A.	"When Esau was forty years old, he took to wife Judith, the daughter of Beeri, the Hittite, and Basemath, the daughter of Elon the Hittite; and they made life bitter for Isaac and Rebecca" (Gen. 26:34-35):
	B.	"The swine out of the wood ravages it, that which moves in the field feeds on it" (Ps. 80:14).
	C.	R. Phineas and R. Hilquih in the name of R. Simon: "Among all of the prophets, only two of them spelled out in public [the true character of Rome, represented by the swine], Asaf and Moses.
	D.	"Asaf: 'The swine out of the wood ravages it.'
	E.	"Moses: 'And the swine, because he parts the hoof' (Deut. 14:8).
	F.	"Why does Moses compare Rome to the swine? Just as the swine, when it crouches, puts forth its hoofs as if to say, 'I am clean,' so the wicked kingdom steals and grabs, while pretending to be setting up courts of justice.

	G.	"So Esau, for all forty years, hunted married women, ravished them, and when he reached forty, he presented himself to his father saying, 'Just as father got married at the age of forty, so I shall marry a wife at the age of forty.'
	H.	"'When Esau was forty years old, he took to wife Judith, the daughter of Beeri, the Hittite, and Basemath the daughter of Elon the Hittite.'"

How long would Rome rule, when would Israel succeed? The important point is that Rome was next to last, Israel last. Rome's triumph brought assurance that Israel would be next – and last:

LXXV:IV

2.	A.	"And Jacob sent messengers before him:"
	B.	To this one [Esau] whose time to take hold of sovereignty would come before him [namely, before Jacob, since Esau would rule, then Jacob would govern].
	C.	R. Joshua b. Levi said, "Jacob took off the purple robe and threw it before Esau, as if to say to him, "Two flocks of starlings are not going to sleep on a single branch' [so we cannot rule at the same time].'"
3.	A.	"...to Esau his brother:"
	B.	Even though he was Esau, he was still his brother.

Esau remains Jacob's brother, and that Esau rules before Jacob will. The application to contemporary affairs cannot be missed, both in recognition of the true character of Esau – a brother! – and in the interpretation of the failure of history.

To conclude: Genesis Rabbah reached closure, people generally agree, toward the end of the fourth century. That century marks the beginning of the West as we have known it. Why so? Because in the fourth century, from the conversion of Constantine and over the next hundred years, the Roman Empire became Christian – and with it, the West. So the fourth century marks the first century of the history of the West in that form in which the West would flourish for the rest of time, to our own day. Accordingly, we should not find surprising sages' recurrent references, in the reading of Genesis, to the struggle of two equal powers, Rome and Israel, Esau and Jacob, Ishmael and Isaac. The world-historical change, marking the confirmation in politics and power of the Christians' claim that Christ was king over all humanity, demanded from sages an appropriate, and, to Israel, persuasive response.

VIII. Differentiating among Documents
4. Rome in Leviticus Rabbah

What we see in Leviticus Rabbah is consistent with what we have already observed in Genesis Rabbah: how sages absorb events into their system of classification. So it is sages that make history through the thoughts they think and the rules they lay down. In such a context, we find no interest either in the outsiders and their powers, or in the history of the empires of the world, or, all the more so, in redemption and the messianic fulfillment of time. What is the alternative to the use of the sort of symbols just now examined? Let us turn immediately to the relevant passages in Leviticus Rabbah:

XIII:V
1. A. Said R. Ishmael b. R. Nehemiah, "All the prophets foresaw what the pagan kingdoms would do [to Israel].
   B. "The first man foresaw what the pagan kingdoms would do to Israel].
   C. "That is in line with the following verse of Scripture: 'A river flowed out of Eden [to water the garden, and there it divided and became four rivers]' (Gen. 2:10). [The four rivers stand for the four kingdoms, Babylonia, Media, Greece, and Rome]."
2. A. R. Tanhuma said it, [and] R. Menahema [in the name of] R. Joshua b. Levi: "The Holy One, blessed be He, will give up the cup of reeling to the nations of the world to drink in the world to come.
   B. "That is in line with the following verse of Scripture: 'A river flowed out of Eden' (Gen. 2:10), the place from which justice [DYN] goes forth."
3. A. "[There it divided] and became four rivers" (Gen. 2:10) – this refers to the four kingdoms.
   B. "The name of the first is Pishon (PSWN); [it is the one which flows around the whole land of Havilah, where is gold; and the gold of the land is good, bdellium and onyx stone are there]" (Gen. 2:11-12).
   C. This refers to Babylonia, on account [of the reference to Babylonia in the following verse:] "And their [the Babylonians'] horsemen spread themselves (PSW)" (Hab. 1:8).
   D. [It is further] on account of [Nebuchadnezzar's being] a dwarf, shorter than ordinary men by a handbreath.
   E. "[It is the one which flows around the whole land of Havilah" (Gen. 2:11).
   F. "This [reference to the river's flowing around the whole land] speaks of Nebuchadnezzar, the wicked man, who came up and surrounded the entire Land of Israel, which places its hope in the Holy One, blessed be He.
   G. That is in line with the following verse of Scripture: "Hope in God, for I shall again praise him" (Ps. 42.5).
   H. "Where there is gold" (Gen. 2:11) – this refers to the words of Torah, "which are more to be desired than gold, more than much fine gold" (Ps. 19:11).
   I. "And the gold of that land is good" (Gen. 2:12).
   J. This teaches that there is no Torah like the Torah that is taught in the Land of Israel, and there is no wisdom like the wisdom that is taught in the Land of Israel.

From Enemy to Sibling

	K.	"Bdellium and onyx stone are there" (Gen. 2:12) – Scripture, Mishnah, Talmud, and lore.
4.	A.	"The name of the second river is Gihon; [it is the one which flows around the whole land of Cush]" (Gen. 2:13).
	B.	This refers to Media, which produced Haman, that wicked man, who spit out venom like a serpent.
	C.	It is on account of the verse: "On your belly will you go" (Gen. 3:14).
	D.	"It is the one which flows around the whole land of Cush" (Gen. 2:13).
	E.	[We know that this refers to Media, because it is said:] "Who rules from India to Cush" (Est. 1:1).
5.	A.	"And the name of the third river is Tigris (HDQL), [which flows east of Assyria] (Gen. 2:14).
	B.	This refers to Greece [Syria], which was sharp (HD) and speedy (QL) in making its decrees, saying to Israel, "Write on the horn of an ox that you have no portion in the God of Israel."
	C.	"Which flows east (QDMT) of Assyria" (Gen. 2:14).
	D.	Said R. Huna, "In three aspects the kingdom of Greece was in advance (QDMH) of the present evil kingdom [Rome]: in respect to ship-building, the arrangement of camp vigils, and language."
	E.	Said R. Huna, "Any and every kingdom may be called 'Assyria (ashur), on account of all of their making themselves powerful at Israel's expense.
	F.	Said R. Yosé b. R. Hanina, "any and every kingdom may be called Nineveh (NNWH), on account of their adorning (NWY) themselves at Israel's expense."
	G.	Said R. Yosé b. R. Hanina, "Any and every kingdom may be called Egypt (MSRYM), on account of their oppressing (MSYRYM) Israel."
6.	A.	"And the fourth river is the Euphrates (PRT)" (Gen. 2:14).
	B.	This refers to Edom [Rome], since it was fruitful (PRT), and multiplied through the prayer of the elder [Isaac at Gen. 27:39].
	C.	Another interpretation: "It was because it was fruitful and multiplied, and so cramped his world.
	D.	Another explanation: Because it was fruitful and multiplied and cramped his son.
	E.	Another explanation: Because it was fruitful and multiplied and cramped his house.
	F.	Another explanation: "Parat" – because in the end, "I am going to exact a penalty from it (PR!c!)."
	G.	That is in line with the following verse of Scripture: "I have trodden (PWRH) the winepress alone" (Is. 63:3).
7.	A.	[Gen. R. 42:2] Abraham foresaw what the evil kingdoms would do [to Israel].
	B.	"[As the sun was going down,] a deep sleep fell on Abraham; and lo, a dread and great darkness fell upon him]" (Gen. 15:12).
	C.	"Dread" (YMH) refers to Babylonia, on account of the statement, "Then Nebuchadnezzar was full of fury (HMH)" (Dan. 3:19).
	D.	"Darkness" refers to Media, which brought darkness to Israel through its decrees: "To destroy, to slay, and to wipe out all the Jews" (Est. 7:4).

	E.	"Great" refers to Greece.
	F.	Said R. Judah b. R. Simon, "The verse teaches that the kingdom of Greece set up one hundred twenty-seven governors, one hundred and twenty-seven hyparchs and one hundred and twenty-seven commanders."
	G.	And rabbis say, "They were sixty in each category."
	H.	R. Berekhiah and R. Hanan in support of this position taken by rabbis: "Who led you through the great terrible wilderness, with its fiery serpents and scorpions and thirsty ground where there was no water], (Deut. 8:15).
	I.	"Just as the scorpion produces eggs by sixties, so the kingdom of Greece would set up its administration in groups of sixty."
	J.	"Fell on him" (Gen. 15:12).
	K.	This refers to Edom, on account of the following verse: "The earth quakes at the noise of their [Edom's] fall" (Jer. 49:21).
	L.	There are those who reverse matters.
	M.	"Fear" refers to Edom, on account of the following verse: "And this I saw, a fourth beast, fearful, and terrible" (Dan. 7:7).
	N.	"Darkness" refers to Greece, which brought gloom through its decrees. For they said to Israel, "Write on the horn of an ox that you have no portion in the God of Israel.
	O.	"Great" refers to Media, on account of the verse: "King Ahasuerus made Haman [the Median] great" (Est. 3:1).
	P.	"Fell on him" refers to Babylonia, on account of the following verses: "Fallen, fallen is Babylonia" (Is. 21:9).
8.	A.	Daniel foresaw what the evil kingdoms would do [to Israel].
	B.	"Daniel said, I saw in my vision by night, and behold, the four winds of heaven were stirring up the great sea. And four great beasts came up out of the sea, [different from one another. The first was like a lion and had eagles' wings. Then as I looked, its wings were plucked off....And behold, another beast, a second one, like a bear....After this I looked, and lo, another, like a leopard....After this I saw in the night visions, and behold, a fourth great beast, terrible and dreadful and exceedingly strong; and it had great iron teeth]" (Dan. 7:3-7).
	C.	If you enjoy sufficient merit, it will emerge from the sea, but if not, it will come out of the forest.
	D.	The animal that comes up from the sea is not violent, but the one that comes up out of the forest is violent.
	E.	Along these same lines: "The boar out of the wood ravages it" (Ps. 80:14).
	F.	If you enjoy sufficient merit, it will come from the river, and if not, from the forest.
	G.	The animal that comes up from the river is not violent, but the one that comes up out of the forest is violent.
	H.	"Different from one another" (Dan. 7:3).
	I.	Differing from [hating] one another.
	J.	This teaches that every nation that rules in the world hates Israel and reduces them to slavery.
	K.	"The first was like a lion [and had eagles' wings]" (Dan. 7:4).
	L.	This refers to Babylonia.

From Enemy to Sibling

M. Jeremiah saw [Babylonia] as a lion. Then he went and saw it as an eagle.
N. He saw it as a lion: "A lion that came up from his thicket" (Jer. 4:7).
O. And [as an eagle:] "Behold, he shall come up and swoop down as the eagle" (Jer. 49:22).
P. People said to Daniel, "What do you see?"
Q. He said to them, "I see the face like that of a lion and wings like those of an eagle: 'The first was like a lion and had eagles' wings. Then, as I looked, its wings were plucked off, and it was lifted up from the ground [and made to stand upon two feet like a man and the heart of a man was given to it]' (Dan. 7:4).
R. R. Eleazar and R. Ishmael b. R. Nehemiah:
S. R. Eleazar said, "While the entire lion was smitten, its heart was not smitten.
T. "That is in line with the following statement: "And the heart of a man was given to it' (Dan. 7:4)."
U. And R. Ishmael b. R. Nehemiah said, "Even its heart was smitten, for it is written, 'Let his heart be changed from a man's (Dan 4:17).
X. "And behold, another beast, a second one, like a bear. [It was raised up one side; it had three ribs in its mouth between its teeth, and it was told, Arise, devour much flesh]" (Dan. 7:5).
Y. This refers to Media.
Z. Said R. Yohanan, "It is like a bear."
AA. It is written, "Similar to a wolf" (DB); thus, "And a wolf was there."
BB. That is in accord with the view of R. Yohanan, for R. Yohanan said, "Therefore a lion out of the forest [slays them]' (Jer. 5:6) – this refers to Babylonia.
CC. "'A wolf of the deserts spoils them' (Jer. 5:6) refers to Media.
DD. "'A leopard watches over their cities' (Jer. 5:6) refers to Greece.
EE. "'Whoever goes out from them will be savaged' (Jer. 5:6) refers to Edom.
FF. "Why so? 'Because their transgressions are many, and their backslidings still more' (Jer. 5:6)."
GG. "After this, I looked, and lo, another, like a leopard [with four wings of a bird on its back; and the beast had four heads; and dominion was given to it]" (Dan. 7:6).
HH. This [leopard] refers to Greece, which persisted impudently in making harsh decrees, saying to Israel, "Write on the horn of an ox that you have no share in the God of Israel."
II. "After this I saw in the night visions, and behold, a fourth beast, terrible and dreadful and exceedingly strong; [and it had great iron teeth; it devoured and broke in pieces and stamped the residue with its feet. It was different from all the beasts that were before it; and it had ten horns]" (Dan 7:7).
JJ. This refers to Edom [Rome].
KK. Daniel saw the first three visions on one night, and this one he saw on another night. Now why was that the case?
LL. R. Yohanan and R. Simeon b. Laqish:
MM. R. Yohanan said, "It was because the fourth beast weighed as much as the first three.
NN. And R. Simeon b. Laqish, said, "It outweighed them"

	OO.	R. Yohanan objected to R. Simeon b. Laqish, "'Prophesy, therefore, son of man, clap your hands [and let the sword come down twice; yeh, thrice. The sword of those to be slain; it is the sword for the great slaughter, which encompasses them]' (Ezek. 21:14-15). [So the single sword of Rome weighs against the three others]."
	PP.	And R. Simeon b. Laqish, how does he interpret the same passage? He notes that [the threefold sword] is doubled (Ezek. 21:14), [thus outweighs the three swords, equally their strength].
9.	A.	Moses foresaw what the evil kingdoms would do [to Israel].
	B.	"The camel, rock badger, and hare" (Deut. 14.7). [Compare: "Nevertheless, among those that chew the cud or part the hoof, you shall not eat these: the camel, because it chews the cud but does not part the hoof, is unclean to you. The rock badger, because it chews the cud but does not part the hoof, is unclean to you. And the hare, because it chews the cud but does not part the hoof, is unclean to you, and the pig, because it parts the hoof and is cloven-footed, but does not chew the cud, is unclean to you" (Lev. 11:4-8.]
	C.	The camel (GML) refers to Babylonia, [in line with the following verse of Scripture: "O daughter of Babylonia, you who are to be devastated!] 'Happy will be he who requites (GML) you, with what you have done to us" (Ps. 147:8).
	D.	"The rock badger" (Deut. 14:7) – this refers to Media.
	E.	Rabbis and R. Judah b. R. Simon.
	F.	Rabbis say, "Just as the rock badger exhibits traits of uncleanness and traits of cleanness, so the kingdom of Media produced both a righteous man and a wicked one."
	G.	Said R. Judah b. R. Simon, "The last Darius was Esther's son. He was clean on his mother's side and unclean on his father's side."
	H.	"The hare" (Deut. 14:7) – this refers to Greece. The mother of King Ptolemy was named "Hare" [in Greek: lagos].
	I.	"The pig" (Deut. 14:7) – this refers to Edom [Rome].
	J.	Moses made mention of the first three in a single verse and the final one in a verse by itself [(Deut. 14:7, 8]. Why so?
	K.	R. Yohanan and R. Simeon b. Laqish.
	L.	R. Yohanan said, "It is because [the pig] is equivalent to the other three."
	M.	And R. Simeon b. Laqish said, "It is because it outweighs them."
	N.	R. Yohanan objected to R. Simeon b. Laqish, "Prophesy, therefore, son of man, clap your hands [and let the sword come down twice, yea thrice]' (Ezek. 21:14)."
	O.	And how does R. Simeon b. Laqish interpret the same passage? He notes that [the threefold sword] is doubled (Ezek. 21:14).
10.	A.	[Gen. R. 65:1:] R. Phineas and R. Hilqiah in the name of R. Simon: "Among all the prophets, only two of them revealed [the true evil of Rome], Assaf and Moses.
	B.	"Assaf said, 'The pig out of the wood ravages it' (Ps. 80:14).
	C.	"Moses said, 'And the pig, [because it parts the hoof and is cloven-footed but does not chew the cud]' (Lev. 11:7).
	D.	"Why is [Rome] compared to a pig?

From Enemy to Sibling

    E.   "It is to teach you the following: Just as, when a pig crouches and produces its hooves, it is as to say, 'See how I am clean [since I have a cloven hoof],' so this evil kingdom takes pride, seizes by violence, and steals, and then gives the appearance of establishing a tribunal for justice."

    F.   There was the case of a ruler in Caesarea, who put thieves, adulterers, and sorcerers to death, while at the same time telling his counsellor, "That same man [I] did all these three things on a single night."

11. A.   Another interpretation: "The camel" (Lev. 11:4).

    B.   This refers to Babylonia.

    C.   "Because it chews the cud [but does not part the hoof]" (Lev. 11:4).

    D.   For it brings forth praises [with its throat] of the Holy One, blessed be He. [The Hebrew words for "chew the cud" – are now understood to mean "give praise." GRH is connected with GRWN, throat, hence, "bring forth [sounds of praise through] the throat."

    E.   R. Berekhiah and R. Helbo in the name of R. Ishmael b. R. Nahman: "Whatever [praise of God] David [in writing a psalm] treated singly [item by item], that wicked man [Nebuchadnezzar] lumped together in a single verse.

    F.   "Now I, Nebuchadnezzar, praise and extol and honor the King of Heaven, for all his works are right and his ways are just, and those who walk in pride he is able to abase' (Dan. 4:37).

    G.   "'Praise' – 'O Jerusalem, praise the Lord' (Ps. 147:12).

    H.   "'Extol' – 'I shall extol you, O Lord, for you have brought me low' (Ps. 30:2).

    I.   "'Honor the king of Heaven' – The Lord reigns, let the peoples tremble! He sits enthroned upon the cherubim, let the earth quake' (Ps. 99:1).

    J.   "'For all his works are right' – 'For the sake of thy steadfast love and thy faithfulness' (Ps 115:1).

    K.   "'And his ways are just' – 'He will judge the peoples with equity' (Ps. 96:10).

    L.   "'And those who walk with pride' – 'The Lord reigns, he is robed in majesty, the Lord is robed, he is girded with strength' (Ps. 93:1).

    M.   "'He is able to abase' – 'All the horns of the wicked he will cut off' (Ps. 75:11)."

    N.   "The rock badger" (Lev. 11:5) – this refers to Media.

    O.   "For it chews the cud" – for it gives praise to the Holy One, blessed be He: "Thus says Cyrus, king of Persia, 'All the kingdoms of the earth has the Lord, the God in heaven, given me" (Ezra 1:2).

    P.   "The hare" – this refers to Greece.

    Q.   "For it chews the cud" – for it gives praise to the Holy One, blessed be He.

    R.   Alexander the Macedonian, when he saw Simeon the Righteous, said, "Blessed be the God of Simeon the Righteous."

    S.   "The pig" (Lev. 11:7) – this refers to Edom.

    T.   "For it does not chew the cud" – for it does not give praise to the Holy One, blessed be He.

	U.	And it is not enough that it does not give praise, but it blasphemes and swears violently, saying, "Whom do I have in Heaven, and with you I want nothing on earth" (Ps. 73:25).
12.	A.	Another interpretation [of GRH, cud, now with reference to GR, stranger:]
	B.	"The camel" (Lev. 11:4) – this refers to Babylonia.
	C.	"For it chews the cud" [now: brings up the stranger] – for it exalts righteous men: "and Daniel was in the gate of the king" (Dan. 2:49).
	D.	"The rock badger" (Lev. 11:5) – this refers to Media.
	E.	"For it brings up the stranger" – for it exalts righteous men: "Mordecai sat at the gate of the king" (Est. 2:19).
	F.	"The hare" (Lev. 11:6) – this refers to Greece.
	G.	"For it brings up the stranger" – for it exalts the righteous.
	H.	When Alexander of Macedonia saw Simeon the Righteous, he would rise up on his feet. They said to him, "Can't you see the Jew, that you stand up before this Jew?"
	I.	He said to them, "When I go forth to battle, I see something like this man's visage, and I conquer."
	J.	"The pig" (Lev. 11:7) – this refers to Rome.
	K.	"But it does not bring up the stranger" – for it does not exalt the righteous.
	L.	And it is not enough that it does not exalt them, but it kills them.
	M.	That is in line with the following verse of Scripture: "I was angry with my people, I profaned my heritage; I gave them into your hand, you showed them no mercy; on the aged you made your yoke exceedingly heavy" (Is. 47:6).
	N.	This refers to R. Aqiba and his colleagues.
13.	A.	Another interpretation [now treating "bring up the cud" (GR) as bring along in its train" (GRR)]:
	B.	"The camel" (Lev. 11:4) – this refers to Babylonia.
	C.	"Which brings along in its train" – for it brought along another kingdom after it.
	D.	"The rock badger" (Lev. 11:5) – this refers to Media.
	E.	"Which brings along in its train" – for it brought along another kingdom after it.
	F.	"The hare" (Lev. 11:6) – this refers to Greece.
	G.	"Which brings along in its train" – for it brought along another kingdom after it.
	H.	"The pig" (Lev. 11:7) – this refers to Rome.
	I.	"Which does not bring along in its train" – for it did not bring along another kingdom after it.
	J.	And why is it then called "pig" (HZYR)? For it restores (MHZRT) the crown to the one who truly should have it [namely, Israel, whose dominion will begin when the rule of Rome ends].
	K.	That is in line with the following verse of Scripture: "And saviors will come up on Mount Zion to judge the Mountain of Esau [Rome], and the kingdom will then belong to the Lord" (Ob. 1:21).

To stand back and consider this vast apocalyptic vision of Israel's history, we first review the message of the construction as a whole.

This comes in two parts, first, the explicit, then the implicit. As to the former, the first claim is that God had told the prophets what would happen to Israel at the hands of the pagan kingdoms, Babylonia, Media, Greece, Rome. These are further represented by Nebuchadnezzar, Haman, Alexander for Greece, Edom or Esau, interchangeably, for Rome. The same vision came from Adam, Abraham, Daniel, and Moses. The same policy toward Israel – oppression, destruction, enslavement, alienation from the true God – emerged from all four.

How does Rome stand out? First, it was made fruitful through the prayer of Isaac in behalf of Esau. Second, Edom is represented by the fourth and final beast. Rome is related through Esau, as Babylonia, Media, and Greece are not. The fourth beast was seen in a vision separate from the first three. It was worst of all and outweighed the rest. In the apocalypticizing of the animals of Lev. 11:4-8/Deut. 14:7, the camel, rock badger, hare, and pig, the pig, standing for Rome, again emerges as different from the others and more threatening than the rest. Just as the pig pretends to be a clean beast by showing the cloven hoof, but in fact is an unclean one, so Rome pretends to be just but in fact governs by thuggery. Edom does not pretend to praise God but only blasphemes. It does not exalt the righteous but kills them. These symbols concede nothing to Christian monotheism and biblicism. Of greatest importance, while all the other beasts bring further ones in their wake, the pig does not: "It does not bring another kingdom after it." It will restore the crown to the one who will truly deserve it, Israel. Esau will be judged by Zion, so Obadiah 1:21. Now how has the symbolization delivered an implicit message? It is in the treatment of Rome as distinct, but essentially equivalent to the former kingdoms. This seems to me a stunning way of saying that the now-Christian empire in no way requires differentiation from its pagan predecessors. Nothing has changed, except matters have gotten worse. Beyond Rome, standing in a straight line with the others, lies the true shift in history, the rule of Israel and the cessation of the dominion of the (pagan) nations.

To conclude, Leviticus Rabbah came to closure, it is generally agreed, around A.D. 400, that is, approximately a century after the Roman Empire in the East had begun to become Christian, a half a century after the last attempt to rebuild the Temple in Jerusalem had failed – a tumultuous age indeed. Accordingly, we have had the chance to see how distinctive and striking are the ways in which, in the text at hand, the symbols of animals that stand for the four successive empires of humanity and point towards the messianic time, serve for the framers' message.

IX. The Result of Differentiating Issues of Symbolization and their Documentary Differentiation

When the sages of the Mishnah and the Tosefta spoke of Edom and Edomites, they meant biblical Edom, a people in the vicinity of the land of Israel. By Rome they meant the city – that alone. That fact bears meaning when we turn to documents produced two centuries later, and one hundred years beyond the triumph of Christianity. When the sages of Genesis Rabbah spoke of Rome, it was not a political Rome but a messianic Rome that is at issue: Rome as surrogate for Israel, Rome as obstacle to Israel. Why? It is because Rome now confronts Israel with a crisis, and, I argue, Genesis Rabbah constitutes a response to that crisis. Rome in the fourth century became Christian. Sages responded by facing that fact quite surely and saying, "Indeed, it is as you say, a kind of Israel, an heir of Abraham as your texts explicitly claim. But we remain the sole legitimate Israel. the bearer of the birthright – we and not you. So you are our brother Esau, Ishmael, Edom." And the rest follows.

By rereading the story of the beginnings, sages discovered the answer and the secret of the end. Rome claimed to be Israel, and, indeed, sages conceded, Rome shared the patrimony of Israel. That claim took the form of the Christians' appropriation of the Torah as "the Old Testament," so sages acknowledged a simple fact in acceding to the notion that, in some way, Rome too formed part of Israel. But it was the rejected part, the Ishmael, the Esau, not the Isaac, not the Jacob. The advent of Christian Rome precipitated the sustained, polemical, and, I think, rigorous and well-argued rereadings of beginnings in light of the end. Rome then marked the conclusion of human history as Israel had known it. Beyond? The coming of the true Messiah, the redemption of Israel, the salvation of the world, the end of time. So the issues were not inconsiderable, and when the sages spoke of Esau/Rome, as they did so often, they confronted the life-or-death decision of the day.

When we come to Leviticus Rabbah, we find ourselves several steps down the path explored by the compilers of Genesis Rabbah. The polemic represented in Leviticus Rabbah by the symbolization of Christian Rome, therefore, makes the simple point that, first, Christians are no different from, and no better than pagans; they are essentially the same. Second, just as Israel had survived Babylonia, Media, Greece, so would they endure to see the end of Rome (whether pagan, whether Christian). But of course the symbolic polemic rested on false assumptions, hence conveyed a message that misled Jews by misrepresenting their new enemy. The new Rome really did differ from the old. Christianity was not merely part of a succession of undifferentiated modes of paganism. True, the symbols assigned to Rome attributed worse, more dangerous traits than those assigned to the earlier empires. The pig pretends to be clean, just as the Christians give the signs of adherence to the God of Abraham, Isaac, and Jacob. That much the passage concedes. But it is not enough. For out of symbols should emerge a useful public policy, and the mode of thought represented by symbols in the end should yield an accurate confrontation with that for which the symbols stands.

This survey of four documents read one by one, then in pairs, yields a simple result. A striking shift in the treatment of Rome does appear to take place in the formative century represented by work on Genesis Rabbah and Leviticus Rabbah. In earlier times Rome symbolized little beyond itself, and Edom, Esau (absent in the Mishnah, a singleton in Tosefta), and Ishmael were concrete figures. In later times these figures bore traits congruent to the fact of Christian rule. The correspondence between the modes of symbolization – the pig, the sibling – and the facts of the Christian challenge to Judaism – the same Scripture, read a new way, the same messianic hope, interpreted differently – turns out to be remarkable and significant when we compare what the earlier compilers of canonical writings, behind the Mishnah and the Tosefta, produced to the writings of the later ones, behind the two Rabbah compilations. When we differentiate one document from the next, the details of each document turn out to cohere to the systematic traits of the document as a whole. And, furthermore, what a document says about the common topic turns out to bear its own messages and meanings. That, in a single sentence, justifies the route of canonical differentiation I advocated at the outset.

X. The Result of Not Differentiating: Missing a Distinction that Makes a Difference

When I originally worked on this problem, I took the view that the rabbinic canon, from beginning to end, fails to effect differentiation when it treats the outsider.[7] I maintained that the recognition of the outsider depends upon traits that, so far as the framers of the writings at hand are concerned, remain not only constant but uninteresting. The

---

[7] I refer to "Stable Symbols in a Shifting Society: The Delusion of the Monolithic Gentile in Documents of Late Fourth-Century Judaism, " *History of Religions* 1985, 25: 163-175. cf. also Jacob Neusner and Ernest S. Frerichs, eds., *To See Ourselves as Others See Us:" Christians, Jews, "Others" in Late Antiquity* (Atlanta, 1985: Scholars Press Studies in the Humanities, pp. 373-396.

outsider is just that – not worthy of further sorting out. And, as a result of that premise, in the unfolding of canonical doctrine on the outsider, I did not discern substantial change from one document to the next. So, I concluded, people put out of mind that with which they cannot cope, and the outsider stood for the critical fact of Israelite life, the nation's weak condition and vanquished status. So for the same fundamental cause that accounts for the persistence among the founders of the Mishnah's system of the priestly conception of Israelite life, so too a single tight abstraction masked the detailed and concrete features of the other. All "others" looked alike – and posed a threat. The less response to that threat, the more comforting the illusion of inner control over the outer world wholly beyond one's power. Ignoring what could not be sorted out and focusing upon what could, the sages' Israelite kept at a distance a hostile world and retained command of a universe of rule and order. But I believe that in approaching matters as I did, I failed to compare what the Mishnah and the Tosefta say about the same matter. And the reason was that it never entered my mind that Christianity would make much difference to Judaism – a point to which I shall come back at the end.

Now to return to the methodological question. I can display the repertoire of results attained by the labor of harmonization simply by citing my own uncomprehending words. By seeing things without distinguishing among sources, what conclusions did I draw? Here, alas, are my *ipsissima verba*:

> What demands attention is the failure of people to reimagine a symbol that no longer corresponds to, or conveys, perceived reality. When, to be specific, people continue to speak in the same language about something that has in fact produced drastic change, we must ask why. For reason suggests symbols serve to construct an imaginary world that, for the structure to serve, must in some way correspond to the world out there. When, therefore, a critical area of social experience undergoes vast transformation, the symbols also should undergo metamorphosis. The one thing that should change is the character of the symbols through which people portray in their minds what is going on in that world that their minds and imaginations propose to mediate and to interpret.
>
> ...I point out that the mode of symbolization of the outsider, perceived as a nation and great power equivalent to Israel, remained stable during that period that marked Israel's complete transformation from one thing to something else.

As we have seen, this is simply not true. The opposite is the case. The movement from the Mishnah and its companion to the two Rabbah compilations suggest no failure to reimagine a symbol, but a careful reconsideration of Scripture to find and appropriate a useful symbol to

From Enemy to Sibling

make sense of perceived reality. Scripture supplied the rules of history as much as the laws of society, and in Genesis sages found those rules, hence, Jacob and Esau told them the historical laws governing the relationship of Israel and Rome. In consequence, we see not a failure but an enormously imaginative and successful intellectual initiative.

> At the outset of the period at hand, before A.D. 70, Israel in its land constituted a small political entity, a state, like many others of its time and place. It was subordinate to a great empire, but was a distinct and autonomous unit, a part of the political structure of that empire. I had working institutions of self-government and politics. At the end of the same period, by the seventh century, Israel in no way constituted a political entity. Such institutions of a political or juridical character that it had had, had lost the recognition and legitimacy formerly conferred upon them.
>
> Moreover, when Israel looked outward, toward the world beyond its limits, the changes proved no less stunning. At the outset, Rome, and at the end, Rome, but what a different Rome! In the first three centuries, Rome was what it had always been, what its predecessors in the Middle East had always been: pagan, essentially benign toward Israel in its land. From the fourth century, Rome became something unprecedented: a kind of Israel and canny enemy, a brother.
>
> The modes by which the Jews, or, more to the point, the rabbis whose writings survive, proposed to symbolize the world had therefore to take up two contradictory worlds. On the one hand these "symbols of the stranger," of Israel's history and destiny, and of Israel's relationship to the outsider, dealt with a world in which Israel was like the outsider: a nation among nations, a political entity confronting another such entity, thus history among other histories. At the end, these symbols had to convey the reality of an Israel that was essentially different in genus from the outsider: no longer a nation in the sense in which other groups constituted a nation, no longer a political entity like others, no longer standing at the end of a history essentially consubstantial with the history of the nations.
>
> What we shall see is the surprising fact that, so far as we are able to tell, the modes of political and social symbolization remained essentially stable in a world of change. More to the point, the outsider remained what he had always been, a (mere) pagan, part of a world demanding from Israel no effort whatsoever at differentiation. The "nations" were all alike, and Israel was still not essentially different from them all: consubstantial, thus judged by the same standards, but to be sure guiltless while the rest were guilty. What makes so puzzling the stability of the modes of symbolization of Israel and the nations, Israel's history and destiny, and the substance of Israel's doctrine, is a simple fact. In the interval, Christianity had not only come to full and diverse expression, it also had reached power.

But the modes of symbolization as revealed by the canonical writings read one by one show enormous and surprising change. Imagination, an act of extraordinary daring – these characterize the later fourth and fifth century thinkers. They confronted an unprecedented challenge, and they responded in an unprecedented way, by determining the equivalence of the two powers of the world, Israel and Rome. Of course there was nothing equivalent about the two, either in Heaven (from sages' viewpoint on God's view) or on earth (from everyone else's viewpoint. But that is part of the amazing work at hand. Once more, therefore, we observe: the preceding statement is simply false. I missed the difference among the source, therefore I saw everything as pretty much the same thing when it was not. And, to proceed:

> In coming to power, Christianity drew upon essentially the same symbolic heritage to which Israel had long had access. To Christianity as much as to Judaism the pagan was a pagan, not differentiated; history began in Eden and led through Sinai to the end of time; the Messiah stood at the climax and goal of this world's history; revelation ("Torah") came from one God to unique Israel. True, for all forms of Christianity, the values assigned to the repertoire of symbols at hand hardly corresponded to those imputed by the Jews. But the symbols remained the same, and so Israel now resorted to what had become a shared symbolic system and structure to express its history and politics.
>
> Under such circumstances, who would be surprised to learn that deep thought went into the revision of the available symbols, a restatement in such wise as to differentiate what had been treated as uniform, to redefine what had been grasped as settled? Surely the Christian, in the symbolic system of Judaism, should look like something other than pagan, maybe worse but at least different. Certainly history as a mode of social symbolization should proceed on a somewhat different path from the one it had taken when the one God had not yet come to rule, when Israel's ancient Scriptures had not yet come to define the nature and destiny of humanity. Reckoning with the profound political changes at hand, we might imagine, should lead at least some profound thinkers to reconsider the symbolic system that had formerly prevailed or, at the very least, the nature and definition of symbols that had gone forward into the new age and remained vivid. After all, social change should generate symbol change, political change should make its mark upon the symbols of politics and society.

I now see that the thinkers at hand did reconsider the available system and effect considerable revisions of it – at precisely the right points. And what follows also is simply wrong, and for the reasons now amply spelled out:

> But if that is what reason dictates we should expect, it is not how things actually happened....It would take the rabbis of the canon of Judaism nearly a millennium to take seriously the specific character and claims of Christianity and to begin to counter in a systematic way

From Enemy to Sibling

the concrete assertions of that religious tradition. Before the High Middle Ages, Judaism would have nothing to say about, let alone to, Christianity. More probative, Jewish thinkers would maintain the fantastic pretense that nothing important happened in either the first or the fourth century, that is, in either the supernatural or the political world at hand. As we shall now see, one important indicator of that fact is the unwillingness of the rabbinic exegetes of the fourth and early fifth centuries to concede that Christians were different from pagans. On the contrary, the rabbinic sources treat all pagans as essentially faceless, and Christianity not at all, except as part of that same blank wall of hostility to God (and, by the way, to Israel).

When we consider the movement from the first two documents we examined to the third and the fourth, we realize that every word in the preceding discussion is wrong. In fact the documents brought to closure in the fourth century say something entirely different from those concluded earlier.

XI. Conclusion
The Methodological Upshot

What went wrong? The answer is simple. I began my research with perfect faith in a dogma of Judaism and therefore also of scholars of Judaism. It is that Christianity never made any difference to Judaism. So I took for granted, without knowing it, that I too would find that Christianity never made any difference. My original results then conformed to the premise with which I had commenced work. That is how I could earlier conclude, reflecting a consensus I myself simply took for granted instead of questioning:

> In fact it would be many centuries before Jews would take seriously, and in its own terms, the claim of Christianity to constitute a kind of Judaism, and not a kind of paganism. It would take a long time for Jews to distinguish the Christian from the outsiders. When that differentiation began to emerge, it would be in Christian Europe, on the part of Joseph Kimhi and Moses Nahmanides and others who had no choice. By that time, to be sure, "paganism" had long disappeared from the world of Israel's residency, on the one hand, and any expectation that Roman rule would give way to Israelite hegemony had lost all worldly credibility. Then, but only then, we find Jews confronting in a systematic way and with solid knowledge of the other side the facts of history that had emerged many centuries earlier.

> Whether a different symbolic system would have produced a more realistic and effective policy for the confrontation with triumphant Christianity we shall never know. For so long Israel had pretended nothing happened of any importance, not in the first century, not in the fourth. By the time people came around to concede that, after all, Christianity was here to stay and was essentially different from anything Israel had earlier encountered, it was an

awareness too late to make such a difference in Israel's framing of its picture of the outsider and its policy toward the alien."

We now recognize that this statement is not only wrong, it is wrongheaded. The error is not niggling and it is not inconsequential. It is fundamental, because it is methodological. The methodological error is both general and specific. In general I erred by believing other people instead of asking how people knew the things they took for granted. I took over a prevailing attitude of mind – and I did not even realize it. The specific error was that I failed to work along the lines I myself had already discovered. I homogenized what should be analyzed and differentiated. I gave "the talmudic view of...," having spent too many years trying to show that there is no such thing.

What is at stake? It is the progress of knowledge, learning as an active, continuing, progressive tense. I not only do not mind pointing out where I have erred, I take pleasure in doing so. That is why I do it all the time, and why I wonder at how little colleagues follow suit, that is, how little some people seem to learn both from others and from their own mistakes. They deprive themselves of both learning and enjoyment. Why do I call it deprivation? Because I indulge myself with the pleasure of rethinking things, reworking conclusions and reconsidering questions earlier settled in my own mind. It is one of the joys of learning as an ongoing and continuing, never-ending process – that progressive present tense of life to which I alluded in my encomium of Ben Zion Bokser. Anyone who does not enjoy that process – does not give himself or herself that same pleasure – knows nothing of the pleasures of scholarship.

Let me in conclusion return to the questions with which we began and answer them:

> [1] *If we find that each one of the documents says on its own essentially what all of the documents say together, so that the parts do turn out to be interchangeable, then imposing distinctions suggests differences where there is none...In that case, differentiation proves misleading.*

The outcome is that failing to differentiate among documents and to listen to the message of each on its own, I missed what in fact was a striking and fresh trait in one set of compilations. Not having heard the evidence of one canonical statement, I did not recognize the originality, the unprecedented nature, of another. So harmonization misled me. Now to turn to the opposite:

> [2] *If, by contrast, when viewed one by one, our documents in fact do not say the same thing by themselves that all of them say*

> when read together, our category, failing to recognize differences, suggests a unity and a cogency where there is none....In that case, not effecting a considerable labor of description of the documents one by one will obscure the very center and heart of matters: that the documents, components of the whole are themselves autonomous, though connected (if that can be shown) and also continuous (if that can be shown).

Clearly, the documents read one by one do yield insight that combining all their statements on a given topic does not bring to light. So, in sum, differentiating among documents shows us things that not differentiating among them obscures. Not seeing the books as individual statements obscured for me those shifts and turnings that now appear to respond to the movement of the wheel of history. And, it follows, the thinking at hand, concerning both the outsider in general and Rome in particular, the history of humanity but especially the history and destiny of Israel – that thinking turns out, properly analyzed, to respond in a deep and systematic way to the single most considerable challenge the Jewish people in the Land of Israel was to face for the next fifteen hundred years: the rise of the Christian West as brother and enemy to Israel, the Jewish people.

Do we learn only from the matter of method? No, I think we learn also from the substance of things. I speak now only as a faithful Jew, who takes as an ideal the model of Ben Zion Bokser's faith. We who stand at the other side of the abyss mark the first generation to know that the siblings, Jacob and Esau, Israel and Rome, Judaism and Christianity, may learn to exchange the kiss of peace. And, as in the time of the meeting and reconciliation of the first Jacob and the first Esau, so today, it is at the very moment that Jacob, having labored in exile for so long, once more enters upon the land and the patrimony that is his.

I like to think that our dear friend, Ben Zion Bokser, would have found agreeable this brief and modest homily in his memory, for in his person he straddled the abyss: he suffered in the suffering of Israel in the Shoah, but he also rejoiced in the twentieth century, and ours was the blessing of sharing that century, and that life, with him.

16

What, Exactly, Do We Mean by "An Event" in Judaism?

Address to College de France, Paris
February 1990

In an exact sense, "event" has no meaning at all in Judaism, since Judaism forms culture through other than historical modes of organizing existence. Without the social construction of history, there also is no need for the identification of events, that is, individual and unique happenings that bear consequence, since, within the system and structure of Judaism, history forms no taxon, assuredly not the paramount one, and, it must follow, no happening is unique, and, on its own, no event bears consequence. These statements rest upon modes of the analysis of history as the fabrication of culture, including a religious culture, and require us to review the recent formation of thought on history as culturally ordered, and on the event as "contingent realization of the cultural pattern," for it is only in that context that we may make sense, also, of the representation of both history and its raw materials, events, in Judaism in its definitive canon.

Until modes of historical thinking of a social-scientific character got under way – beginning, as a matter of fact, in this most distinguished collegium – narrative history, ordinarily a paraphrastic chronicle, served as a medium for organizing and explaining perceived experience. That kind of history enjoyed the status of objective truth, a principle of explanation of self-evident validity. Its generative data, events, meaning, happenings of (self-evident) consequence, defined the foci of learning, an episteme ultimately formulated as the search for precisely what happened. When people contemplated the past, it was because they proposed through such precise knowledge to explain whatever mattered in the present. What they chose to interpret in the present then defined their curiosity about the past. They then identified out of the unlimited agenda of the past those things that mattered, and these they called events, occasions of consequence, as distinct from undifferentiated and unperceived happenings – from eating breakfast to losing one's keys – which of course bear no material consequence in the explanation of the world.

Now it hardly mattered, in the long era during which historical study predominated as the medium for the explanation of the social order, that the received manner of doing history as a mode of organizing and explaining experience involved a series of logical fallacies. Explaining the outcome by reference to a sequence of ordered events, after all, formed an intellectually legitimate way of appeal to the intellectually illegitimate argument, *post hoc, ergo propter hoc.* So too, explanation without verification through a process of generalization, interpretation without a process of comparison and contrast, analysis as mere paraphrase of received accounts – these traits of historical learning did not attract attention. Historical explanation of the world, specific and ad hoc and episodic, found no competition and enjoyed the standing of self-evident truth. The notion that the mere paraphrase of "happenings," identified by ourselves as a matter of fact, as events, could account for the perceived present demands for credulity an innocence so childlike that we must wonder how historical explanation of society and culture served for as long as it did. All the more reason to admire the towering intellects, so many of them collected in this one place, whose independence of mind impelled them to ask, why so? when everyone held, indeed, why not? and how otherwise? But they persisted. In consequence we now understand that the very notion of an "event," and with it the vast superstructure of the ordering of intellect and the explanation of society built upon historical explanation of sequences of events, then to now, there to here, all rational, all obvious, all self-evidence, come to us as the gifts of naive credulity.

It would carry us far afield to trace the long history of historical explanation of the social order by appeal to the definition, selection, and sequence of events. Chronicles and other exercises in *Listenwissenschaft,* of course, go back to remote antiquity. But history as arbiter of truth, history as mediator of sensibility and source of explanation – these honored roles in the court of intellect came to history only in the formative centuries of our own civilization. We should, after all, have to trace the path back to the Protestant Reformation, with its insistence on the priority of historical fact, deriving from a mythic age of perfection, in dictating the legitimacy of social reality in the present moment. Cutting through the detritus and sediment of the long centuries of increment and accumulation, therefore appealing not to *Listenwissenschaft,* but to a different, more autonomous kind of judgment altogether, for the logic of their discourse, the Reformation theologians identified history, the record of what happened (in this case) in Scripture, as the instrument for the validation of reform. Reform then would accomplish the renewal of times past, times perfect, appealing therefore to the court of appeal formed by history.

But history of a particular order, events of a very specific character, reaching their definition in the second way station, beyond the Reformation, in our quest for the self-evidence of history as a medium of social explanation. And that, of course, is the nineteenth century with its interest in historical explanation of not merely the life of faith but the reality of society, above all, the formation of the nation. Here again, I stand in the right place to speak of the appeal to history, once more with its canon of well-chosen events, in explanation of the social order, this time, the "we" of the nation, the other-ness of other peoples. If history with its prooftexts in self-evidently probative events served the purpose of religious reform, it provided a still more abundant source for explaining the self-evidence of the nation-state. No wonder, then, that in the American State of Texas, once an independent nation, all school children must study Texas history in three sequences, but American history in only one. No wonder, too, that Zionism precipitated the massive rewriting of the histories of Jews as a single, unitary Jewish history, with a beginning, middle, and end, with the self-evident message of Zionism as its ubiquitous proposition. The State of Texas and the State of Israel exemplify the uses that for so long guaranteed for history a principal place in the academy, for both appeal to facts to validate the claims of social ideology.

Now it is only in the recent past that we have begun to recognize that history forms a discourse of contemporary taste and judgment, events become eventful only because we make them so, and, in all, history is culturally ordered, and events are defined and identified as statements of an intensely contemporary perception. It follows, we now understand, that all histories are the creation of an eternal present, that is, those moments in which histories are defined and distinguished, in which events are identified and assigned consequence, and in which sequences of events, "this particular thing happened here and therefore...," are strung together, pearls on a string, to form ornaments of intellect. And, with that understanding well in hand, fully recognizing that history is one of the grand fabrications of the human intellect, facts not discovered but invented, explanations that themselves form cultural indicators of how things are in the here and now, we find ourselves no longer historians of ideas of history, or analysts of the history of culture, let alone practitioners of the dread narrative history that makes of historical writing a work of elegant imagination. We find ourselves, rather, archaeologists, working from the surface that is known, through the detritus of the unknown, in quest of a material understanding of a reality that is not known but for its artifacts, not susceptible of explanation and understanding except in categories and terms that are defined by those same artifacts. And that quest is, we all recognize, not a very smooth one.

The metaphor of archaeology for historical study, chosen for obvious reasons, is jarring, because, after all, nearly all historical evidence is in writing, and we are used to thinking of archaeology in terms of the pick and the shovel. But it is an apt metaphor, nonetheless, for it teaches us how to examine the written evidence on which most of us work in our cultural analysis of we know not what. The archaeologist (in theory at least) peels back from the surface to the underneath, and so must we. The archaeologist knows no categories other than the boundaries of the dig and the strata of the dig, knows no categories, imposes no categories, invents no categories that are not there. Then the things dug up define the categories and impose their own questions, their location *in situ* defining their "text," by which I mean, their circumstance, their relationships with other artifacts *in situ* defining their context, their stratum *in situ* dictating the matrix of interpretation. For us, the site is the document, and our task is to treat the document as not a candidate for paraphrase, that is, for descriptive historical study within the premise of explaining how things were and how they got to be the way they are. For us the task is to treat the document – as we have all learned from the faculty of this college – as a cultural artifact, as evidence for the working out of a social order in small detail.

Now if these remarks have suggested in your mind, however generous your spirit, that I have come to Paris to reinvent the intellectual wheel that, after all, has already been invented here, then consider how fresh and remarkable are the initial results of the antihistoricistic revolution you have sparked. For the consequences for hermeneutics, which I have outlined in the analogy of the archaeology of knowledge, are such that just now we cannot have too many examples of what only recently has become obvious. In sustaining the self-evidence of a new order of learning, I mean to take part in the task of rereading cases and reconsidering problems long thought settled. In the present instance, at stake is the proposition that the definition of events forms an acutely concrete statement of the larger systemic principles, and when we understand how a system defines events, we grasp the working of that system.

The task is important, even though narrative history in the academy no longer enjoys immediate recognition as how things must be done. For still, as a matter of fact, in the English language at least, the annual lists of new historical writings devote the larger part of the catalogue to narratives of how things were, explaining how they now are. Analytical history does not yet predominate, and the anthropology of history has achieved its greatest successes in the study of not Europe and its overseas dependencies in North America but the Pacific. And it is equally true that we are trying to teach ourselves to regard written evidence as a cultural artifact, no less than the broken sherd dug up in the field. But as a matter of fact, in entire ranges of learning the urgent question remains, did it really happen? And the urgency of the question derives from the conviction that, if so, certain important consequences must follow. The self-evidence of a connection between past and present competes with the view of the systemic character of culture, and we who propose to hold the whole together in a different way from the historical may not yet claim to hold the field. Consequently, we do not waste our energy by exercises in the rehearsal of other modes of reading the writing of prior ages than the historical-historicistic ones.

One fresh way of reviewing old things is to ask how the historical invention of history defines and identifies its raw materials. I mean to say, when we know what literary site presents to us as its artifacts, and when we can read those artifacts in our vocation as archaeologists of knowledge, rather than as historians of how things were (perhaps then theologians or storytellers of how things are connected and so what they mean), then we gain perspective on the new way by contrast to the old. No more telling indicator of the shift in the processes of understanding than the definition of an event comes to hand. For the event is to the composition of history as the atom is to the molecule, the thread to the fabric, or the steel beam to the building. And yet, these diverse metaphors reverse matters. The molecule defines the atoms that it wants (to impute teleology to the inanimate, in the manner of historians), the fabric requires that thread and no other, the building dictates the requirements, as to tensile strength, of its beams. And so, I wish to show, the culture identifies the events that explain and justify the culture. And, in consequence, we must ask ourselves, are not the literary records of events so constituted as to dictate the shape of the parts by appeal to the necessities of the whole? For it is my view that the system forms its events, not as a matter of mere consciousness, but as a *diktat* of culture. History therefore emerges as not the source for the explanation of culture, but rather as the best evidence for the shape, structure, and system that a culture comprises.

Let us take as our initial instance not Judaism but a different matter altogether, one that gives us perspective on our question, what, in Judaism, is an event, and how, from Judaism, do we learn about the hermeneutics of events? It is the clash of cultures that produced a long-remembered event indeed, the death of Captain Cook in Hawaii two hundred years ago. Marshall Sahlin argues[1] in behalf of the view, adumbrated in my remarks, that "history is culturally ordered, differently so in different societies, according to meaningful schemes of things."[2] Sahlin further cites Clifford Geertz's observation that "an event is a unique actualization of a general phenomenon, a contingent realization of the cultural pattern." Sahlin selects as his probative case the death of Captain Cook, because he is able, through his analysis of exactly what happened, to show the cultural indicators to which "events" testify – and which explain "events." To state matters briefly, "When the English anchored next year at Kealakekua, Hawaiian priests were able to objectify their interpretation of Cook as the Year-God Lonon, on his annual return to renew the fertility of the land." Then, when Cook came back to repair the broken main-mast, he violated the rules and had to be, and was, killed. In his "Anthropology of History," Sahlin states the upshot with lapidary clarity: "Different cultural orders have their own modes of historical action, consciousness, and determination – their own historical practice."[3] That is not to argue in favor of historical, let alone intellectual, relativity. It is only to insist upon the study of what a culture, as represented by its documents, defines as its past: the events, their order and connection, the meanings to be derived from them. History therefore serves as a capital indicator of the hermeneutics, and hermeneutics defines the system and structure – theirs but ours too – that all together form intellect.

When we come to the case of Judaism, we bring with us a substantial intellectual heritage, composed, as a matter of fact, of misinformation or no information. First, we wrongly take for granted that Judaism (whatever else it may be) is the religion of the Old Testament. Then we have as an established fact the utter misrepresentation that Judaism is a historical religion, in that it appeals for its worldview to not myth about gods in Heaven but the history of Israel upon earth – interpreted

---

[1] In his landmark work, *Islands of History* (Chicago, 1985: The University of Chicago Press).
[2] Ibid., p. vii.
[3] Ibid., p. 34.

What, Exactly, Do We Mean by "An Event" in Judaism?

in relationship to the acts of God in Heaven to be sure. Whether history in this form materially differs from myth in the Greek form is not at issue here. I take it as a broadly held conviction, third, that Judaism is a religion that appeals to history, that is, to events, defined in the ordinary way, important happenings, for its source of testing and establishing truth.

True, what the Old Testament writers deem events is not to be gainsaid: God descending to Sinai surely proves more dramatic than the failure of rain on a village, but to Amos, what does not happen defines an event as rich in revelation as, to the Yahwist, Elohist, and Priestly authors of the strands of the Pentateuch, what does happen defines an event. The fundamentally historical character of the Old Testament narratives, with their beginnings, middles, ends, their lessons and their demonstrations – that basic historical character is so broadly held as not to require comment. And so I shall refrain from comment, even though I doubt that anyone in this august assembly can concur, as I cannot concur, that there is a shred of historical consciousness, as distinct from mythic fantasy, in the Old Testament. But then, I need hardly rehearse Professor Paul Veyne's arguments on "the constitutive imagination," in his *Did the Greeks Believe in their Myths?* – a book waiting to be written for ancient Israel as well.

But Judaism, of course, is not only the religion of the Old Testament, and, as a case in the study of the cultural definition of events, only in its full canonical expression does Judaism serve to show us how culture identifies events through its own cognitive processes. Judaism is the religion of not the Old Testament but the Torah, and the canonical Torah encompasses the Old Testament only as it is reworked, as an object of rewriting and revision, in the vast canon of the two Talmuds and the Midrash compilations that took shape in late antiquity, the first seven centuries A.D., under the title, the Oral Torah. That labor of rewriting and recasting of one thing in light of something else that produced the Judaism of the Dual Torah forms a rich set of cases in cultural transformation, in the determination, by a system, of its own past, in the identification, within a system, of its own resources. For, after all, while a system speaks through its canon, and while theologians commonly read the canon to describe the system, in point of fact it is the canon that recapitulates the system, the system that speaks, in detail to be sure, through the canon.

When, therefore, we can affirm, with Sahlin, that "the different cultural orders studied by anthropology have their own historicities," the result of that affirmation is not a conclusion (the relativity of historical knowledge) but a question: how shall we frame history into a cultural indicator? In the case of the Judaism of the Dual Torah, the answer to that question proves quite accessible, for that Judaism makes ample use of the Old Testament in its account of itself. We should therefore anticipate that the canon of the Dual Torah will encompass narrative history, but it does not. We should expect to find therein accounts of events of not only times past but also the present explained by the past, but we do not. We should go in search of the description of one-time, unique happenings – events in the conventional sense – but, if we did, we should return disappointed. The result will be quite opposite. When we read matters properly, we shall find out how to read. For the archaeology of texts uncovers abstract structure in the identification and explication of the concrete event.[4]

This brings me directly to the problem at hand, what exactly does Judaism mean by events? To answer that question succinctly is simple. When we know how Judaism classifies events, we shall have the answer to the question of definition. So too, when we know how Judaism utilizes events, the heuristic value, the probative standing, of events, we once again shall have our answer. What I shall show is that, in the canonical literature of the Judaism of the Dual Torah, formed between the second and the seventh centuries and authoritative to this day, events find their place, within the science of learning of *Listenwissenschaft* that characterizes this literature, along with sorts of things that, for our part, we should not characterize as events at all. Events have no autonomous standing; events are not unique, each unto itself; events have no probative value on their own. Events form cases, along with a variety of other cases, making up lists of things that, in common, point to or prove one thing. Not only so, but events do not make up their own list at all, and this is what I found rather curious when I first noted that fact. Events will appear on the same list as persons, places, things. That means that events not only have no autonomous standing on their own, but also that events constitute no species even within a genus of a historical order. For persons, places, and things in our way of thinking do not belong on the same list as events; they are not of the same order. Within the logic of our own minds, we cannot classify the city, Paris, within the same genus as the event, the declaration of the rights of man, for instance, nor is Sinai of the same order of things as the Torah.

What then will you make of a list that encompasses within the same taxic composition events and things? One such list made up of events, persons, and places, is as follows: [1] Israel at the sea; [2] the ministering angels; [3] the tent of meeting; [4] the eternal house [=the Temple]; [5] Sinai. That mixes an event (Israel redeemed at the sea), a

---

[4] cf. Sahlin, p. 72.

category of sensate being (angels), a location (tent of meeting, Temple), and then Sinai, which can stand for a variety of things but in context stands for the Torah. In such a list an event may or may not stand for a value or a proposition, but it does not enjoy autonomous standing; the list is not defined by the eventfulness of events and their meaning, the compilation of matters of a single genus or even a single species (tent of meeting, eternal house, are the same species here). The notion of event as autonomous, even unique, is quite absent in this taxonomy.

Another such list moves from events to other matters altogether, finding the whole subject to the same metaphor, hence homogenized. First come the events that took place at these places or with these persons: Egypt, the sea, Marah, Massah and Meribah, Horeb, the wilderness, the spies in the Land, Shittim, for Achan/Joshua and the conquest of the Land. Now that mixture of places and names clearly intends to focus on particular things that happened, and hence, were the list to which I refer to conclude at this point, we could define an event for Judaism as a happening that bore consequence, taught a lesson or exemplified a truth, in the present case, an event matters because it is the mixture of rebellion and obedience. But there would then be no doubt that "event" formed a genus unto itself, and that a proper list could not encompass both events, defined conventionally as we should, and also other matters altogether.

But the literary culture at hand, this textual community proceeds, in the same literary context, to the following items: [1] the Ten Commandments; [2] the show-fringes and phylacteries; [3] the *Shema* and the Prayer; [4] the tabernacle and the cloud of the Presence of God in the world to come. Why we invoke, as our candidates for the metaphor at hand, the Ten Commandments, show-fringes and phylacteries, recitation of the *Shema* and the Prayer, the tabernacle and the cloud of the Presence of God, and the mezuzah, seems to me clear from the very catalogue. These reach their climax in the analogy between the home and the tabernacle, the embrace of God and the Presence of God. So the whole is meant to list those things that draw the Israelite near God and make the Israelite cleave to God. And to this massive catalogue, events are not only exemplary – which historians can concede without difficulty – but also subordinated.

They belong on the same list as actions, things, persons, places, because they form an order of being that is not to be differentiated between events (including things that stand for events) and other cultural artifacts altogether. A happening is no different from an object, in which case "event" serves no better, and no worse, than a hero, a gesture or action, recitation of a given formula, or a particular locale, to establish a truth. It is contingent, subordinate, instrumental. I can think of no more apt illustration of Geertz's interesting judgment: "an event is a unique actualization of a general phenomenon, a contingent realization of the cultural pattern." And why find that fact surprising, since all history comes to us in writing, and it is the culture that dictates how writing is to take place; that is why history can only paraphrase the affirmations of a system, and that is why events recapitulate in acute and concrete ways the system that classifies one thing that happens as event, but another thing is not only not an event but is not classified at all. In the present instance, an event is not at all eventful; it is merely a fact that forms part of the evidence for what is, and what is eventful is not an occasion at all, but a condition, an attitude, a perspective and a viewpoint. Then, it is clear, events are subordinated to the formation of attitudes, perspectives, viewpoints – the formative artifacts of not history in the conventional sense but culture in the framework of Sahlin's generalization, "History is culturally ordered, differently so in different societies, according to meaningful schemes of things."

To make more concrete the evidence on which I have drawn to join the public discussion, let me refer to one important compilation of lists, of the sixth century A.D., Song of Songs Rabbah, a reading of the Song of Songs as a metaphorization of God's relationship of intense love for Israel, and Israel's relationship of intense love for God. In that document we find sequences, or combinations, of references to Old Testament persons, events, actions, and the like. These bear the rhetorical emblem, "another matter," in long lists of composites of well-framed compositions.[5] Each entry on a given list will be represented as "another matter," meaning, another interpretation of reading of a given verse in the Song of Songs. As a matter of fact, however, that "other matter," one following the other, turns out to be the same matter in other terms. These constructions form lists out of diverse entries. When in Song of Songs Rabbah we have a sequence of items alleged to form a taxon, that is, a set of things that share a common taxic indicator, of course what we have is a list. The list presents diverse matters that all together share, and therefore also set forth, a single fact or rule or phenomenon. That is why we can list them, in all their distinctive character and specificity, on a common catalogue of "other things" that pertain all together to one thing.

Since, on these lists, we find classified within a single taxon events, persons, places, objects and actions, it is important to understand how

---

[5] I estimate that approximately 80% of the document in bulk is comprised of "another-matter" compositions. The list in this form defines the paramount rhetorical medium and logical structure of the document.

they coalesce. The rhetoric is the key indicator since it is objective and superficial. When we find the rhetorical formula, "another matter," that is, *davar aher*, what follows says the same thing in other words, or at least something complementary and necessary to make some larger point. That is why I insist the constructions form lists. William Scott Green states the matter, in his analysis of a single passage, in these words:

> Although the interpretations in this passage are formally distinguished from one another...by the disjunctive device *davar aher* ('another interpretation'), they operate within a limited conceptual sphere and a narrow thematic range....Thus rather than 'endless multiple meanings,' they in fact ascribe to the words 'doing wonders' multiple variations of a single meaning....By providing multiple warrant for that message, the form effectively restricts the interpretive options.[6]

When we have a sequence of *davar-aher* passages forming a *davar-aher* construction, the message is cumulative, and the whole as a matter of fact forms a sum greater than that of the parts; it will then be that accumulation that guides us to what is implicit yet fundamental in the exact sense: at the foundation of matters; there is where we should find that system, order, proportion, cogency that all together we expect a theology to impart to discrete observations about holy matters.

In general, "another matter" signals "another way of saying the same thing"; or the formula bears the sense, "these two distinct things add up to one thing," with the further proviso that both are necessary to make one point that transcends each one. Not only so, but in Song of Songs Rabbah the fixed formula of the *davar-aher* compilation points toward fixed formulas of theological thought: sets of coherent verbal symbols that work together. These "other things" encompass time, space, person and object, action and attitude, and join them all together, for instance, David, Solomon, Messiah at the end of time; this age, the age to come; the Exodus from Egypt, Sinai, the age to come all may appear together within a single list. Let me give a single example of the list that makes it possible to redefine "event" into a category of quite ahistorical valence.

Chapter Five. Song of Songs Rabbah to Song 1:5
V:i
1. A.   "I am very dark, but comely, [O daughters of Jerusalem, like the tents of Kedar, like the curtains of Solomon]" (Song 1:5):

---

[6]In Jacob Neusner with William Scott Green, *Writing with Scripture. The Authority and Uses of the Hebrew Bible in the Torah of Formative Judaism* (Minneapolis, 1989: Fortress Press), p. 19.

	B.	"I am dark" in my deeds.
	C.	"But comely" in the deeds of my forebears.
2.	A.	"I am very dark, but comely:"
	B.	Said the Community of Israel, "'I am dark' in my view, 'but comely' before my Creator."
	C.	For it is written, "Are you not as the children of the Ethiopians to Me, O children of Israel, says the Lord" (Amos 9:7):
	D.	"as the children of the Ethiopians" – in your sight.
	E.	But "to Me, O children of Israel, says the Lord."
3.	A.	Another interpretation of the verse, ""I am very dark:" in Egypt.
	B.	"but comely:" in Egypt.
	C.	"I am very dark" in Egypt: "But they rebelled against me and would not hearken to me" (Ezek. 20:8).
	D.	"but comely" in Egypt: with the blood of the Passover offering and circumcision, "And when I passed by you and saw you wallowing in your blood, I said to you, In your blood live" Ezek. 16:6) – in the blood of the Passover.
	E.	"I said to you, In your blood live" (Ezek. 16:6) – in the blood of the circumcision.
4.	A.	Another interpretation of the verse, "I am very dark:" at the sea, "They were rebellious at the sea, even the Red Sea" (Ps. 106:7).
	B.	"But comely:" at the sea, "This is my God and I will be comely for him" (Ex. 15:2) [following Simon's rendering of the verse].
5.	A.	"I am very dark:" at Marah, "And the people murmured against Moses, saying, What shall we drink" Ex. 15:24).
	B.	"But comely:" at Marah, "And he cried to the Lord and the Lord showed him a tree, and he cast it into the waters and the waters were made sweet" (Ex. 15:25).
6.	A.	"I am very dark:" at Rephidim, "And the name of the place was called Massah and Meribah" (Ex. 17:7).
	B.	"But comely:" at Rephidim, "And Moses built an altar and called it by the name 'the Lord is my banner' (Ex. 17:15).
7.	A.	"I am very dark:" at Horeb, "And they made a calf at Horeb" (Ps. 106:19).
	B.	"But comely:" at Horeb, "And they said, All that the Lord has spoken we will do and obey" (Ex. 24:7).
8.	A.	"I am very dark:" in the wilderness, ""How often did they rebel against him in the wilderness" (Ps. 78:40).
	B.	"But comely:" in the wilderness at the setting up of the tabernacle, "And on the day that the tabernacle was set up" (Num. 9:15).
9.	A.	"I am very dark:" in the deed of the spies, "And they spread an evil report of the land" (Num. 13:32).
	B.	"But comely:" in the deed of Joshua and Caleb, ""Save for Caleb, the son of Jephunneh the Kenizzite" (Num. 32:12).
10.	A.	"I am very dark:" at Shittim, "And Israel abode at Shittim and the people began to commit harlotry with the daughters of Moab" (Num. 25:1).
	B.	"But comely:" at Shittim, "Then arose Phinehas and wrought judgment" (Ps. 106:30).
11.	A.	"I am very dark:" through Achan, "But the children of Israel committed a trespass concerning the devoted thing" (Josh. 7:1).

What, Exactly, Do We Mean by "An Event" in Judaism?

	B.	"But comely:" through Joshua, "And Joshua said to Achan, My son, give I pray you glory" (Josh. 7:19).
12.	A.	"I am very dark:" through the kings of Israel.
	B.	"But comely:" through the kings of Judah.
	C.	If with my dark ones that I had, it was such that "I am comely," all the more so with my prophets.

V:ii
5.	A.	[As to the verse, "I am very dark, but comely," R. Levi b. R. Haita gave three interpretations:
	B.	"'I am very dark:' all the days of the week.
	C.	"'But comely:' on the Sabbath.
	D.	"'I am very dark:' all the days of the year.
	E.	"'But comely:' on the Day of Atonement.
	F.	"'I am very dark:' among the Ten Tribes.
	G.	"'But comely:' in the tribe of Judah and Benjamin.
	H.	"'I am very dark:' in this world.
	I.	"'But comely:' in the world to come."

The contrast of dark and comely yields a variety of applications; in all of them the same situation that is the one also is the other, and the rest follows in a wonderfully well-crafted composition. What is the repertoire of items? Dark in deeds but comely in ancestry; dark in my view but comely before God; dark when rebellious, comely when obedient, a point made at Nos. 3, for Egypt, 4 for the sea, and 5 for Marah, 6 for Massah and Meribah, 7 for Horeb, 8 for the wilderness, 9 for the spies in the Land, 10 for Shittim, 11 for Achan/Joshua and the conquest of the Land, 12 for Israel and Judah. But look what follows: the week as against the Sabbath, the weekdays as against the Day of Atonement, the Ten Tribes as against Judah and Benjamin, this world as against the world to come. Whatever classification these next items demand for themselves, it surely will not be that of events. Indeed, if by event we mean something that happened once, as in "once upon a time," then Sabbath as against weekday, Day of Atonement as against ordinary day form a different category; the Ten Tribes as against Judah and Benjamin constitute social entities, not divisions of time; and this age and the age to come form utterly antihistorical taxa altogether.

Events not only do not form a taxon, they also do not present a vast corpus of candidates for inclusion into some other taxon. The lists in the document at hand form selections from a most limited repertoire of candidates. If we were to catalogue all of the exegetical repertoire encompassed by *davar-aher* constructions in this document, we should not have a very long list of candidates for inclusion in any list. And among the candidates, events are few indeed. They encompass Israel at the Sea and at Sinai, the destruction of the first Temple, the destruction of the second Temple, events as defined by the actions of some holy men such as Abraham, Isaac, and Jacob (treated not for what they did but for who they were), Daniel, Mishael, Hananiah, and Azariah, and the like. It follows that the restricted repertoire of candidates for taxonomic study encompasses remarkably few events, remarkably few for a literary culture that is commonly described as quintessentially historical!

Then what taxic indicator dictates which happenings will be deemed events and which not? What are listed throughout are not data of nature or history but of theology: God's relationship with Israel, expressed in such facts as the three events, the first two in the past, the third in the future, namely, the three redemptions of Israel, the three patriarchs, and holy persons, actions, events, what-have-you. These are facts that are assembled and grouped; in Song of Songs Rabbah the result is not propositional at all, or, if propositional, then essentially the repetition of familiar propositions through unfamiliar data. What we have is a kind of recombinant theology, in which the framer ("the theologian") selects from a restricted repertoire a few items for combination, sometimes to make a point (e.g., the contrast of obedient and disobedient Israel we saw just now), sometimes not. What is set on display justifies the display: putting this familiar fact together with that familiar fact in an unfamiliar combination constitutes what is new and important in the list; the consequent conclusion one is supposed to draw, the proposition or rule that emerges – these are rarely articulated and never important. True, the list in Song of Songs Rabbah may comprise a rule, or it may substantiate a proposition or validate a claim; but more often than not, the effect of making the list is to show how various items share a single taxic indicator, which is to say, the purpose of the list is to make the list. The making of connections among ordinarily not-connected things is then one outcome of *Listenwissenschaft*. What I find engaging in *davar-aher* constructions is the very variety of things that, on one list or another, can be joined together – a list for its own sake. What we have is a kind of subtle restatement, through an infinite range of possibilities, of the combinations and recombinations of a few essentially simple facts (data). It is as though a magician tossed a set of sticks this way and that, interpreting the diverse combinations of a fixed set of objects. The propositions that emerge are not the main point; the combinations are.

That seems to me an important fact, for it tells me that the culture at hand has defined for itself a repertoire of persons and events and conceptions (e.g., Torah study), holy persons, holy deeds, holy institutions, presented candidates for inclusion in *davar-aher* constructions, and the repertoire, while restricted and not terribly long, made possible a scarcely-limited variety of lists of things with like taxic indicators. That is to say, the same items occur over and over again, but there is no pattern to how they recur. By a pattern I mean that items of the repertoire may appear in numerous *davar-aher* constructions or not; they may keep company with only a fixed number of other items, or they may not. Most things can appear in a *davar-aher* composition with most other things.[7]

---

[7]To make this point concrete, here is a survey of sequences of components of such lists:

Joseph, righteous men, Moses, and Solomon;

patriarchs as against princes, offerings as against merit, and Israel as against the nations; those who love the king, proselytes, martyrs, penitents;

first, Israel at Sinai; then Israel's loss of God's presence on account of the golden calf; then God's favoring Israel by treating Israel not in accord with the requirements of justice but with mercy;

Dathan and Abiram, the spies, Jeroboam, Solomon's marriage to Pharaoh's daughter, Ahab, Jezebel, Zedekiah;

Israel is feminine, the enemy (Egypt) masculine, but God the father saves Israel the daughter;

Moses and Aaron, the Sanhedrin, the teachers of Scripture and Mishnah, the rabbis;

the disciples; the relationship among disciples, public recitation of teachings of the Torah in the right order; lections of the Torah;

the spoil at the Sea = the Exodus, the Torah, the Tabernacle, the ark;

the patriarchs, Abraham, Isaac, Jacob, then Israel in Egypt, Israel's atonement and God's forgiveness;

the Temple where God and Israel are joined, the Temple is God's resting place, the Temple is the source of Israel's fecundity;

Israel in Egypt, at the Sea, at Sinai, and subjugated by the gentile kingdoms, and how the redemption will come;

Rebecca, those who came forth from Egypt, Israel at Sinai, acts of loving kindness, the kingdoms who now rule Israel, the coming redemption;

fire above, fire below, meaning heavenly and altar fires; Torah in writing, Torah in memory; fire of Abraham, Moriah, bush, Elijah, Hananiah, Mishael, and Azariah;

the Ten Commandments, show-fringes and phylacteries, recitation of the Shema and the Prayer, the tabernacle and the cloud of the Presence of God, and the mezuzah;

the timing of redemption, the moral condition of those to be redeemed, and the past religious misdeeds of those to be redeemed;

Israel at the sea, Sinai, the Ten Commandments; then the synagogues and school houses; then the redeemer;

the Exodus, the conquest of the Land, the redemption and restoration of Israel to Zion after the destruction of the first Temple, and the final and ultimate salvation;

the Egyptians, Esau and his generals, and, finally, the four kingdoms;

Moses's redemption, the first, to the second redemption in the time of the Babylonians and Daniel;

the litter of Solomon: the priestly blessing, the priestly watches, the Sanhedrin, and the Israelites coming out of Egypt;

The upshot is simple. List-making is accomplished within a restricted repertoire of items that can serve on lists; the list-making then presents interesting combinations of an essentially small number of candidates for the exercise. But then, when making lists, one can do pretty much anything with the items that are combined; the taxic indicators are unlimited, but the data studied, severely limited. And that fact returns us to our starting point, the observations on history as a cultural artifact that form the premise for the study of history within the archaeology of knowledge. In fact, in Judaism history serves the theological sciences and therefore cannot be said to constitute history in any ordinary sense at all; but that is a trivial and obvious observation. More to the point, history, in the form of events, contributes to a rather odd way of conducting theological science.

For, forming part of the *davar-aher* construction, history constitutes one among a variety of what I call, for lack of more suitable language at this point, theological "things,"[8] – names, places, events, actions deemed to bear theological weight and to affect attitude and action. The play is worked out by a reprise of available materials, composed in some fresh and interesting combination. When three or more such theological "things" – whether person, whether event, whether action, whether attitude – are combined, they form a theological structure,

---

Israel at the sea and forgiveness for sins effected through their passing through the sea; Israel at Sinai; the war with Midian; the crossing of the Jordan and entry into the Land; the house of the sanctuary; the priestly watches; the offerings in the Temple; the Sanhedrin; the Day of Atonement;

God redeemed Israel without preparation; the nations of the world will be punished, after Israel is punished; the nations of the world will present Israel as gifts to the royal messiah, and here the base verse refers to Abraham, Isaac, Jacob, Sihon, Og, Canaanites;

the return to Zion in the time of Ezra, the Exodus from Egypt in the time of Moses;

the patriarchs and with Israel in Egypt, at the Sea, and then before Sinai;

Abraham, Jacob, Moses;

Isaac, Jacob, Esau, Jacob, Joseph, the brothers, Jonathan, David, Saul, man, wife, paramour;

Abraham in the fiery furnace and Shadrach, Meshach, and Abednego, the Exile in Babylonia, now with reference to the return to Zion.

[8] I find myself at a loss for a better word choice and must at this stage resort to the hopelessly inelegant, "'theological' things," to avoid having to repeat the formula that seems to me to fit the data, namely, "names, places, events, actions deemed to bear theological weight and to affect attitude and action." Still, better a simple Anglo-Saxon formulation than a fancy German or Greek or Latin one. And Hebrew, whether mishnaic or modern, simply does not serve for analytical work except when thought conceived in some other language is translated back into that language, should anyone be interested.

and, viewed all together, all of the theological "things" in a given document constitute the components of the entire theological structure that the document affords. The propositions portrayed visually, through metaphors of sight, or dramatically, through metaphors of action and relationship, or in attitude and emotion, through metaphors that convey or provoke feeling and sentiment, when translated into language prove familiar and commonplace. The work of the theologian in this context is not to say something new or even persuasive, for the former is unthinkable by definition, the latter unnecessary in context. It is rather to display theological "things" in a fresh and interesting way, to accomplish a fresh exegesis of the canon of theological "things."

The combinations and recombinations defined for us by our document form events into facts, sharing the paramount taxic indicators of a variety of other facts, comprising a theological structure within a larger theological structure: a reworking of canonical materials. An event is therefore reduced to a "thing," losing all taxic autonomy, requiring no distinct indicator of an intrinsic order. It is simply something else to utilize in composing facts into knowledge; the event does not explain, it does not define, indeed, it does not even exist within its own framework at all. Judaism by "an event" means, in a very exact sense, nothing in particular. It is a component in a culture that combines and recombines facts into structures of its own design, an aspect of what I should call a culture that comes to full expression in recombinant theology.

We have been prepared for such a result by Jonathan Z. Smith, who has made us aware of critical issue of the recombinancy of a fixed canon of "things" in his discussion of sacred persistence, that is, "the rethinking of each little detail in a text, the obsession with the significance and perfection of each little action." In the canonical literature of Judaism, these minima are worked and reworked, rethought and recast in some other way or order or combination – but always held to be the same thing throughout. In this context I find important Smith's statement:

> An almost limitless horizon of possibilities that are at hand...is arbitrarily reduced...to a set of basic elements....Then a most intense ingenuity is exercised to overcome the reduction...to introduce interest and variety. This ingenuity is usually accompanied by a complex set of rules.[9]

---

[9] "Sacred Persistence: Towards a Redescription of Canon," in William Scott Green, ed., *Approaches to Ancient Judaism* 1978, 1:11-28. Quotation: p. 15.

The possibilities out of which the authorship of our exemplary document has made its selections are limited not by the metaphorical potential of the Song of Songs (!) but by the contents of the Hebrew Scriptures as the textual community formed of the Judaic sages defined those contents within their Torah.

For every Abraham, Isaac, and Jacob that we find, there are Job, Enoch, Jeroboam, or Zephaniah, whom we do not find; for every Sea/Sinai/entry into the Land that we do find, there are other sequences, for example, the loss of the ark to the Philistines and its recovery, or Barak and Deborah, that we do not find. Ezra figures, Haggai does not; the Assyrians play a minor role, Nebuchadnezzar is on nearly every page. Granted, Sinai must enjoy a privileged position throughout. But why prefer Shadrach, Meshach, and Abednego, Hananiah, Mishael, and Azariah, over other trilogies of heroic figures? So the selection is an act of choice, a statement of culture in miniature. But once restricted through this statement of choice, the same selected theological "things" then undergo combination and recombination with other theological things, the counterpart to Smith's "interest and variety." If we know the complex set of rules in play here, we also would understand the system that makes this document not merely an expression of piety but a statement of a theological structure: orderly, well-composed and proportioned, internally coherent and cogent throughout.

The canonical, therefore anything but random, standing of events forms a brief chapter in the exegesis of a canon. That observation draws us back to Smith, who observes:

> The radical and arbitrary reduction represented by the notion of canon and the ingenuity represented by the rule-governed exegetical enterprise to apply the canon to every dimension of human life is that most characteristic, persistent, and obsessive religious activity....The task of application as well as the judgment of the relative adequacy of particular applications to a community's life situation remains the indigenous theologian's task; but the study of the process, particularly the study of comparative systematics and exegesis, ought to be a major preoccupation of the historian of religions.[10]

Smith speaks of religion as an "enterprise of exegetical totalization," and he further identifies with the word "canon" precisely what we have identified as the substrate and structure of the list. If I had to define an event in this canonical context, I should have to call it merely another theological thing: something to be manipulated, combined in one way or in another, along with other theological things.

---

[10]*Ibid.*, p. 18.

What, Exactly, Do We Mean by "An Event" in Judaism?

Have we access to other examples of cultures that define for themselves canonical lists of counterparts to what I have called "theological things"? Indeed, defining matters as I have, I may compare the event to a fixed object in a diviner's basket of the Ndembu, as Smith describes that divinatory situation:

> Among the Ndembu there are two features of the divinatory situation that are crucial to our concern: the diviner's basket and his process of interrogating his client. The chief mode of divination consists of shaking a basket in which some twenty-four fixed objects are deposited (a cock's claw, a piece of hoof, a bit of grooved wood,...withered fruit, etc.). These are shaken in order to 'winnow out truth from falsehood' in such a way that few of the objects end up on top of the heap. These are 'read' by the diviner both with respect to their individual meanings and their combinations with other objects and the configurations that result.[11]

In Song of Songs Rabbah, Abraham, Isaac, Jacob, or the Sea and Sinai, or Hananiah, Mishael, and Azariah, are the counterpart to the cock's claw and the piece of hoof. The event, in Judaism, is the counterpart to a cock's claw in the Ndembu culture. Both will be fixed, but will combine and recombine in a large number of different ways. But then what of "the lessons of history," and how shall we identify the counterpart to historical explanation? I find the answer in the Ndembu counterpart, the mode of reading "the process of interrogating the client"? Again Smith:

> The client's situation is likewise taken into account in arriving at an interpretation. Thus...there is a semantic, syntactic, and pragmatic dimension to the 'reading.' Each object is publicly known and has a fixed range of meanings....The total collection of twenty-four objects is held to be complete and capable of illuminating every situation....What enables the canon to be applied to every situation or question is not the number of objects....Rather it is that, prior to performing the divination, the diviner has rigorously questioned his client in order to determine his situation with precision....It is the genius of the interpreter to match a public set of meanings with a commonly known set of facts...in order to produce a quite particular plausibility structure which speaks directly to his client's condition, which mediates between that which is public knowledge and the client's private perception of his unique situation.[12]

That concludes our inquiry, since it draws us to the task of the exegesis of exegesis. Events then form a problem of exegesis, in which, from what a culture defines as a consequential happening, we find our way back to the system and structure that that culture means to form. The

---

[11]*Ibid.*, p. 25.
[12]*Ibid.*, p. 25.

work before us will teach us, in the case of Judaism, how from the study of what are defined as events to describe the process of interrogation that has produced the result we see before us, this particular plausibility structure that has persuaded holy Israel, from then to now (as indeed all the Israels that revere the Song of Songs have been persuaded), to read the erotic as the best, the only way to express precisely who is God in relationship to Israel, and who is Israel in relationship to God. The theology of this Judaism – that is to say, our account of the worldview that comes to expression within this literary culture and textual community – will take shape within the exegesis of that exegesis.

Epilogue
A LECTURE NOT GIVEN

17

Methodology in Talmudic History

[Written for the Historical Society of Israel. Conference in celebration of its journal, *Zion*, on the occasion of its fiftieth volume. Jerusalem, Israel. Scheduled for July 2, 1984. This paper was mailed to Jerusalem on January 27, 1984, and the invitation to present it was withdrawn in a letter dated March 5, 1984. The facts speak for themselves, but I prefer not to suggest what they say.]

I. Methodology

When we speak of methodology, we may mean many things. To specify the very few things under discussion here, let us begin with the simplest possible definition. The method by which we work tells us the questions we choose to pose and the means we use to find the answers. Our method tells us what we want to know and how we can find it out. Method then testifies to the point at which we begin, the purpose for which we work. A sound method will guide us to questions both pertinent to the sources under study and also relevant to broader issues of the day. The one without the other is merely formal, on the one side, or impressionistic and journalistic, on the other. Proper method will tell us what sources we must read and how to interpret them. Above all, sound method will match the issues we raise to the information at hand, that is, will attend especially to questions of historical epistemology: *what we know and how we know it.*

We cannot raise in the abstract the issues of historical methodology in talmudic history. Talmudic history is a field that people practice. We cannot ignore what people actually do in favor of some preferred theory of what we think they should do. It furthermore would defy the honorable occasion at hand to speak about talmudic history without paying appropriate attention to the journal we celebrate here and now. Accordingly, let us first of all turn our attention to *Zion* itself and ask how talmudic history is practiced in its pages: the methodology demonstrated here.

The answer is in three parts. First, talmudic history constitutes a strikingly unimportant field in *Zion*. From 1935 (Vol. 1) to 1983 (Vol. 48), the journal published 476 articles, at the rate of approximately 10 per volume. Of these, no more than 28 in all fall into the category of talmudic history, approximately one article for every two volumes. Talmudic history accounts, in all, for little more than 5% of all articles published in the 50 years we celebrate – a strikingly small proportion.[1]

---

[1]My student, Paul Flesher, supplied the following footnote:

A list of all the articles of Talmudic History appearing in the journal, *Zion*, since its inception. I have divided the articles into two categories, General Talmudic History, and the use of the rabbinic literature for the study of the second Temple period.

I. Talmudic History
1. E. Bickermann, "Notes on the Megillath Taanith," vol. 1.
2. G. Allon, "How Yabneh became Rabbi Johanan ben Zakkai's Residence," vol. 3.
3. M. Stein, "Yabneh and her Scholars," vol. 3.
4. A. Kaminka, "Rabbi Johanan ben Zaccai and his Disciples," vol. 9.
5. G. Allon, "Concerning the History of Juridical Authorities in Palestine during the Talmudic Period," vol. 12.
6. E.E. Urbach, "Political and Social Tendencies in Talmudic Concepts of Charity," vol. 16.
7. E.E. Urbach, "Halakhot Regarding Slavery as a Source for the Social History of the Second Temple and the Talmudic Period," vol. 25.
8. M. Beer, "The Exilarchs in Talmudic Times," vol. 28.
9. B.Z. Dinur, "The Tractate Aboth (Sayings of the Fathers) as a Historical Source," vol. 35.
10. J. Florsheim, "The Establishment and Early Development of the Babylonian Academies, Sura and Pumbeditha," vol. 39.
11. J. Geiger, "The Ban on Circumcision and the Bar-Kokhba Revolt," vol. 41.
12. Moshe David Herr, "The Causes of the Bar-Kokhba War," vol. 43.
13. S. Safrai, "Kiddush Ha-Shem in the Teachings of the Tannaim," vol. 44.
14. M.D. Herr, "Continuum in the Chain of Torah Transmission," vol. 44.
15. Z.W. Falk, "On the Historical Background of Talmudic Laws Regarding Gentiles," vol. 44.
16. A. Wasserstein, "Rabban Gamaliel and Proclus the Philosopher (Mishna Aboda Zara 3.4)," vol. 45.
17. D. Goodblatt, "New Developments in the Study of the Babylonian Yeshivot," vol. 46.
18. I. Gafni, "On D. Goodblatt's Article," vol. 46.

Yet, in fact, these figures overstate the importance accorded to talmudic history in the journal. How so? Of the 28 articles at hand, seven deal with Second Temple times, using rabbinic literature for the treatment of the period before 70 (five of the seven by I. F. Baer, as a matter of fact). Now since a vast range of sources, outside of the Talmud, pertain to the period before 70, and since the bulk of the talmudic writings do not speak of that period, we can hardly concur that that period falls into talmudic history at all. Strictly speaking, talmudic history encompasses the period from the second century A.D. onward. Accordingly, when we ask how many articles in *Zion* dealt with problems on which the Talmuds and related documents provide first-hand evidence, rather than merely referring to things that happened long ago of which the authors have no direct knowledge of their own, and on which (by definition) the Talmuds constitute the principal corpus of evidence, the figures change. Specifically, only 21 of the 476 articles – four percent of the total, at the rate of somewhat less than one article every two years – attend to the field at hand. So we see in a rather dramatic way that talmudic history – the history of the Jewish people in its formative centuries beyond 70 and up to the rise of Islam – enjoys little attention in *Zion*.[2] I need hardly add that were

---

    19. O. Irsai, "R. Abbahu said: If a man should say to you 'I am God' – He is a Liar," vol. 47.
    20. B. Rosenfeld, "The Activity of Rabbai Simlai: A Chapter in the Relations Between Eretz Israel and the Diaspora in the Third Century, vol. 48.
    21. R. Kimelman, "The Conflict Between the Priestly Oligarchy and the Sages in the Talmudic Period (An Explanation of PT Shabbat 12:3, 13C = Horayot 3:5, 48C))," vol. 48.
II. The Use of Rabbinic Literature for the Study of Second Temple Times
    1. G. Allon, "The Attitude of the Pharisees Toward Roman Rule and the Herodian Dynasty," vol. 3.
    2. I.F. Baer, "The Historical Foundations of the Halakha," vol. 17.
    3. I.F. Baer, "On the Problem of Eschatological Doctrine During the Period of the Second Temple," vol. 23-24.
    4. I.F. Baer, "The Historical Foundations of the Halakha," vol. 27.
    5. J. Amir, "Philo's Homilies on Fear and Love in Relation to Palestinian Midrashim," vol. 30.
    6. I.F. Baer, "Jerusalem in the Times of the Great Revolt," vol. 36.
    7. I.F. Baer, "The Service of Sacrifice in Second Temple Times," vol. 40.

Zion began in 1935. This study begins with volume one and ends with number 3 of volume 48 (1983). The total number of articles in these volumes is 476.

[2]We note that no articles on the period from ca. 70 to ca. 640 deal with any topic outside of talmudic history, as defined in Flesher's catalogue in n. 1. So

we to examine other scholarly journals[3] in this country [*viz.*, the State of Israel, where the paper was supposed to be presented] and overseas, the proportions might change somewhat, but the picture would emerge pretty much the same.

The second and third observations about the status and methodology of talmudic history in *Zion* require less exposition.

The second is that when people practice talmudic history in *Zion*, they limit their discussion to talmudic history in particular. The field does not encompass its period, but only one set of sources emergent from its period. While many of the scholars represented in *Zion* draw upon *sources* outside the Talmud, none of the articles deals with a *problem* outside the Talmud. Accordingly, talmudic history in the journal at hand finds definition as the study of historical problems pertinent to a given *source*, rather than to a chronological *period* to which that source attests.[4] (In this regard, Baer's articles form an exception to the rule.) It follows that talmudic history severely limits itself, in *Zion*, to literary evidence. While, once again, we may find allusion to archeological data, no article in the past half-century has entered the category of inquiry in which archeology, as much as literature, defines the problem or contributes to its solution.

The third observation is that the methodology of reading the literary sources, which define the problems and solutions of talmudic history in *Zion*, begins in an assumption universally adopted by the scholars of the journal (and not only there). Whatever the Talmud says happened happened. If the Talmud attributes something to a rabbi, he really said it. If the Talmud maintains that a rabbi did something, he really did it. So among the twenty-one articles under discussion, I find not a single one that asks the basic critical questions with which historical study normally commences: how does the writer of this source know what he tells me? How do I know that he is right? On the contrary, the two Talmuds serve, in *Zion*, as encyclopedias of facts about rabbis and other Jews in the Land of Israel and Babylonia. The task of the historian is to mine the encyclopedias and come up with

---

talmudic history is the only history of the Jews as a group in the period at hand on which *Zion* published articles as all.

[3] I omit reference to *Sinai*, which in no ways strikes me as a journal responsive to the critical agenda of modern scholarship. That is not to say a handful of articles of scholarly quality have not been printed there. But *Sinai* serves a learned constituency out of all relationship to academic learning as it is practiced in the West and may be ignored in the present context. *Tarbiz* presents a separate set of problems entirely and requires analysis in its own context.

[4] I return to this matter below.

important observations on the basis of the facts at hand. The work of the historian, then, is the collection and arrangement of facts, the analysis of facts, the synthesis of facts. It is not in the inquiry into the source and character of the facts at hand. Just as, for the literary scholar, the text constitutes the starting point of inquiry, so for the historian, the text at hand defines the facts and dictates the character of inquiry upon them. This is the case, beginning and end, from Allon to Kimelman.

Whether it is Allon, telling us what Yohanan ben Zakkai meant in his conversation with Vespasian in August 70, on the assumption that Vespasian and Yohanan were attended by secretaries who wrote down their every word, or whether it is Kimelman, telling us about the politics of the priesthood and exilarchate as reported by a story in Yerushalmi Shabbat 12:3, the method is the same. Now I hasten to add that the prevailing assumption need not deprive of all interest and value a given study in *Zion*. For instance, where the meaning of a story is subject to interpretation, without attention to whether or not the story took place, the article stands on its own, as in the case of Wasserstein on Gamaliel and Proclus and Israi on Abbahu's saying. Again, when the author deals with events on which the Talmud by definition constitutes a primary source, as in the case of Goodblatt's study of the Babylonian yeshivot, we deal with a very high level of critical acumen. But the bulk of the articles could not have been written in the way that they were written had the authors first of all taken up the critical program of contemporary historical scholarship.

II. The First Century of Talmudic History

No one should suppose that the work of *Zion* met a lower standard of critical acumen than articles and books published elsewhere. The contrary is the case. My impression is that the great Gedaliahu Allon, to name the premier Israeli talmudic historian of all time, published his best work in *Zion*. In fact, from the beginning of talmudic history in modern times, things scarcely have changed. The work of talmudic history began with three books, all of them completed within approximately one decade, from 1850 to 1860: A. Geiger's *Urschrift und Uebersetzungen der Bibel* (1857), an effort to correlate the history of biblical translation with the history of Israelite sects in the period at hand; Z. Frankel's *Darkhei HaMishnah* (1859), a collection of thumbnail biographies of talmudic rabbis and some other historical observations; and H. Graetz's *History of the Jews*, volume 4, on the talmudic period (the first book to be published of his general history of the Jews) (1853). These were the first systematic inquiries into the

Talmud as a historical document, as distinct from an interest in the Talmud as a source of law for Judaism.

From the very beginnings of talmudic history, the critical program of ancient history and of biblical studies remained remote. By the 1850s, biblical studies had attained a quite critical program. From the time of Geiger, Graetz, and Frankel, down to nearly our own time, by contrast, it has been taken for granted that a story in a holy book about an event accurately portrays exactly what happened. The story itself has no history, but it is history. No special interests or viewpoints are revealed in a given historical account. Everything is taken at face value. Since historians and storytellers stand together within the same system of values, it was unthinkable that anyone would either lie or make up a story for his own partisan purposes. No one ever would wonder, *Cui bono?* To whose interest is it to tell a given story? Obviously, if a learned rabbi told a story, he said it because he knew it to be so, not because he wanted to make up evidence to support his own viewpoint.

In modern times – beginning long before the Enlightenment – by contrast, people learned to take a skeptical position *vis-à-vis* the sacred histories and holy biographies of the earlier generations. They asked about the tendencies of stories, the point the storyteller wished to make, and wondered not about whether a story "really" happened, but rather, about the situation to which a given story actually supplies accurate testimony. They asked how the storyteller knew the facts of the case. Who told him? If he was an eyewitness, on whose side did he stand in a situation of conflict? No reporters were present to take down verbatim what was said and done at the various incidents recorded in the rabbinic traditions. If that is so, then all we have are traditions about such events, given both form and substance on some other, later occasion than that of which they speak. But often we have not traditions but mere legends, fabrications quite unrelated to the events they purport to report.

Such a skeptical attitude had been well established in biblical studies done by non-Jews by the early nineteenth century. Western scholarship in these and related fields had furthermore shown the necessity of analyzing the components of stories and asking how each element took shape and where and when the several elements were put together. But with rabbinic materials, aside from some reservations about obvious miracles, one rarely discerns among nineteenth or even most twentieth century scholars an appreciation of the necessity to understand the historical background of texts in a manner other than that narrated in the texts themselves. And when the rabbinic scholars

Methodology in Talmudic History 347

tried to stand outside the presuppositions of the texts, they did so chiefly for exegetical, not historical purposes.

III. Examples of Established Methodologies

One cannot, however, attempt to refute histories made up on the basis of talmudic tales. One can only point out that such histories are seriously deficient because they are wholly uncritical and gullible, omit all reference to the internal evidence revealed by the talmudic sources, and exclude from discussion the literary evidence available in cognate literature. Nor need one refute the nineteenth- and twentieth-century historians, who, using the talmudic materials, go on to reinterpret them, to posit new "postulates" about their meaning, to reject one detail of a story in favor of another – in all, to lay claim to a "critical" position toward a literature whose historical usefulness is never in the end called into question. In such histories we have the pretense of critical scholarship but not its substance. The bulk of the work of nineteenth and twentieth century historians must be regarded as pseudocritical, critical in rhetoric but wholly traditional in all its presuppositions; and in the main, primitive and puerile. Like the "critical" fundamentalists, who agree that the whale did not really swallow Jonah, but only kept him in his cheek, or like the pseudo-orthodox who say it was for three hours, not three days, the "critical" scholars of the modern period have scarcely improved upon the traditional picture. They have merely rearranged some of its elements. *"Plus ça change, plus c'est la même chose."* Nothing has changed, but much is made of the changes.

Two specific examples of the primitivism of the scholarship of so-called "scientific" scholars will suffice.

First, Zecharias Frankel, the founder of the modern study of the Mishnah, the first component of the Talmud, is still taken seriously, as shown by the reprinting of his books and their use in contemporary Israeli scholarship to this day. But Frankel operates in a world of private definitions, circular reasoning, and capricious postulates. For him it is unnecessary to prove much, for one may, through *defining* things properly, obviate the need for proof. For Frankel, medieval commentaries constitute primary sources for the study of the Mishnah. He furthermore claims that Seder *Toharot* is old because it is the largest order (!); that the ancient Jews were all students of the rabbinic Torah; that the structure of the Mishnah was revealed by divine inspiration; and numerous other marvels. In what way then is he to be regarded as "modern"? The reception of his book supplies the answer. His enemies accused him of treating the Mishnah in a secular spirit and not as a divinely revealed document, the Oral Torah. They said he regarded the Mishnah as the work of men and as a time-bound document. He even explained mishnaic laws otherwise than through the Babylonian Talmud. For this Frankel was condemned by the traditionalists of his day. That his work today is taken seriously among traditionalists tells us that what is said in the name of tradition changes from one century to the next. But scarcely a line of his *Darkhei Hammishnah* can be taken seriously as history.

Second, H. Albeck, in his *Mabo Lammishnah* (1959) looks upon the Mishnah and Talmud as the culmination of the process of "oral tradition" beginning in ancient times. He takes for granted that anything reflective of non-scriptural (= oral) tradition, whether in biblical or apocryphal, pseudepigraphic, or Septuagintal literature, is *The Oral Tradition* of pharisaic-rabbinic Judaism. While Albeck is critical of earlier students of the history of the Oral Torah, he does not depart from their frame of reference. Indeed, Albeck takes pretty much the position of Sherira Gaon, founder of talmudic history in the ninth century, altering details but not the main points. What is striking is that for Albeck the scholarly agenda formulated by Sherira remains uncriticized and unchanged: "When was the Mishnah written?" He extensively reviews and criticizes the ideas of earlier scholars, as if they had supplied him with a viable agenda. So we find ourselves once again in the midst of debates on the work of the Men of the Great Assembly, although we have not the slightest shred of evidence about what they had actually done, let alone a document produced by them or in their days. While Y. N. Epstein demonstrated for example, in his *Introduction to Tannaite Literature* (1957) that the tractate Eduyyot was produced by the disciples of Aqiba at Usha – they are explicitly named throughout – Albeck takes seriously what the traditions from talmudic times assert, that Eduyyot was produced at Yavneh: "It was ordered according to the names of the sages and the work was done at Yavneh." But he never proves this is so. One may easily show that Eduyyot is *different* from other tractates, but that difference does not mean it is *earlier* than the others. Whatever a talmudic tradition alleges about a tractate is taken as fact. Albeck seldom looks in a thorough and critical way for internal evidence. Again and again one finds circular reasoning. For example, Albeck holds that Rabbi Judah the Patriarch, author of the Mishnah, arranged the material he had received according to a single principle, content, and he did not change anything he had received. How do we know this? Because Judah ordered the material only according to the content of the laws and any material not collected according to this principle was formed into units before Judah received them. We know that they were formed into units

Methodology in Talmudic History

in Judah's sources because Judah ordered his material only according to the content of the laws. Likewise, Judah did not change any of the material he received because the sources are not changed. We know the sources are not changed because Judah did not change any of the sources. And so forth. Albeck further disputes the view of Epstein that the Mishnah yielded numerous variations in texts. He says once the Mishnah was edited, it was never again changed. I am not clear on how Albeck understands the work of the early Amoraim, for they seem not only to have changed the Mishnah, but to have stated explicitly that they changed the Mishnah.

Though separated by a century, Frankel and Albeck exhibit the same credulousness and lack of critical acumen. Considering the achievements of scholarship in the intervening hundred years, one may be astonished at how little Albeck's perception of the critical task and definition of the problems has been affected. But Frankel, too, exhibits little mastery of the critical conceptions of his own day.

IV. Principal Errors of Prevailing Methodologies in Talmudic History

Let me now generalize from these two examples. I focus discussion on the concrete errors that render useless for historical purposes nearly all work on the Talmud, with the two exceptions specified earlier, namely, interpretation of talmudic texts in historical context, typified by Wasserstrom's splendid article, and study of talmudic institutions in historical reality, exemplified by that of Goodblatt. The bulk of the articles in *Zion*, as well as elsewhere, have taken for granted that the numerous specific stories concerning what given rabbis and other Jews actually said and did under specific circumstances – on a given day, at a given place, in a given setting – tell us *exactly the way things were*. I speak, then, of a species of the genus, fundamentalism.

The philological fundamentalists have generally supposed that once we have established a correct text of a rabbinic work and properly interpreted its language, we then know a set of historical facts. The facticity will be proportionately greater the earlier the manuscript and the better its condition. These suppositions are correct. But these facts will concern *only* what the compiler of the text wished to tell us. Whether or not the original text was veracious is to be settled neither by textual criticism nor by philological research, valuable though both of these ancillary sciences are for the historical inquiry.

The fundamentalists further suppose that any story, whether occurring early or late in the corpus of rabbinic literature, may well contain valuable information, handed on orally from generation to generation, until it was finally written down. I cannot accept the unexamined opinion held in rabbinical circles, both scholarly and traditional, that all rabbinical material was somehow sent floating into the air, if not by Moses, then by someone in remote antiquity (the Men of the Great Assembly, the generation of Yavneh); that it then remained universally available until some authority snatched it down from on high, placed his name on it, and so made it a named tradition and introduced it into the perilous processes of transmission. By this thesis nothing is older than anything else: "there is neither earlier nor later in the Torah."

Synoptic studies of the traditions of Yohanan b. Zakkai and of the Pharisees before 70[5] indicate that versions of a story or saying appearing in later documents normally are demonstrably later than, and literarily dependent upon, versions of the same story or saying appearing in earlier documents. This is important, for it shows that what comes late is apt to be late, and what comes in an early compilation is apt to be early. Admittedly, these are no more than probabilities – extrapolations from a small number of demonstrable cases to a large number in which no demonstration is possible. But at least there are grounds for such extrapolation.

I therefore suggest that the fundamentalists' convictions about the nature of the historical evidence contained in the Babylonian Talmud are likely to be false. Whether true or false, the primary conviction of fundamentalism is that the story supplies an accurate account of what actually happened. It is difficult to argue with that conviction. A study of rabbinic sources will provide little, if any, evidence that we have eyewitness accounts of great events or stenographic records of what people actually said. On the contrary, it is anachronistic to suppose the talmudic rabbis cared to supply such information to begin with. Since they did not, and since they asserted that people had said things of which they had no sure knowledge, we are led to wonder about the pseudepigraphic mentality. By the time we hear about a speech or an event, it has already been reshaped for the purpose of transmission in the traditions. It is rarely possible to know just what, if anything, originally was said or done. Sometimes we have an obvious gloss, which tells us the tradition originated before the time the glossator made his addition. But knowing that a tradition was shaped within half a century of the life of the man to whom it was attributed helps only a little bit. It is very difficult to build a bridge from the tradition to the event, still more difficult to cross that bridge. The fact

---

[5]*Development of a Legend. Studies on the Traditions Concerning Yohanan ben Zakkai* (Leiden, 1970: E.J. Brill) and *The Rabbinic Traditions about the Pharisees Before 70* (Leiden, 1971: E. J. Brill) I-III.

is that the entire Babylonian Talmud is a completely accurate record of the history of those who are responsible for it. But the specification of those people, the recognition of the viewpoint of a particular group, place, and time to which the Talmud's various facts pertain – these remain the fundamental task still facing us.

V. Toward a Reconsideration of Appropriate Methodology

I now wish to offer an alternative set of problems and solutions, a program of inquiry in my judgment more appropriate to the sources under study and to the sort of information we may ask those sources to supply us. In order to offer such a fresh program, I naturally have to begin at the beginning. Let us start with the character of historical study – the field of history itself, the place of talmudic history within the historical field. History is the noun, the genus, talmudic history the adjective, the species. Before we can deal with the species, we surely must first attend to the genus.

A subdivision of the vast realm of historical learning marked off solely by information contained in a particular book finds the definition of its program and tasks in the pages of that book. The field of historical study bearing the adjective "talmudic" covers the age in which the talmudic canon took shape and to which it refers. That field of history attends to the places in which the people of that document flourished. So the time and place conform to the limits set by the principal source of historical study. The boundaries of topics, too, fall within the bindings of one book. Now to those who study other realms of historical learning, the one at hand must appear artificial, merely theological. In general people define a range of historical inquiry through limits posed by geography, political change to denote beginnings and endings, surely in addition to national or ethnic traits that include some and exclude others. More to the point, the pertinent historical information will derive from many different sources, not from a single book. Accordingly, anyone opening a book of history will find puzzling the particular sort of historical study under way here. Specifically, such a person will ask what sort of history may bear the adjective "talmudic," as distinct from "American," "medieval," or "African," thus national, chronological, or regional, not to mention economic, social, or political. Indeed, who has ever heard of a field of historical study defined by a particular book, unless it is what is in the book that is studied, for example, constitutional history or the history of New England as seen through Cotton Mather's sermons!

By "the Talmud," all agree, we mean the entire canon of writings of the Jewish sages of Babylonia and the Land of Israel ("Palestine"), a canonical corpus beginning with the Mishnah, closed at ca. A.D. 200, and ending with the Talmud of Babylonia, completed at ca. A.D. 600. These documents to be sure refer to events spread over a longer period of time, specifically from the creation of the world onward to the end of history. They cover, in their scope of commentary, things that are supposed to have happened throughout much of the known world of their day. But in chronology, the account becomes particular to the first-hand knowledge of its authors and editors at ca. A.D. 70 or so, and, in geographical area, it covers the affairs of the Jews in the specified provinces, the one under Iranian, the other under Roman, rule.

In all, talmudic history cannot be said to deal with great affairs, vast territories, movements of men and nations, much that really mattered then. Even the bulk of the women and men of Israel, the Jewish nation, in the time of the composition of the canonical writings at hand, by the testimony of the authors themselves falls outside of the frame of reference. Most Jews appeared to the sages at hand to ignore – in the active sense of willfully *not knowing* – exactly those teachings that seemed to the authors critical. To use the mythic language, when God revealed the Torah to Moses at Mount Sinai, he wrote down one part, which we now have in the Hebrew Scripture ("the Old Testament"), and he repeated the other part in oral form, so that Moses memorized it and handed it on to Joshua, and then, generation by generation, to the contemporary sages. Now, to the point, the contemporaries of the sages at hand did not know this oral half of the Torah, only sages did, and that by definition. Only sages knew the whole of the Torah of Moses. So, it follows, the talmudic corpus preserves the perspective of a rather modest component of the nation under discussion.

How could we define a subject less likely to attract broad interest than the opinions of a tiny minority of a nation about the affairs of an unimportant national group living in two frontier provinces on either side of a contested frontier? Apart from learning, from the modest folk at hand, some facts about life on the contested frontier of the ancient world – and that was only the one that separated Rome from Iran, the others being scarcely frontiers in any political sense – what is to be learned here that anyone would want to know must seem puzzling.

VI. Latent and Manifest History in the Talmud

Self-evidently, no one can expect to find stories of great events, a continuous narrative of things that happened to a nation in war and in politics. The Jews, as it happens, both constituted a nation and sustained a vigorous political life. But the documents of the age under discussion treat these matters only tangentially and as part of the periphery of a vision of quite other things. But if manifest history scarcely passes before us, a rich and complex world of latent history – the long-term trends and issues of a society and its life in imagination and emotion – does lie ready at hand. For the talmudic canon reports to us a great deal about what a distinctive group of people were thinking about issues that turn out to prove perennial and universal, and, still more inviting, the documents tell us not only what people thought but how they reasoned.

That is something to which few historians gain access, I mean, the philosophical processes behind political and social and religious policy, class struggle and popular contention. For people do think things out and reach conclusions, and for the most part, long after the fact, we know only the decisions they made. Here, by contrast, we hear extended discussions, of a most rigorous and philosophical character, on issues of theory and of thought. In these same discussions, at the end, we discover how people decided what to do and why. That sort of history – the history of how people made up their minds – proves particularly interesting, when we consider the substance of the story. The Jews in the provinces and age at hand adopted the policies put forward by the sages who wrote the sources we consider. The entire subsequent world history of the Jews – their politics, social and religious world, the character of the inner life and struggle of their community-nation – refers back to the decisions made at just this time and recorded in the Talmud.

A further aspect of the character of the principal sources for Talmudic history, moreover, will attract attention even among people not especially concerned with how a weak and scattered nation explained how to endure its condition. The talmudic canon bears the mark of no individual authorship. It is collective, official, authoritative. Now were it to hand on decisions but no discussion, that collective character would not mark the literature as special. We have, from diverse places and times, extensive records of what legislative or ecclesiastical bodies decided. But if these same bodies had recorded in detail how they reached their decisions, including a rich portrait of their modes of thought, then we should have something like what the Talmud gives us.

But the points of interest scarcely end there. The talmudic corpus stands in a long continuum of thought and culture, stretching back, through the biblical literature, for well over a thousand years. Seeing how a collegium of active intellectuals mediated between their own age and its problems and the authority and legacy of a vivid past teaches lessons about continuities of culture and society not readily available elsewhere. For their culture had endured, prior to their own day, for a longer span of time than separates us in the West from the Magna Charta, on the one side, and Beowulf, on the other. If these revered documents of our politics and culture enjoyed power to define politics and culture today, we should grasp the sort of problem confronting the Talmud's sages. For, after all, the Talmud imagined as normative a society having little in common with that confronting the sages – isolated, independent, free-standing, and not – as the sages' Israel was – assimilated in a vast world-empire, autonomous yet subordinate, and dependent upon others near and far.

VII. Topics for Talmudic History

Proceeding from the explanation of why the species *talmudic* belongs in the genus *history* to the logical next question, we ask ourselves just what sort of history we may expect to compose. The Babylonian Talmud and related literature contain two sorts of historical information: first, stories about events occurring within an estate of clerks; second, data on the debates of those who produced the Talmud. How are these to be used for historical purposes? It is important to specify what those purposes are. We must at the outset recognize that there are many kinds of information we simply do not have, and never shall have, on Jews and Judaism in late antiquity. The Talmud contains very little information on such questions, for instance, as the nature of the inner life, the consciousness and personal hopes of Jews of the day. It has no autobiographical materials, no record of what people thought and felt as private individuals. No one person stands behind a simple sentence. All has been refracted through a shared prism. The whole is a public record, publicly redacted and communally, hence politically, transmitted. Few individuals play a manifest part in the redaction of their own thoughts, much less in their transmission. This seems to me a significant fact: autobiography, letters, the records of individual life are simply not present. It means at the outset that we cannot ask questions about the motives of individuals, their feelings and intentions – the essence of historical inquiry. But there is, in compensation, the record of the collectivity of sages, and, as I have argued, that permits a remarkably contemporary kind of historical study.

Our information on various kinds or groups of Jews, moreover, is limited. The Talmud is not a historical document and was never intended as such. It is the record of the laws and logic, exegesis and episodic theology, of a relatively small group of Jews. One may estimate that about three hundred names of Babylonian Amoraim are mentioned, yet we may guess that a minimum of two hundred thousand, and probably more like half a million, Jews lived in Babylonia and Mesopotamia in Parthian and Sasanian times. Whatever judgments one may make about the rabbis' being "normative" or "more significant" than others are fundamentally theological, not historical. Moreover, when we take seriously the facts of rabbinical life – that the rabbis lived within a relatively limited institutional framework, somewhat like the contemporary monastic communities of Mesopotamian and Babylonian Christianity – we may wonder how far what we do know represents what we do not know. Whatever archaeological data we have of the same place and period – the Dura synagogue and the magical bowls – bear little obvious relationship to what we learn in the Babylonian Talmud. So we cannot ask a great many questions about Jews who are other than rabbis, except in relationship to the rabbis themselves.

The third and most important specification is this: We must at the outset isolate and identify the *viewpoint* of the texts we study and attempt to separate ourselves from that viewpoint for the purposes of historical inquiry. As I said earlier, we must always wonder, *Cui bono?* Who is served? What interest advanced? If we neglect to do so, we simply repeat, in modern language, the viewpoint of our sources, rather than attempt to understand and evaluate that viewpoint. When, for example, we concentrate attention on the issues set by the texts, when we merely generalize in historical language the specific stories and ideas presented by the text, then we are doing little more than repeating what is before us in the same propagandistic, tendentious, and partisan spirit in which it was originally composed. This will not serve any useful purpose, for if all we hope for from history is to participate in the worldview of the documents that supply us with information, why study history at all? Why not remain in the tradition of the classical and modern exegetes, who may add their episodic philological *hiddushim* (artificial refinements, fictional distinctions that make no difference, and other artifices) but contribute nothing new and comprehend nothing more than they are told by the discrete texts they study?

What purposes then do we have in reading the Babylonian Talmud for the writing of history? It will not suffice, alas, to say we want to know just how things were. This is naive, since "things" encompasses information about trivialities as well as important matters. We must acknowledge at the outset the values and interests shaping our mind and imagination and isolate what we regard as important issues. We must criticize those values and interests. And then we may proceed to the historical problems. What we must seek to know is not just how things were, but *just how those things were which interest us*, and *which the documents in their present state may reveal*. What interests us is, naturally, a reflection of our, and not their, situation. So the *we* is decisive. And we who read the Babylonian Talmud for historical purposes are modern historians, who want to know things of no interest whatever to classical Jews, or who want to know the same things but in different ways, in ways congruent to our knowledge and understanding of all aspects of reality.

What I want to know, first, is how a community actually functioned: the dynamics of the relationships among various power groups, and between those groups and the inchoate masses. In many ways my *History of the Jews in Babylonia*[6] is an essay not merely in historical knowledge – though that lies at the foundation of everything historians do – but an essay in *power*. What earlier interpreters saw as ethics I see as power. What they saw as objective and eternal truths I see as statements of a particular viewpoint, serving a particular group and its interest; statements reflecting the values and ideals, the imagination, of the special interest groups represented in the documents available to us.

Alongside concern for power is an interest in *myth:* namely, the stories people told, the beliefs they held, to verify and justify the power relationships they experienced. Why did people do what they did? Earlier, I denied that we can investigate individual motivation. But we can ask many questions about ideas widely held, characteristics of specific groups; issues investigated by historians of religion: What were the beliefs that people referred to in order to understand and explain reality? What were the fundamental convictions about reality that underlay all their actions? How did they justify themselves to other people – Israel, gentiles – and before God? In line with my earlier emphasis on the record of the collective consensus of individuals, I further want to know what happened to many people so as to present as self-evident the mythic world at hand. How do we account for the formation of the consensus of myth and of power, expressed in a distinctive mode of powerful discourse, achieved in an iron consensus within the estate of the clerks, but then, among the nation at large.

These two, then, power and myth, represent the theoretical interests of our day, these and still a third – *function:* How did things work? Granted the existence of power, the ability of some men to coerce others to say and do their will, either by force or, more amiably, by moving them through an internalization of values; and granted the knowledge of the imagination of those men and their community,

---

[6]Leiden, 1965-1970: E. J. Brill, I-V.

knowledge of their mythic life – granted these two, we ask ourselves, how did the system work? What defined adaptive behavior in such a power structure? What sort of *history* took place? What institutions embodied the power and the myth, what programs carried them forward, what was their thrust and dynamism, and what were the events that at specific times and places embodied these abstract forces of power and of myth in historical facts?

These then are the questions in my mind as I do my work. I should confess that at the outset I could not have specified them. On the contrary, it was in response to the materials I found pertinent to my *History* that I began to discern what I wanted to know. I began with chaos, the chaos of the texts and of my own limited historical understanding. Whatever order and sense emerged came forth unanticipated and uninvited.

VIII. Foundations of Talmudic History

But does the Babylonian Talmud serve to answer these questions, and if so, how? What are the principles of historical knowledge by which I can justify historical results? First, it seems to me important to form a view of the whole, rather than to allow oneself to be paralyzed by the exegesis and eisegesis of the discrete texts within the whole that historians supposed were historical, primarily because of their contents and themes. Earlier historians of the Talmud took for granted that what a man was said to have done is what actually was done. What was attributed to him is what he really said. What people claimed happened actually took place. And the record before us is the accurate, detailed, account of what *really* was said and done. The legal scholar or textual exegesis is interested in the content of the texts; it would not matter to him whether a man *really* said what is attributed to him, for he wants only to know the legal principles at issue and to trace the rabbis' discussion of those principles through legal literature. The literary critic – and the classical scholars produced brilliant literary criticism of a kind – takes at face value the text before him. He so concentrates on the meaning of words and sentences and their relationships to other words and sentences, that he cannot but accept their content as true. The exegesis and explication of texts, whether by Talmudists or by biblical scholars, in the very nature of things, tend to produce a fundamentalist spirit.

But if it is time to attempt a critical characterization of the whole, not merely a gullible reprise of suggestive parts, what to characterize? Here, as I said earlier, we need to locate questions both pertinent to our own imagination *and* appropriate to the Talmud. These questions obviously could not concern what the Talmud purports to tell: Was Aqiba really ignorant until he was forty? Did Rabbah b. Nahmani really get taken up to Heaven because his Torah was needed in the heavenly academy? On the other hand, the Talmud does accurately tell what those responsible for compiling it thought about the world around them. It contains substantial materials given *en passant*, not in a polemical or tendentious spirit. For example, it preserves numerous reports of what rabbinical courts decided in specific cases. These seem to me to possess great historical value, for, while we may never know whether such a decision was actually made on a given day concerning a given litigation, the fact that the tradents certainly believed such decisions *could* be made is of some sociological interest. The shape of such beliefs, after all, cannot have greatly diverged from the configuration of everyday life, if no polemical or theological interest intervenes.

While the beliefs of the rabbis about times past may be of slight consequence for the description of those times, the belief of the rabbis about what they themselves did every day in their courts seems to me very important in analyzing what the courts actually did. So I do not know whether a man named Samuel really decided thus-and-so in court. But I think the conviction of the generation and school responsible for shaping the story that he had done so accurately portrays how *they* saw things, and therefore provides us with valuable information on how they viewed the state of their courts and the range of their authority and power. And if, further, we find evidence of a consistent picture, extending for several hundred years, we may then conclude that the courts in general could accomplish pretty much what the rabbis claimed in their behalf. If a picture of an effective court system emerges, we may then proceed to speculate on the basis for the ability of a group of men to force others to do what they wanted. Obviously, we must take into account not only how the rabbis explained things, but also the facts known to us from quite separate sources of information. In the case of Babylonian Jewry, we need to know about the policies of successive Iranian governments toward the minority communities and *their* government, and also about other groups and institutions within the Jewish community likely to be able to exercise authority, which are not described in much detail in rabbinical sources.

When it comes to the mythic life of the rabbinical group, we are on still firmer ground, for the Talmud is a rich resource for information on how the rabbinical circles in particular viewed reality. Here again, we may well have the record only of the final period of talmudic literature. Only through specific and careful investigation can we distinguish what is peculiarly characteristic of the last group of talmudic tradents and redactors, and what also characterized earlier groups in sequence.

IX. The Promise and Prospects of Talmudic History

What will persuade someone primarily interested in historical study, rather than in continuities and changes in culture and society, that the document at hand demands sustained attention in particular as a problem for historians? It is the simple fact that the Talmud provides a striking example, for close analysis, of a problem of acute interest in historical debates even in our own day. I refer to the debates on how we study not the individual but human societies, organized groups, that engage historians from the *Annales* of the 1920s through *Social Science History* today. Let me explain.

In describing and interpreting the life of peoples, we seek to generalize about attitudes and shared conceptions, using the French word, "*mentalité*," for example, to explain that about which we speak. Specifically, we want to know how people form a shared conception of themselves so as to see themselves as a group, and how, further, what they conceive in common relates to how they each, as individuals, confront and experience life. Louise A. Tilly, writing on "People's History and Social Science History"[7] frames matters in terms of shared emotions and, citing Lucien Febvre, founder, with Marc Bloch, of the *Annales*, quotes Febvre as follows:

> Emotions imply relations between men, collective relationships. They are doubtless born within the organic depths specific to a given individual....But their expression is the result of a series of experiences of common life, or similar and contemporaneous reactions to the shock of identical situations and encounters of the same nature....Little by little... by linking many participants in turn as initiators and followers – these end by becoming a system of interindividual motivations that differ according to circumstances and situations...and a true system of emotions is built. They become something like an institution.

Febvre copes with the deep problems of how peoples' emotions so take shape as to fit a common pattern. That is why he speaks of experiences of common life, identical situations, encounters of the same nature. Now if we take up the same issue framed in terms not of feelings but of the ideas and doctrines that give expression to attitudes and feelings, we find ourselves raising exactly the same questions. The thesis at hand, that collective relationships expressed through mutually comprehensible emotions emerge, not from what is specific to the given

---

[7]*Social Science History*, 1983:7, 458.

individual, but from what is shared and common, becomes all the more pertinent. Specifically, we take up the social expression of attitudes. We turn, then, to matters of doctrines and institutions, and issues of governance of groups based on a compact of common values. These all together constitute politics, for the secular world, and theology, for the religious one. In the setting of Judaism, with its interest in what people do as much as in what they think, the whole reaches the surface of everyday life in what we call *halakhah*, the rules and laws of life. If, then, we can trace the context of consensus and the progress through which consensus is achieved, we find ourselves providing an exceptionally suggestive example for the inquiry into the interplay between the individual and the group, specifically the formation of collective attitudes out of individual experiences.

In the talmudic corpus we have the end result of half a millennium of the process of attaining concurrence, the achievement of what was at first a caste and class consensus but what was at the end a national compact and agreement. Israel, the Jewish people, in late antiquity produced a minority, the sages under discussion, which to begin with coalesced on its own, and then won adherence to its views, through coercion and persuasion alike, among the nation as a whole. So when we ask what sort of history we may expect from the sources at hand, we find a remarkably relevant sort of discourse. We deal with an example of the long-term formation of collective doctrine, social theory shared among people in diverse times and places, subject to transmission, moreover, from the special circumstances in which the theory took shape to distant and wholly other conditions confronted by the Jewish nation later on. The sources at hand come down from late antiquity because people agreed to copy and preserve them. They came to that agreement because what they found in the sources laid claim to truth and authority. The fundamental thesis of the sources attained that status of utter self-evidence that made possible debate on everything but the fundamental issues. These were settled in late antiquity. Where, when, how they were settled, what sort of "experiences of common life, of similar and contemporaneous reactions to the shock of identical situations and encounters of the same nature," in Febvre's language, produced these components of a common consensus and endowed them with self-evidence – these are the issues at hand.

In the conditions of contemporary debate on the nature of historical study, the interest in generalization and the analysis of collectivities, the concern for comparison of group to group, the interest in small details and how these typify large trends, the concern for politics and the influence of ideology – in these conditions the talmudic historian finds remarkably relevant what in itself is remote, particular, and rather special. What we have is a collective biography of a well-organized political and religious estate. But the constant reference to individual opinion characteristic of the sources at hand allows for attention to the individual as well. The vigorous debate, the close study of modes of argument as much as of substance, likewise allow us to address the formation of shared modes of thought. *Self-evidence*, in the documents at hand, is not conferred by politics alone but achieved by argument. Professor Tilly concludes her article with the following words:

> The genius of social science history is twofold. First, its central method — collective biography of one kind or another — preserves individual variability while identifying dominant social patterns. Second, its focus on social relationships rather than psychological states remains our surest guarantee of reconstructing how ordinary people of the past lived out their days and made the choices that cumulate into history. Social science history, properly conceived, is the ultimate people's history.

So far as we wish to trace collective biography, our documents exemplify precisely the sort of sources that make that work feasible. So far as we take up the issues of social relationships, both within a social group and also between that group and the outsider, the sources of the talmudic canon address precisely the issue at hand. That is why I claim that, by criteria of contemporary historical debate, the kind of history that bears the adjective "talmudic" and that emerges from a rather circumscribed body of sources indeed falls smack in the center of historical learning today.

X. My Own Program

Let me close with a few remarks about how I have tried to carry out the program outlined here. Since my work has never been read and reviewed in this particular setting — in *Zion*, I mean — or indeed in any other journal in this important center of Jewish learning, it is surely appropriate to introduce it to people who do not know it.[8] My work began with precisely the methodology I have rejected, with a history of the Jews in Babylonia and some parallel studies, all of which rest upon the givens that the sources mark the beginning of study, not the focus, and that their facts define the task at hand.

From all that has been said, the reader will realize that there is not a page, not a paragraph, not a sentence in my early books that I

---

[8] I call attention to the forthcoming Hebrew translation by Sifriat Poalim of my *Judaism: The Evidence of the Mishnah* (Chicago, 1981: University of Chicago Press).

could write today exactly as I did twenty-five or even fifteen years ago. The very fundamental category at hand – "the Jews in Babylonia" – yields a program that stands entirely asymmetrical with the characteristics of the sources. The division by particular periods, for instance, is simply implausible. In order to speak of "the Parthian period" or "the early Sasanian period," I have to take for granted that stories told about events before the rise of Sasanian rule, in the early third century, really took place in the time and circumstances in which the storyteller narrates them. What is attributed to rabbis of the period before 200 really was said, before 200, by those rabbis. None of this has been or can be either demonstrated or disproved. And, it goes without saying, in those early studies everything Josephus tells us is fact, pure and simple. But Josephus was not eyewitness to the stories cited here, and we do not know how he found out about these events. To state matters simply, I here assume as data for the composition of manifest history what in fact serve as constituents for that very different, latent history I described earlier.

More to the point, the sources at hand – stories and sayings – cannot be read distinct from the documents that contain those sources. We begin from the whole and work back to the parts. We start with, not the Jews in Babylonia in Parthian or Sasanian times, but Josephus, the Mishnah, the Tosefta, the Talmud of the Land of Israel ("Yerushalmi") and the Talmud of Babylonia ("Bavli"). Let me state with appropriate emphasis. *Each of the components, the documents, of the talmudic canon requires attention as a whole and on its own terms.* And if we pay attention to the documents, we shall not find interesting the remnants and shards that these documents contain on the history of the Jews in Babylonia in Parthian times. The documents tell their own story. It is to that story that we must teach ourselves to listen. The documents (except for Josephus) constitute artifacts of culture, testimonies to the inner life of people who expressed their consensus through them – facts of politics, indicators of collective doctrine and dogma, expressions of a small community of clerks and their imagination.

So I think it quite correct to say that we need to find out just what happened, what came first and what came afterward. But what happened is not what I described, analyzed, and interpreted in my earlier books. It is the documents that constitute the principal events: social events, cultural and intellectual events. The history must then be the history of the cultural life of a well defined social group and its encounter with the politics and condition of the larger nation of which it formed an active and aggressive component. When we know how the community of sages framed its ideas in the context of its historical and social setting, we shall have learned from the books that community endorsed and transmitted precisely the kind of history they allow us to recover. And, as I argued at the outset, that is exactly the sort of historical inquiry that in our own day proves urgent and compelling.

Let me conclude by referring to the two trilogies that bring to fruition twenty years of reflection and further study of exactly the same texts and problems of historical description, analysis, and interpretation, on which I worked at the outset.

These are, first, the trilogy on the reading of each of three individual documents as historical testimonies: *Judaism: The Evidence of the Mishnah; Judaism in Society: The Evidence of the Yerushalmi;* and *Judaism and Scripture: The Evidence of Leviticus Rabbah* (all: Chicago, The University of Chicago Press, 1981, 1983, and 1985, respectively). Second is the trilogy in which, reading documents as a whole on critical issues, I carry out the first work of stage-by-stage restoration and renewal: *Foundations of Judaism: Method, Teleology, Doctrine,* as follows: *I. Midrash in Context: Exegesis in Formative Judaism, II. Messiah in Context: Israel's History and Destiny in Formative Judaism;* and *III. Torah: From Scroll to Symbol in Formative Judaism* (all: Philadelphia, Fortress Press: 1983, 1984, and 1985, respectively). The double trilogy shows rather strikingly that talmudic history enjoys prospects unimagined in its first century, the one that began with Geiger, Graetz, and Frankel, and ended with my *History.* So let the old – whether in *Zion* or in my *History* – find its way as a model, not of what to do, but of what not to do. Alas, since most of the historical work on the documents at hand even now remains bound to the old ways, the claim that my *History of the Jews in Babylonia* marks the epitaph may appear premature. But in fact it is where things indeed did end, and it marks the point from which the future began.[9]

---

[9]My student, Mrs. Judith Romney Wegner, made useful comments on this paper, for which I express thanks.

Index

Abba b. Abba 265, 278, 280
Abbaye 143
Abner 93, 94
Aboth de R. Nathan 111
Abraham 33-35, 91, 133, 169, 242, 298, 299, 303, 309-311, 332-334, 336, 337
Abraham bar Hiyya 106
Abraham ibn Ezra 106
Achemenids 204, 264, 267
Adam 136, 171, 309
Adiabene 214, 259, 263, 275, 276
Ahiah 269
Akiba 276
Albeck, H. 348, 349
Alexander 59, 127, 131, 207, 262, 268, 307-309
Allon, Gedaliahu 342, 343, 345
Almond, Philip C. 26-28
American Jewry 171, 282, 283
American Reform [Jews] 81, 196
Amoraic 241, 250, 258, 265, 285
Anan 208, 271
Anilai 205, 206, 208, 210, 268
Anileus 268

Anthropologist(s) 5, 60, 61, 68, 69, 72-74, 80
anthropology 57, 58, 60, 61, 68, 70, 72, 73, 76, 133, 135, 139, 323-325
anti-Semitic 37
Antoninus Pius 207
Apocrypha 41
Aqiba 210, 232, 234, 248, 250, 251, 295, 308, 348, 358
Arda 211, 270
Ardavan 267
Aristotle 120, 122-124, 126, 127, 129, 130, 132, 135, 138, 237, 238, 254
Armenia 206, 208, 263, 267, 268, 272, 275
Arsacid 204, 206, 207, 209, 210, 262, 264, 272
Arta 211, 270
Artaxerxes 217, 262, 268
Artaxerxes Ochus 262
Asa 215, 218
Asinai 205, 206, 208, 210, 268
Asineus 268
Assimilation 57, 58

Augustine 97, 130, 136

Avi-Yonah, Michael 59

Azariah 256, 298, 332, 333, 336, 337

B'ne Bathyra 275

Babylonia 38, 59, 71, 85, 86, 93, 121, 135, 152, 154, 170, 180, 186, 193, 194, 197, 198, 200, 201, 205-216, 251, 255, 257-263, 265-285, 302-310, 334, 344, 351, 352, 355, 356, 361-363

Babylonian Jewry 194, 197, 203, 205, 207, 209, 257, 258, 262, 263, 265, 271-274, 280-283, 285, 358

Babylonian Talmud 58, 157, 197, 198, 204, 255, 257, 348, 350, 351, 354-357

Baer, I.F. 343

Bar Hutah 298

Bar Kokhba War 59, 210, 276-278

Baron, Salo Wittmayer 59, 105-107, 139, 141-144, 208

Bavli 83, 85, 86, 93, 94, 96, 98-110, 114, 115, 121, 152-163, 362

Ber, M. 259, 269

Berekhiah 299, 304, 307

Bible 34, 35, 37, 41, 42, 121, 136, 283, 329

biblical 7, 47, 48, 69, 76, 107, 126, 136, 143, 158, 242, 243, 245, 252, 255, 256, 273, 274, 294, 296, 297, 299, 310, 345, 346, 348, 353, 357

Blood 46, 48-51, 69, 222, 232, 270, 330

Bokser, Ben Zion 287, 316, 317

Bowie, E. L. 131

Brooks, Roger 130

Brown, Peter 68

Buddhism 21, 25-29, 43, 60

Buechler, A. 245

Canada 70, 168, 169, 171, 246

Canon 23, 25, 40, 41, 86, 96, 121, 150, 159-161, 291, 292, 311, 314, 319, 321, 325, 326, 335-337, 351, 353, 361, 362

Catholics 30, 149

Charax Spasinu 262, 265

Cherniss, Harold 237, 238, 254

Christ 22-24, 27, 34-36, 42, 43, 301

Christian theology 21, 29, 36, 43, 238

Christianity, Christianities 18, 19, 21-27, 29, 33-45, 59, 64, 97, 120, 132, 135, 148, 166, 172, 179, 196, 246, 247, 276, 284, 288, 292, 293, 296, 297, 310-315, 317, 355

Christians 18, 19, 21-23, 25-27, 30, 34, 36, 38, 43, 44, 64, 142, 179, 188, 214, 218, 296, 297, 310, 311, 315

Chronicles, Chron. 199

Church 19, 20, 24, 25, 33-38, 41, 42, 82, 97, 148, 149, 176, 179, 188, 193, 194, 196, 203, 204

Clagett, Marshall 96, 97

Classification 27, 101, 102, 123, 128, 291, 292, 302, 331

Cohen, Gerson D. 57, 136

Conservative [Jews] 81, 166, 195

Constantine 22, 23, 25, 34, 137, 288, 297, 301

Cross, Jr., Frank 273

Ctesiphon 205, 206, 214, 260, 262

Cult 45, 47, 48, 50, 51, 53, 67, 121, 186, 222-224, 226-231, 284, 285, 293

Cyrus 307

Daiches, Samuel 279

Daniel, Dan. 88, 270, 294, 303-305, 307-309, 332, 333

Davar-aher [compilation] 329, 331-334

David 59, 93-95, 157, 171, 200-205, 208, 211, 212, 218, 307, 329, 334, 342

Day of Atonement 166, 170, 181-183, 331, 334

Days of Awe 181-184

Dead Sea 41

Deut. Sifre 267

Deuteronomy, Dt., Deut. 50, 86, 87, 90, 91, 160, 216, 235, 267, 280, 300, 304, 306, 309

Dosetai b. R. Yanna 270, 278, 281

Douglas, Mary 5, 72, 74, 75, 80

Dual Torah 42, 81-83, 85, 86, 93, 96, 97, 99, 102, 104-106, 110, 112, 116, 121, 122, 124, 150, 151, 154, 161, 162, 165-167, 169-172, 175-178, 180, 181, 185-188, 325, 326

Dubnow, Simon 258

Dura 198, 262, 265, 270, 274, 279, 285, 355

Dura Europos 270, 285

East 17-19, 28, 48, 49, 59, 97, 123, 124, 127, 128, 131, 206, 208, 260, 263-265, 268, 303, 309, 313

Easter 35, 179

Economics, distributive 121, 123-127, 129, 131-135, 137, 138

Economics, market 119, 124-130, 132, 134, 135, 138

Eden 172, 174, 187, 302, 314

Edessa 265, 276

Edom 23, 293, 294, 296, 298, 303-307, 309-311

Eleazar 46, 50, 51, 63, 305

Eleazar ben Pedat 199

Eleazar b. R. Simeon 50, 51, 55, 271

Eleazar ben Azariah 63, 256

Eliezer b. Jacob 49, 50, 55

Eliezer b. Shamua 267, 277

Eliezer ben Hyrcanus 247, 255

Elijah 54, 333

Epstein, Y. N. 139, 348, 349

Esau 23, 293, 294, 296-301, 308-311, 313, 317, 333, 334

Essene(s) 41, 137, 223-228, , 230, 231, 233, 234

Esther, Est. 273, 303, 304, 308

Ethnos 39, 42

Eucharist 179

Europe 18, 37, 70, 128, 167-169, 171, 180, 181, 187, 188, 195, 246, 260, 315, 323

Eusebius 34

Exegesis 23, 30, 40, 41, 55, 59, 60, 67, 70, 79, 84, 95, 108, 121, 122, 158, 159, 161, 218, 219, 230, 248, 273-275, 280, 292, 335-338, 354, 357, 363

Exilarch 198-205, 207-215, 217-219, 259, 266, 269-272, 276, 279, 283

Exodus 174, 186, 329, 333, 334

Ezekiel, Ezek. 257, 260, 274, 281, 306, 330

Ezra 106, 216, 217, 257, 258, 268, 270, 273, 279, 307, 334, 336

Febvre, Lucien 359
Finkelstein, Louis 60
Finley, M. I. 131
First Man [Adam] 34, 302
Fixed associative [logic] 83, 86, 90, 114, 115
Fox-Genovese, Elizabeth 120
Frankel, Zechariah 240-245, 247, 249, 254, 345-349, 363
Free association 92, 101, 108-110, 112, 114
Frerichs, Ernest S. 311
Friedman, Shamma 157
Funk, S. 208, 259
Gamaliel 91, 119, 207, 248, 254, 266, 271, 275, 276, 342, 345
Gamaliel I 275
Gamaliel II 207
Gaon, Sherira 106, 281, 348
Geertz, Clifford 70-72, 74
Geiger 240, 241, 345
Geller, Markham J. 219
Genesis Rabbah, Gen. Rabbah 159, 248, 265, 292, 297, 298, 301, 310, 311
Geniva 198-200, 202
Getzav, Nahman Zvi 258, 259
Ginzberg, Louis 60, 254, 260
God 3, 9, 19, 21-23, 34, 36, 37, 39, 40, 43, 44, 50, 52, 62, 69, 73, 87, 88, 91, 116, 128-130, 132-135, 150, 151, 154, 163, 167, 168, 170, 174-178, 182-184, 186, 187, 189, 193-197, 201-203, 205, 212, 219, 224, 226, 229, 284, 285, 288, 298, 300, 302-305, 307, 311, 314, 315, 325, 327, 328, 330, 331, 333, 334, 338, 352, 356
Goodblatt, D. 342, 349
Goodenough, Erwin 285
Gospels 41, 136, 242, 243
Graetz, Heinrich 111, 240-245, 247, 249, 256, 345, 346, 363
Greco-Roman 59, 88, 121, 285
Greece 81, 97, 127, 131, 302-310
Greek 58, 64, 96, 97, 107, 114, 136, 206, 207, 238, 262, 264, 268, 285, 306, 325, 334
Greeley, Andrew M. 149
Gross, Nachum 144, 145
Hadas-Lebel, Mireille 288
Haggai 265, 299, 336
Hagiography 65, 246
Hakoken, Mordecai 279
Halevy, Y. I. 208
Halivni, David Weiss 59, 157
Hamnuna 280
Hananiah 254, 257, 269, 270, 276, 332, 333, 336, 337
Hanina b. Hama 267, 278, 280
Harris, Marvin 61
Heave-offerings 143
Heaven 34, 37, 63, 130, 201, 203, 222, 229, 283, 304, 307, 308, 314, 324, 325, 358
Hebrew 25, 34, 40, 58, 72, 109, 114, 121, 144, 145, 157, 160, 183, 238, 243, 244, 246, 253, 257, 268, 288, 307, 329, 334, 336, 352, 361
Hebrew Scriptures 25, 34, 40, 58, 72, 238, 243, 246, 257, 336

Index

Helbo 307
Hellenism, Hellenistic 59, 262, 264
Hermeneutic(s) 34-40, 42, 59, 84, 160-162, 222, 322, 324
Heschel, Abraham J. 133
Hillel 64, 65, 69, 201, 238, 261, 274
Hillelite 204, 271
Hilqiah 306
Hisda 198, 200, 216, 217
Historians 59, 62, 65-69, 73, 196, 242, 243, 247, 252, 262, 322, 323, 327, 346, 347, 353, 356, 357, 359
History 3-5, 8, 11, 12, 20, 23-26, 30, 34, 35, 37-39, 41, 54, 57, 59-63, 65-67, 70, 71, 73, 77, 78, 80, 97, 99, 103-106, 108, 117, 122, 124, 135, 136, 139-142, 144, 145, 151, 156, 162, 171, 178, 181, 191, 193, 194, 196, 198, 200, 201, 211, 215, 218, 219, 221, 223-230, 235-248, 250-256, 289, 293, 294, 296-298, 301, 302, 308-311, 313-315, 317, 257-259, 265, 271, 273, 279, 281, 282, 285, 319-326, 328, 332, 334, 337, 341-346, 348, 349, 351-357, 359-363
Hiyya 106, 200, 201, 208, 210, 265-267
Holy of Holies 48
Holy One 87, 205, 285, 302, 307
Holy Place 49
Holy Things 234
Horton, Robin 114, 115
Hosea 216, 217
Humphreys, Sally C. 135, 238
Huna 198, 200, 208-210, 219, 271, 299, 303

Huna b. Nathan 219
Huzal 276-280
Hyrcanus 51, 247, 255, 268
Iranian(s) 58, 59, 197-199, 204, 207, 209, 216, 217, 261, 263, 264, 267, 268, 273, 284, 285, 292, 352, 358
Isaac 34, 94, 95, 169, 196, 216, 217, 276, 298-301, 303, 309-311, 332-334, 336, 337
Isaiah, Is. 5, 9, 11, 18-20, 25, 27, 29, 31, 35, 36, 38-40, 44, 48, 49, 51, 52, 59, 61, 62, 64, 67, 68, 76-78, 80, 83, 87, 89-91, 93, 95, 96, 98, 101-103, 108, 111, 116, 119, 125-127, 130, 132, 135, 149, 151, 153, 154, 156, 160, 161, 165, 168, 172, 177, 179, 193, 194, 197, 199, 201-203, 208, 221, 225, 230, 232, 245, 248, 249, 252, 253, 257, 259, 289-292, 295, 296, 298, 299, 303, 304, 306, 308, 309, 315, 316, 319, 321, 322, 325, 328, 329, 335, 341, 354, 356
Ishmael 23, 143, 210, 248, 255, 277, 280, 294, 296-298, 301, 307, 310, 311
Ishmael b. R. Nehemiah 302, 305
Ishmael b. R. Yosi 271
Islam 18, 19, 21, 26, 43, 45, 81, 97, 105, 107, 246, 343
Islamic 18, 26, 58, 76
Israel 3, 21-25, 34-38, 40, 42-44, 46, 47, 52, 62, 69, 74, 75, 81, 87, 88, 91, 94, 106, 116, 126, 127, 129, 130, 132-136, 160, 165-167, 169-178, 180-189, 195, 201-204, 208, 224, 225, 227, 229, 234-236, 242, 246, 253, 256, 257, 267, 282, 285, 287-289, 308-310, 312-315, 317,

321, 326, 328, 330-334, 338, 341, 343, 344, 351, 352, 354, 356, 360, 362

Israelite(s) 22, 25, 52, 69, 126, 129, 130, 132-134, 223, 224, 231, 292, 293, 312, 315, 327, 333, 345

Issi b. Akavya 279

Issi b. Gur Arye 279

Issi b. Judah 278

Issi b. Mehallel 279

Issi ben Judah 277

Jacob 34, 49, 50, 55, 69, 165, 169, 200, 208, 255, 259, 296, 299-301, 310, 311, 313, 317, 329, 332-334, 336, 337

Jehoiachin 205, 208

Jeremiah, Jer. 200, 257, 260, 299, 304, 305

Jesus 22-24, 34-36, 38, 42, 43, 64, 65, 148, 196, 204, 233, 242, 243, 246

Jewish Babylonia 194, 213

Jewish People 11, 33, 38, 57, 79, 169, 178, 238, 239, 317, 343, 360

Jewry 96, 99, 166, 167, 169, 171, 176, 177, 181, 184, 188, 194, 196-198, 200, 203-205, 207, 209, 210, 212, 243, 253, 257, 258, 260, 262, 263, 265, 269, 271-274, 280-283, 285, 358

Jews 11, 18, 19, 21, 24, 25, 30, 35-37, 41-44, 59, 64, 69, 71, 77, 78, 81, 85, 105, 107, 111, 112, 121, 127, 129, 135, 139-146, 165-178, 180, 181, 184-188, 193, 196-201, 203-211, 213-219, 239-241, 245, 253, 255-257, 261-271, 273, 279, 281-285, 291, 297, 310, 311, 313-

315, 343-345, 347, 349, 352-356, 361-363

Jonah 63, 113, 347

Jonathan 267, 277, 279, 334

Jonathan b. Eliezer , 267, 278, 280

Joseph ibn Saddik 106

Joseph the Babylonian 277, 279

Josephus 62, 205, 208, 262, 268, 272, 362

Joshua 151, 248, 254, 257, 269, 327, 330, 331, 352

Joshua b. Hananiah 276

Joshua b. Levi 301, 302

Josiah 276, 277, 279, 280

Judah b. Bathyra 267, 277

Judah b. Bava 276

Judah bar Ila'i 143

Judah ben Bathra 275

Judah hal-levi 106

Judah I 142

Judah the Patriarch 236, 250, 348

Judah the Prince 200, 208, 212, 257, 261, 266, 267, 270, 271, 278, 279, 283

Judaic 21, 23, 24, 29, 30, 35-39, 42, 65, 76, 77, 80, 105, 108-110, 114, 119, 130, 134, 136, 141, 147, 148, 154, 166, 167, 169, 171, 173, 179, 180, 237, 254, 256, 289, 336

Judaism(s) 1, 15, 18, 21-23, 25, 31, 33-45, 58, 60, 63-68, 72, 73, 75-78, 80-86, 90, 93, 96-100, 102, 104-108, 110, 112, 114-117, 119-124, 127, 129-133, 135, 138, 139, 141, 143, 147, 149-154, 156, 160-163, 165-182, 184-188, 191, 194-197,

Index 371

210, 213, 220, 221, 223, 237-241, 243, 244, 246, 247, 250, 251, 253-257, 264, 276, 280-282, 284, 285, 287-289, 291-293, 297, 311, 312, 314, 315, 317, 319, 324-327, 329, 334, 335, 337, 338, 346, 348, 354, 360, 361, 363

Judaism of [the] Holocaust and Redemption 166, 167, 171-173, 175-178, 180, 187, 188

Judaism of the Dual Torah 42, 81-83, 85, 86, 93, 96, 97, 99, 102, 104-106, 110, 116, 121, 122, 124, 150, 151, 154, 161, 162, 165-167, 170-172, 175-178, 180, 181, 185-188, 325, 326

Kadushin, Max 66, 71, 254

Kahana 262

Kasowski, Chaim Josua (see Kosovsky, H. Y.)

Kimhi, Joseph 315

King 54, 87, 93, 94, 182, 199, 204, 205, 208, 215, 216, 264, 268, 270, 301, 304, 306-308, 333

King Messiah 54

Kings 73, 126, 198-203, 205, 215, 264, 270, 331

Kosovsky, H. Y. 294, 296

Krauss, Shmuel 264, 288

Krochmal, Nahman 241-243, 247

Land of Israel 22, 42, 127, 129, 132-135, 160, 186, 208, 257, 282, 288, 293, 297, 302, 310, 317, 344, 351, 362

Lasch, Christopher 239, 254

Lazarus, Felix 208, 259

Leach, Edmund 69, 72, 80

Lekachman, Robert 122

Levi b. Sisi 267, 274, 278, 280, 284

Levine, Baruch 261

Leviticus 72, 126, 134, 159, 160, 186, 230, 235, 248, 260, 292, 293, 300-302, 309-311, 363

Leviticus Rabbah 159, 160, 248, 292, 293, 300-302, 309-311, 363

Lieberman, Saul 110-114, 141

List-making 334

Listenwissenschaft 320, 321, 326, 332

Literary critics 69

Liturgy, liturgies 111, 170, 179-184, 186-189, 281

Loewe, H. 244

Logic 9, 41, 62, 71, 83, 85-96, 99, 101, 102, 105, 106, 108-110, 113, 152-156, 160, 162, 234, 239, 251, 288, 289, 292, 321, 326, 354

Logic(s) of cogent discourse 83, 86, 90

Logic of fixed association 90-93, 96, 101, 102, 105, 108-110, 113

Luke 233

Maccabees 262, 268

Magi 204, 264, 273

Maimonides 54, 106

Mantel, H. 10, 259

Mar 'Uqba 198, 199, 200

Mar Ukban 270

Marcus Aurelius 207

Mark 125, 158, 166, 172, 182, 200, 233, 237, 241, 257, 297, 314, 317, 353, 361

Matt 233

Mattia 267

McNeill, W. H. 213
Meir 238, 250, 251, 269
Mekhilta 277, 280
Merkavah 274, 281
Mesopotamia 126, 262, 263, 266-269, 355
Messiah 22, 24, 25, 54, 163, 193, 200, 202-204, 219, 220, 225, 293, 310, 314, 329, 334, 363
Metaproposition 90
Metapropositional [logic] 83, 86, 93, 114
Middle East 17, 59, 123, 127, 131, 264, 265, 268, 313
Midrash 111, 113, 208, 266, 288, 297, 325, 363
Mishnah 41, 45-51, 58, 67, 71, 74, 77, 78, 80, 83, 86, 90, 93-96, 99, 101, 103, 104, 121-124, 126-132, 134-138, 145, 155-161, 186, 212, 213, 221, 226-228, 230-232, 240, 241, 247-250, 254, 255, 257, 274, 281, 282, 291-294, 296, 297, 303, 310-312, 333, 347-349, 352, 361-363
Mishnaic 48, 49, 54, 64, 123, 130, 133, 221, 223, 226-236, 238, 241, 248, 250, 255, 256, 281, 334, 348
Mishnaic system 133, 221, 226-236
Mongols 26, 264
Montefiore, C. G. 244
Moore, George F. 254
Moses 37, 39, 54, 88, 91, 148, 150, 151, 154, 160, 167, 186, 187, 195, 197, 201, 211, 212, 217, 300, 306, 309, 315, 330, 333, 334, 350, 352
Mount of Olives 49-51
Muslims 30, 188

Nahman b. Isaac 216, 217
Nahman b. Jacob 200
Nahman b. R. Hisda 216, 217
Nahman bar Isaac 95
Nahmanides, Moses 315
Nahum 208, 209
Narrative 64, 86, 89, 206, 208, 240, 242, 297, 319, 322, 323, 326, 352
Nathan 111, 208, 210, 219, 269, 270, 276, 277, 280, 281
Nathan b. Yehiel 58
Natural philosophy 82, 97, 101, 103-107, 116
Near East 18, 59, 124, 128
Nebuchadnezzar 261, 302, 303, 307, 309, 336
Nehardea 206, 207, 212, 268, 269, 271, 272, 276, 280
Nehemiah 268, 275, 276, 279, 299, 302, 305
Nehunyon 269
Nestorians 26
Neusner, J. 57, 58, 165, 211, 215, 218, 219, 254, 255, 289, 311, 329
New Testament 34-38, 42, 148, 246
New Year 170, 181, 182
Newman, Louis E. 134, 265
Nisibis 207, 263, 265, 266, 269, 271, 274-277, 279, 280
Noah 37
Numbers, Num. 46, 47, 52, 55, 81, 86, 126, 159, 179, 185, 186, 295, 262, 263, 265, 267, 275, 282, 297, 330
Obadiah 309
Obermeyer, Jacob 259

Ohrenstein, Roman A. 136, 139

Old Testament 22, 24, 25, 34, 36, 37, 40, 41, 43, 69, 121, 310, 324-326, 328, 352

Oral Torah 37, 42, 65, 107, 195, 258, 325, 348

Oral Tradition 65, 197, 272-275, 278, 348

Orthodox [Judaism] 38, 41, 75, 82, 166-169, 180, 185, 194

Orthodoxy 41, 167, 169, 170, 195, 220

Palestine 22, 45, 59, 69, 110, 127, 145, 201, 204, 206, 207, 209, 210, 212, 251, 265-268, 270, 271, 273, 274, 276-282, 297, 342, 351

Palestinian Jewry 200, 271

Palestinian Talmud 111-113

Papa 204

Parthian(s) 59, 193, 197, 204, 205, 207, 209-211, 259-273, 276, 282, 355, 362

Passover seder 166, 171, 182, 185

Paul 34-36, 38, 42, 61, 72, 97, 131, 237, 325, 342

Penner, Hans H. 115

Pentateuch 127, 242, 325

Persia 26, 204, 288, 307

Persians 215, 218, 260, 262

Peter 42

Peters, F.E. 59

Pharisaic party [at Yavneh] 207, 271, 275

Pharisaism 52, 225, 227, 274, 275

Pharisees 51, 60, 65, 226, 227, 230, 255, 271, 275, 343, 350

Philo 41

Philosophy 3-5, 8, 66, 67, 82, 83, 89, 97, 101, 103-107, 114-116, 122, 131, 237, 238, 241, 249, 254, 256, 262

Phineas 300, 306

Pil-y Barish 211, 270

Pinhas b. Yair 54, 225, 227

Plato 122, 130, 138, 237, 238, 254

Polanyi, Karl 120, 123, 124, 135

Pope(s) 18, 26, 33

Priest 46-51, 94, 232-235, 268, 276

Priestly 46-48, 52, 53, 55, 126-129, 131, 136, 137, 143, 186, 216, 224, 229-231, 233, 234, 312, 325, 333, 334, 343

Priestly Code 126-129, 131, 136, 137, 224, 230, 231

Propositional discourse 89, 93, 95, 102, 112

Propositional logic 86, 87, 89, 95, 106

Protestant(s) 21, 30, 35, 37, 82, 97, 148, 166, 175, 176, 180, 187, 188, 221, 320

Proverbs, Prov. 198, 202

Psalms, Ps. 88, 92, 199, 298-300, 302, 304, 306-308, 330

Pseudepigrapha 41

Qumran 137, 223-225, 227, 228, 230, 231, 233

Rab 94

Rabba b. Hana 265, 267

Rabbah b. Nahmani 358

Rabbi(s) 36-38, 43, 45, 53-55, 58, 62, 66, 67, 69, 70, 73, 77, 78, 94, 110-112, 139, 141-143, 154, 158, 174, 195, 197-203, 205, 210-219,

236, 241, 243-252, 255, 287, 304, 306, 313, 314, 333, 342, 344-346, 348-350, 355, 358, 362

Rabbinic Judaism 45, 66, 68, 75, 197, 240, 241, 250, 251, 254

Rashi 258, 272

Ratzinger, Cardinal 34, 38

Rav 199, 200, 208-210, 216, 217, 258, 262, 265-267, 270, 272, 274, 277-283

Rava 215-217, 219

Rebecca 299, 300, 333

Reform Judaism 36, 196, 220, 240

Reformation 18, 19, 35-37, 97, 148, 202, 235, 320, 321

Religion(s) 3, 5, 12, 15, 17-22, 26-28, 30, 31, 37-43, 45, 60, 66, 69-71, 74-76, 78, 81, 82, 115, 120, 136, 138, 139, 147, 148, 150-153, 162, 168, 169, 171-176, 180, 186-189, 193, 196, 203, 213, 236, 237, 246, 256, 264, 280, 283-285, 288, 292, 311, 324, 325, 336, 356

Religious systems 17, 20, 30, 41, 42, 136, 148, 166

Renaissance 63, 97, 239

Rite 20, 46-53, 55, 56, 165-168, 171, 173, 176, 181, 185, 186, 188

Ritual 45, 46, 48, 51, 53-56, 172, 183, 194, 196, 211

Roman Catholic 21, 33, 35, 41, 82, 97, 147, 148, 179

Roman Empire 22, 24, 25, 135, 208, 272, 292, 301, 309

Rome 23, 34, 58, 136, 206, 208-210, 263, 264, 266, 268, 269, 271, 272, 275, 287-289, 291-303, 305, 306, 308-311, 313, 314, 317, 352

Rosh Hashshanah 181, 182

Rostovtzeff 264

Saadiah Gaon 106

Sabbath 42, 53, 168, 174, 181-185, 193, 296, 331

Sacrifice(s) 50, 51, 53, 55, 67, 119, 201, 219, 229, 343

Sadducees 275

Safavids 213

Sages 23, 24, 33, 66, 82, 119, 121, 123, 129-131, 138, 144, 195, 197, 201, 208, 210, 212, 215, 216, 219, 226, 233, 235, 236, 244, 245, 258, 273, 276, 292, 294, 296-299, 301, 302, 310, 313, 336, 343, 348, 351-354, 360, 362

Sahlin, Marshall 324-326

Samuel, Sam. 87, 93, 94, 208, 209, 212, 258, 265, 266, 278-281, 283, 284, 358

Sanders, E. O. 37, 198

Sandmel, Samuel 63-65, 255

Sarah 35, 298

Sasanian(s) 59, 71, 193, 197, 204, 211, 214, 215, 261, 263, 265, 273, 282, 355, 362

Saul 87, 94, 110, 114, 119, 141, 334

Schechter, Solomon 195, 244, 256

Schorsch, Ismar 240, 241, 256

Science 38, 60, 61, 67, 81-83, 96-98, 100-107, 114, 115, 120, 122, 140, 141, 237, 284, 326, 334, 359, 361

Scott, D. A. 26, 115, 157, 329, 335

Scripture 23, 24, 36, 38, 41, 49, 51, 78, 91-96, 99, 104, 121, 126, 132, 148, 152, 157-160, 200, 202, 215, 216, 222, 228, 231-233, 235, 248,

Index

281, 292, 294-296, 298, 302, 303, 306, 308, 311-313, 321, 329, 333, 352, 363

Second Sophistic 123, 131

Second Temple 52, 54, 144, 208, 247, 253, 331, 342, 343

Seder 59, 166, 171, 182, 185, 208, 209, 347

Seleucia 206, 260, 262, 263, 266, 268

Semites 33, 34, 37, 43, 269

Semitics 58

Sevus Alexander 207

Shammai 64, 238

Shamua 267, 277

Shapur 193, 214, 217, 284

Shekhenaiah 208

Shemaiah 208

Sifra 86, 159, 160, 248

Sifré 86, 87, 91, 159, 248

Sifré to Deuteronomy 86, 87, 91

Sifré to Numbers 86, 159

Silver, Morris 124, 136

Simeon b. Abba 113

Simeon b. Gamaliel 91, 119, 266, 271

Simeon b. Laqish 113, 299, 305, 306

Simeon ben (b.) Nanos 295

Simeon ben Yohai 143

Simeon the Righteous 307, 308

Sinai 38, 39, 43, 62, 81, 98, 115, 121, 131, 150, 151, 154, 159, 163, 167, 187, 195, 197, 201, 212, 220, 279, 314, 325-327, 329, 331, 333, 334, 336, 337, 344, 352

Smallwood, Mary 59, 256

Smith, Jonathan Z. 256, 335-337

Smith, Morton 249, 256

Solomon 69, 244, 256, 329, 333

Solomon ibn Gabirol 106

Sombart, Werner 139, 140

Song of Songs 57, 328, 329, 332, 336-338

Song of Songs Rabbah 328, 329, 332, 337

Soviet Jewry 166, 176, 188

Spinoza 242

Spiro, Melford 60, 72

State of Israel 81, 166, 167, 169, 171, 172, 176, 177, 180, 187, 188, 246, 321, 344

Storyteller 69, 242, 346, 362

Strack-Billerbeck 37, 38

Sukkot 182

Sura 272, 342

Syllogistic 88, 94, 104, 152, 155, 162

Synagogue 20, 92, 148, 165, 167, 170, 172, 174, 180, 181, 184-186, 198, 237, 265, 274, 279, 285, 355

Taboos 47, 51-53, 56, 125, 126, 128, 194

Tacitus 62

Talmud 11, 36, 38, 57-63, 66-68, 70, 71, 73-80, 85, 86, 93, 96, 111-113, 121, 135, 139, 145, 152, 154, 157, 160, 170, 180, 186, 195, 197, 198, 204, 219, 237-246, 250, 252, 253, 255-258, 261-263, 267, 270, 273, 275, 277, 288, 297, 303, 343-359, 362

Talmud as history 63, 237, 240, 242, 245, 253

Talmud of Babylonia 38, 85, 86, 93, 121, 135, 152, 154, 170, 180, 186, 352, 362

Talmudic 58-63, 66-68, 71, 76-78, 80, 96, 101, 106-108, 121, 136, 139, 142, 144, 193, 195, 197, 240-247, 252, 257-259, 261, 272, 273, 288, 291, 316, 341-354, 357-363

Talmudic history 78, 242, 243, 245, 246, 258, 341-346, 348, 349, 351-354, 357, 359, 363

Talmudic literature 59-63, 66, 67, 71, 76, 80, 96, 136, 139, 241, 244, 272, 273, 358

Talmudic studies 59, 246, 247

Talmudists 62, 68, 71, 243, 357

Tanhuma 302

Tannaim 210, 212, 213, 247, 265, 267, 272, 276-278, 280, 283, 342

Tannaite 94, 157, 299, 348

Tarfon 248, 254, 295, 296

Tarn 264

Telegdi, S. 263

Teleological [logic] 83, 86, 93, 108, 114, 117, 139

Teleology 23, 25, 89, 293, 323, 363

Temple 20, 45, 47-55, 67, 121, 125-129, 132, 133, 135, 138, 144, 186, 197, 206-208, 211, 216, 223-236, 247, 253, 262, 271, 272, 275, 276, 285, 288, 296-298, 309, 326, 327, 331, 333, 334, 342, 343

Temple cult 47, 48, 51, 67, 186

Ten Tribes 275, 331

Tent of Meeting 46, 51, 186, 326, 327

"the other" 17, 18, 21, 22, 93, 134, 169

Theologian(s) 21, 23, 24, 36, 66, 67, 73, 74, 136, 137, 148, 240, 321, 323, 325, 332, 335

Theology 21, 26, 29-31, 34, 36-39, 43, 54, 57, 67, 73, 74, 76, 79, 100, 122, 124, 129, 131-133, 153, 160, 162, 170, 179, 180, 193, 194, 197, 200, 205, 238, 244, 283, 329, 332, 335, 338, 354, 360

Tilly, Louise A. 359, 361

Torah 2, 22, 24, 25, 34, 37-39, 42, 43, 62, 64, 65, 69, 78, 81-83, 85, 86, 93, 96, 97, 99, 102-107, 110, 112, 115-117, 121, 122, 124, 143, 144, 148-151, 154, 161-163, 165-167, 169-172, 175-178, 180-182, 185-188, 195, 197, 198, 200-203, 205, 212, 216, 217, 245, 257, 258, 273, 274, 282, 283, 285, 291, 296, 298, 302, 310, 314, 325-327, 329, 332, 333, 336, 342, 347, 348, 350, 352, 358, 363

Tosafists 258, 272

Tosefta 49-51, 110, 112, 157-160, 186, 247-250, 292-294, 296, 297, 310-312, 362

Tradition 21, 35, 36, 41, 44, 65, 69, 76-78, 81, 88, 97, 98, 102, 103, 105, 106, 108, 112, 115, 147-159, 161, 162, 195-197, 209, 211, 220, 238, 240, 248, 251, 255, 256, 262, 264, 272-275, 278, 281, 282, 284, 288, 315, 348, 350, 355

Traditional 59, 98, 115, 147, 149-154, 156, 161-163, 195, 258, 262, 268, 273, 275, 284, 347, 350

Trajan 207, 210, 263, 267, 275

Twersky, Isadore 106

Ulla 95, 216

Index

Uncleanness 47, 74, 221-224, 226-236, 293, 306
Urbach, Ephraim 66, 244, 245, 342
USA 70, 172, 180
Usha 277, 348
Veyne, Paul 325
Vologases I 206, 207, 268, 269, 271
Vologasia 206, 260
Wansbrough, J. 124
Weiss, J.H. 59, 157, 258
West 19, 23, 25-28, 48, 49, 88, 90, 97, 114, 138, 166-168, 170, 180, 185, 194, 213, 238, 246, 268, 285, 288, 295, 301, 317, 344, 354
Western 19, 21, 25-28, 63, 67, 70, 81, 115, 167-169, 180, 263, 274, 282, 287, 346
Widengren, George 215, 259, 263
Wolski 204, 264
Written Torah 24, 25, 34, 37, 43, 197, 201, 212

Yadin, Yigael 225
Yavetz, Ze'ev 258, 259, 274
Yavnean(s) 232-235, 248, 250, 251
Yavneh 52, 207, 230, 232, 233, 235, 247, 251, 254, 276, 348, 350
Yerushalmi 111, 158, 160, 345, 362, 363
Yeshivot 59, 70, 342, 345
Yohanan ben Zakkai 207, 218, 219, 247, 255, 271, 275, 345, 350
Yom Hakkipurim 181
Yosé 250, 295, 303
Yosi b. Halafta 271
Yosi b. Kefar 270, 276-278, 280, 281
Yudan bar Shillum 298
Zab 222, 232
Zion 341-345, 349, 361, 363

DATE DUE

MAY 2 0 1994			

HIGHSMITH # 45220